Contents

THE ARCHAEOLOGY
OF ARGYLL

THE ARCHAEOLOGY OF ARGYLL

Graham Ritchie

Editor

RCAHMS

EDINBURGH UNIVERSITY PRESS

© Edinburgh University Press, 1997

Transferred to Digital Print 2011

Edinburgh University Press
22 George Square, Edinburgh

Reprinted 2002

Typeset in Monotype Plantin Light
by Nene Phototypesetters, Northampton,
Printed and bound in Great Britain by
CPI Antony Rowe, Chippenham and Eastbourne

A CIP record for this book is available
from the British Library

ISBN 0 7486 0645 9 (paperback)

Figures

Tables

Foreword by Sir William Fraser

*Chairman of the Royal Commission on the Ancient
and Historical Monuments of Scotland*

The seven *Inventories* of the Ancient and Historical Monuments of Argyll
published by the Royal Commission on the Ancient and Historical Monuments of Scotland between 1971 and 1992 occupy a space of about ten inches
on the bookshelf, comprise some 2312 pages and describe 2286 monuments
of all ages. This fundamental source material, complemented by more recent
work in the National Monuments Record of Scotland, lies at the heart of the
present volume. The Royal Commission is delighted by the suggestion of
Edinburgh University Press that the present contributors be approached to
create a study of the environment and prehistory of Argyll that will set the
findings of fieldwork within the context of further research and in a way that
will be available to all.

The monuments of Argyll are among the most important in Scotland and
have been studied from the earliest days of archaeology. There is still much
to learn, but the consistent description and mapping of sites is an important
beginning. Some excavation has revealed the complexity of disentangling the
evidence of the past from the surviving remains. The cairns, standing stones,
rock carvings and fortifications are testimony to the ingenuity, artistic and
engineering skills of the early peoples of Argyll.

It is a county I know well personally in landscape terms, though archaeologically less so. With this volume I feel that my understanding of the way
the land was formed is clearer; I shall make better sense of the notations on
Ordnance Survey maps that denote antiquities. Many peoples have contributed to the make-up of Argyll, though we can only give names to the
later Celtic tribes, the *Epidii* and the like, then the *Scotti*, then the Norse; but
the archaeological evidence illustrates the firm foundation created by the
fishermen, farmers, and craftsmen and craftswomen from periods for which
we have no written records.

The Royal Commission has moved away from the sort of publications from which this volume draws much of its material, to those that provide a distillation of the results of field endeavour in accessible format, with the detailed descriptions added to the National Monuments Record of Scotland. We fully support Edinburgh University Press in their creation of this volume which brings together the prehistoric and early historic archaeology of Argyll in a way in which the distinctiveness of the area can be illustrated, and I am particularly grateful to contributors from beyond the Royal Commission for joining in this project.

Acknowledgements

No composite volume would be possible were it not for the assistance of many people. First of all the editor is grateful to the contributors, particularly those that were timely in the production of papers and those that rose to the challenge to prepare contributions at a late stage. Secondly thanks are due to colleagues who assisted with the preparation of illustrations; in the National Monuments Record of the Royal Commission on the Ancient and Historical Monuments of Scotland this has been achieved through Lesley Ferguson and Kevin McLaren and the good offices of the Photographic Department. Gordon Thomas, Department of Archaeology, University of Edinburgh, undertook the preparation of many of the maps, which are based on the maps published by the Royal Commission in the *Inventories* of Argyll, complemented by information in the National Monuments Record of Scotland manipulated through its Geographic Information System by David Easton and Peter McKeague. The contribution of Mrs Betty Naggar in many excavation photographs is gratefully acknowledged. Dorothy Kidd, Scottish Ethnological Archive, National Museums of Scotland, provided the illustrations of tinker tents; figure 4.1 from Miss M. E. M. Donaldson's collection and figures 4.2–4 from the *Scotland's Magazine* collection, all four with the permission of the Trustees of the Royal Museums of Scotland. The final preparation of illustrations was in the hands of John Borland. The processing of the text benefited greatly from the advice of Christine Allen, both in scanning and in patiently advising the editor on aspects of word-processing technology. The editorial advice of Anna Ritchie and W. F. Ritchie is gratefully acknowledged. Dr Ritchie's assistance in advising on the archaeological content is acknowledged both by the editor and by Miss Brown. The assistance of Dr I. D. L. Clark in the preparation of the text is also gratefully acknowledged.

Grants from the Russell Trust and the Binks Trust made possible the preparation of illustrations for the volume, the gathering of new photographs and assistance over the preparation of the finished text. The volume would not have been illustrated as comprehensively without this generous assistance.

Dr MacKie wishes to thank Dr Alan Lane for his courtesy in showing him a copy of his 1988 paper in advance of publication, and also Dr Margaret Neike for permission to quote from her PhD thesis. He is also grateful to Dr Richard Jones for advice on the technicalities of Ishbel Gair's report and to Dr Rupert Housley for advice on radiocarbon dating and for providing the data for table 8.5.

We are grateful to Mr John Barber, Dr Steven Mithen and Dr Anna Ritchie for permission to quote as yet unpublished radiocarbon dates.

Colleagues in the Department of Archaeology, National Museums of Scotland have provided both assistance and advice, notably Dr Alison Sheridan, Mr Trevor Cowie, Mr Alan Saville and Miss Caroline Richardson. The advice of Miss A. S. Henshall on matters relating to chambered cairns is gratefully acknowledged. Colleagues and former colleagues within the Royal Commission have done many hours of field survey and recording, the results of which are brought together here, notably Mr A. MacLaren, Mr G. B. Quick and Mr I. G. Scott.

The illustrations are largely drawn from the collections of the Royal Commission on the Ancient and Historical Monuments of Scotland and are Crown Copyright. We are grateful to the following for their assistance in providing illustrations: Clive Bonsall, figures 3.1–4; D. W. Harding, figures 7.1–8; E. W. MacKie, figures 8.1–8; National Museums of Scotland, Scottish Ethnological Archive, figures 4.1–4, and Department of Archaeology, figures 5.15 and 5.22; I. G. Scott, figure 4.7; D. G. Sutherland, figures 2.1–3; and Gordon Thomas figures 1.1, 2.1, 3.1–2, 3.4, 5.1, 5.16, 5.19, 6.7 and 7.1–8.

1   Introduction

Graham Ritchie

Excavation is often seen as the major way in which archaeological information is gathered, but structured field-survey is equally vital; the presentation of such results is important not only for the understanding of past landscapes, but also to assist in seeking the best ways to look after what survives. What remains visible is clearly but a tiny part of the picture of past landuse, and how we interpret what we see is tempered by many approaches. In Argyll and the adjacent islands of Arran and Bute the dilemma is acute because the land available for development may be the same restricted patch between the sea and the higher ground that early folk have lived in and farmed for generations. The sense of custody felt by farmers, crofters, landowners and factors has been borne home to the editor and his colleagues in the Royal Commission on the Ancient and Historical Monuments of Scotland in the course of more than thirty years of recording and surveying in Argyll, and this volume stems from the belief that the results of such work should be distilled in a way that is accessible to the community at large.

TOPOGRAPHY

The geographical area of our volume does not follow a precise administrative boundary. We have included the whole of the former county of Argyll, that being the coverage of the seven *Inventories* of the Royal Commission, even though Northern Argyll (Ardnamurchan, Morvern, Sunart and Ardgour) and the northern portion of Lorn (South Ballachulish, Glen Etive and Rannoch) have been part of Highland since 1975; Arran and Bute are included for geographical integrity, but that part of Dumbarton that will transfer to the new authority in April 1996 has not been included. Indeed when this project began the new boundaries had not been decided. Where

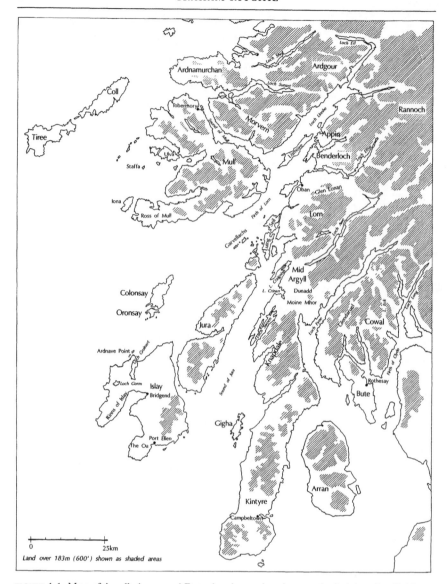

FIGURE 1.1. Map of Argyll, Arran and Bute showing major places and administrative divisions.

appropriate, the administrative subdivision of Argyll has been added to a place-name, for this not only helps to relate a place to a published *Inventory,* but also narrows down what are often rather similar names. Thus the use of the terms 'Argyll' and 'county' should be taken to mean 'the area under discussion', rather than anything too exclusive. The distribution maps are based on those published in the *Inventories*, updated for Argyll and composed for Arran and Bute from the database of the National Monuments Record of

Scotland. The illustrations have been largely taken from Royal Commission sources in order to maintain a degree of uniformity of style.

The area extends from Ardnamurchan in the north to Kintyre in the south, with the islands of the Southern Inner Hebrides in the west, Coll and Tiree, Mull, Colonsay and Oronsay, Jura, Islay and Gigha (figure 1.1). Groome's *Gazetteer* evokes the topography in superlatives (1882, 69): 'The outlines are so exceedingly irregular, the projections of mainland into ocean so bold, the intersections of mainland by sea-lochs so great, the interlockings of mainland and islands so intricate, and the distributions everywhere of land and sea so manifold and erratic, that no fair notion of them can be formed except by examination of a map.' The spectacular scenery, the delight of 'summer visitors and transient tourists', is vividly described, but the 'excessive humidity of the climate' not ignored. For the prehistoric traveller Groome's notes about weather conditions would have been more apposite: 'A great drawback, though operating vastly more in the summer than in the winter months, is occasional, fitful, severe tempestuousness; and this combines with the prevailing boldness and rockiness of the shores to render navigation perilous'(1882, 70). The sea, the deeply indented sea-lochs, and inland Loch Awe must all have played a vital role in communication between communities from earliest times.

The interplay of island and mainland communities was certainly important in early prehistoric times, when calmer seas allowed passage for the exchange of architectural notions about the building of chambered cairns between people on Arran, Kintyre and Islay. The little passage-grave at Achnacreebeag, in Lorn, like that at Greadal Fhinn, in Ardnamurchan, is so comparable to examples in the Western Isles that close contact seems clear. Yet for other types of site, stone circles for example, very restricted foci are evident from the distribution maps.

We have sought to concentrate on the distinctive aspects of the archaeology of Argyll, most often the field monuments, but have not attempted to straitjacket the material into chapters with chronological labels that are inappropriate. Thus after setting the scene with the formation of the topography and vegetation in the period before the arrival of the first groups of hunters and foragers, the examination of the interpretation of the remarkable shell-middens and associated artefacts explores one facet of mesolithic activity. Subsequent chapters look at the evidence for sites associated with settlement and agriculture, monuments associated with death and ritual from earliest times to the beginning of the first millennium AD, and the remarkable prehistoric rock carvings of Argyll. Our attempt has been to avoid any cultural distinction between chambered cairns as being 'neolithic' and thus standing stones and rock art being consigned to a compartment of time called 'Bronze Age', but to try to create in the mind of the reader the impression one has on the ground of several interrelated groups of monuments, created, altered and reassessed over time, that form landscapes of ritual and ceremony. The forts, duns and brochs of Argyll are notable features in the landscape of Argyll in a very different way, for their hilltop or stack-top locations isolate them from the surrounding area. Few have been excavated to modern standards, and the mechanics of preservation mean that bone or environmental evidence rarely survives. Campaigns of excavation in the Hebrides, notably Dun Vulan on South Uist, and Berie on Lewis, will markedly increase knowledge about the construction, date and economy of the period, the latter particularly because of the presence of water-logged deposits. The only stratigraphically recorded broch to have been examined is Dun Mor Vaul on Tiree, the results of which were published in 1974. The way that the report has been used and re-interpreted in the intervening period is explored as a case study in the presentation and use of 'evidence'. There are differences of nuance and interpretation throughout the study of the prehistory and early history of any area, and it is important in a volume such as this not to pretend that there is but one approach. On the other hand, care in the use of archaeological material is essential. It is for this reason too that the partiality and irrationality of the surviving remains have been highlighted on more than one occasion; in creating broad tapestries of change we have to be aware that many stitches are missing.

The Early Christian and Norse remains in Argyll are among the most important in Scotland, but this is the first time that the disparate elements throughout the county have been brought together. They form the link between the archaeology of prehistory and that of the beginnings of historical times. The organisation of the *Scotti* in the *Senchus Fer nAlban*, a tenth-century compilation with some earlier material, underlines the importance of sea-borne communication witnessed again during the Lordship of the Isles. The Gaulish trader mentioned by Adomnán in his *Life of Columba* (Anderson and Anderson 1961, 263) shows how far flung such contacts might be. This is more difficult to understand in prehistoric times, but the links of trade or exchange with areas beyond Argyll have been noted wherever relevant.

RADIOCARBON DATING

Radiocarbon dating is one of the principal methods available for the provision of a chronological framework for the west of Scotland. In some cases preservation of bone or charcoal in stratified excavation contexts is good, and thus a series of radiocarbon determinations can be obtained. A considerable number of radiocarbon dates are now available for Argyll, Arran and Bute, and these are listed here for the first time in totality. The determination does not in itself provide a true calendar date, but has to be calibrated in order to take account of atmospheric variations over time. That calibration in turn provides a span within which the event took place in calendar years BC. The dates are thus given in a way that allows the raw 'date' to be viewed in one column, and the calibrated date BC in terms of a span within which there is a 95 per cent chance that the true date lies. Considerable thought went into the way that the list should be laid out: should all determinations from the same site be listed together, or should the dates be listed in chronological order, in order to allow the broad juxtaposition of events to be appreciated? The latter course has been adopted, and thus the beginnings of the early history of Argyll have been set in place.

The view has now been taken by some researchers into the dating method that the practice of publishing uncalibrated dates (that is the convention that uses bc or ad) is not as helpful as first appeared, and that either the date BP should be used or else it should be given in its calibrated form, either within a span, or as a generalised date. Neither method makes it very easy to write general statements that rely on radiocarbon dates as their chronological pegs. The presentation of archaeological evidence in uncalibrated terms has never found favour with the editor, for no one has the notional construct of un-calibrated time in their heads; it was a science fiction horror. The currently approved method may appear cumbersome, but it is closer to the spirit of the dating technique by underlining the breadth of the span, and perhaps more importantly by emphasising the length of time we may envisage particular events occurring in our personal chronological construct of the past. The archaeologist has to act not only as the news-reporter for an individual event, but also as the distant interpreter of fashions and change; often this is only possible by a series of juxtapositions of pieces of evidence, with changing social or ritual attitudes implied, but rarely understood. Dates BP, Before Present, are preferred in considerations of the early environment (Chapters 2 and 3). In some instances, however, presentation in terms of uncalibrated dates may be helpful, especially where comparisons are being made with earlier discussions, as in Chapter 8.

Similarly, although the measurements used in this volume are mostly metric, imperial measurements have been used in certain sections where the original research was undertaken using imperial measurements. Accentua-tion of Gaelic place-names has generally been avoided for simplicity, but has been included for periods where accentuation is accepted practice (notably Chapter 9). Ranging poles and scales in photographs are metric, except where noted in the caption.

It will be clear from the chapters that the contributors believe that a close involvement and engagement with the material on the ground and in the museum is an essential prerequisite to the articulation of the processes of change in social or theoretical terms. The Dun Mor Vaul chapter is important in this regard both in terms of the discussion of the stratigraphy of the broch and as an example of artefact analysis. The examination of forts and duns equally addresses the alternative possibilities of date. On the other hand the limitations of the evidence, for the Iron Age for example, reflect the absence of modern excavation and intensive landscape survey. Perhaps our volume, while showing the strength of past research, will also demonstrate the potential for future work.

Earlier Work on the Archaeology of Argyll, Arran and Bute

The study of the archaeology of the area is as old as the subject itself. Edward Lhuyd's drawing of the cairns and standing stone at Kintraw, Mid Argyll, made in about 1699, is a clear depiction of a monument now sadly ruined (RCAHMS 1988, 64–7, no.63). Interest in the antiquities of the area often found focus in a visit to Iona, but passing mention of the many monuments on the way may be found in the accounts of Thomas Pennant and Dr Samuel Johnson. The contributors to the *Statistical Account* and to the *New Statistical Account* frequently make mention of the earliest antiquities of the parish, as well as of ecclesiastical and medieval monuments. Agricultural improvements of the earlier nineteenth century resulted in the destruction of many cairns particularly, but lost monuments were sometimes documented in the Name Books compiled by the first map makers of the Ordnance Survey. In 1864 Canon Greenwell and Dean Mapleton undertook the first excavations in Argyll to be recorded in the *Proceedings of the Society of Antiquaries of Scotland* at Nether Largie South and Kilchoan, Mid Argyll (1866; 1866). In 1868 the decorated rock surfaces of Kilmartin were drawn to antiquarian attention for the first time by Sir J. Y. Simpson (1868). On Oronsay, excavations between 1879 and 1882 by Symington Grieve uncovered the shell-mounds of the island, which, with the discoveries in the caves at Oban in the latter part of the century, set the material of the hunters and foragers apart from the rest of Scotland, eventually to be accorded the label 'Obanian' (the subject of Chapter 3) (figures 1.2–3). The history of Bute was detailed in J. K. Hewison's *Bute in the Olden Times* in 1893, with full illustration of what were then thought of as 'Monuments of Unrecorded Times' (36–83). A comprehensive examin-

FIGURE 1.2. Oronsay shell mound, with the Paps of Jura in the background.

FIGURE 1.3. Oban, Lorn, excavation of McArthur Cave in 1894.

ation of the prehistory and history of Arran was published in 1910 and 1914, the former detailing the archaeology of the island under the editorship of J. A. Balfour. The long chapter on the sepulchral remains was contributed by Professor T. H. Bryce, and that on the cup-and-ring markings on Stronach Ridge, Brodick, by Fred R. Coles.

Three remarkable field-surveys and two campaigns of excavation form the basis, in very different ways, for the evolution of knowledge about how the archaeology of the county has evolved. David Christison published surveys of the forts and duns in Lorn and Mid Argyll (1889; 1904); Christison's artistic style, developed in the recording of the forts of the Borders, exaggerates aspects of the natural rock formations, but his observations are important in assessing any change in the condition of the monuments today. Angus Graham undertook an archaeological survey of his family estate at Skipness, Kintyre, which was published in 1919, and which was later followed up by excavations at Dun Breac; the breadth of Graham's recording in chronological terms was impressive, including cupmarks, bloomeries and whisky-stills. After a period in Canada, Graham returned to Scotland to become Secretary to the Royal Commission on the Ancient and Historical Monuments of Scotland, and later, as a Commissioner, he was clearly instrumental in encouraging the Royal Commission to take up the task of making an *Inventory* of the whole county. Systematic survey of Mid Argyll was undertaken by Miss Marion Campbell of Kilberry and Miss Mary Sandeman;

exhaustive cartographic, bibliographic, and most importantly field research resulted in a definitive list of sites (1962). Such work has acted as the inspiration to other groups or individuals, with comprehensive surveys being undertaken by local societies in Cowal, Kintyre and Lorn. The inspiration of Eric Cregeen, in helping to re-create local societies, and Jack and Margaret Scott, in tackling the upgrading of museums and in undertaking excavations to meet rescue and research needs must also be fully acknowledged. On Bute, Miss D. N. Marshall held high the standard raised by her father, who had invited the Glasgow archaeologist Ludovic Mann to examine the vitrified (timber-laced) fort at Dunagoil (Marshall, J. N. 1915), by continuing the recording and excavation of the antiquities of the island. Undoubtedly the most comprehensive museum in the area is that of the Buteshire Natural History and Antiquarian Society in Rothesay. The only other museums with considerable archaeological collections are those founded by the Kintyre Antiquarian Society in Campbeltown, and more recently the Museum of Islay Life at Port Charlotte and the Isle of Arran Heritage Museum in Brodick.

Major campaigns of excavations were mounted by the Society of Antiquaries of Scotland in 1904–5 and later in 1929; in the course of the former campaign, Duntroon, Ardifuir and Dunadd were explored, and many artefacts subsequently added to the National collection (Christison et al. 1905). However we view the published report today, Lord Abercromby was sufficiently critical of the work to be thought to have changed his will from one that benefited the Society, to one that encouraged the study of European archaeology through the creation of a Chair of Prehistoric Archaeology in the University of Edinburgh (Piggott and Robertson 1977, no.90). The excavation campaigns of Hewat Craw, and later of Gordon Childe, on the cairns at Kilmartin were partly designed to make the monuments more understandable; Craw had another reason as well, for 'dry weather being essential for the riddling of soil at Dunadd, arrangements were made for work at other sites in the event of rain. The Bronze Age cairns were selected for this purpose' (1930, 127). The exceptional nature of the monuments of Kilmartin was clear, although the method of the excavation of some of them has left tantalising gaps in our knowledge.

The publication of the results of field survey in Argyll by the Royal Commission on the Ancient and Historical Monuments of Scotland in a series of *Inventory* volumes from 1971 until 1992 provides a county-wide basis against which the distribution of all classes of prehistoric sites can be assessed. The provision of plans to consistent scales allows comparison of groups of monuments over the whole area, and this makes possible the sort of regrouping of types of fort and dun, for example, undertaken in Chapter 7 (figure 1.4). What the *Inventory* format cannot do is to link various classes of monument into landscapes of interconnected ritual monuments, nor evoke the mass of artefacts that have been found in the course of excavation. Most objects are now in museums far from their original findspots; the British Museum, London, holds the Greenwell Collection, the National Museums of Scotland

FIGURE 1.4. Tirefour Broch, Lismore.

have an extensive collection that results from excavations undertaken by the Society of Antiquaries of Scotland. Glasgow Art Gallery and Museum, Kelvingrove, and the Hunterian Museum, University of Glasgow, both have important holdings, the former with the decorated cist slab from Badden, Mid Argyll, and the latter with the material from the broch at Dun Mor Vaul, Tiree, and Balnabraid, Kintyre. The chapters that follow seek to draw together the landscape, the wealth of field monuments, and the diversity of artefacts that constitute our evidence for the earliest peoples of Argyll.

2 The Environment of Argyll

Donald G. Sutherland

Argyll is an area of diverse geology and topography comprising a mountainous mainland and adjacent hilly or mountainous islands and peninsulas (figure 1.1). The coastline is several thousand kilometres long and very irregular, with numerous major indentations such that no land point is more than 30 km from the sea. These factors, interacting with major climatic changes, have resulted in a complex history of environmental change during the Quaternary. The record of environmental change, however, is only understood in detail for the last 13,000 years or so, that is since the decay of the last ice sheet to cover the area. Over this period a complex interplay in marine and atmospheric climates, sea-level movement, terrestrial vegetational change and geomorphological processes have been established and form the major part of this review. The impact of man on the environment can only be discerned at other than the local level during the last 4000–5000 years. However, ice-sheet glaciations prior to 13,000 BP are the events which have had the most notable impact on the topography and scenery of Argyll, and the glacial inheritance must first be considered in gaining an understanding of the opportunities offered to man by the environment.

GLACIAL INHERITANCE

In Argyll, the great majority of the evidence for former glaciation is erosional. Large-scale glacial erosion has not only produced the characteristic deep Highland valleys and their continuation in the fjord-like sea lochs which permit the sea to penetrate so far inland, but it has also been responsible for the isolation of many of the islands. Thus, for example, prior to glaciation it is most probable that Mull was joined to Morvern and possibly Ardnamurchan, and that Islay, Jura and Scarba were part of a long peninsula.

10

At the time of the maximum of the last ice sheet (about 18,000 BP) the whole of Argyll was covered in ice which, from its zone of maximum thickness over the south-west Highlands, flowed westwards on to the outer continental shelf, southwards into the Irish Sea basin and eastwards into the North Sea basin. Ice-sheet retreat was progressive, such that by around 13,000 BP any ice remaining was only to be found in the higher mountain valleys and inner sea lochs (Sutherland 1984).

Along all of the mainland and island coasts sea level was high as the ice retreated, and consequently the lower parts of many valleys were inundated. During the major part of the ice retreat the marine climate was severe, the sea being covered by ice in winter and dotted with icebergs in summer. The marine fauna was restricted to a few species of arctic molluscs and a limited range of foraminifera and ostracods. Elsewhere in Scotland arctic seal remains have been found from this period, and these may be presumed to have occurred along the Argyll coast at this time.

During these cold conditions, and presumably during similarly cold conditions at previous times during the Quaternary, rock platforms were eroded along parts of the western coasts of the islands and western mainland (figure 2.1) (Sissons 1982; 1983a). Glacio-isostatic depression at the time of their formation has resulted in these platforms and in the accompanying cliffs and caves now occurring at altitudes of between 15 m and 50 m OD. These high rock platforms are conspicuous features of the coastlines of the western islands. Some of them are overlain by glacial deposits and others are apparently unaffected by glaciation. Occasional caves, such as on Ulva (Bonsall et al. 1991; 1992) have been found to be related to these high sea-level stands. In addition, at the time of ice-sheet retreat, depositional littoral features were formed, including the spectacular 'staircases' of unvegetated shingle ridges along the west coast of Jura and the large deltas that occur at the mouths of many small valleys.

During deglaciation relative sea level was at its maximum (the 'marine limit') adjacent to the retreating ice margin, and the altitude of the marine limit generally slopes upwards towards the area of maximum isostatic depression (and latest deglaciation) from altitudes of around 20 m to 25 m in the western islands to over 40 m in the neighbourhood of the Firth of Lorn and the head of the Firth of Clyde.

The majority of the ice sheet melted during a time of intense cold, and this implies that deglaciation resulted from a combination of lack of precipitation and iceberg calving, which was promoted by rising world sea level. The deglaciated land surface was bequeathed a covering of impoverished mineral soils and bare rock surfaces. At around 13,000 BP, however, the North Atlantic oceanic polar front rapidly moved northwards of Scotland (Ruddiman and McIntyre 1973; Duplessy et al. 1981), and the influence of the warmer waters of the North Atlantic Drift was felt throughout the country. This marked climatic change ushered in the 3000 years of the Devensian Lateglacial period, the final part of the last ice age.

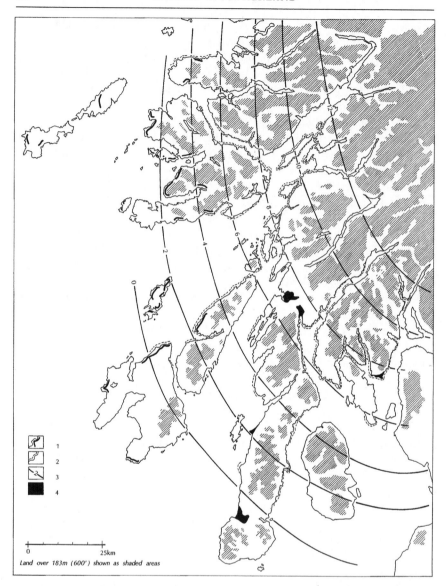

FIGURE 2.1. Aspects of the coastal history of Argyll. 1. Coasts with high rock platforms or clifflines; 2. Coasts where the Main Rock Platform is developed; 3. Isobases (lines of equal altitude) of the Main Rock Platform (in m OD); 4. Large areas of littoral deposition at time of Main Postglacial Shoreline.

LATEGLACIAL ENVIRONMENTAL CHANGE

Climatic change during the Lateglacial

The return of warm waters to the western coasts was accompanied by a marked rise in air temperatures, to close to present levels (Atkinson et al. 1987). This warm period occurred between 13,000 and 12,700 BP, after which there was a decline in both summer and winter temperatures, with summer temperatures falling to 1–3°C below present values and the temperature of the coldest winter month being well below 0°C. After around 11,400 BP a further steady temperature decline occurred, leading to the onset of the very cold Loch Lomond Stadial between approximately 11,000 and 10,000 BP. During the stadial arctic climate was experienced again throughout Scotland with mean summer temperatures some 9–10°C below present and winter temperatures being perhaps as low as −20°C.

These temperature trends are largely mirrored by those in the nearshore marine environment with the exception of a brief period at around 11,000 BP, just before the onset of the cold stadial, when the seas warmed slightly to within 1–2°C of present-day temperatures (Peacock 1983; 1989). Evidence from deep-sea cores in the Atlantic (Ruddiman and McIntyre 1973; Duplessy et al. 1981) makes it clear that the cold Loch Lomond Stadial was the product of the cessation of the North Atlantic Drift as the oceanic polar front once again moved south of the British Isles.

Lateglacial Interstadial terrestrial environment

Despite the relative mildness of the opening of the interstadial, the skeletal soils and the time required for vegetation to spread from more southerly, non-glaciated areas meant that the initial vegetational cover was that of pioneering species of grasses, sedges, mosses and other plants (Lowe and Walker 1986; Tipping 1989; 1991a). Subsequently, grasslands and dwarf-shrub heaths (with crowberry and juniper well represented) developed as soils matured and became more acidic. In Argyll, tree birch was only locally present during the interstadial. A significant factor in determining the vegetational mosaic was most probably wind, with more exposed localities having no tree birch and lower incidence of juniper (Lowe and Walker 1986). In a number of pollen diagrams from Argyll (and elsewhere in Scotland) there was a significant decline in juniper pollen at around 12,000 BP which lasted for about 200 years. This decline was accompanied by increased mineral sedimentation in some lake basins and an increase in the occurrence of certain plants indicative of disturbed ground (Tipping 1991a). Thus during the middle part of the interstadial there appears to have been a short period of more severe climate. Comparison with the temperature trends established for the interstadial (Atkinson et al. 1987) suggests that this fluctuation was in response to more severe winters rather than a decline in summer temperatures (Walker et al.1992).

There are no records from Argyll of the terrestrial animals which may have lived during the Lateglacial interstadial. However, the recovery of bones of reindeer of Lateglacial age from the site at Croftamie south of Loch Lomond (Jack 1875) implies that reindeer were very probably present farther west at that time.

Lateglacial Interstadial marine environment

Throughout the interstadial there was abundant marine fauna, species including *Arctica islandica, Chlamys islandicus, Modiolus modiolus* and *Mytilus edulis*. Given that for much of the interstadial marine temperatures were mild, but 2–3°c below present, winter sea-ice would have been likely to be both more frequent and thicker than in recent times (note that upper Loch Fyne was sufficiently frozen in 1758 and 1786 for people to cross from Inveraray to St Catherines). This contention is borne out by the occurrence in marine sediments deposited during the interstadial of cobbles and boulders partially covered in barnacles, with the barnacles facing downwards where they had been dropped into the sea-bed sediments.

Around much of the coasts of Argyll sea level was falling rapidly at the onset of the interstadial due to the high rate of isostatic uplift which exceeded the concurrent rise in world-wide sea level. Figure 2.2 shows this fall for lower Loch Fyne and this is typical for much of the western mainland coast of Argyll. For the outer islands a large part of the fall in sea level would have been accomplished prior to the opening of the interstadial, but the general form of this part of the curve would be the same, only shifted back in time. In lower Loch Fyne, the average rate of emergence of the land was about 1.8 m per century which, while high, is still less than the rate of emergence experienced today in certain areas of Arctic Canada (Andrews 1970). With the slowing of isostatic uplift during the stadial and the continuing rise of world sea level, the rate of emergence gradually came to a halt, possibly about 11,500–11,000 BP, although this period is not well studied because subsequent changes in sea level have resulted in the burial or erosion of much of the nearshore sediment and landforms for this time. In areas such as lower Loch Fyne the sea level during this later part of the interstadial was several metres above its present position whilst in the outer areas it was probably some way below present sea level.

Loch Lomond Stadial glaciation

It is not known whether the inner mountainous part of Argyll was completely deglaciated during the Lateglacial Interstadial, because this area was completely covered by the ice which expanded during the cold Loch Lomond Stadial and the relevant evidence was destroyed. However, if, as seems possible, there was a significant mass of ice still present in the south-west Highlands at the time of the onset of the interstadial and that summer

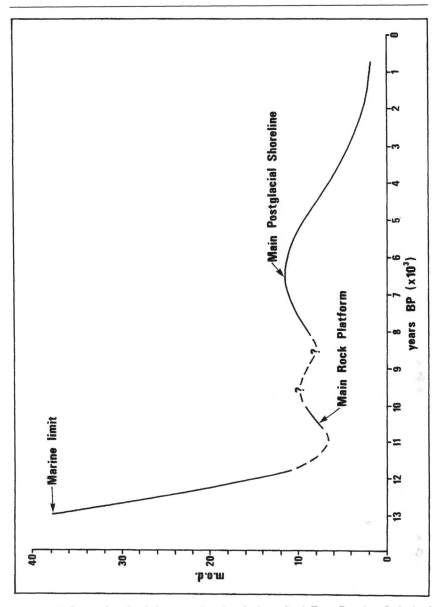

FIGURE 2.2. Curve of sea-level change against time for lower Loch Fyne. Based on Sutherland (1981).

temperatures fell back to 1–2°C below present after only a few centuries into the interstadial, then survival of small ice bodies in the high corries seems possible. Subsequent glacier expansion probably started during the latter part of the interstadial, at a time when temperatures were declining, and reached its maximum during the stadial.

At its maximum the ice inundated the Rannoch basin, where it was up to 400 m thick (Thorp 1986), and the mountainous areas to the north and south with outlet glaciers flowing along all the major sea lochs (Peacock 1971a; Gray 1975a; 1992; Thorp 1986; 1991). An independent ice cap developed on Mull (Gray and Brooks 1972) and small glaciers occurred in the corries of the Cowal (Sutherland 1981) and the Morvern peninsulas (Wain-Hobson 1981). The outlet glaciers over-rode, picked up and transported the shelly sands and silts that had been deposited in the sea lochs during the interstadial, and radio-carbon dating of these shells has confirmed that the readvance reached its maximum after 11,000 BP and possibly as late as 10,100 BP (Peacock 1971b; Gray and Brooks 1972; Sutherland 1981; Peacock et al. 1989).

Close to the maximum positions of the larger outlet glaciers a number of large outwash plains and associated glaciofluvial terraces were deposited (McCann 1961; Peacock 1971a; Gray 1975a). These are particularly striking at the mouth of Loch Etive, at Corran Ferry on Loch Linnhe, at Ballachulish on Loch Leven, and at the mouth of Loch Creran. Retreat of the glaciers was likely to have been progressive and rapid and has bequeathed to the Highland valleys a characteristic suite of apparently irregular, hummocky landforms. In places, such as to the north-west of Sgurr Dearg on Mull (Gray and Brooks 1972, pl.1), these moraines have a strong alignment in the direction of glacier flow, but more typically they are irregular or elongated across a valley and enclose now-peat-filled depressions. Such moraines with their associated poor drainage are one of the principal reasons for the low agricultural potential of many of the highland valleys in Argyll.

Stadial terrestrial non-glacial environment

The harsh conditions of the Loch Lomond Stadial resulted in the vegetation of the interstadial being replaced by a tundra with grass- and sedge-dominated communities. The acid soils developed during the stadial were eroded and plants indicative of bare soils and unstable ground occurred (Lowe and Walker 1986; Tipping 1989; 1991a). High precipitation apparently resulted in considerable snow cover, for certain species of *Artemisia*, which are chiono-phobic (snow-fearing) and which are found in great abundance during the stadial in drier parts of Scotland (Tipping 1985), were less common in the south-west Highlands and adjacent islands. The proportion of *Artemisia* in the pollen spectra from the stadial is greater in the later than in the earlier stadial, suggesting that precipitation may have diminished as the stadial pro-gressed (Lowe and Walker 1986; Tipping 1991a and b). In the mountains above and beyond the glacier margins there was considerable frost weathering with the production of mountain top débris (Thorp 1986) and valley-side talus slopes. Scree production at low levels is also indicated by the burial of barnacles of Lateglacial Interstadial age at Oban (Gray 1975b).

Loch Lomond Stadial marine environment

As on land, the marine environment of the Loch Lomond Stadial was marked by the disappearance of warmth-demanding species and their replacement by a restricted fauna, the principal elements of which are now found in arctic regions (Peacock et al. 1978). Particularly characteristic of this time is the mollusc *Portlandia arctica* which prefers muddy waters close to glacier margins.

During this latter part of the Lateglacial there was a notable period of marine erosion which resulted in the fashioning of a prominent cliffline and rock platform around the greater part of the Argyll coastline (figure 2.1). This shoreline, termed the Main Rock Platform, is absent or only poorly developed within the inner sea lochs due to occupation during or subsequent to its formation by glaciers of the Loch Lomond Readvance (Gray 1974a; Suther-land 1981). The shoreline is isostatically tilted towards the west and south-west (figure 2.2) and accordingly disappears below sea level in the outer parts of the Argyll coasts (Gray 1974a; 1978; Dawson 1980; 1988; Sutherland 1984). The cliffline, with its accompanying caves, undercuts and stacks, is perhaps the single most prominent feature of the coastline around much of Loch Linnhe, eastern and southern Mull and the outer parts of the sea lochs at the head of the Firth of Clyde.

It is likely that the particular clarity of the shoreline in these areas is due to a longer period of balance between isostatically and eustatically induced sea-level movements than in the areas more peripheral to isostatic uplift. How-ever, it is also likely that the rock platform owes some of its prominence to the existence of older rock platforms at approximately the same altitude (Suther-land 1981; Gray and Ivanovic 1988): such platforms still occur along the Kintyre peninsula at altitudes above those of the Main Rock Platform (Gray 1978).

HOLOCENE ENVIRONMENTAL CHANGE

Climatic change during the Holocene

The opening of the Holocene (10,000 BP) coincides broadly with the tran-sition from the arctic conditions of the Loch Lomond Stadial to the mild climate of the present 'interglacial'. The change in conditions occurred rapidly with air temperatures perhaps rising by 0.3–0.7° per decade (Atkin-son et al. 1987). As with the opening of the Lateglacial Interstadial this rapid rise in temperatures is a consequence of the retreat of the oceanic polar front from south of the British Isles to north of Iceland with the accompanying resumption of the North Atlantic Drift (Ruddiman and McIntyre 1973). The oceanic circulation may not immediately have assumed its present-day configuration, however, for the nearshore marine climate was slightly cooler than that of today for several hundred years prior to reaching present-day temperatures at around 9600–9800 BP (Peacock 1989; Peacock and Harkness 1990).

During the Holocene, in contrast to the Lateglacial Interstadial, the milder climate, once attained, was maintained during the following millennia. Curiously, given the wealth of information on the development of vegetation during the Holocene, there has been relatively little work on the changes in temperature and precipitation during that period. On the basis of the maximum northern penetration of certain plants during the mid-Holocene, it has been suggested that the climate of north-west Europe at that time may have been 2–3°C warmer in summer and 1–2°C warmer in winter (Iversen 1944). Rather similar inferences have been suggested for the nearshore marine climate on the basis of the occurrence of certain molluscs north of their present known limits (Robertson, D. 1877). However, as demonstrated by S. M. Smith (1971) for the east coast of Scotland, such inferences were based on poorly documented present-day distributions and hence must be treated with caution.

Precipitation is generally held to have increased after about 4000 BP and isotopic analyses of fossil pine stumps led Dubois and Ferguson (1985) to infer periods of higher precipitation at around 7500 BP, between 6300 and 5800 BP, 4300 and 3900 BP and around 3300 BP.

Wind exposure is today a major limiting factor on vegetational development, and there is some evidence that during the mid-Holocene winds may have been less intense (Andrews et al. 1987), perhaps increasing after around 4000 BP (Birks 1987).

Forest expansion during the early and mid-Holocene

The rapid amelioration in climate at the opening of the Holocene was not immediately reflected in the vegetation. This was initially characterised by plants typical of the bare, disturbed alkaline soils left by the arctic conditions of the Loch Lomond Stadial (Walker et al. 1992). However, vegetational development followed a similar sequence throughout Argyll with initial expansion of juniper heaths being followed by a progressive spread of tree birch from the south and, in the coastal zones, the almost simultaneous spread of hazel. The early expansion of juniper is not well dated (Tipping 1987), but probably took place between 10,000 and 9600 BP. Birch spread through most of the mainland and inner islands between 9800 and 9500 BP (Birks 1989), but hazel had a curious and rapid expansion along the western coastal zone prior to 9500 BP and only spread into the mainland interior at a later date, reaching the Rannoch basin at around 9000 BP (Haggart and Bridge 1992). Such behaviour may have been due to quick sea-borne propagation of hazel nuts (Birks 1989), in contrast to the slower methods of tree spreading across land. Of the major tree species, elm and oak both spread from the south and south-east, the former reaching southern Argyll prior to 8500 BP and spreading rapidly along the west mainland coast, but being apparently slower into the islands, reaching the western islands only after 7500 BP. Oak showed a similar but later pattern and was slower to expand into the islands, not reaching some till perhaps as late as 6000 BP.

Of all the major trees, pine is perhaps the most anomalous, for it did not migrate into the Scottish Highlands from the south (Birks 1977, 1989; Bennett 1984) but appeared initially in the north-west Highlands and then spread southwards and eastwards. It reached and then became the dominant tree species in the forests of the Rannoch Moor area by 6800 BP (Haggart and Bridge 1992), but never achieved dominance in the coastal areas. In the south of Argyll there is little evidence that pine was ever present (Bennett 1984). Alder may have been a minor element in the forests during the early Holocene, but it expanded rapidly into southern Argyll at around 7500 BP and then spread northwards and westwards to reach its maximum extent by around 6000 BP (Birks 1989). It is apparent that the development of the forests was not the result of simple expansion from the south. Tree species spread by different mechanisms, from different 'source' areas and in response to different soil as well as climatic conditions. Further, competition between the species can also be expected to have limited their final extent.

Vegetational pattern during the mid-Holocene

Between 6000 and 5000 BP the forests had reached their greatest extent, and an estimation of the distribution of the different dominant tree species is given in figure 2.3 (Bennett 1989). Note that figure 2.3 shows dominant species and does not preclude the existence of stands of other trees in particular areas. The non-forested upland areas would have been grasslands and heathlands. Particular factors that controlled the distribution of trees were climate (wind exposure and rainfall as well as temperature), geology and topography (and hence soil type) and soil moisture. The extent of the forest cover at about this time should also not be regarded as static. For example, Bridge et al. (1990) have indicated that there was probably significant change in the extent of the pine forest on Rannoch Moor, with two periods of greatest extent at 6800–6500 BP and 5000–4600 BP.

Reduction of forest cover during the late Holocene

A decline in elm pollen values has been noted in many sediment profiles at around 5000 BP in Argyll (and over a much wider area). This has been attributed either to a precursor of elm disease or to human impact, the latter perhaps being the preferred mechanism of the majority of authors. Whatever the mechanism involved, by 4000 BP the forests were reducing in area and

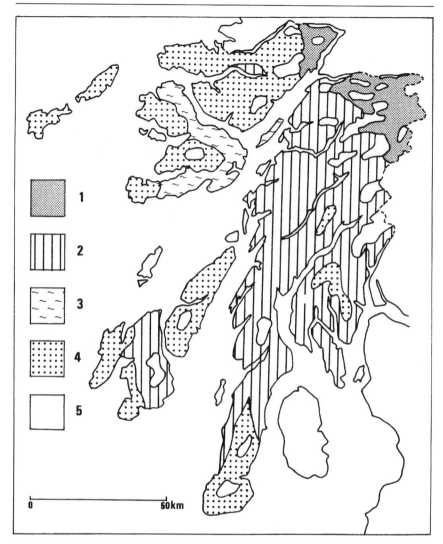

FIGURE 2.3. Provisional map of the distribution of forest types in Argyll 5000 BP. 1. Pine-dominated; 2. Oak-dominated; Hazel-dominated; 4. Birch-dominated; 5. Unforested (within Argyll boundary). Based on Bennett (1989).

blanket bog was expanding. This was also probably aided by the apparent increase in storminess and precipitation at around this time (Birks 1987). It may also be noted that the natural processes of soil development during the Holocene led to increased acidification which would be inimical to the continuation of the forest cover in its contemporaneous state (Romans and Robertson 1975; Birks 1986). It therefore seems likely that a complex of factors at around 5000–4000 BP combined to produce a reduction in the forest cover. However, this period also witnessed the expansion of ash throughout much of Argyll (by 3000 BP), probably colonising areas of forest clearance (Birks 1989).

Fluvial and slope geomorphic activity during the Holocene

On the retreat of the glaciers of the Loch Lomond Readvance, the mountainous parts of Argyll inherited a bare environment with abundant unconsolidated débris resting on or adjacent to steep bedrock slopes. As a consequence there was a period of quite intense geomorphological activity while a new equilibrium was sought as vegetation spread, soils developed and débris was redistributed into more stable parts of the landscape. Landslides were probably relatively common during the early Holocene (Holmes 1984; Ballantyne 1984) with a particular concentration in the Cowal peninsula. Additionally, during the early to mid-Holocene débris flows were likely to have been active along many of the steeper mountain slopes (Brazier et al. 1988). The development of scree beside many steep slopes that were ice-covered during the Loch Lomond Readvance indicates that rock-fall activity has also occurred, even at quite low altitudes, during the Holocene. However, talus slopes outside the limits of the Loch Lomond Readvance are frequently vegetated and gullied, indicating that rock-fall activity has been muted compared to that of the Lateglacial period (Ballantyne and Eckford 1986). Many of the low-altitude, bouldery slope deposits can therefore be inferred to have been formed during the Loch Lomond Stadial (cf. Smith, S. M. 1971).

During the mid- to late-Holocene the geomorphological environment appears to have been relatively quiescent. In the lower valleys systems of river terraces have been constructed in response to the fall of sea level since around 6500 BP. Few corresponding features have been reported from the upland areas. During the last several hundred years, however, there has been a distinct upsurge in geomorphological activity. This has been characterised by renewed, often intense, débris-flow activity (Innes 1983; Brazier 1992) together with the fluvial reworking of the lower parts of previously deposited débris cones (Brazier et al. 1988). The reasons for this renewed activity could be climatic – 'the Little Ice Age' – or increased grazing pressure.

Holocene marine environment

As noted earlier, the beginning of the Holocene coincided with a return of North Atlantic Drift waters to the western coasts of Scotland. Initially, however, a full 'interglacial' oceanic circulation pattern was not established, and the period up to approximately 9600 BP had a marine climate comparable to that during the middle part of the Lateglacial Interstadial (Peacock and Harkness 1990). Thereafter the oceanic circulation was similar to that of today.

The course of sea-level change during the early Holocene is poorly documented around the Argyll coasts, although analogy with other areas in Scotland may suggest an initial positive movement (from the altitude of the Main
Rock Platform, figure 2.1), at least in the areas closest to the centre of isostatic
uplift, followed by a regression which may have reached its nadir at between
8000 and 8500 BP (Sissons 1983b; Sutherland 1984).

Thereafter sea level rose rapidly (figure 2.2) during the Main Postglacial
Transgression, and marine sediments were deposited upon peat layers which
have been dated along the coasts of Loch Fyne to between 8000 and 7200 BP
(Sutherland 1981). The time of the maximum of this transgression has not
been defined precisely on the Argyll coasts, but has been placed at between
7200 and 6600 BP on Oronsay (Jardine 1987), at slightly prior to 6700 BP in
the Oban area (Bonsall and Sutherland 1992) and after 7200 BP around the
head of the Firth of Clyde by Sutherland (1981). The altitude reached by the
sea at the maximum of the transgression was greater than that attained at any
time since the early part of the Lateglacial Interstadial, and hence depositional
coastal features dating from the intervening period were largely reworked with
only sporadic preservation in coastal embayments.

The maximum of the transgression is marked by a distinct shoreline, the
Main Postglacial Shoreline, which attains an altitude of over 14 m around
the inner parts of the mainland sea lochs. It slopes southwards and westwards
in conformity with isostatic uplift at a gradient of about 0.05 m per km in
the Firth of Lorn area (Gray 1974b) and 0.06 m per km in the Firth of
Clyde area (Sutherland 1981). At this time along the Argyll coast there were
a number of moderate sized marine embayments (such as near Crinan,
figure 2.1), in which generally fine-grained littoral or estuarine sediments
were deposited.

Subsequent to the formation of the shoreline there has been a general fall
in sea level (figure 2.2), probably marked by slight halts during which other
shorelines were formed. In the Firth of Lorn area, Gray (1974b) identified
four such shorelines; at the head of the Firth of Clyde, Sutherland (1981)
found five shorelines. The difference is largely due to the variations in coastal
configurations and the relative closeness to the centre of isostatic uplift of the
two areas. The fall in sea level and the associated shorelines are poorly dated,
but Sutherland (1981) and Haggart and Sutherland (1992) have suggested
that one shoreline at around 4 m OD was formed at about 4000 BP. Coastal
sand-dune systems are only sporadically developed along the inner Argyll
coasts, but on the western isles and the southern Kintyre peninsula they are
more widespread. They have developed in response to sea-level change and
the availability of sediment in the immediate offshore zone. Any dune systems
deposited during the early Holocene would have been reworked during the
Main Postglacial Transgression, and hence the earliest wind-blown sand deposits that have been encountered were formed close to the Main Postglacial
Shoreline (Jardine 1987). Wind-blown sand deposits have continued to
develop during the mid- and late-Holocene period of falling sea levels.

IMPLICATIONS FOR HUMAN SETTLEMENT

Man, self-evidently, is opportunistic, and prehistoric man can be expected to have made such a living as would be possible from the environment at any one time. The opportunities since the retreat of the last ice sheet, however, have not been uniform as is indicated in table 2.1.

	Lateglacial Interstadial (13,000–11,000)	Loch Lomond Stadial (11,000–10,000)	Holocene (10,000–present)
Climate	mild, within 1–3°c of today, summer. Winter colder than present	snowy	mild, broadly similar to present, slightly warmer, drier and less windy prior to 4000 BP
Vegetation	grasslands, heaths, trees (birch) only locally	treeless tundra	forests expanding pre-6000 BP: heath and peat expanded post-4000 BP
Soils	initially poor, alkaline, later acid	shallow, disturbed	early development forest soils, later acid soils and blanket peats
Marine life	abundant, diverse nearshore fauna	poor, low diversity	abundant, diverse nearshore fauna
Glaciation	possible small mountain glaciers	ice caps, small glaciers	none
Modern analogues	middle Norway above treeline, sw Iceland	Spitzbergen, N Norway, E Greenland	

Table 2.1 Summary of environmental changes in Argyll during the period since the disappearance of last ice sheet.

The modern analogues in the final row of table 2.1 suggest that none of the environments were such that it would not have been possible for man to have survived, although the Loch Lomond Stadial would have had the most adverse conditions. The Lateglacial Interstadial would have offered a relatively benign climate together with reasonable terrestrial and nearshore marine food resources, and there would appear to have been no environmental constraints on human settlement in Argyll during this 2000-year period. That there is little evidence for the presence of man at this time (Morrison and Bonsall 1989) may partly be due to the lack of chance discoveries of the isolated occupation sites of a thin population. However, it may be noted that after about 12,500–12,000 BP on most of the mainland coast, and earlier than that on the outer islands, sea level was lower than that of the later Main Postglacial Transgression. Moreover, erosion associated with the formation of the Main Rock Platform at the end of the Lateglacial would have resulted in truncation of the

Lateglacial Interstadial coastal zone. Consequently, if the shoreline and its immediate hinterland had formed a focus for human activity, as occurred during the Mesolithic, then the preservation potential of such sites would be very low. Additionally, inland sites would clearly have been completely eroded in areas of subsequent glaciation during the Loch Lomond Readvance, whilst, beyond the margins of the glaciers, slope instability would further have destroyed many surface features. It may be speculated that the most likely sites to find evidence of human activity during the Lateglacial Interstadial would be in caves associated with the High Rock Platform and on the deltas, littoral terraces or shingle ridges formed during the period of rapidly falling sea level prior to about 12,500 BP.

The Main Postglacial Transgression would have had a similar effect on evidence for settlement near early Holocene shorelines, and it is notable that direct evidence for occupation prior to 7000 BP comes only from cave and rock-shelter sites which were above the altitude of the Main Postglacial Shoreline (Bonsall et al. 1992; Bonsall and Sutherland 1992). The second half of the Holocene presents much greater opportunity for preservation of evidence for human settlement. The sea was in general regressing, and this led to the isolation and preservation of shell middens as well as permitting access to the many caves associated with the Main Rock Platform. In addition, the expansion of coastal sand-dunes and blanket peats provided excellent sealed contexts for the preservation of organic remains.

3 Coastal Adaptation in the Mesolithic of Argyll. Rethinking the 'Obanian Problem'

Clive Bonsall

Direct evidence for the exploitation of coastal resources in the mesolithic of western Scotland is restricted to a small number of sites on which shell-midden deposits are preserved. These sites are generally referred to as 'Obanian' after the initial discoveries around Oban Bay in Argyll (figure 3.1). The Obanian sites share a number of features: faunal assemblages dominated by the shells of marine molluscs, but including crustacean remains and bones of fish, sea birds, sea mammals, and wild land mammals such as red deer and pig; lithic assemblages of flint and quartz in which retouched tools are often rare or absent and bipolar cores and débitage well represented; and a distinctive range of implements made from antler or bone which include bevelled tools, points ('awls') and, occasionally, harpoon heads and perforated mattock-heads.

A contrast is often drawn between the artefact assemblages from the Obanian middens and the microlithic industries recovered from a large number of mesolithic sites in western Scotland. The latter are invariably surface sites where soil conditions are unsuitable for the preservation of organic materials, and mesolithic activity is indicated mainly by the occurrence of one or more lithic scatters. Compared to Obanian toolkits, the lithic scatters are often characterised by a higher incidence of platform cores and blade débitage and the presence of microliths, scrapers and other retouched tools regarded as typical of mesolithic sites. This contrast in assemblage types is at the heart of long-standing debate in Scottish archaeology between those workers who believe the evidence justifies the recognition of an Obanian culture or phase within the west Scottish mesolithic, and those who consider that the assemblage types are most readily explained in functional terms. This chapter examines the background to this debate and offers a possible solution to the 'Obanian problem'.

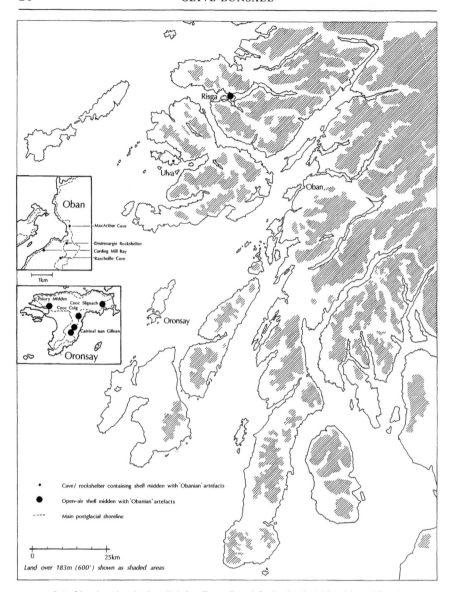

FIGURE 3.1. Obanian sites in Argyll (after Bonsall and Sutherland 1992, with revisions).

OBANIAN SHELL MIDDENS: THE DEVELOPMENT OF IDEAS

Early work on the Obanian between 1881 and 1926 focused on small caves and rockshelters around Oban Bay and a series of open-air sites on the islands of Oronsay and Risga. Joseph Anderson, in his account of the excavations at Druimvargie Rockshelter in Oban, was in effect the first to suggest that the Obanian sites were sufficiently distinctive to warrant their isolation as a distinct 'culture' (Anderson, J. 1898), although the term 'Obanian culture' did not come into general usage until several decades later (Movius 1940). Most subsequent workers have followed this interpretation, although there have been disagreements over the origins of the Obanian. Anderson, Breuil (1922) and Clark (1956) interpreted the style of the barbed points as evidence of a link with the Azilian, while Movius (1942) and Lacaille (1954) favoured an origin in the Irish mesolithic. Further work on the Oronsay middens was undertaken by Paul Mellars in the 1970s designed primarily to recover information on the economic basis of the Obanian occupation of the island (Mellars 1987). Mellars' excavations also provided the first radiocarbon dates for Obanian sites – multiple dating of each of the five excavated sites indicated that the Oronsay middens had been deposited between c.6200 and c.5400 BP. Radiocarbon determinations for microlithic industries available at that time ranged from c.8600–6000 BP (figure 3.2).

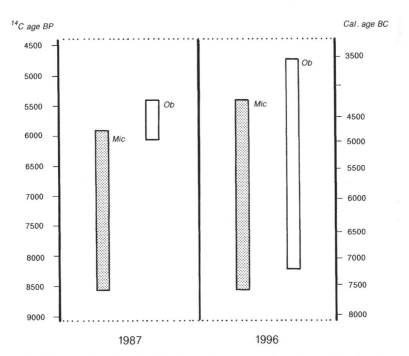

FIGURE 3.2. The changing chronological relationship between microlithic and Obanian site types in western Scotland. Knowledge of the Obanian time-range has been transformed mainly through direct dating of individual bone and antler artefacts using the AMS ^{14}C technique.

From this evidence, several authors have concluded that the Obanian sites are a very late manifestation of the mesolithic in western Scotland, post-dating the sites with microlithic industries and possibly overlapping in time the earliest neolithic sites. Woodman (1989) argued that the use of microlithic armatures in hunting equipment had been abandoned in favour of the production of barbed projectile points of bone and antler (see also Woodman 1990). Jacobi (1982) suggested that the adoption of barbed points, mattock-heads and other elements of the Obanian toolkit was the result of contact with the earliest farming communities of the region. Mellars (1972, 92) reserved judgement on the relationship between the Obanian and microlithic sites, but suggested that the Obanian artefact assemblage represented 'a highly specialized toolkit adapted to the intensive exploitation of coastal economic resources'.

THE OBANIAN IN PERSPECTIVE

Most previous interpretations of the Obanian are underpinned by five basic assumptions:

1. The Obanian has a limited geographical distribution, occurring only in coastal areas of Argyll.
2. The Obanian middens belong to a very late stage in the development of the mesolithic in this part of western Scotland, after c.6500/6000 BP.
3. The manufacture of microliths was not characteristic of the human groups responsible for the Obanian middens.
4. Certain artefact types found in Obanian assemblages are not characteristic of other coastal mesolithic sites in Scotland.
5. Obanian sites are found only on coasts where sites with microlithic industries do not occur, and vice versa.

Results of recent research on shell midden and microlithic sites in western Scotland, coupled with a reassessment of existing evidence, raise doubts about the validity of most, if not all, of these assumptions.

It has long been recognised that certain artefact types regarded as characteristic of the Obanian are not confined to shell midden sites on the west coast of Scotland. Isolated finds of flat harpoon-heads and perforated mattock-heads are known from a number of coastal locations in northern Britain (Movius 1942; Mellars 1972), while a shell midden excavated at Morton on the east coast of Scotland produced bevelled tools of bone similar to those from the west coast middens (Coles, J. M. 1971). Stone bevelled tools have a wide distribution along the western seaboard of Britain and have recently been reported from a microlithic site at Kinloch on the island of Rum in western Scotland (Wickham-Jones 1990).

Bone tools of typical Obanian form have been found recently at An Corran on the island of Skye in apparent association with a lithic assemblage which contains microliths, scrapers and other retouched tools (Rees et al. 1994;

Saville and Miket 1994), and at Ulva Cave on an island off the west coast of Mull in conjunction with platform cores and blade débitage (Bonsall et al. 1994). The An Corran site also extends the distribution of known Obanian middens along the western seaboard to significantly north of the 'core area' in Argyll.

Knowledge of the chronology of the Obanian has been vastly improved by the use of AMS radiocarbon dating to obtain direct age estimates on individual antler and bone artefacts from sites that were previously undated (Bonsall and Smith 1990; 1992; Bonsall et al. 1995). A large series of AMS and conventional radiocarbon determinations are now available for sites with Obanian artefacts (included in the lists in Chapter 11). These dates range from c.8350 to c.4750 BP and can be compared with (reliable) dates for sites with microlithic industries of between c.8600 and c.5450 BP (Morrison and Bonsall 1989; Hedges et al. 1989). The radiocarbon evidence therefore demonstrates a substantial chronological overlap between Obanian and microlithic assemblage types in western Scotland (figure 3.2). The dates from Carding Mill Bay I (the latest of the Obanian sites) are similar to those for the earliest dated neolithic sites in western Scotland and suggest that the economic system represented by the Obanian middens persisted until, and possibly after, the adoption of farming in the region.

Until recently, no microlithic sites were known to occur in close proximity to any of the known Obanian shell middens. At Lón Mór, near Oban, microlithic and shell midden sites have been recorded on the margins of a former marine embayment (Bonsall and Robinson 1992; Bonsall et al. 1993), while research on the island of Colonsay has revealed several sites with microlithic industries within 6 km to 8 km of the Oronsay shell middens (Mithen and Finlayson 1991).

Results of recent research, therefore, do not support the view that Obanian and microlithic assemblage types were the product of populations that were differentiated culturally or chronologically. Other possible explanations need to be considered. It can be argued that much of the variability exhibited by mesolithic sites in western Scotland is a consequence primarily of the conditions of preservation at the sites and the nature of the activities undertaken there.

SHELL MIDDENS AND SITE FUNCTION

Shell middens will accumulate where refuse from shellfish gathering is deposited on a regular basis. They will only survive, however, under favourable circumstances. In western Scotland shell midden deposits are preserved mainly in two geological situations – in coastal caves and rockshelters, the entrances to which were sealed by talus accumulations, and on open-air sites where the middens were subsequently buried beneath blown sand deposits. Among ethnographically-known shellfish gatherers, shellfish are rarely the principal source of food. But shellfishing is a regular activity, often undertaken by women and children, which normally is integrated with other economic tasks such as fishing, hunting (of land and sea mammals) and plant gathering. In her study of the Anbarra of the north coast of Australia, Meehan (1982) described three types of site at which shellfish remains accumulate: home bases, processing camps and 'dinnertime' camps. Processing camps and dinnertime camps are normally located near to the shell beds; the former being special-purpose sites where shellfish are gathered and cooked, and the flesh carried back to the home base; and the latter 'small campsites used during the middle of the day while people are engaged in [collecting] trips away from their home base' (Meehan 1982, 26), where food procured up to that time is cooked and eaten – some of the food prepared at these sites may also be carried back to the home base for later consumption. The existence of special-purpose 'processing camps' has been reported for other con- temporary shellfish gatherers in different parts of the world (Waselkov 1987), and they may be assumed to have archaeological counterparts in a similarly wide range of coastal situations.

From ethnographic evidence, archaeological 'processing camps' can be hypothesised to exist where the main habitation sites are some distance from the shell beds and to occur close to the contemporaneous shoreline; they are also likely to lack evidence of substantial structures, and to be characterised by a more restricted range of cultural equipment than at residential base camps (cf. Waselkov 1987, 145).

Ethnographically-known 'dinnertime camps' are typically small and were often used on only a single occasion; it follows that their prehistoric open-air equivalents are likely to be less visible archaeologically than either base camps or processing sites. However, if dinnertime camps were located in coastal caves, the chances of survival and discovery would be greatly enhanced; and if such locations were used repeatedly over a long period of time, then significant amounts of food refuse can be expected to have accumulated there.

SHELL MIDDENS IN THE MESOLITHIC OF WESTERN SCOTLAND

These observations drawn from ethnographic data can serve to guide in- terpretation of mesolithic shell middens in western Scotland. Mesolithic coast-dwelling communities in western Scotland had access to abundant and varied shellfish resources, and it is probable that most groups were in some degree shellfish gatherers. It is also likely that women and children played an important role in this economic activity. Shellfish on the rocky coasts that characterise much of western Scotland constitute a highly dispersed resource (see below). It is unlikely, therefore, that shellfishing activities would have been confined to base camps. Thus, it may be suggested that in addition to residential camps the use of processing camps and dinnertime camps was a feature of the mesolithic settlement-subsistence system, and that individual middens will relate to one or other of these site categories.

The quality of the data from the Obanian sites is highly variable, but a number of general features can be discerned which have a bearing on the question of site function. All of the known shell middens (whether within caves or in the open air) appear to have been deposited in close proximity to the contemporaneous shoreline; and at two sites, MacArthur Cave (Oban) and Cnoc Sligeach (Oronsay) the midden deposits were interstratified with storm beach gravels (Anderson, J. 1895; Mellars 1987). The sites often occur on open, relatively exposed coasts; and six of the twelve known sites are on small islands (Oronsay, Risga) that could not have sustained resident populations of deer or other large herbivores, and where access to land-based resources generally would have been limited. Conversely, such locations maximise access to shellfish and other shore-based resources.

In contrast to mesolithic coastal shell middens in some parts of Europe, the Obanian sites are very small – rarely exceeding 25 m across or 1.5 m in thickness. Yet radiocarbon dating and stratigraphic evidence from several recently excavated sites suggest that they were used repeatedly over long periods; on Oronsay this use appears to have followed a seasonal pattern (Mellars and Wilkinson 1980; see below). At Druimvargie Rockshelter in Oban and Caisteal nan Gillean I and Priory Midden on Oronsay midden accumulation occurred over several hundred radiocarbon years, while the Ulva Cave midden (only 8 m across) was deposited over 2000–3000 radiocarbon years (Russell, Bonsall and Sutherland 1995).

Although the faunal evidence indicates that seals, otters and sea birds were sometimes procured from the sites, the processing of shellfish and fish appears to have been the main economic activity undertaken. Bones of wild land mammals (principally red deer and pig) occur in all of the middens, but there is no unequivocal evidence that these were procured from the sites, or that major processing of their carcasses or hides occurred there (but see Finlayson 1995). From a study of the Cnoc Coig assemblage, Grigson concluded that antlers and bones of red deer and bones and tusks of wild boar had been introduced to the site primarily as a source of raw material for tool manufacture (Grigson and Mellars 1987).

None of the sites has produced convincing evidence of dwelling structures or storage facilities. The only site with extensive structural remains is Cnoc Coig on Oronsay, where two stake-hole settings and a series of hearths, small pits and concentrations of heat-affected stones were associated with a former land surface underneath the midden (Mellars 1987). These features appear to have resulted from frequent reuse of the site, and their occurrence with burnt shells and fish bones suggests that they were connected essentially with food preparation activities.

Many of the artefacts recovered from the Obanian middens appear to reflect 'expediency' in design, manufacture and raw material procurement. Reduction strategies applied to flint and quartz frequently involved use of the bipolar technique. At the majority of sites nearly all of the lithic artefacts and most of those made from bone, antler or shell, are simple, easily made (and hence 'disposable') items which were probably manufactured at the sites for immediate use; as such they offer an interesting parallel to the 'situational gear' of the Nunamiut which tends to be well represented at their special-purpose sites (Binford 1979). The frequent absence of retouched pieces, such as microliths and scrapers, commonly found at other mesolithic sites in western Scotland, implies that activities (production, use, maintenance) involving such artefacts were not normally undertaken at the shell midden sites. Occasionally, elaborate artefacts such as harpoon- and mattock-heads made of bone or antler are represented in the middens. These are items that can be expected to have been 'heavily curated' (cf. Binford 1979). In some cases, they may have been brought to the sites for use there. In many instances, however, they were probably introduced as broken items intended for recycling. Some of the broken harpoon heads from MacArthur Cave, for example, appear to have been converted into bevelled tools.

The principal categories of artefacts with an 'expedient' aspect occurring in Obanian sites are unretouched flakes of flint and/or quartz often produced by the bipolar technique, bevelled tools, and small bone points. There has been little systematic research on the possible uses of these artefacts. Finlayson (in Connock et al. 1993) has observed that a bipolar reduction strategy applied to small pebbles of flint or quartz produces numerous flat, sharp flakes which could be used without further modification as 'knives' for processing fish. Experimental studies of bevelled tools and bone points are being undertaken at the University of Edinburgh. Pending the results of this research, the present writer favours the view advocated by some previous workers (e.g. Grieve 1885; Bishop 1914) that the bevelled tools were used in the processing or collection of limpets. In this context it is worth noting that 'Asturian picks' from mesolithic shell middens along the north coast of Spain, usually interpreted as 'limpet hammers', often exhibit a degree of bevelling at the tip. The small bone points which occur in large numbers in some Obanian middens may also have been used in the processing of shellfish, e.g. for removing the soft parts of periwinkles and dog-whelks from their shells, and for piercing shellfish/fish meat so that it could be strung up for drying.

From the similarities in their location and in the character of their artefactual and faunal assemblages, it can be argued that the known Obanian sites fulfilled a specific role in the mesolithic settlement-subsistence system of the region. The absence of major architectural features, and the lack of certain categories of industrial and food refuse that can be expected to have been discarded inside residential camps, suggest that the middens do not represent the disposal of refuse from nearby base camps. From the available evidence it can be inferred that they mark the locations of special-purpose processing camps associated with the exploitation of sea food resources, principally fish and shellfish, and that food prepared at the sites was carried back to residential camps located some distance away. As noted above, it is likely that women and children played a dominant role in this economic activity and at some sites, perhaps, an exclusive one. The age/sex composition of the task group occupying a site is likely to have some influence on the character of the resulting artefact assemblage. The incidence of bipolar débitage is likely to be greater where women and children were more actively involved than men in the use of the site, on the assumption that generally they were less skilled flint knappers. Similarly, items traditionally made and used by men (e.g. remains of hunting equipment) ought to be poorly represented at sites where men and teenage boys were not present or only occasionally participated in the activities of the site.

Processing of shellfish and other food items occurred at all of the known Obanian sites. However, differences in the content of the midden deposits suggest that there was significant variation in the frequency, range, scale and intensity of the processing activities undertaken. The midden in Ulva Cave (figure 3.3) is substantially smaller than those on Oronsay, is unusually heavily dominated by shells of marine molluscs and contains comparatively few artefacts or mammalian bones (Russell, Bonsall and Sutherland 1995). Yet evidently it represents refuse from numerous visits to the site over several millennia, implying that the site was used less frequently than those on Oronsay, or for shorter periods, or that particularly small amounts of material were processed during individual occupations. Such differences suggest that the Obanian sites perhaps represent a spectrum of human activities between dedicated processing camps and repeatedly-used dinnertime camps.

The midden at An Corran on Skye is unusual in possessing what Saville and Miket (1994) have termed a 'conventional' mesolithic assemblage with blade débitage, microliths and other retouched artefacts. But the site is also unusual in respect of access to lithic resources. Compared to other Obanian sites a wider range of materials was available locally, including large pieces of high quality volcanic rock; a significant proportion of the microliths and blade débitage is apparently made from this volcanic material. In addition to 'normal' processing activities, therefore, An Corran was possibly important for raw material procurement, and stages in the production of lithic items related to the manufacture or repair of personal gear may have been undertaken there. Such tasks are likely to have involved men and could have been performed in conjunction with the processing of fish and shellfish or at other times.

SHELL MIDDENS AND SITE LOCATION

It was noted above that mesolithic shell middens in western Scotland occur in coastal caves/rockshelters and on open-air sites. Among ethnographically-known shellfish gatherers the processing of shellfish for food often involves cooking (roasting or boiling) 'in, over, under or around open fires' (Waselkov 1987, 100). If climatic conditions in Scotland during the mesolithic were similar to today – with high rainfall and strong winds – then processing activities would necessitate the frequent use of some form of shelter. It follows

FIGURE 3.3.1. Ulva Cave, Isle of Ulva, Argyll.

FIGURE 3.3.2. Close-up of the shell midden in the entrance zone of the cave.

that where caves existed near to the shell beds they would have been used occasionally for processing activities (Russell, Bonsall and Sutherland 1995), and that construction of artificial shelters is likely to have occurred on open-air processing sites. The existence of stake-hole settings, hearths and pits in association with shell refuse at Cnoc Coig on Oronsay (Mellars 1987) is consistent with this hypothesis, and a similar interpretation can be placed on the structural remains excavated at Morton on the east coast of Scotland (Coles, J. M. 1971).

The shell middens on Oronsay and around Oban Bay occur at intervals along the shoreline that was formed at the maximum of the Main Postglacial Transgression, c.6000–7000 BP (figure 3.1). Radiocarbon dating and stratigraphic evidence indicate that most of the sites post-date or are contemporaneous with the maximum of the transgression. Since the middens are likely to have been deposited in close proximity to the shoreline of the time, it is highly probable that many sites predating the maximum of the transgression (and possibly some that were contemporaneous with it) are likely to have been destroyed during that event (Bonsall and Sutherland 1992). Therefore, the known sites are most probably only a partial record of shellfish-gathering activities along those coasts during the mesolithic.

From a study of the length distributions of otoliths in the Oronsay middens, Mellars and Wilkinson (1980) have shown that fish were procured from the different sites at specific times of the year. Equivalent seasonality data are not available for the shellfish, but it seems reasonable to assume that they were collected and processed at the sites at the same times of year. Although shellfish probably contributed less to the overall food supply than either fish or sea mammals, it may be suggested that they exercised a significant influence on site location. On Oronsay, as on many coasts in western Scotland, there is a rocky shoreline. As Waselkov (1987, 115) has observed, shellfish associated with such shorelines constitute a dispersed resource which can be exploited most effectively at numerous points. Thus, the choice of location for the processing sites on Oronsay may have been determined primarily by the need for seasonal scheduling of the shellfish resources (figure 3.4).

From the ethnographic and archaeological evidence discussed, it can be predicted that remains of mesolithic processing camps will occur at numerous points around the coasts of western Scotland, around or above the level of the Main Postglacial Shoreline. Unlike the coast of Oronsay, many other coasts have no blown sand deposits which could preserve open-air shell middens. The former locations of such middens, however, can be expected to be represented by residual scatters of lithic artefacts similar in character to those from known shell midden sites. Such sites are likely to be of limited extent, and hence difficult to locate. Moreover, in the absence of microliths or other diagnostic artefacts, it is doubtful if they would be immediately identifiable as mesolithic. In a recent survey of the island of Ulva, several such scatters were recognised (Russell, Bonsall and Sutherland 1995, fig.2). None of the sites, however, has been investigated further and their ages are unknown.

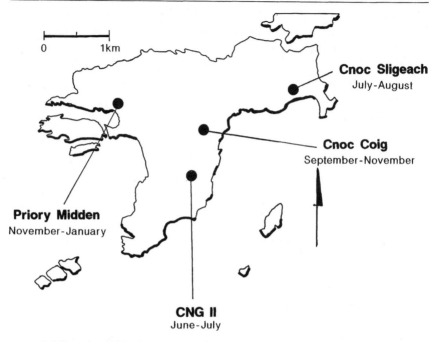

FIGURE 3.4. Location of Obanian shell middens on Oronsay showing the main seasons at which processing of fish was undertaken at the sites, based on the size distribution of otoliths of saithe (after Mellars and Wilkinson 1980). The flesh of fish and shellfish processed at these special purpose sites would have been carried back to a home base for later consumption. Residential sites relating to the Oronsay processing camps were probably located some distance away, possibly on the neighbouring island of Colonsay.

CONCLUSIONS

In this chapter it has been argued that the contrast between Obanian sites and sites with microlithic industries evident in the mesolithic of western Scotland cannot be explained satisfactorily in cultural or chronological terms, but is primarily a reflection of differences in the conditions of preservation at the two types of site and the nature of the activities undertaken there.

A case can be made for interpreting most, and possibly all, of the known Obanian sites as remains of special-purpose processing camps associated primarily with the exploitation of shellfish and fish. The use of such logistic camps appears to have been an integral part of an economic system that operated in western Scotland (if not more widely in northern Britain) throughout the greater part of the mesolithic and into the period after c.5000 BP and the widespread adoption of farming in the region. The model proposed explains a number of 'unusual' features of Obanian sites, such as their frequent occurrence on open coasts and on small islands which lacked resident populations of large land mammals, and the prevalence in the middens of expediently designed and manufactured tools.

The existing evidence, however, has obvious limitations. Although there has been a marked increase in research activity over the past twenty-five years, with new excavations at sites on the islands of Oronsay, Skye and Ulva, and on the mainland around Oban Bay, the full results of this research are not yet available. Consequently, there is a lack of detailed information on the faunal composition of the majority of Obanian sites and on functional and technological aspects of the Obanian toolkit. There is also a need for additional research, including studies to determine the seasonality of shellfish gathering at individual sites like those conducted by Margaret Deith (1983; 1985; 1986) at sites in eastern Scotland and northern Spain, and for more extensive excavations to expose areas adjacent to middens in order to test for associated architectural features and to recover information on site structure in general. The interpretation of the Obanian sites presented in this chapter should, therefore, be viewed as a 'working hypothesis' which can be tested, and modified, as new data become available.

4 Early Settlement in Argyll

Graham Ritchie

MESOLITHIC EVIDENCE

The earliest settlement of the Atlantic coasts and islands of Scotland is indicated both by scatters of tiny flint tools, or microliths, together with the waste material discarded in the course of their manufacture, and by midden débris, including mounds of shells and occupation deposits in caves. The early hunters, whose processing sites are indicated by such flint scatters, were drawn by the natural resources that the area had to offer, game, fish, seals, and rich vegetation, which could provide nuts, berries, and the material for shelter and for making boats. There were also many caves and rock-shelters that could offer an occasional or seasonal base for hunting or fishing expeditions. Only rarely, as in the sites of Chapter 3, is there a greater range of artefactual material than flint- or stone-work or anything by way of structural remains, other than hearths. This is a consequence of differing levels of preservation, rather than cultural distinction. Frequently the discovery of flint scatters is a matter of chance, but on Jura the systematic work of John Mercer and Susan Searight has uncovered sites as a result of deliberate field examination (the references are in Searight 1993); on Islay and Colonsay many new sites have been discovered as a result of careful field-walking undertaken by the Southern Hebrides Research Project, directed by Steven Mithen (e.g. Mithen 1989; 1996; Mithen and Finlayson 1991). Larger-scale area excavation has, however, been undertaken at Kinloch, on the island of Rum, to the north of Ardnamurchan, and thus beyond the boundary of Argyll, but today's administrative boundaries have little meaning in an evocation of activities of some 9000 years ago.

The excavations at Kinloch are important because several aspects of the evidence – chronological, structural and artefactual – provide links to sites in

38

Argyll (Wickham-Jones 1990). To take the chronological evidence first, a series of radiocarbon dates showed that the activities of the hunting and gathering communities spanned about a thousand years from about 7000 BC, but whether continuously or not was impossible to suggest. Comparable artefacts found on sites with similar radiocarbon dates include microliths from Newton, Islay, and Lussa Wood, Jura.

At Kinloch the structural evidence, which is our principal concern, was revealed because a larger area was uncovered than has usually been possible in past excavations, and the individual stake-holes, pits, and hollows could be seen in a broader, if still tentative, context. Thus arcs of stake-holes indicate the positions of wind-breaks, shelters, or fragments of stake and skin huts. Certainly there were the timber resources to provide the framework for a covering of skins or thatch of twigs. Although hearths were not found, the presence of burnt artefacts shows that there must have been fires in the vicinity of the structures. The preservation of organic material was not good, and the exploitation of the resources of the surrounding sea and the animals of the uplands has to be assumed.

Comparable stake shelters have been found at Cnoc Coig, on Oronsay, where stake-holes suggest a diameter of 3 m – 3.5 m for the hut or wind-break around a central hearth (Mellars 1987, 237–9). Again the covering material can only be surmised, but intertwined branches with animal skins or grass have been suggested. These features were probably connected with activities connected with food preparation.

The fugitive structural remains at Kinloch and Cnoc Coig were interpreted using ethnographic parallels from African or Eskimo groups. Until recent times several of the lay-bys of Mid Argyll saw summer encampments of tinker groups, whose wooden-framed (or latterly metal-framed) and tarpaulin-covered tents weighted down with stones formed remarkably spacious and weather-proof seasonal accommodation, for which there will be no archaeological evidence at all. Photographs from the Scottish Ethnological Archive, National Museums of Scotland, give a vivid impression of the range of size of such shelters, the framework of birch, hazel or ash branches and the covering of felt, sailcloth or tarpaulin (figures 4.1–4) (Leitch 1989). The structural branches might be taken from site to site along with the necessary covering; alternatively the various components might be found anew, with thatch from local resources of twigs and reed. Although work and cooking was clearly carried on in front of the shelter, it is recorded that for winter quarters, often on traditional sites, a more substantial tent contained a hearth of flat stones and a number of straw beds (M. E. M. Donaldson in Telfer Dunbar 1980, 57), but evidence for sites such as these in the mesolithic period in Argyll is entirely lacking.

The excavations at Kinloch also highlight the possibilities of the exchange of resources over broad areas, demonstrating contact and movement across the sea to neighbouring communities. Rum has an outcrop of a very distinctive type of siliceous rock known as bloodstone which can readily be knapped

FIGURE 4.1. Tinker encampment on the west coast, c.1910; photograph by M. E. M. Donaldson.

to create implements. Bloodstone was used at several periods, and certainly not all those found belong to the initial phase of activity at Kinloch, but bloodstone artefacts have been found on the adjacent islands of Canna, Eigg and Skye, and further afield bloodstone has been found associated with flint scatters in Ardnamurchan and Morvern (Wickham-Jones 1990, 151–3; Ritchie et al. 1975, 28). Although the mechanisms for such exchange are not clear, the presence even of small amounts of bloodstone over a wide area help

FIGURE 4.2. Tinker family on the move, c.1900s, with the boy carrying the supports for the family tent.

FIGURE 4.3. A tinker at work beside his camp fire.

to underline the possibilities of sea-borne travel, with communities moving about in search of the most abundant game or other natural resources at different seasons of the year.

In Jura, the remains of a campsite at Lussa Wood included conjoined circular stone settings, each about 1.5 m in diameter, containing hazelnut shells and other burnt material; radiocarbon determinations show that the cooking place was in use about 6000 BC (Mercer 1980). At Newton, on Islay, occupation débris in a subrectangular depression associated with numerous hearths appears to belong to broadly the same date (McCullagh 1989, 25–7). At Kilellan, Islay, mesolithic activity is associated with patches of deliberately laid stones and at least one shallow pit (pers. comm. A. Ritchie).

The artefactual sequences of the various forms of microliths or stone and bone tools are not relevant to our examination of the surviving structural

FIGURE 4.4. Two tinkers working in front of their tents.

remains, and the possible inferences in terms of site interpretation have been explored in the previous chapter. The distribution of flint scatters and shell-midden accumulations that may broadly be dated to between 7500 and 3500 BC shows the favoured areas of activity at that time to have been the Southern Inner Hebrides (Colonsay, Oronsay, Jura, Islay), Mull and the adjacent mainland round Oban and Campbeltown. Clearly the whole extent of the coastline and the immediate hinterland of Argyll offered the early hunter and gatherer communities potential resources, and our understanding of their settlement pattern is limited by the partial nature of prospective field-survey and by the small number of chance finds that have been followed up by excavation as at Kilmelfort (Coles, J. M. 1983).

It is important to evoke the early prehistory of Argyll because of the part it has to play in the understanding of the distinctive archaeology of the west of Scotland and the notion of Atlantic archaeology in a European context. Emergency excavations undertaken around Oban in the late 19th century produced an array of artefacts including barbed antler points, scrapers and borers, as well as distinctive stone tools, known as 'limpet-hammers' and hammer-stones. Subsequent excavations on Oronsay revealed a similar range of finds (Smith, C. 1992, 147–57). Discussion of the discoveries in a contemporary context is provided in Chapter 3. What is relevant here is the way that these distinctive objects could be viewed within a European dimension, and the early occupation of the Atlantic coast set within a context of comparable finds from the south of France and northern Spain. Childe's evocation caught the imagination:

> In other words the colonists who have settled near Oban and on Oronsay in Atlantic times must have arrived by sea, ultimately from Northern Spain and South-western France. It sounds fantastic to bring primitive fishers and hunters who did not even possess an axe from so far afield, especially when intermediate finds are lacking. But we do not envisage a single voyage direct from the mouth of the Garonne to Galloway. On the contrary the fishers would have progressed very slowly, halting at many points on the way, perhaps for several generations at each. (1935, 17)

No archaeologist would paint the early settlement of the west of Scotland in such vivid terms today, but the tentative nature of the arrival of groups of people and the length of time involved in coming to understand the resources of any particular area are still relevant. Nor is the adjective 'primitive' appropriate to what is now known of the sophistication of hunter-gatherer communities, and it suggests that a settled agricultural economy is somehow a preferable and less 'primitive' existence. Ethnographic parallels can be adduced to show the complexity of such societies and their success in meeting their objectives (Sahlins 1974, 1–39), and at the same time they illustrate the wealth of everyday objects that can be made from wood, bark, skins, woven grass, nothing of which will survive in the archaeological record in western

Scotland, except in unusual circumstances (as for example in Alaska, Kaplan and Barsness 1986).

The wider archaeological understanding of the economic basis and burial practices of hunting and gathering peoples resulting from excavations in England and Denmark show such societies to be anything other than 'primitive'. Once a rhythm of movement and exploitation is achieved that meets the expectations of a group, natural forces alone need dictate change. Thus it should come as no surprise that the radiocarbon dates from several shell middens and caves demonstrate continuing activity of such groups at periods in the third and fourth millennia when early agricultural activity was underway in other parts of Argyll. Nor is there any reason to think that the early agriculturalists were immediately successful in meeting economic sufficiency. There is likely to have been a change in the pattern of movements of the hunting and gathering groups, for the rhythm of subsistence had evolved over some four millennia; in some areas the natural vegetation would be cut down to make way for fields and grazing, and passage between one seasonal campsite and another might become impossible. It is perhaps not surprising therefore that the sites from which such radiocarbon dates have been determined are mainly on the periphery of early agricultural activity, in areas where natural resources were assured, and the benefits of an agricultural economy were at best limited.

The background to the discovery of the deposits in the caves at Oban and to the relationship between the different approaches to hunter/gatherer and agricultural economies in the light of current theoretical approaches was reviewed by Pollard (1990). The programme of radiocarbon dating undertaken on the skeletal material demonstrates, however, that the burial deposits overlying the mesolithic layers result from renewed interest in the caves in the later first millennium BC rather than implying any mesolithic/neolithic interaction (Saville and Hallen 1994). The potential of coastal resources in an agricultural economy, not necessarily only at times of crisis, is a valuable one, for the balanced economy of any region must take account of readily available natural resources as well as those under the more immediate control of the farmer and pastoralist, as any crofter will testify today. The ritual deposits of marine shells at the chambered cairn at Crarae, Mid Argyll (Scott, J. G. 1961), or fish bones at Holm of Papa Westray North, Orkney (Ritchie, A. 1995, 63), help to emphasise this.

Theoretical approaches to the gradual change in economic practice have been outlined by Zvelebil (1986): the wave of advance model, the pioneer colonisation model, and the availability model. The availability model has much to recommend it when set within the broken terrain of uplands and islands that make up Argyll; the long period during which the change took place, with a phase of forager/farmer interaction, and a gradual increase in the importance of domesticated animals and cultivated cereals in the economic cycle (Zvelebil and Rowley-Conwy 1984; Zvelebil 1986, 71–5). In Argyll, as in many other areas, the economic change is difficult to explain analytically, for the reality was almost certainly one with myriad local facets. The complexity of hunter/gatherer society must be invoked without the benefit of much archaeological evidence. The uncertainty of early farming practice is often understated because of the permanence of the associated burial monuments (though not necessarily with the very earliest stages). The economy of the coast must always have depended on skills with a boat and tenacity in gathering the riches from the shore; while for the farmer to ignore the woodland game would be to forgo a valuable source of food, skin, and raw material, as well as reducing the numbers of potential competitors for the growing crops. It may be that it is in the expression of the relationship of people to the land they occupy that the greatest change occurs.

The concept of the 'agricultural frontier' is also important, although in the absence of palynological evidence, that is the understanding of the vegetational history through an examination of the pollen, the approach relies on the distribution of chambered cairns and small finds; there is very little avowedly neolithic material from the more northerly islands of Argyll, one chambered cairn apiece on Mull and Jura, none on Tiree, Coll or Colonsay, and merely a scatter in Northern Argyll. Certainly there are finds of axes and flint artefacts, sometimes in the course of forestry ploughing (pers. comm. Roy Douglass)(RCAHMS 1980, 7); but did the advantages of a hunting and gathering economy outweigh agriculture in the eyes of communities to the west of the Lynn of Lorn? Later neolithic Beaker pottery has been found, however, in some quantity in the sandhill sites of Coll, Tiree and Ardnamurchan. There seems no reason to doubt that the whole of Argyll was within the agricultural frontier by the middle of the third millennium BC (Ritchie and Crawford 1978; for ploughing associated with Beakers see e.g. Shepherd and Tuckwell 1977).

HOUSES OF EARLY FARMING COMMUNITIES

Richard Bradley has explored the nature of the change in the structural record that accompanied the adoption of agriculture; the megalithic burial cairns are the most enduring monuments of the third and second millennia BC, yet they are clearly not essential to a prosperous farming economy (1993, 17). The change is one of attitude of mind to the space or place in which the economic activity is carried out. Burial rituals and the monuments associated with them are the subject of a later chapter, but the small number of settlement sites found in Argyll should be considered here. Argyll has no Skara Brae, no stone-built icon of early domestication of the landscape. The remains are of houses that were largely timber-built. At Ardnadam, Cowal, for example, excavation revealed a sequence of occupation on an alluvial fan on one side of a stream (Rennie 1984); the two earliest phases were separated by a layer of gravel and silt, which suggested that the first houses had been destroyed by flooding. The houses are represented by post-holes, cobbled areas, and hearths; although it was difficult to be certain of the overall dimensions, sizes of about 7.5 m by

5.5 m, 3.5 m by 3 m, and 6 m by 6 m were proposed. House 5 had been re-built or modified on several occasions, three floor levels for example being distinguished by distinct layers of cobbling, but the position of the hearth re-mained constant. Neolithic pottery was found associated with all three levels and a radiocarbon determination associated with the lowest hearth has a span of between 3699 and 3342 BC (GU–1549). A later house, apparently oval and about 12 m in length overall, could be made out from the pattern of post-holes and the base of a surrounding stone bank.

At Auchategan, Cowal, on a terrace above the River Ruel, the structures associated with neolithic pottery were also represented by post-holes and hearths as well as many other characteristic artefacts of flint and stone (Marshall, D. N. 1978). The insubstantial nature of the structural evidence belies, perhaps, the stability of the settlement, if such can be inferred from the large number of neolithic vessels recovered. Sherds from about sixty vessels were recovered within what was quite a restricted excavation area. A radiocarbon determination from charcoal in a hearth from the second phase of neolithic settlement provides an indication of date, between 3254 and 2500 BC (I–4705).

The discovery of the settlements of the early agricultural communities of Argyll has been the result of the excavation and careful recording of sites where there have been surface traces of later occupation. It is the location of such sites on alluvial fans and valley terraces that suggests areas of future research. The discovery of a considerable number of sherds of distinctive neo-lithic vessels in the course of excavation of the fort on Balloch Hill, Kintyre, though unassociated with any structure, indicates another type of area of early settlement (Peltenburg 1982); the discovery of Arran pitchstone at Balloch Hill may be an indication of the wide-ranging contacts possible at this time. At Newton, Islay, there was clear evidence for neolithic activity, with pottery, pits, and gullies and conformable radiocarbon dates, but too little of the site could be excavated for the nature of the settlement to be interpreted (figures 10.1–2)(McCullagh 1989, 27–31). The available radiocarbon dates from Argyll provide only a tentative chronological guide. The beginning of an economy based more on agriculture and stock-rearing is, from evidence be-yond our area, taken to have been underway by about 4000 BC. An occupation horizon below the chambered cairn at Port Charlotte, Islay, associated with carbonised hazelnut shells, sheep bones and flint objects, has a date in the second quarter of the fourth millennium, while dates from the chamber itself fall in the second half of the millennium.

The neolithic artefacts from Kintyre form the best-studied group for Argyll as a whole, partly because the pottery assemblage from the chambered cairn at Beacharra is so distinctive and that from Balloch Hill so comprehensive, but also because of the work of J. G. Scott (1969, 240–3). A brief discussion of the relevant pottery styles has been included in the section on burial monu-ments (Chapter 5), but here it is pertinent to mention the sources of the material from which the axeheads that formed such an important part of the toolkit of the farming communities were made. Scott identified axes of porcellanite, probably from Tievebulliagh or Rathlin Island from the adjacent shores of Ireland; others were likely to be of Lake District origin, from Great Langdale. It is likely that some axes were of local material. The participation of the communities of the area in trade and exchange is clear, but the slight archaeological evidence is ill-suited to explain the mechanisms of how this took place. Equally tantalising is the discovery of carved stone balls, a most distinctive neolithic artefact, with a distribution mainly in north-eastern Scotland, on the shore at Dunaverty, Kintyre, at Dunadd, Mid Argyll, and in Glen Masson, Cowal (Marshall, D. N. 1977, 1983; Edmonds 1992).

There is an uncertain contrast between the structural evidence of settlements and burial cairns of Argyll and those of Orkney, where the settlements are largely constructed in stone. There, a parallel has sometimes been seen between the houses of the living and the resting places of the dead, between the hearths of houses and the ritual features of henge monuments. In Argyll no such parallel can be adduced; from the archaeological evidence, the houses appear to have few architectural pretensions and certainly few of the statements of monumentality made by the contemporary chambered cairns.

SAND-HILL SITES

The present sand-hills of the western islands of Argyll and of mainland Ardnamurchan contain evidence of activity throughout the occupation of the seaboard; scatters of pottery, flint, metalwork, hearths, burials and stone foundations have been discovered, sometimes recorded, sometimes forgotten. The disturbance of a burial in a grave pit in the sand-dunes at Sorisdale, Coll, in 1976 is one example. The discovery of a skull and an all-over-cord ornamented Beaker vessel left no doubt that the deposit was that of an inhumation burial; a rescue excavation was set in train, the burial carefully recorded and a radiocarbon date obtained (Ritchie and Crawford 1978). In fact the date is the earliest so far obtained for such a vessel in Scotland, its span being 2468–2197 BC (BM–1413), and it is an important indication of the date of the spread of such pottery to the islands. An immediately adjacent fragmentary arc of stones and floor deposit could be interpreted as one end of a 'house', comparable to those found at Northton, Harris (Simpson, D. D. A. 1976). Here low drystone walling associated with stake-holes, set within the sand-dunes and measuring about 8.5 m by 4.3 m, was interpreted as being the revetment for the stance for a light tent or hut (ibid., 222–4). If this interpretation is valid, the surviving structural evidence of activity in such environments is likely to be limited: stone settings and hearths perhaps, but little more.

The remains at Ardnave, Islay, were more substantial (Ritchie and Welfare 1983); a hollow in the sand had been faced with drystone walling, forming a house about 6.5 m in diameter with a central hearth (figure 4.5). Few of the internal post-holes were large enough to support a weighty timber roof, but

FIGURE 4.5. Ardnave, Islay, stone house set into the sand-dunes, with Nave Island in the background.

a lighter roofing, of skins for example, could readily have been created. Part of the interior was subsequently reused to form a smaller house measuring about 3.3 m by 4.5 m internally with stone walls outlining the interior and distinct settings of post-holes indicating several periods of rebuilding. The posts were merely driven into the sand and there was no attendant stone packing. Immediately in front of the entrance a small pit covered by a layer of flat slabs was found to contain a complete Food Vessel (figure 4.6); there was no associated burial, and it may be that the deposit is by way of a foundation offering. The artefacts associated with the structures include flint and stone tools, together with shovels made from ox scapulae. Preservation of bone allowed the economic basis of the little community to be suggested: cattle and sheep bones were discovered as well as red deer; shell fish and crabs showed that the resources of the nearby shore were not ignored; and the cultivation of six-row barley and emmer was attested. The stone structures were later engulfed by a thick layer of blown sand, and subsequent occupation of the site is represented by hearths and midden deposits. The archaeological importance of this occupation débris lies in the range of highly decorated pottery vessels that was present, a range that is unexpected for a community that might otherwise be seen as operating in a marginal environment at the tip of Islay (figure 4.6). Many of the vessels are large and are unlikely to have been made far from the settlement, yet the decoration and shapes belong to wider ceramic traditions linking the west of Scotland to Ireland. Also important is the series of radiocarbon dates, which help to set the pottery styles

FIGURE 4.6. Ardnave, Islay, pottery, above, a Food Vessel from a special deposit in front of the entrance; below, Food Vessels from the midden layers (scale 1:4).

of the west into a chronological framework, rather than depending on individual determinations from burial deposits. The settlement remains at nearby Kilellan are less readily interpretable, but palisade slots and what appeared to be a house floor were found; the pottery recovered has an even greater range of decoration than that from Ardnave, though there are similarities between the two assemblages and again the links with Irish styles is clear (pers. comm, A. Ritchie).

HUT-CIRCLES

Understanding of the settlement archaeology of Argyll was slow to develop; hut-circles as a class were not recognised in the course of RCAHMS survey in Kintyre or Lorn in the later 1960s and early 1970s, partly because they did not fit into the accepted pattern of the times and partly because broadly similar monuments in the Borders had been seen as of comparatively recent agricultural origin, although a few certainly exist (for example at Corputchechan, Kintyre, NR 679334). The identification of the field-boundaries at Achnacree,

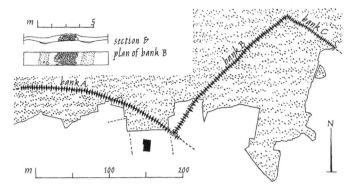

FIGURE 4.7. Achnacree, Lorn, field-boundaries and peat-cover.

which hinted at land-divisions in prehistoric times before the growth of the blanket peat (Ritchie et al., 1974; Barrett et al. 1976), alerted subsequent field-workers to the possibility of a wider range of evidence, and this coupled with the knowledge of the results of survey and excavation on Arran helped to change approaches to field recording (figure 4.7).

Similarly the identification of burnt mounds, the piles of discarded stones that result from a cooking process that involves heating water in a trough to permit a form of 'slow cooking', was made in Islay in the early 1980s. Sample excavations have been undertaken on Bute, Arran and Islay with radiocarbon dates in the third and second millennia BC (Russell-White and Barber 1990; Lehane 1990). There is no reason to suppose that this form of food preparation was not much more widespread than the recorded examples suggest, and such sites have been found to be important elements in the landscape of many parts of upland Scotland recently surveyed; undoubtedly many burnt mounds remain to be discovered in Argyll.

Advances in survey techniques in the 1970s also had a part to play in the more comprehensive presentation of the field evidence, for it was increasingly possible to piece the disparate elements of the landscape together on a single plan, and thus to present a more integrated picture than previously. In fact this is more difficult in the broken topography of the west of Scotland than it sounds, for the parcels of fields may not be intervisible, and the natural rock outcrops, which may be an integral part of the way an area was farmed, may be time-consuming to draw. Nevertheless surveys in Colonsay and Oronsay in the late 1970s and on Islay in the early 1980s set the hut-circles of Argyll within the framework of associated field-walls, small cairns, while parallel excavations on Jura and Islay (as well as earlier work on Arran) provided material that set such sites into firmer chronological contexts. At Druim Mor, Oronsay, for example, a series of field-banks and rather later small cairns occupy the southern tip of the island, at the mid point of which there is a well-preserved hut-circle some 6 m in diameter within a bank some 0.75 m in height (RCAHMS 1984, 135–5, no.257). At Beinn Arnicil, Colonsay, a more

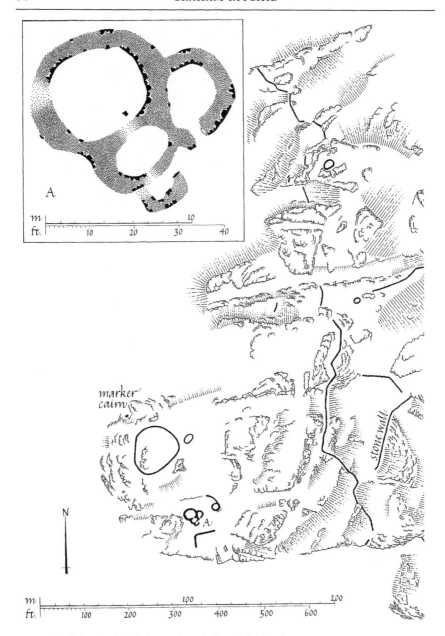

FIGURE 4.8. Beinn Arnicil, Colonsay, hut-circle and field-walls.

complex cellular house is associated with low stone walls which form a series of terraces on the eastern flanks of the rocky hill (figure 4.8) (RCAHMS 1984, 130–1, no.244).

Excavation of a hut-circle and associated enclosure on the slopes of Cul a'Bhaile, Jura, demonstrated the chronological depth of the use of individual settlement locations (Stevenson, J. B. 1984). The surrounding stone-walled enclosure measures about 78 m by 65 m and is now largely masked by peat that has formed over much of the site. The excavation showed that the area had been under the plough before the building of the house, for there were distinct traces of ard-marks beneath the stones of the wall. The wall of the hut-circle (figure 4.9), which encloses a central area about 7.5 m in diameter, comprised a carefully laid stone foundation with a capping of earth and turf; immediately within the inner facing-stones excavation revealed a ring of small stake-holes, which probably supported a wattle screen. Within the interior there is a ring of post-holes for the uprights that would have been required to take the ring-beam needed to support the roof. Two later phases of construction, remodelling of the wall and replacement of the posts, together with the radiocarbon dates point to a lengthy occupation spanning the late second millennium BC and the early first millennium BC. The artefactual evidence was meagre, flint and stone objects offering evidence for cutting, scraping and bashing, but as has been stressed for earlier periods paucity of surviving material in such acidic conditions is of little help in evoking the range of environmental resources that were to hand. A paved area outside the doorway suggests that many activities took place, as in later times, in the open air at the front of the house. Indeed the doorway of the majority of hut-circles is frequently on the south-east side in order to allow as much light into the interior as possible; the interior floor levels, however, are unlikely to offer the range of archaeological evidence that a contemporary external midden can provide. In a number of examples the entrance into a hut-circle appears to be further protected by a low hook-like bank, and it may be that this formed the foundation for a wind-break to shelter the multitude of outside activities.

The ard-marks beneath the wall show the use of simple ploughs without mould-boards. Evidence of this form of ploughing can be found in two ways; the parallel groups of scores in the subsoil that have filled in with material of a different colour can be seen in the course of excavation, and the stone ard points, often showing heavy wear at the tip, can be found. Ard-marks can most readily be seen in sandy situations, among the most fully recorded being at Rosinish, Benbecula (Shepherd and Tuckwell 1977; Halliday et al. 1981, 55). Sample excavations have been undertaken on Bute, Arran and Islay with radiocarbon dates in the third and second millennia BC (Russell-White and Barber 1990; Lehane 1990). An extensive area of ard marks was recovered at Machrie Moor, Arran, in stratigraphical relationship that placed the ploughing between ritual timber circles and later stone circles; there were also lines of stake holes apparently forming land divisions (Haggerty 1991). An extensive area of ard marks was recovered at Machrie Moor, Arran, in

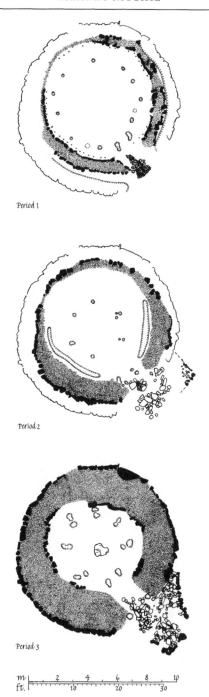

FIGURE 4.9. Cul a'Bhaile, Jura, showing the suggested sequence of construction.

FIGURE 4.10. Ardnave, Islay, traces of spade cultivation in plan and in section.

stratigraphical relationship that placed the ploughing between ritual timber and subsequently stone circular monuments; there were also lines of stake holes apparently forming land divisions (Haggerty 1991). Spade cultivation can also show as a distinct colour difference in sand, and a section was excavated at Ardnave, Islay, where the individual actions of spading – digging and turning – could clearly be seen, and a date early in the first millennium seems likely (figure 4.10) (Halliday in Ritchie and Welfare 1983, 315f). Ridged plots were revealed by excavation at Kilpatrick and Machrie, Arran, the area at the latter site measuring some 300 m by 100 m (Barber 1982, 362–3). Nothing is, however, known of the find circumstances of a wooden yoke, presented to the Society of Antiquaries of Scotland in 1890, beyond the fact that it came 'from a peat-moss at Loch Nell' (*Proc. Soc. Antiq. Scot.*, *24*, 443). Its shape shows that it was attached to the shoulders of a pair of oxen. Radiocarbon analysis has been undertaken by the National Museums of Scotland, with the exciting result that it has been found to belong to the span of 1937–1517 BC (OXA–3541) (pers. comm. Alison Sheridan). Thus the elements that will provide a much fuller picture of prehistoric agriculture than has previously been possible are being assembled little by little.

Excavation at Cul a'Bhaile and on Arran allowed the attribution of comparable monuments to a broad horizon in the second millennium BC, and the settlement pattern, particularly of Islay and Colonsay, was mapped with some degree of confidence. One concept, however, that lies behind many a settlement locational analysis is that the favoured sites for settlement have always been so, and thus the likely location for the farm/settlement for the area is under the present farm/township. Settlements that can be identified in 'less favoured' areas must represent movement into marginal environments at times of more favourable climate or population pressure. Good anchorages are vital locations for settlement on the coasts of Argyll, and the presence of the early settlement of places for which there is little other evidence may be found from the chance discovery of cist burials; a good example is that from Salen, Mull, one of which was associated with a Beaker vessel, two fragments of copper and two flint implements (RCAHMS 1980, 63, no.80). The burials at Lagg, Jura, a stage in the droving routes of much later times, indicate the importance of a sheltered bay as the focus for settlement many millennia earlier (RCAHMS 1984, 59, no.57). In terms of distribution maps of settlement evidence this means that we should add in the dots for areas where there is almost certainly occupation in prehistoric times, for which the physical evidence has been swept away many times over.

The fact that many of the surviving hut-circles and associated field-walls are now partly hidden by peat or in areas of rough moorland attests to deteriorating climate and soil conditions; such factors are confirmed by the evidence of pollen studies where these have been possible. Something of the complexity of settlement can be seen at An Sithean, Islay, where there are eight hut-circles within a pattern of field-walls and cairns of field-gathered stones (figure 4.11) (Barber and Brown 1984). The basal walls of the hut-circles are so clear that they were originally interpreted as shielings of pre-improvement times; a date in the late second millennium and the early first millennium BC has been indicated both by radiocarbon determination and by environmental evidence. Several of the hut-circles have low banks at the entrance, which may have been designed to support a wind-break; others have banks that are concentric to the main wall that may suggest the foundation of an ancillary, perhaps lean-to structure.

COPPER AND BRONZE ARTEFACTS

Copper and bronze artefacts do not play an important part in the archaeological evidence of Argyll, but the range of objects and their chronological spread shows that the area enjoyed access to metal objects throughout the later third and second millennia BC and indeed later. The copper fragments associated with a Beaker in a cist at Salen, Mull, have already been mentioned. A bronze blade was found with two Beakers in a cist at Callachally, Mull. A fine riveted dagger accompanied a burial in a cist at Kilmore, Lorn. Two bronze armlets and a jet necklace were found in a cist at Melfort, Lorn (*Inventaria Archaeologica*, 5th set, GB.25). Such examples demonstrate that Argyll was participating in exchange with a much wider world than the surviving monuments themselves can suggest. The individual discoveries of copper, bronze or gold are listed in the relevant *Inventories* following the broad

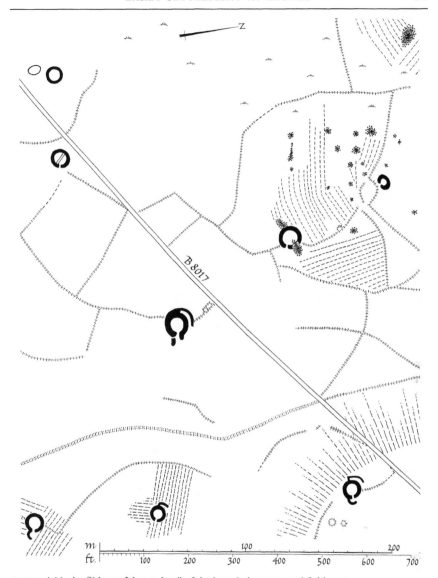

FIGURE 4.11. An Sithean, Islay, a detail of the hut-circle group and field-system.

categories outlined by J. M. Coles (1960; 1964; 1970). Something of the wealth of the early first millennium BC in Kintyre, which cannot be illustrated by other evidence, is seen in the two deposits of bronzework found at Kil-leonan in about 1884 and 1908 (figure 4.12); on the first occasion five bronze swords, a chape, a spearhead and eleven flint flakes were uncovered, while on the second, a further sword was found along with the prongs and butt of a fleshfork. Such a discovery bears with it the evocation of warrior élites, in-deed the 'champion's portion' of 'Celtic' feasting of later periods. Whatever

FIGURE 4.12. Killeonan, Kintyre, the bronze deposits of about 1884 and 1908 (scale 1:4).

the interpretation of the deposit or deposits, a passing bronze-worker or merchant concealing some of his wares, or a local magnate making a propitious offering, the surviving objects show that Kintyre was part of an economic and social network for which settlement evidence is lacking (RCAHMS 1971, 12). The chance elements of archaeological discovery have perhaps been stressed too much, and yet it is a vital part of our ability to draw broad conclusions from the material at our disposal to realise how fragmentary the evidence is: the important hoard at Torran, Mid Argyll, has its origin in 'digging out a ferret' in 1885, while the excavation of an ornamental pond at Ballimore House, Cowal, resulted in the recovery of a spectacular hoard of eight socketed axes, seven spearheads, two swords and a cast bronze tube.

KILMARTIN

The exceptional number of large burial monuments, expanses of decorated rock surfaces, standing stones, and cist burials around Kilmartin will be discussed in later chapters, but the expression of such prestige or wealth, religious or economic authority is also a matter for consideration among the more mundane aspects of the archaeological record. Some commentators have seen the monuments as situated in an area set apart for ritual of the disposal of the dead with ceremonies that involved the deposition of objects denoting the wealth of the dead and more so of the living. The standing stone settings and cupmarks somehow evoke intercession of the rock and the sky. The absence of structures associated with settlement is thus readily explicable; it was elsewhere. The fragmentary evidence for houses, farms, industrial activity, has been stressed throughout; the dearth of settlement sites around Kilmartin is thus no surprise, and the interpretation of the concentration of sites as the result of the economic success of a powerful social group controlling access to economic resources has much to recommend it. The central position of Kilmartin in the network of seaways, lochs and natural land routes is clear, and from neolithic times had clearly been the focus of activity represented by chambered cairns, the Temple Wood circles, and cupmarkings. The artefacts laid out with ceremony in some of the cist burials of the burials of the Early Bronze Age in the early centuries of the second millennium BC show contact with other parts of Britain, Ireland and Yorkshire, and suggest that control of trade may be at the heart of the wealth that we can sense through the artefacts associated with burials and perhaps with the carvings of axes on some of the constructional slabs of the burial cists.

SETTLEMENT IN THE FIRST MILLENNIUM BC
AND THE FIRST MILLENNIUM AD

The settlement archaeology of the later first millennium BC and the earlier first millennium AD is largely represented by the structures customarily interpreted in terms of defence – the forts, brochs and duns described in greater detail in later chapters. Some duns are certainly no more than houses in terms of size (see Chapter 7). Nieke rightly draws attention to the absence of discussion of how the stone-walled structures of Argyll integrated with their landscape setting and with each other (1990, 139). To an extent the presentation of the plans of the individual monuments was limited by the technology available to plan them in earlier volumes of the *Inventory*, and there was certainly a reticence to attribute an early date to landscape remains that were, without excavation, undatable. But the relationship with cultivable land was certainly an important element in field prospection for duns particularly, and the relationships with adjacent sites and with relief at least can be sensed from the various distribution maps in the relevant volumes. The style of survey evoked here by the plans of Beinn Arnicil, Colonsay, and An Sithean, Islay (figures 4.8 and 4.11) would certainly give a better sense of relationship of many a dun to its economic base in the surrounding landscape. The unsatisfactory *Inventory* category of Enclosures may well also conceal less well 'defended' settlements, although some are certainly no more than slight circular structures of uncertain date.

The partiality of archaeological survival means that we are sometimes influenced by site terminology rather than by the surviving evidence; to think of Duntroon, Mid Argyll, as a 'fort' may well be correct; it is in a highly defensible location protected on one side by steep cliffs, and it had on at least one occasion caught light to judge by the heavily vitrified wall-débris, but excavation recovered no less than thirty-six saddle querns as well as a very unwarlike assemblage of flint and stone artefacts. Peltenburg summed up the evidence from the excavations on Balloch Hill, Kintyre, the only fort to have been explored in detail in recent years: 'the assemblage is typically impoverished with few signs of external contact. It is primarily associated with the pursuits of a small residential community that exploited local material for such domestic activities as grinding barley and oats, presumably from the fields below the fort' (1982, 204–5). Specialist activities, iron-working and copper-working, were certainly represented. There were few artefacts that suggested external contacts, but these included a knobbed bronze brooch, glass beads, and lignite objects. It may well be that to be dogmatic in the interpretation of the function of such sites and to link such interpretations to social structure based on war or peace does not allow for the changing and partial archaeological evidence.

It is for this reason that the transient fragments of the settlement evidence have been stressed, for these are frequently forgotten. At Ardnave, Islay, the presence of a hearth associated with exotic metalwork, a rosette-headed pin and a brooch, possibly of third or fourth century AD date, can be interpreted in several ways. Is it the archaeological remnant of a well-to-do refugee family eking out an impoverished existence on the edge of society? Perhaps it represents the seasonal home of a family for whom a period at the seaside was a welcome change from the restrictive life on a rock stack, the local dun or fort, coupled with the advantages of the rich resources of Loch Gruinart in terms of fish and birdlife nearby. Perhaps it is the winter camp of a trader for whom Loch Gruinart is an ideal berth? If a single hearth allows such a legitimate range of interpretation, we should beware of being too dogmatic in our interpretation of more complex evidence.

The distinctive pottery of the Hebridean Iron Age has been found only on Tiree, Coll, and at Dun Cul Bhuirg, on Iona (Ritchie and Lane 1980), and the various styles are examined later. Other objects that indicate trade or exchange have been found in the exploration of brochs and duns in Argyll, but the interpretation of their significance is rarely clear and is discussed in greater detail in Chapters 7 and 8.

The impressive forts, brochs and duns of Argyll focus attention away from other forms of settlement, for open settlement is attested by scatters of pottery in sand dune areas, by well-built hearths (Ardnave, Islay; Ritchie and Welfare 1983, 313f), and by industrial activity (Sanaigmore, Islay, *Discovery and Excavation in Scotland 1979*, 30). Nor was the potential of caves ignored, for at Keil Cave, at the south end of Kintyre, excavation uncovered a series of distinctive objects, including combs, a weaving tablet, bronze brooch, and colour-coated Roman pottery of fourth-century manufacture. The discovery of considerable quantities of iron slag suggested that the occupation was, perhaps only intermittently, associated with iron working; indeed in the last century it was recorded that there was a smithy at the front of the cave and an illicit still at the back (Ritchie 1967b). Iron Age occupation is also attested in the King's Cave, Jura, though the most dramatic use of the cave is by tradition that of Irish Franciscan missionaries in the early 17th century (Mercer 1978). Underground structures, clearly comparable to souterrains in Ireland and eastern Scotland, have been found on Coll and on Tiree, but there is no satisfactory evidence of date; from the location of the surviving souterrain at Arnabost, Coll, it is indeed likely that it was associated with an upstanding house, for which there is now no trace; it is about 11.6 m long with an end-chamber about 2.1 m in diameter (RCAHMS 1980, 118, no.231). At Kilellan, Islay, the souterrain appears to be of late Iron Age date and was about 2 m in width and 1 m in depth, but its total length was not recorded (RCAHMS 1984, 143, no.270). Crannogs, or island-dwellings, are discussed in Chapter 7.

The eclectic collection of objects found either in middens associated with forts and duns or as stray objects may be interpreted more as demonstrating the advantage of the individual location chosen for occupation, either peacefully or defensively or both, than as firm indicators of chronology or far-flung contacts. Pottery styles are more useful indicators of broad patterns and these are discussed in detail in a later chapter. Representative examples of other types of artefact have been selected, both to show the variety and unexpected richness of such material, and as a reminder that the settlement archaeology of Argyll has yet to be built on reliable sequences of material with associated radiocarbon and tree-ring chronologies. There are coins, although few need be ancient losses; an Athenian tetradrachm of about 450 BC was found in

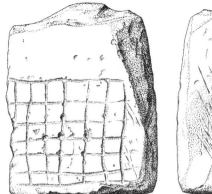

FIGURE 4.13. Dun Chonallaich, Mid Argyll, gaming-board (scale 1:4).

about 1885 when digging the foundation of a new villa at Tarbert, Kintyre (Robertson, A. S. 1971, 119). A hill-walker found a very worn sestertius of Hadrian (AD 118–28) near Loch Goil close to the site of a crashed American bomber (Robertson, A. S. 1983, 410). Sherds of Roman pottery have been found at Ardifuir and Dunadd, Mid Argyll, and at Dun an Fheurain, Lorn. A stone gaming-board of Early Historic date was discovered in the course of the survey of Dun Chonallaich, Mid Argyll, a hilltop fort that may well have seen several phases of activity (figure 4.13). The midden associated with the small rock-stack of Dun an Fheurain is a valuable example of the range of date that is implied by the artefactual evidence alone (Ritchie 1971a). The top of the stack is small, only 23 m by 12 m, with few surviving structural remains; it would surely in Harding's terminology have been a house-dun, and thus the chronological range of use of the site is all the more telling: a ring-headed pin, spiral finger ring and sherd of samian ware could belong to the first or second century AD, while a beautifully made little object has been identified as an pottery stamp of Anglo-Saxon origin probably of sixth-century AD date (figure 4.14). The faunal remains, though not attributable to any specific period of occupation, are of importance in showing the range of material that might be expected where conditions of preservation permit. Sheep, pig, ox, horse, deer; birds are represented by the hindquarters of a crane, while fish bones are those of mackerel and salmon. Any number of hypotheses can be created from such a random series of artefacts.

CELTS, PICTS, SCOTS AND VIKINGS

The writings of Roman and Greek travellers and geographers mean that from the first century AD something of the names by which tribes or places were known has been recorded, although we have no means of knowing what names the local populations themselves used. Nevertheless Argyll and Bute gradu-

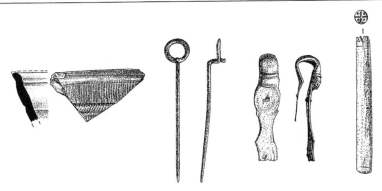

FIGURE 4.14. Dun an Fheurain, Lorn, Roman pottery, ring-headed pin, Roman strap-end, Anglo-Saxon potter's stamp (scale 1:2).

ally emerge from anonymous prehistory into a world where we can think of the Southern Inner Hebrides as *Ebudae Insulae,* Bute as *Botis Insula,* and the inhabitants of Kintyre and Mid Argyll are described as the *Epidii,* with the Mull of Kintyre as *Epidium Promontorium.* But the names and the adjectives derived from them are used in different ways and with different nuances by archaeologists and linguists, and are understood in a variety of ways by other people. 'Celtic' is primarily a language or group of languages, and from the evidence at our disposal from place-names, for example, there is reason to accept that the Iron Age people of Argyll spoke a form of Celtic known as P-Celtic. The archaeological remains belong to the broad body of material that may be thought of as 'Celtic', through similarities of style or the social order represented by forts and duns, but it has to be admitted that in Agryll there are no pieces of highly ornamented metalwork, with the exception of the armlet from Lismore, that might help to draw the surviving material into the world of 'Celtic art'. There is only the massive armlet from Newfield, Lismore (*Discovery and Excavation in Scotland 1995,* 66) and a few brooches to indicate a degree of 'Celticity'. Moulds for the manufacture of distinctive bronze knobbed spearbutts at Dunagoil, Bute (Mann 1915), show that the accoutrements of the Celtic warrior were not unknown in the area, and suggest that the small number of finds reflects the low chances of preservation of iron and bronze artefacts. Harding has stressed the broad cultural continuum from the later Bronze Age into the Iron Age in Atlantic Scotland, and the contrast that this represents with what is known from other parts of Europe at the same time (1990, 16). Confusingly the term 'Celtic' is in more general use for the art styles of the mid first millennium AD from Early Christian contexts, particularly the crosses and decorative interlace of that period (Chapter 9).

There was no Roman penetration into Argyll, Arran or Bute, but trade or exchange may be assumed; Agricola ordered the Roman fleet to circumnavigate the islands following the battle of Mons Graupius in AD 83 and essential provisioning *en route* must have brought the peoples of the islands into sudden contact with Roman power. However, the Roman fleet serving the west end of the Antonine Wall through the Firth of Clyde may have looked with some awe at the looming mass of Arran and the steep hill-sides of Cowal, which were beyond the control of the Empire. The map of the Greek geographer Ptolemy, using information of largely first-century date, shows the tribe known as the *Caledones* as occupying territory between the Moray Firth and Loch Linnhe (though other lochs have been proposed, including Lochs Long and Fyne). The 'Picts' are first mentioned in AD 297, and in a rather later reference to 'the *Caledones* and other Picts' there is the impression that the northern tribes together were thought of as Picts, of whom the *Caledones* were but a part.

Throughout the middle centuries of the first millennium the authority of the Pictish ruling classes was strengthened, and the Pictish kingdom is recognisable historically from the mid sixth century and they were to remain the political rulers of northern and eastern Scotland till about AD 843. The *Scotti* came originally from the coastal part of Co. Antrim, and were suffficiently well established for the tradition that the capital of the kingdom of Dál Riata under Fergus Mor, son of Erc was moved from Dunseverick, on the Antrim coast, to Scotland. There is no sense of dislocation in the archaeological record at this time, and it may be that there was a social affinity amongst the peoples across the North Channel that cannot be documented either by artefact or monument similarities in the two areas in the preceding centuries. The Scots introduced a different form of Gaelic, that found in Ireland and known as Q-Celtic, the precursor of Scots Gaelic today. Like the Picts (and many peoples of this period) the political institutions of the Scots became more codified and organised, doubtless under the influence of the Christian Church, introduced by Columba to Iona in AD 563. Brief annalistic accounts tell of sieges and thus raiding between the Picts and the Scots, but there was also political and dynastic contact, and about AD 843 the peoples were brought together under the kingship of Kenneth, son of Alpin, the ruler of the Scots.

Viking raids on Iona are recorded in the annals for AD 795, with a 'burning' of the monastery in 802. The term 'Viking' is used for such marauders from Norway, but the settlers who followed them in subsequent decades and began to take up land in the Northern and Western Isles, Colonsay and Islay, are usually termed 'Norse', to emphasise that the raiding phase was past, hence the title of Chapter 10 (Crawford, B. E.1987, 2).

Waves of people initiating change have been invoked in the earlier parts of this chapter in terms of the arrival of hunters and foragers, and many millennia later groups of people with knowledge of agriculture, but the knowledge of metal working or new ceramic skills seems to have found its way into the economic life of the communities of Argyll more by way of absorption than by displacement of people. Whatever social changes are present during the first millennium BC are as much a matter of our perception today as they are of an evaluation of the surviving material. At any period, movement of people can be inferred only ambiguously from the archaeological record.

DUNADD, DUNOLLIE AND MACHRINS

Dunadd, Mid Argyll, was identified as the capital of Dál Riata by W. F. Skene in 1850, and the rocky massif has had a special place in the mythology of early Scottish history since that time. The discussion of the significance of the carved footprint on a rock outcrop near the summit in ceremonies of inauguration of the kings of the Scots, and the subsequent discovery of a carved boar generated interest in a monument whose structural remains were yet little understood. Three separate campaigns of excavation, in 1904–5, 1929, and 1980–1, have been summarised in RCAHMS 1988 (149–59, no.248). These produced a comprehensive series of artefacts principally of Early Historic date, which give an impression of the range of contacts that a high status centre might have. There was also some earlier material, and there is now a range of radiocarbon dates showing that occupation of the hill was underway by the early centuries BC. Crucibles and moulds show the production of brooches and pins of eighth- and ninth-century date (figures 4.15–16). Few objects are more exotic than the small piece of orpiment, a yellow pigment sometimes used in manuscript illumination. An inscribed stone disc bears a Christian dedication in a style of lettering that is of eighth-century date. The fullest summary of the excavations of 1980–1 is in Campbell and Lane 1993, where there is discussion both of the structural sequence and the radiocarbon dates; the top-most defence is taken to belong to the fifth–sixth century, with the rebuilding of the south-east end and the immediately adjacent walls belonging to the sixth to seventh century; the outer and the best-preserved wall and the gateway defile, which must have had a timber doorway like that of Bruide's royal fortress, near Inverness, is of eighth to ninth century AD date. Metalwork in Anglo-Saxon, Germanic and Irish styles underlines the breadth of the cultural milieu in which the Dunadd craftsmen were working; the wide-ranging contacts can thus clearly be seen in secular contexts as well as in the the ecclesiastical world discussed in Chapter 9. A quern from Dunadd links the two, for it is decorated with a cross in a distinctive style that can be paralleled on Iona, Eileach an Naoimh, and in caves at Scoor and Carsaig on Mull, which can be interpreted as the retreats of anchorites (Campbell, E. 1987).

Excavations at Dunollie, at the north end of Oban Bay, have demonstrated that the summit area was occupied in the seventh to ninth centuries AD (Alcock and Alcock 1987). The finds show Dunollie to have been the seat of a potentate or a person of importance and, like Dunadd, various industrial activities were undertaken within this high-status site: blacksmithing, bone- and antler-working certainly, craftsmanship in bronze and precious metals possibly. Pottery imported from western or northern Gaul (Class E) was present, as it was at Dunadd and at the crannog at Loch Glashan (RCAHMS

FIGURE 4.15. Dunadd, Mid Argyll, metal working crucible and moulds.

1988, 205–8, no.354). Such imported pottery, like the Anglo-Saxon potter's stamp from Dun an Fheurain, are reminders of the long-range contacts that are precursors of the better documented maritime routes of the Viking Age.

There are few traces of open settlement of comparable date, though doubtless some of the slight secondary structures in duns and forts indicate occupation at this time, as for example at Dun Eibhinn, Colonsay (figure 4.17). In the machair at Machrins, Colonsay, erosion revealed a small settlement of four houses, not necessarily contemporary (Ritchie 1981); the best preserved was squarish in plan and about 4.2 m across with a central hearth that had seen many periods of use (figure 4.18). The bottom of the walls were formed by upright slabs set into a shallow groove in the sand and must merely have

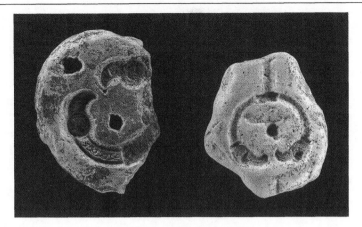

FIGURE 4.16. Dunadd, Mid Argyll, brooch moulds (scale 1:1).

been the outline for a timber framework covered by turf or skins. Such impermanent structures may have been seasonal, certainly temporary, for there were no signs of any post-holes. A radiocarbon date and comparisons for the surviving artefacts suggest a date of around AD 800; the iron knives are closely comparable to those from Dunadd and Dunollie. Close by, there was a Norse burial of comparable date, but there is no evidence to connect the burial and settlement.

This chapter has tried to evoke the disparate evidence for the settlement of Argyll during the period when physical remains provide the only source of information. The strands are thus tenuous; the environmental background in

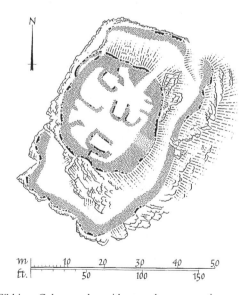

FIGURE 4.17. Dun Eibhinn, Colonsay, dun with secondary occupation.

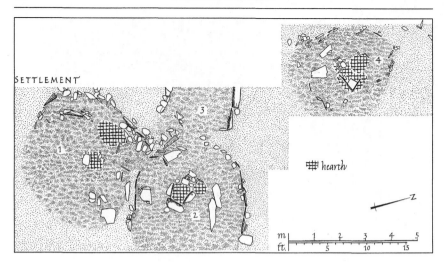

FIGURE 4.18. Machrins, Colonsay, settlement.

which this would be set in many other parts of Britain is largely lacking or is so site-specific as to be unhelpful in general terms. The range of sites, however, is unusually wide, with mesolithic shelters, timber houses of both neolithic and Bronze Age date, the substantial stone-walled foci of later defences.

5 Monuments Associated with Burial and Ritual in Argyll

Graham Ritchie

In Argyll, as in the rest of Scotland, the rituals associated with death have archaeological expression only with the arrival of people whose economy was based on agriculture and stock rearing, rather than on hunting native animals, birds and fish, and gathering the existing vegetation of the forests and moorland. Excavations of burials in Denmark and elsewhere have shown levels of attentive sophistication in the interment of members of hunting and foraging communities that the surviving artefacts alone cannot evoke. At the same time, a heightened understanding of the relationship of travelling communities to their countrysides, through the increasingly political involvement of Australian and North American native peoples, means that the potential depths of feeling of the hunting and foraging communities of Argyll to the land and animals around them should not be underestimated, although the casual disposal of human bones on Oronsay gives little hint of this (Mellars 1987). We accept without question, however, that Celtic peoples enjoyed the rituals of pools and groves, rather than stone-built temples; that the early settlers of Argyll had an equally complex cosmology is just as likely.

CHAMBERED CAIRNS

The early agricultural communities of Argyll are represented not by the relict landscapes of their fields and stock enclosures, nor to any extent by their farms, but by the burial places of their dead. The burial chambers were constructed of massive upright slabs and were covered by large cairns; an entrance at the edge of the mound allowed repeated access into the vault. Chambered cairns are found in many parts of Europe, notably the Atlantic seaboard from Iberia, Brittany, England, Wales and Ireland, but also in North Germany and Denmark. Not all are contemporary, nor are the rituals involved the same in all areas, but the various groups of these remarkable monuments bear testimony to the cohesion of the regional neolithic communities at least in terms of architectural styles. The construction of even a small tomb involved the manoeuvring of very large slabs, a task that was probably beyond the capabilities of a single family. The chambered cairns of Argyll, Bute and Arran are probably one of the most studied classes of archaeological monuments; early antiquaries recognised the potential of the tombs to produce artefacts, and in 1864 Canon Greenwell and Dean Mapleton excavated the chambers of Nether Largie South and Kilchoan. T. H. Bryce, Professor of Anatomy at the University of Glasgow, excavated several chambers on Arran in the early nineteenth century, initially in a search for anatomical remains, but latterly with a well-informed archaeological interest. The major excavations of J. G. Scott extended our understanding of burial deposits and tomb construction. The chambered cairns of Argyll have been reviewed by J. G. Scott (1969; 1973), Henshall (1972), and in the relevant volumes of the Royal Commission's *Inventory*. The similarities and differences with court tombs or court cairns found in the northern half of Ireland have most recently been outlined by Henshall, and the debate about the primacy of the Irish or Scottish sites examined in the light of typological and devolutionary approaches. The approach favoured by Henshall and Scott is that *Clyde Cairns*, the major category of cairn found in Argyll, Bute and Arran, should be studied as an independent group and that the internal dynamics of construction and use can lead to a greater understanding of the earliest architectural monuments of our area (figure 5.1). Recent excavations, notably Scott's work at Temple Wood, have underlined the greater complexity of the neolithic ritual landscape, with other forms of stone settings and decorated stones all having a part to play.

   Current interpretation of the plan-forms of chambers and the artefactual or burial deposits found within them involves two complementary tenets: cairns and chambers, particularly the more complex in ground-plan, are likely to be the result of several periods of building or reconstruction, rather in the manner of a church with a medieval core; secondly there is evidence to suggest that the deposits found inside the chamber may have been cleared out or pushed to one side on many occasions before the final deposition was made, and of course this last is the one that remains for archaeologists to excavate. The first means that only for the few excavated sites can we demonstrate the likely evolution; the excavations undertaken by Corcoran at Mid Gleniron in Wigtownshire, and Scott's reinterpretation of Piggott and Powell's excavation at Cairnholy I, Kirkcudbrightshire, provide corroboration for the hypothesis (Corcoran 1969; Scott, J. G. 1969). Although sequences of construction can be proposed for other cairns, we cannot be sure of their validity, nor of course of the length of time involved. Nor need all simple sites, for example, be contemporary, for a simple tomb may be all that is required for a new community setting up in virgin territory many centuries after the earliest such monuments were being built. Corcoran's excavations also showed that adjacent com-

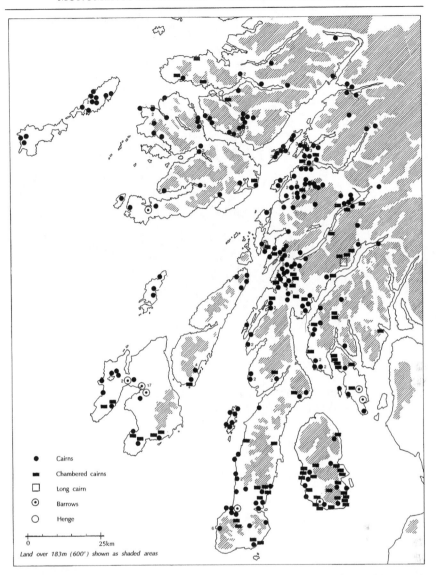

FIGURE 5.1. Distribution map of chambered cairns, long cairns, henges, cairns and barrows in Argyll, Arran and Bute.

paratively simple monuments might by a process of amalgamation create a more complex one; small chambered cairns might in effect be subsumed within larger mounds. An independent chamber as first constructed might become the ancillary chamber of a more complex site. Perhaps the process of deconstructing chambered cairns subsequently went too far, but it was also part of the realisation in the later 1960s and 1970s that the short chronology of pre-radiocarbon days (epitomised by Piggott, S. 1954) had to be radically

FIGURE 5.2. Ardnadam, Cowal, chambered cairn showing the portal stones.

revised and that new frameworks could accommodate longer structural sequences and much longer periods of use. The second tenet demands caution in the interpretation of the limited pottery and skeletal evidence (Piggott, S. 1973). Clearly it is unfortunate that there are so few radiocarbon dates to help to inform the span of use of the tombs in firmer chronological terms.

The convincing typological sequence proposed by Scott postulates simple closed chambers, often with portal stones, followed by single compartment chambers with an open entrance, which frequently have large portal stones in relation to the size of the chamber. Examples of the first category include Ardachearanbeg and Ardmarnock in Cowal (RCAHMS 1988, 39–40, nos 3–4). An important feature of the latter is the use of a cup-and-ring marking and an opposed cupmarking on the septal-slab (figure 6.8). Both cairns were first planned with comparatively small cairns, but at Ardmarnock, recent clearance has shown that the covering mound, at least in its final phase, was originally much larger. Impressive examples of simple chambers include Ardnadam, Cowal (figure 5.2) (RCAHMS 1988, 40, no.5) and Loch Nell South or Dalineun, Lorn (RCAHMS 1975, 43, no.6; Ritchie 1972). Here small-scale excavation was designed to explore the composite nature of the site, for it was clear that both a simple *Clyde Cairn* and a massive cist were present in the same mound (figures 5.3–4). Excavation revealed that the chamber, constructed of six large upright stones and a substantial capstone had in fact been subdivided into two parts by a cross-slab, for which only the stone-hole remained. The lintel that had originally spanned the portal-stones was found

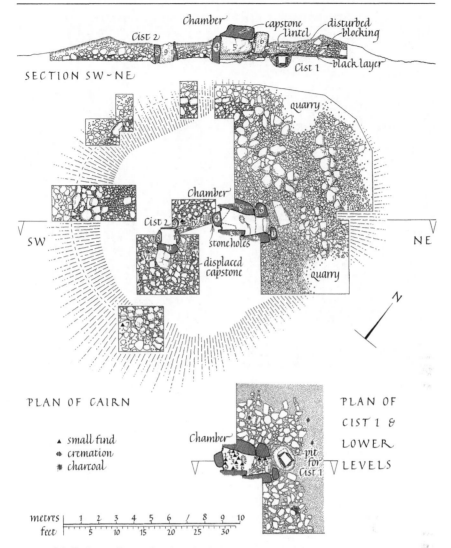

FIGURE 5.3. Dalineun, Lorn, chambered cairn, excavation plan showing the main chamber and the two later cists.

cast down in front of them. Dug into a pit immediately in front of the entrance there was a well-built cist which will be discussed in greater detail below. Because in some places the cairn was too disturbed and in others too little of the lowest levels was excavated, the shape of the original mound could not be determined, but the large cist appeared to have been inserted into the existing cairn material; perhaps the ring of large kerbstones found intermittently around the cairn is the result of remodelling at this time. A rather similar sequence is present at Ardnacross, in Kintyre (*Discovery and Excavation in Scotland 1971*, 10; *1972*, 8–9).

FIGURE 5.4. Dalineun, Lorn, chambered cairn under excavation, showing the chamber and the fallen lintel.

The artefacts recovered from Dalineun illustrate the problems of interpretation outlined above. The neolithic sherds within the chamber were found in disturbed layers, while the sherds of three Beaker vessels were found in what were considered to be undisturbed contexts, including a layer that was thought to represent the final blocking of the chamber with stones. The large cist to the rear of the tomb may have been associated with a fragmentary Food Vessel found to one side of this disturbed part of the cairn. Clearly the disentangling of such structural and artefactual sequences is open to several interpretations.

The way that skills developed in the use of upright slabs to create more complex structures is remarkable, particularly in the way that the edges of side-slabs were overlapped and that cross-bracing slabs were introduced to lengthen the chambers to up to five compartments as at East Bennan, Arran. Cairn forms also evolved with trapeze-shaped cairns sometimes with distinct straight or deeply crescentic façades being created; a fine façade survives at Blasthill, Kintyre (figure 5.5). Only rarely can the ritual activities that took place in such forecourts in front of the chambers be discovered, but fires and the deposition of pottery fragments have been found. A pit containing some 2500 marine shells was found in the forecourt at Crarae, Mid Argyll (Scott,

FIGURE 5.5. Blasthill, Kintyre: the crescentic façade and the main chamber behind a second chamber (scale in feet).

J. G. 1961; RCAHMS 1988, 44–6, no.13). At both Monamore, on Arran (MacKie 1964,13–15), and at Dalineun, Lorn, there were earthy deposits in the area in front of the entrance associated with charcoal and stones, but in neither case could these layers be explained satisfactorily. At Glenvoiden, Bute, careful excavation of the entire cairn made possible the elucidation of the sequence of constuction of a complex monument comprising three chambers within a trapeze shaped cairn. The axial chamber was first in the sequence with a small round cairn; then two lateral chambers were built at the rear of the cairn and these too were covered by stones. These existing cairns were encapsulated within a trapeze-shaped cairn, with a façade of upright stones adding elaboration in front of the axial chamber. After further activity, the chamber was deliberately filled, perhaps with the deposit of pottery vessels at this stage, and the forecourt and the edge of the cairn masked by carefully laid slabs. The pottery from the filling of the inner compartment of the axial chamber is described as *Rothesay Ware*, named after a settlement at Town-head, Rothesay, on Bute. These are simple bowls and carinated bowls with an upper part that is generally upright rather than everted or constricted (J. G. Scott in Marshall and Taylor 1977, 32). Scott sees the *Rothesay* style as late in the sequence of neolithic wares in Argyll, and belonging to a distinct tradition to that of the builders of *Clyde Cairns* as epitomised by the pottery from Beacharra mentioned below. However the differing strands of activity at a late stage in the neolithic period is tellingly evoked by his discussion of the deposit of pottery at Glenvoiden, for here 'the makers of Rothesay pottery had by then achieved some sort of *modus vivendi*, not to say *modus moriendi*, with the builders of these cairns' (ibid., 37). The relationship of the makers of Beaker pottery to the use and blocking of cairns is a matter to which we shall return.

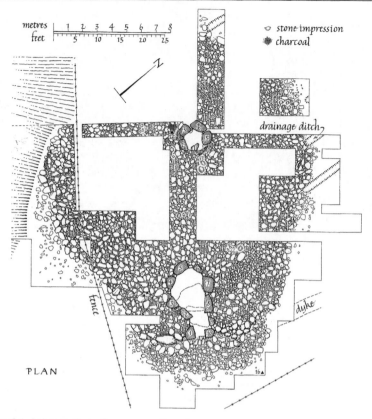

FIGURE 5.6. Achnacreebeag, Lorn, excavation plan.

At Beacharra, Kintyre, there were three chambers in the tomb as well as a short porch or entrance giving access from a straight façade of drystone walling. The chamber had been initially excavated in 1892 and the fine group of well-preserved round-bottomed pottery vessels recovered was well known to writers on neolithic topics because of the way in which they fitted into the nascent pottery typologies of the 1930s (Childe 1935, 65–7) and known as *Beacharra Ware*. The vessels survived in unusual circumstances, however, in that two were found in the three burial chambers within cist-like settings of upright slabs of schist, each 'about the size of an octavo volume'. In general the similarity of deposition inclines to a simultaneous positioning of the vessels in the chamber, and thus the range of vessel shape at any one time can be evoked (Henshall 1972, 166). Alternative chronological sequences of the development of the *Beacharra* style have been proposed, notably by J. G. Scott (1964).

Almost all the chambered cairns in Argyll belong to the *Clyde Cairn* class, but a very few have close parallels among the passage graves of the Hebrides, and at Achnacreebeag, Lorn, excavation demonstrated not only a sequence of building, but also a range of artefacts (figures 5.6–8) (Ritchie 1970). Two

FIGURE 5.7. Achnacreebeag, Lorn, passage-grave and kerb (scale in feet).

burial chambers were visible above the denuded remains of the cairn. An earlier simple chamber, comprising five stones and a large capstone, had been set at the centre of a round cairn some 18 m in overall diameter. There was no means of access from the edge of the cairn, and if the chamber had indeed been used on a number of occasions, the upper part of the cairn would have to have been dismantled to introduce burial deposits to one side of the capstone; perhaps it is most likely that the deposits were introduced at the time of building and the tomb was then closed. A passage-grave was subsequently added to the south-east side of the cairn, which was extended to cover it. A short passage led from the edge of the mound into an oval chamber, in part of which the deposits remained intact from prehistoric times. The earlier deposits, though not necessarily the original deposits, contained sherds of several neolithic vessels, including a carinated bowl of *Beacharra* type, a plano-convex flint knife and other flint flakes; there were no burial remains. Sheridan has drawn attention to the similarities in shape and decoration of the vessels from Achnacreebeag, and Beacharra to those in Ulster at the same time (Sheridan 1995, 11, fig. 2.3). The later phase, in the course of which

FIGURE 5.8. Achnacreebeag, Lorn, showing initial blocking.

FIGURE 5.9. Temple Wood, Mid Argyll; above, as illustrated by William Daniell in 1818, with the chambered cairn of Nether Largie South and the Nether Largie standing stones in the background; right, as it appears today.

the chamber and passage were filled with stones and earth, contained sherds of Beaker pottery, flints, jet disc-beads and some cremated bone. This deposit clearly demonstrates the act of the sealing of the tomb for the last time, for the sherds and disc-beads were found throughout the filling layer. Several large slabs were laid across the entrance and an apron of stones piled in front of the tomb.

The form of the passage grave and the similarities of pottery style underline the contacts that Argyll has enjoyed with the Hebrides and also with Ireland, and also serve as reminders that the archaeological evidence for any area should be seen in as wide a framework as possible.

At several chambered cairns cist burials played a part in what is probably late ritual activity at the tomb, notably at Nether Largie South, Mid Argyll (ARG 23), where Greenwell (1866) found a slab-built cist in the innermost compartment of the chamber, consisting of four upright slabs, a capstone, and, perhaps an unusual feature in such an inserted feature, a basal slab. Although the cist had been disturbed before the formal excavation, Greenwell attributed sherds of Beaker pottery and inhumed bones found nearby to the original burial deposit within it. Beaker pottery found in other compartments also demonstrates interest in the tomb, clearly at that time still accessible. Two cist burials were, however, insertions into the cairn material. One is said to have been about 7 m to the north of the centre of the cairn,

a position just outside the entrance to the tomb, and thus perhaps in the blocking in front of the entrance. The cist appears to have been within the cairn and not set into the old ground surface; there were no traces of any burial, but fragments of a Food Vessel were recovered. The cist to the SSW of the chamber (and visible today) is set into the old ground surface, but was found to be empty. It may well be that the cairn was enlarged to cover these later burial deposits (RCAHMS 1988, 48–51, no.19).

At Dalineun, Lorn, excavation revealed a cist set in a pit immediately in front of the chamber of the cairn discussed above, a position that suggests parallel rituals. The cremated bones were found not only among the gravel filling within the cist, but also deliberately inserted amongst the stones and gravel of the packing at the back of the sides and end slabs. Although there were no accompanying grave-goods, the burials, which were those of an adult and an immature individual, had been deposited with animal bones, particularly pig phalanges. With the increasingly sophisticated examination of cremated material and an understanding of the nature of pyres through experimental work the complexity of the rituals involved is becoming more apparent. This cist and the entrance to the chamber were subsequently sealed by a substantial stone blocking (Ritchie 1972).

TEMPLE WOOD

The dynamics of the creation of the landscape of Kilmartin are complex, and the excavation of the stone circle complex at Temple Wood, Mid Argyll, has been of critical importance in realigning our thinking about the relationships of monuments in the third and second millennia BC (Scott, J. G. 1989) (figure 5.9). Here the discovery of an independent ring of post-holes, with the four largest about 10 m apart, was an unexpected aspect of the examination of this well-known monument. The ring of timber posts had been dismantled to make way for a ring of stones, which was in turn taken down in prehistoric times and the whole area cobbled over. Charcoal from one of the stone-holes provided a radiocarbon determination the span of which begins before

4000 BC and closes in the later third millennium. Temple Wood, the many standing stones, and the expanses of cup-and-ring markings may all be brought into play. A neolithic date for cupmarks in Scotland has been evident since the excavation of a slab with nine cupmarks in the earliest phase of the mortuary structure at Dalladies, Kincardineshire, by Stuart Piggott (1972). The decorative technique, also associated with cairns of the Clava group, should not be thought of as exclusively 'Bronze Age art'. Thus the stone circle of Temple Wood, the stone settings of Nether Largie and Ballymeanoch (where there is also a small kerb-cairn) (Barber 1978), and the impressive cairns on the valley floor, should be viewed together as an inter-related group of monuments spanning perhaps two millennia.

The major stone setting at Temple Wood originally formed a free-standing oval measuring about 13 m by 12 m, two of the uprights bearing pecked decoration – in one case a double oval and in the other a double spiral. Two small cairns were built on the outside of the ring, both incorporating cists containing inhumation burials; the cist to the north-east of the ring also contained a Beaker and three barbed-and-tanged arrowheads. Activity inside the setting is represented by other small independent cairns, the central example containing a large slab-built cist which held cremated bones. The status of the ring of free-standing upright stones was subsequently altered by filling the spaces between them by inserting smaller orthostats; this created a closed ring against which a bank of external stones was piled, and this would have concealed the external cairns. Finally the interior was covered by cairn material. The sequence has been outlined in detail to show the links with sites that have an earlier beginning such as Nether Largie South, but also with the decorated standing stones of Nether Largie and Ballymeanoch (Barber 1978). A landscape that once seemed incremental, in which new elements were added in an orderly fashion, must now be thought of as much more dynamic, with chambered cairns, standing stones and decorated rock surfaces together representing an evolving megalithic cosmology. A little henge monument plays its part at Ballymeanoch (RCAHMS 1988, 52, no.22); the central area, comprising a low stony mound with two cists is surrounded by a shallow ditch with opposing causeways across it. An outer low bank, also with breaks, appears to be composed of stones. In the more central cist there were three inhumations and the upper part of a Beaker (Greenwell 1866; RCAHMS 1988, 52, no.22). The exceptional number of monuments in Kilmartin was immediately apparent to Greenwell, who felt that the area had 'been the centre round which the religious associations of the neighbouring people were drawn; for I cannot but regard the series of standing-stones, three of which still remain, as places of religious and perhaps political assembly' (1866, 337).

CENTRES OF CEREMONIAL

Kilmartin is one of the most accessible concentrations of ancient monuments in Scotland, in part because they were the object of excavation from the earliest days of archaeological interest in the west, and in part because of the interest of the Malcolms of Poltalloch in passing several important sites into State care. The concentration of sites and the intervisibility of many within the confined valley floor allow us to conjure notions of a numinous landscape with an importance that might extend beyond the immediate locality. In different forms such ceremonial centres have been identified at Balfarg, Fife, and around the lochs of Stenness and Harray in Orkney. Unlike these two examples Kilmartin has no dramatic natural feature to equal the Lomond Hills above Balfarg, but it shares a focal relationship to obvious routeways. Similarly the Moss of Achnacree, Lorn, is readily approached from a variety of directions by land and by sea. The mountain of Cruachan looks down from a distance, and the dramatic Falls of Lora, tumbling in different directions depending on the tide, cannot have failed to impress travellers. The two chambered cairns are probably both of multi-period construction, and Achnacree is still one of the largest in the county (RCAHMS 1975, 37, no.1); within a comparatively restricted area between Achnaba and Benderloch, there are numerous cairns and standing stones. Other monuments may now be masked by the growth of peat. The monuments at each end of Loch Nell, a little to the south, lie on an important routeway, and are linked by the loch itself. The chambered cairn at Dalineun, described earlier, is of several periods of construction; there are at least ten round cairns between the loch and the head of Loch Feochan, one situated at one end of a dramatic and sinuous esker known as the Serpent Mound. At Kilmore, one of the best pre-served cairns has a large central cist, which had received two distinct burial deposits: when it was excavated in the 1870s only the uppermost cremation burial was found, which was associated with a bronze riveted dagger; in 1967, a second cremation, probably that of a female, was discovered sealed from that above by layers of clay, sand and gravel (Ritchie 1968). At the north end of the loch there is a small stone circle, the impressive standing stone known as Diarmid's Pillar and a kerb cairn, excavated in 1967 (RCAHMS 1975, 63, no.120; 57, no.78; Ritchie 1971b). On the hillslopes above Loch Nell there are many individual cupmarkings, the majority discovered since the pub-lication of the *Inventory*. A more local centre may be suggested at the head of Lochbuie, Mull, where a stone circle, standing stones, and kerb cairn form a compact group of monuments (RCAHMS 1980, 69–70, no.110; 58, no.49) (figure 5.10). The other ceremonial centre, and the only one to compare with Kilmartin in scale, is at Machrie Moor on Arran; here there are several chambered cairns, six stone circles, some containing cists with Food Vessels, a standing stone and small cairns. Clearly the components of these hypo-thetical centres differ. Cup-markings and cup-and-ring markings play a part at Kilmartin, but not elsewhere. The great concentration of rock-carving on the west side of Kintyre is not matched by any comparable grouping of monuments. There are two enigmatic stone circles at Hogh, on Tiree, but they have not been excavated (figure 5.11).

FIGURE 5.10. Lochbuie, Mull, stone circle.

Bronze Age Cairns

The Bronze Age cairns of the Kilmartin valley are one of the most dramatic expressions of the relationship of death, wealth and authority in Scotland, and, although this can in part be understood by visiting the sites themselves, many in State care and with their informative information boards, the range and sophistication of the accompanying grave-goods is less readily appreciated. However, the chronlogical patterning of sites is less clear-cut than it was a decade ago, and decorated rock surfaces and standing stones are no longer considered to be exclusively 'Bronze Age'. The careful excavation of Temple Wood demonstrated the chronological span that may be expected on even deceptively simple sites. The creation of the ritual landscape may have taken place over a millennium and a half. The number of round cairns and cist burials on the gravel terraces are testimony to the relative importance of Kilmartin.

The excavation of one cairn in Kintyre gives an impression of the burial practices and artefacts of the later third millennium BC and the earlier second millennium BC. The site at Balnabraid was examined with gusto rather than with science in 1910 and 1913, but an important series of finds were re-

FIGURE 5.11. Hogh, Tiree, stone circle.

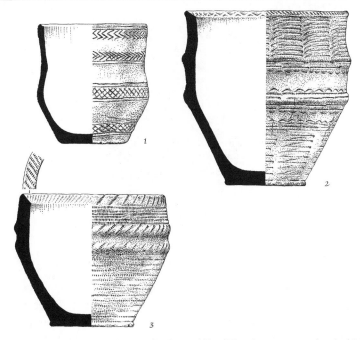

FIGURE 5.12. Balnabraid Cairn, Kintyre, Beaker and Food Vessel pottery associated with burials.

covered; these indicated that the earliest burials were those accompanied by a Beaker, two jet disc-beads and a flint knife, and, rather later, a cremation with a Food Vessel (figure 5.12). Subsequent burials were associated with Food Vessels; one cist, at the edge of the cairn had been used for two distinct burials, the lower being a cremation, and above a layer of clay there was a crouched inhumation with a Food Vessel and two flint flakes. Later Bronze Age burials were cremations in large Cinerary Urns (RCAHMS 1971, 38–9, no.14; Ritchie 1967). The use of the same cairn to receive so many burials is unusual, but the artefacts are of particular interest as they demonstrate that over the centuries the communities in this comparatively remote part of Kintyre were participating fully in the ceramic traditions of western Scotland and Ireland. Such trade or exchange may be key to the wealth that has already been seen in the range of monuments and associated artefacts in Kilmartin. However uncertain, in the absence of radiocarbon dates, the archaeological process of site sequence, not observed at Balnabraid in the stratgraphical sense discussed in Chapter 8, coupled with typological analysis of the pottery gives a hint as to where the site might fit into any overall 'pattern'. The Beaker, to take a single example, belongs to a class, no longer thought to be introduced by folk movements, but more by contact and exchange of ideas, for which a developmental series of broad groupings can suggest synchronous stages of activity. Among the earliest are those with cord ornamentation impressed before the vessel was fired, as for example on the lower part of the

FIGURE 5.13. Campbeltown, Glebe Street, Beaker.

vessel from Glebe Street, Campbeltown (figure 5.13); such a Beaker was found at Sorisdale, Coll, but they have a wide distribution. Taller vessels decorated in zones include those from Nether Largie South and Achnacreebeag chambered cairns. Beakers associated with cist burials occur widely in Argyll, including examples from Poltalloch, Mid Argyll, Glenforsa and Salen, Mull, and here at Balnabraid, the later examples in the postulated sequence being rather more squat (Ritchie and Shepherd 1973). The structural sequence implied at Balnabraid would place the taller and rather stately Food Vessel earlier than the smaller and less carefully decorated examples, but whether this is a general picture cannot be certain.

The Early Bronze Age cairns of Kilmartin demonstrate this sense of sequence, continued reuse and veneration in ways that are difficult to appreciate in other areas of Scotland. The enclosed nature of the valley and the intervisibility of groups of sites of third and early second millennium BC date give the prehistoric monuments a particular sense of place within an agricultural and forested landscape that is largely of ninetenth and twentieth century origin. The sense of sequence is all the more marked as several of the cairns have been constructed in a linear setting with its focus on the chambered cairn of Nether Largie South. To the north are the large cairns of Nether Largie Mid and North as well as the cairn on Kilmartin Glebe, while to the south are the cairn known as Ri Cruin and perhaps two robbed sites. The cairns contained cist burials, some with decorated slabs, which are discussed in Chapter 6. The most complex cairn is Kilmartin Glebe, excavated by Greenwell in 1864, but the report is not altogether clear (RCAHMS 1988, 63–4, no.62); beneath the cairn Greenwell found two concentric circles of stones 11.3 m and 8.2 in diameter (Scott, J. G. 1989, 79).The burials were accompanied by Food Vessels (figure 5.14) and by a jet necklace.

Why the Kilmartin area should contain such a concentration of sites is not

FIGURE 5.14. Kilmartin Glebe Cairn, Mid Argyll, Food Vessel.

clear. It was certainly a centre for ceremony and burial for an extended period, but its authority is also likely to be based on trade or on the control of resources. A major exploration into the symbology of power may be found in Clarke et al. 1985, where the empty 'ritual' nature of the landscape is stressed. Among the most striking examples of the participation of the area in long distance trade are jet necklaces made of material that can be shown to come

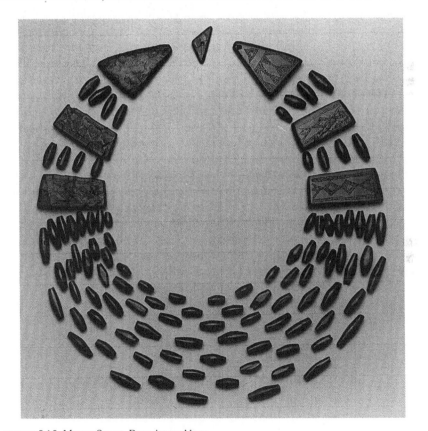

FIGURE 5.15. Mount Stuart, Bute, jet necklace.

from Whitby in Yorkshire; others are made of cannel coal, but that is also not of immediately local origin. One such necklace is from Poltalloch and a second from Mount Stuart, Bute (figure 5.15) (Sheridan and Davis 1995). The concentration of slabs decorated with axe-markings may give a hint that trade in metal might have had an important part to play in creating the wealth that the concentration of monuments implies. Close parallels can be drawn between the shape and decoration of several Food Vessels and examples from Ulster, again an indication of contact between the two areas.

Cists

Burials in small slab-built graves or cists form an important component of the archaeological record of Argyll (figure 5.16), sometimes found singly, sometimes, notably at Clachbreck, Poltalloch and Upper Largie in informal cemeteries (RCAHMS 1988, 76–8, no.86; 80–3, no.104; 84–5, no.109; Mercer and Rideout 1987). Cists or 'Stone Coffins' are amongst the most frequently recorded antiquities on the Initial Survey by the Ordnance Survey in 1862–77; the finding of bones or a pottery vessel clearly caught the imagination of the locality, even if the artefacts may have crumbled on exposure to air, but the distribution recorded in the Name Books prepared in the course of such early mapping, coupled with discoveries since, give a general impression of the areas of settlement in the later third and earlier second millennia BC. That is not to deny that some examples may be of later date, for this is an extremely simple and efficient form of interment, but unlike eastern Scotland there are no certain examples. In general the preservation of bone is not good, although cremated bone is perhaps more likely to leave some trace, and early accounts mention 'black dust', 'unctious matter', with 'urns' and 'crocks'. A crouched inhumation associated with a single funerary vessel, a Beaker or Food Vessel, is by no means the norm, although examples may be instanced from Urugaig, Colonsay, where a small group of three cists was found and carefully recorded in 1882 (RCAHMS 1984, 61, no.65). Two contained crouched inhumations, both accompanied by Food Vessels, one additionally with a flint knife. Many of the cist burials from Argyll have been accompanied by grave-goods of a variety of types, including pottery vessels, a few metal objects and rarely a jet necklace as at Campbeltown (Peltenburg 1979). Equally, long cists, those of proportions that could accommodate an extended inhumation, are by custom assigned an Early Christian date, although some may well be much earlier. The range of interments at Ardyne, Cowal, for example, suggests that this was a focus for burials over a very long period, several of which were certainly covered by cairns, but the majority of which were not (RCAHMS 1988, 54–5, no.28).

There is greater structural variety in cist construction and interment practice than might at first appear; at Glenreasdale, Kintyre, for example, a small cemetery includes simple box-like examples, but also a narrow cist with an internal compartment, as well as a cist one of the side-slabs of which had

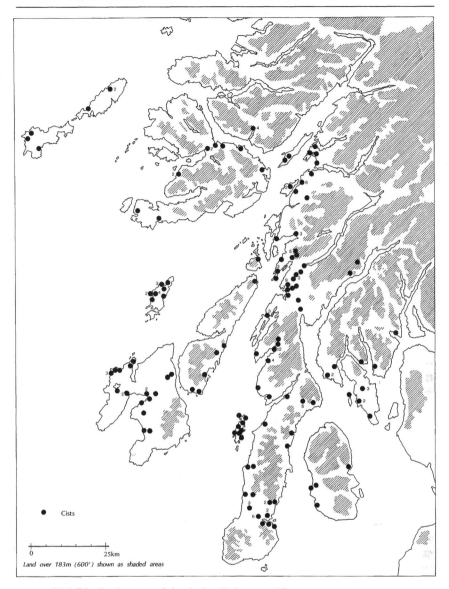

FIGURE 5.16. Distribution map of cists in Argyll, Arran and Bute.

carefully pecked out parallel grooves at each end in order to allow the end slabs to be snugly slotted in, in the manner of tongue-and-groove woodworking (MacLaren 1969; RCAHMS 1971, 48–50, no.70) (figure 5.17). The most dramatic example of this woodworking technique is the slab from Badden in Mid Argyll, which is decorated with double and triple lozenges, the grooves being added after the original designs had been cut (figure 6.26)(Campbell et al. 1961; RCAHMS 1988, 75, no.81). There are twelve grooved and rebated

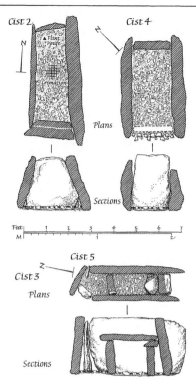

FIGURE 5.17. Glenreasdale, Kintyre, cists.

cists in the Kilmartin area, several with grave-goods, including a crescentic jet necklace and a Food Vessel.

A cist at Traigh Bhan, Islay, illustrates something of the complexity of burial sequence that modern excavation allows us to interpret; the cist had been used on two distinct occasions, the earlier burial, that of a young person, had become defleshed by the time of the second interment and the bones had been neatly gathered to one end, in order to allow the second burial, associated with a Food Vessel, to be inserted. Radiocarbon determinations confirm the observed sequence (Ritchie and Stevenson 1982; RCAHMS 1984, 60–1, no.64) (figure 5.18). A cist, the corners of which were luted with clay to help to seal it, was found at Kentraw, Islay; it contained multiple inhumations and two pottery vessels (Ritchie 1987); the radiocarbon date span is within the first half of the second millennium BC. The discovery of a cist in the course of building-works or agricultural activities is often greeted with dismay by the contractor or farmer, but an immediate archaeological response can deal rapidly with excavation and recording and thus allow work to continue, while at the same time permitting another fragment of evidence to be collected for future study. Where circumstances have allowed, the results of limited rescue excavations such as these have been incorporated into Historic Scotland's

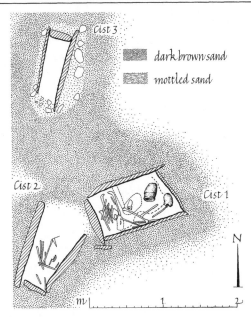

dark brown sand

mottled sand

FIGURE 5.18. Traigh Bhan, Islay, cists.

dating programme in order to add chronological building blocks to our understanding of such burial practices and the associated pottery in Argyll in the second millennium BC, but the links and contrasts with the contemporary settlement sites, like Ardnave and Kilellan, are only now becoming apparent.

STANDING STONES

Standing stones are among the most visible of the field monuments of Argyll, though their purpose is one of the most enigmatic (figure 5.19). The linear stone settings of Argyll are perhaps the most dramatic, yet are the most difficult to evoke as a plan in an *Inventory*; the effect is that of large upright stones in close relationship to one another and in a relationship with a surrounding landscape that we do not know how to evaluate. On plan the setting is merely a line of rectangular blobs, while photographs rarely evoke the sense of presence in the landscape. Standing stones are difficult to excavate around, unless they have fallen, and thus our information as to date is very inadequate. Excavation of the socket of the fallen stone at Kintraw merely revealed how slight it was (Cowie 1980). Linear settings are not just a Kilmartin phenomenon, although these are the best known; the alignment at Escart, Kintyre, retains five stones (RCAHMS 1971, 63, no.143), while Duachy, Lorn, has four stones (RCAHMS 1975, 62–3, no.116). Linear settings are a feature of Mull, with examples from Dervaig and Ardnacross (RCAHMS 1980, 66–7, no.101;

FIGURE 5.19. Distribution map of standing stones and stone circles in Argyll, Arran and Bute.

50–1, no.10); in the latter case the standing stones are associated with kerb cairns, with deliberate deposits of white quartz.

Standing stones and stone circles have been much studied because of the suggestion that they may have been erected using specific units of measure-ment to particular shapes, and that their locations have been carefully chosen to allow an observer at a particular spot to view a movement of the sun and moon in relationship to a distant horizon, and thus to know reasonably precisely the position in the astronomical cycle. Such hypotheses imply a greater degree of mathematical and astronomical knowledge than might be assumed from most of the surviving archaeological evidence. The work of Professor A. Thom led the way in integrating many of the standing stones and stone settings in Argyll into an astronomical framework (1967; 1971; Thom and Thom 1978); MacKie has tested this approach by excavation at Kintraw, Mid Argyll, but his results have not been without challenge (references in RCAHMS 1988, 64–7, no.63). Martlew and Ruggles have also tested by survey and excavated at a number of sites including Ardnacross, Mull (*Discovery and Excavation in Scotland, 1990*, 32; *1991*, 52). A measured and helpful account of the subject is offered by Heggie (1981). We must not dismiss information that is difficult to fathom, nor belittle the possibility of astronomical expertise, when an awareness of natural surroundings was almost certainly more heightened than we can imagine. Papers in two composite volumes will take the reader further than is possible here (Ruggles and Whittle 1981; Ruggles 1984), the former with MacKie's excavations at Cultoon, Islay, and Brainport Bay, Mid Argyll (MacKie 1981).

KERB CAIRNS

The distinct and comparatively localised class of cairn known as kerb cairns has been identified following the excavation of Strontoiller, Lorn (figure 5.20–1); here a small contiguous ring of granite erratics some 4.5 m in diameter was found to be the kerb of a low cairn of earth, gravel and stones. On the old land surface within the kerb there was a layer of burning and there were a few small patches of cremated bones. Unfortunately the central area had been disturbed by the shaft of an earlier attempt to examine what was known as Diarmid's Grave (Ritchie 1971b). One of the most remarkable features of the kerb was the way that chips of white quartz had been scattered round the bases of the stones, presumably before the inner filling of cairn material was inserted; even in the three cases where the stone had been removed the necklace of quartz remained. The stones appear to be graded in height with the tallest pair flanking the stone that is greatest in bulk, this trio situated on the south side.

At Culcharron, Lorn, the cairn had been almost smothered in white quartz. Sadly one half had been swept away in the course of the construction of the Connel to Ballachulish railway, but the surviving arc of stones had originally been about 8 m in diameter and set on a 'carpet' of quartz chips; two stones at right angles to the rest created a 'false-portal' arrangement on the southwest side. In front of this setting was a flat slab with eleven or twelve cupmarks. Subsequently the interior was filled, and external cairn material added to the tops of the uprights along with more quartz (Peltenburg 1972).

The ritual complexity that such apparently simple monuments may hide

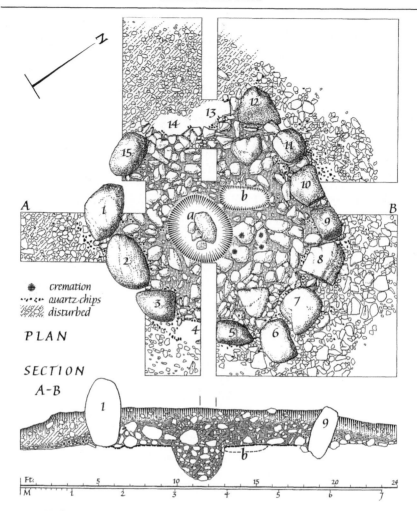

cremation
quartz chips
disturbed

PLAN

SECTION
A-B

FIGURE 5.20. Strontoiller, Lorn, cairn, excavation plan showing cremation deposits and quartz scatters.

was amply demonstrated by the excavation at Claggan, Morvern, in 1973–4 (Ritchie et al. 1975). Here a group of upright stones projecting above cairn material could not be satisfactorily explained, indeed it was possible to think of the site as a ruined passage-grave. Excavation quickly showed that there were three kerb cairns close together. The best preserved had a ring of uprights some 5 m in diameter around a stone setting enclosing a cremation deposit. The ground surface had been severely burnt. The adjacent cairn had been disturbed, but was of the same general dimensions. A tiny cairn, no more than 2 m in diameter, was set between the two. Radiocarbon dates suggest that the cairns belong to the end of the second millennium BC.

FIGURE 5.21. Strontoiller, Lorn, cairn and Diarmid's pillar.

IRON AGE BURIAL AND RITUAL

Burial practice from the second half of the first millennium BC until Early Christian and Norse times would be largely unknown were it not for the programme of radiocarbon dates undertaken by the National Museums of Scotland on the skeletal material from the upper deposits in the caves at Oban. The burials fall within a broad chronological span in the mid to late first millennium BC (Saville and Hallen 1994). They suggest that the burials recorded in a cave at Duntroon may also be of Iron Age date (RCAHMS 1988, 208, no.358), and rightly state that many of the recorded burials without diagnostic ritual or artefacts may belong to this period. Similarly an evocation of beliefs is as uncertain. If we take the people of Argyll as being part of a wider 'Celtic' world at this time, and this is the view envisaged for Ireland (Raftery 1994, 178–99), then the importance of wet sites, lochs, and stands of woodland as places of veneration can be assumed. In 1880 in the moss at North Ballachulish, a large wooden figure was found; it was carved from a beam of alder and had inset eyes of white quartz. 'It lay on its face, covered with a sort of wicker-work; and several pole-like sticks lying near it suggested the idea that it might have been kept in a wattle hut' (Christison, R. 1881, 160f) (figure 5.22). The figure was originally about 1.5 m overall, but because no suitable receptacle could be found to preserve it in moist conditions, it is now almost unrecognisable (Coles, B. 1990, 320). Although worn, the

FIGURE 5.22. Ballachulish, Lochaber, wooden figure.

original illustration shows similarities with some Celtic figures (Piggott, S. 1968, 85, fig.31). Recent radiocarbon analysis, however, has suggested a span of 840–397 BC (HAR–6329), and has confirmed earlier comparisons with the set of figures bearing round shields from Roos Carr, Yorkshire (Piggott and Daniel 1951, 17). A single pagan Celtic stone head was discovered at Port Appin (Cowie 1986). Existing cairns may also have been used to receive later burials, but the manner of excavation of many of them would have precluded the proper recording of bodies in the upper cairn material; in Ireland ancient burial mounds commanded continuing respect. How much we can

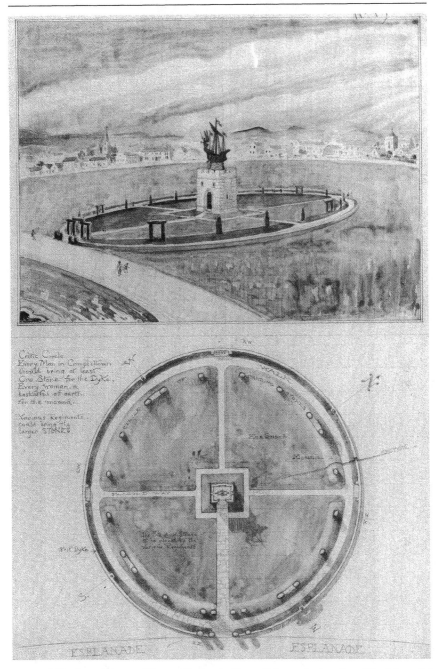

FIGURE 5.23. Campbeltown, Kintyre. Design by James Salmon, Junior, for a War Memorial involving features reminiscent of henge monuments and standing stone settings.

interpolate in this way is clearly open to question; the absence of 'Celtic' metalwork in the area may imply that such links were tenuous.

The tradition of great monuments for ritual and commemoration continues in both national and local war memorials. A design created by James Salmon, Junior, a member of a celebrated dynasty of Glasgow architects, was that for a memorial at Campbeltown, Kintyre, where the central plinth was to be surmounted by a Galley of Lorne, symbol of Argyll's medieval past, at the centre of what is clearly a henge monument. Communal involvement was to be part of the construction, with the women of the community bearing a basket of earth for the bank, men carrying boulders to add to the stability, and the military responsible for shifting and erecting the larger stones that were to form small Stonehenge-like trilithons (figure 5.23).

6 The Prehistoric Rock Carvings of Argyll

J. B. Stevenson

The archaeological richness of Argyll is epitomised by the wealth of its pre-historic rock carvings, and these are, in turn, a reflection of the significance of the county, or at least certain parts of it, from the neolithic period to the end of the Early Bronze Age, a span of time lasting at least two thousand years. Other areas of Britain are well-endowed with cupmarks and cup-and-ring markings, with Galloway and Strathtay rivalling Argyll for the density and number of individual markings; but what is peculiar to Argyll is the presence of a number of carvings belonging to another tradition and dating to the Early Bronze Age. In addition to the two periods of rock carving, the Kilmartin area also boasts an unusually large number of neolithic carvings reused in monuments of the Bronze Age, all of which make this region a crucial area for the study of the nature and context of neolithic and Bronze Age rock art.

The dating of rock art has recently been the subject of considerable debate (MacKie and Davies 1989; Burgess 1990a; 1990b; Morris, R. W. B. 1993), and confusion still remains evident in many archaeological textbooks over the date of the carvings and, by implication, the dating of the monuments on which they are found. The confusion has, in part, been caused as a result of the reuse, both in the neolithic period itself and later in the Bronze Age, of what are almost certainly neolithic carved stones. This has led scholars to believe that the carving of cupmarks and related motifs continued into the Early Bronze Age, alongside the later style. The phenomenon of the reuse of neolithic carvings is not uncommon in many of the regions in which cup-markings are found, but Argyll, and in particular the Kilmartin area, is un-usually rich in examples of this practice.

Although the term 'rock art' (*pace* Morris R. W. B. 1977) has been used to describe a range of prehistoric inscribed rock surfaces, it may be a some-what misleading designation, carrying in its wake a series of connotations that cannot be fully justified. No serious attempt has ever been made to attribute artistic merit to any of the cup-and-ring markings of Argyll, and none rivals the sculptural qualities of the heavily-decorated stones that surround the great chambered tomb at New Grange, Co. Meath (O'Kelly 1982). A similar apparent lack of decorative schemes is evident in the carvings of the Early Bronze Age. However, we have no reason to believe that the carvings were applied randomly, but, by the same token, we have no understanding of the principles which determined the choice of motifs or their disposition on the stones in either the neolithic period or in the Bronze Age.

History of rock art studies in Argyll

The cup-and-ring markings of Argyll seem to have escaped the attention of early travellers and antiquaries, and there is no mention of the remarkable groups in Kilmartin in either the *Statistical Account of Scotland* (1793) or the *New Statistical Account* (1845). The first published reference to 'lapidary art' and 'ring-cuttings' was by Archibald Currie in his *Description of the Antiquities, Etc, of North Knapdale*, published in 1830, in which he gave an account of the cup-and-ring markings at Cairnbaan.

It was not until 1868, with the publication of Sir J. Y. Simpson's remarkable paper in the *Proceedings of the Society of Antiquaries of Scotland*, that cup-and-ring markings became a recognised field of study, and it is from that date that the terms cup, and cup-and-ring markings became the generally accepted terminology. Simpson's paper, which formed a substantial appendix to the *Proceedings* and was also circulated as a free-standing off-print or volume, comprised a comprehensive overview of prehistoric rock carvings in Scotland, as well as setting them in a European context. The paper also contained the first collection of illustrations of Scottish cupmarkings, in which examples from Argyll featured prominently, and it is from this volume that we have the earliest depictions of some of the best known groups in the Kilmartin Valley – Cairnbaan (figure 6.1), Ballymeanoch (figure 6.2) and Achnabreck . The rate of discovery of new sites in Argyll in the immediate wake of Simpson's paper seems to have been surprisingly low. By the early 1880s, Romilly Allen, when compiling a catalogue of all the known cupmarks in Scotland (Allen 1882), could only list fourteen sites in Argyll – the same fourteen that had been identified by Simpson. However, cupmarkings were, by then, a respected field of study, and a selection of those published by Simpson and Allen were amongst the earliest sites to be taken into Guardianship by the Chief Inspector of Ancient Monuments of the then Office of Works.

While the majority of the cup-and-ring markings lie on exposed rock surfaces and, it is normally assumed, were designed to be seen by at least some members of the ancient community, the decorated stones of Early Bronze Age date were deliberately concealed from view in cists or burials. Their discovery is, therefore, dependent on accidental disturbance of the surrounding monument or during the course of archaeological excavation. This has

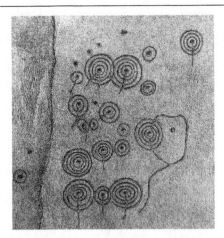

FIGURE 6.1. Cairnbaan, Mid Argyll, cup-and-ring marked rock outcrop (after Simpson 1868).

probably affected the number of such stones found and may distort the numerical ratio of earlier to later stones. In fact, most of the decorated Early Bronze Age stones that have been identified have been recovered as a result of archaeological excavation. The first came from Mapleton's diggings at Ri Cruin Cairn in 1870 (Mapleton 1871), and this set the pattern for the future in the Kilmartin area. Excavations on the large cairns in 1929 (Craw 1930) and 1936 (see RCAHMS 1988, 72–4, no.76) revealed further examples, and all subsequent discoveries have been associated with burial sites.

After the Second World War, the work of recording archaeological sites and monuments in Scotland was underpinned by the countrywide mapping programme of the Archaeology Division of the Ordnance Survey, which was supported by the all-important OS Record Card system. It was through the dedicated routine field-survey of the Division's officers that a basic record of all the decorated stones was built up, and it was on this foundation, albeit unpublished, that all subsequent surveys have been based.

No attempt at a comprehensive assessment of the entire range of prehistoric decorated stones was attempted until the pioneering work carried out by Campbell and Sandeman (1962), as part of their overall survey of the archaeology of Mid Argyll. This survey did not include drawings of individual sites, but listed all the known examples and, for the first time, showed how rich that part of the county was in remains of this type.

Providing a full record of decorated rock surfaces is not an easy matter, nor is it lightly to be undertaken. The decorated surfaces pose problems for drawing and are frequently difficult to photograph under normal lighting conditions. Given these difficulties and the sheer number of cupmarkings, it was not surprising that Ronald Morris, a Glasgow lawyer, chose to restrict his study of the rock art of Britain to only those sites that included rings or other motifs. Understandable though this choice was, it nevertheless produced only a partial view of the overall picture of rock art. During the 1960s and 1970s

FIGURE 6.2. Ballymeanoch standing stones (after Simpson 1868).

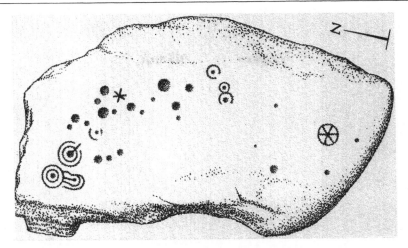

FIGURE 6.3. Braids, Kintyre, cup-and-ring marked boulder (scale 1:25).

Morris published a series of invaluable articles on rock art (for those relating to Argyll see Morris, R. W. B. 1969; 1974) culminating in 1977 with the publication of his volume on *The Prehistoric Rock Art of Argyll* (Morris, R. W. B. 1977). This book did much to stimulate interest in prehistoric rock carving, at both professional and at public levels, combining as it did a descriptive catalogue with simple line drawings, based on full-scale tracings, and black-and-white photographs.

At the same time as Morris was working on his survey, the Royal Commission on the Ancient and Historical Monuments of Scotland was

FIGURE 6.4. Kilmichael Glassary, Mid Argyll, cup-and-ring marked rock outcrop.

FIGURE 6.5. Poltalloch, Mid Argyll, cup-and-ring marked rock outcrop, photographed under artificial light.

undertaking their *Inventory of Argyll* which included entries for all cup- and cup-and-ring markings. Fieldwork by the Commission identified considerable numbers of new cupmarks, working closely with Ronald Morris, as well as with the Ordnance Survey, who continued to maintain a centralised archive of all the discoveries and mapped the position of the known sites. The latter function is particularly important, as in many cases cupmarks are difficult to locate, and over a period of time their locations can be forgotten.

Although the Commission described all the known sites, only a selection was drawn or photographed, and in the earlier volumes a relatively simple drawing technique was used (figure 6.3). By good fortune the exceptional collection of markings in Mid Argyll all fell within one volume and it was decided to use a more sophisticated range of techniques for drawing (figure 6.13) and photographing the markings (e.g. the use of artificial lighting and multiple exposures, figures 6.5–6).

Cup-and-Ring Markings

Plain cups and cup-and-ring markings are widely, but not evenly, distributed throughout the mainland and islands of Argyll (figure 6.7), with a number of pronounced regional concentrations, the principal being in the Kilmartin area. Surprisingly, the island of Arran, with a concentration of neolithic and Bronze Age monuments similar to that in the Kilmartin valley, has no corresponding array of cup-and-ring markings, the only markings of note being found on Stronach Ridge (Balfour 1910, 156–62). Within these regional concentrations, there are more localised groupings which, today, appear to be focused on specific geographical settings, e.g. Ardifuir Glen,

FIGURE 6.6. Colintraive, Cowal, cup-and-ring marked boulder, photographed using multiple exposures.

Glasvaar and Kilbride (RCAHMS 1988, 99–100, no.119, 112–14, no.159, 114–15, no.168 respectively). Looked at in detail, the regional concentration around Kilmartin could be seen as a closely-knit cluster of localised group-ings, but what makes Kilmartin stand out from the other areas is the number of elaborately carved surfaces and the proximity of the cup-markings to monuments which are probably contemporary. If, however, the Kilmartin concentration is seen as a series of localised groups this association, but not the juxtaposition, may be more apparent than real. Nevertheless, the large number and richness of the sites together reinforce the special nature of the Kilmartin area in the neolithic period.

With the exception of some of the cups and cup-and-ring markings on neolithic monuments, most markings do not form prominent features in the landscape, even when carved on rock outcrops. They are normally to be found on level, or gently-sloping surfaces, and appear to shun steeply-sloping, or vertical, faces. Today, the majority of the carvings command extensive views of the surrounding countryside, but, like so many neolithic monuments, they appear to be placed within, rather than being sited to dominate, a landscape. Although attention has been drawn to an affinity for views of the sea, a high proportion of the sites lie well inland and are located in relatively remote locations, often outwith areas of medieval and later cultivation. Richard Bradley (1993, 22–5) has commented on the relatively remote siting of many of the carvings and has noted that the markings may be associated with a pastoral, rather than an agricultural, system, with the sites lying along route-ways and in upland pastures, which would have played an important role in that way of life.

As well as being found on rock outcrops and boulders, a small number of markings in the Kilmartin area has been identified on neolithic stone monu-ments. Surprisingly, the habit of decorating chambered cairns, as seen in Ireland and Brittany, is rare in Argyll, where only one cairn, Ardmarnock,

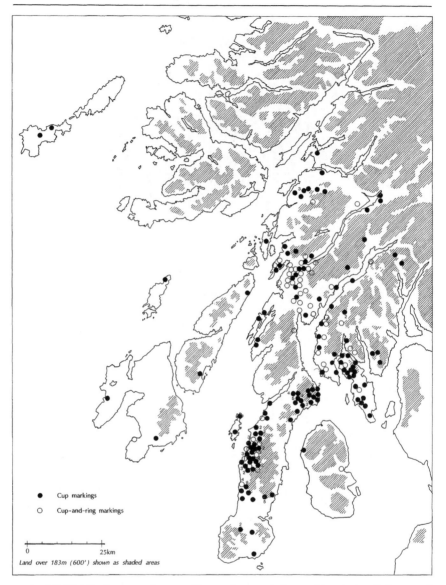

FIGURE 6.7. Distribution map of cup markings and cup-and-ring markings in Argyll, Arran and Bute.

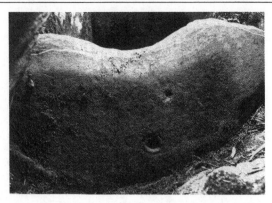

FIGURE 6.8. Ardmarnock, Cowal, chambered cairn with cup-and-ring marked septal slab.

Cowal (figure 6.8), bears any form of carving – in this case a cup-and-ring and a plain cup on the outer and inner face respectively of the septal slab (RCAHMS 1988, 39–40, no.4). Most of the carvings found on monuments have been placed on standing stones, either single monoliths (e.g. Torbhlaran, RCAHMS 1988, 142–3, no.229) or parts of more complex settings (e.g. Bally-meanoch figures 6.2 and 9, and Nether Largie, RCAHMS 1988, 135–7, nos 222 and 229). The form of the decoration ranges from simple cups to more elaborate combinations of cups, and cups-and-rings and grooves (figures 6.10–13); however, the full repertoire of motifs, as used on rock outcrops, does not appear to have been deployed on standing stones. The only other decorated neolithic monument is the stone circle at Temple Wood (Scott, J. G. 1989); there, three of the stones of the circle and one of the interval slabs bear marks. Two of the stones have plain cups on them, the third has two rings but no cup, while the fourth is decorated with a most unusual double spiral spread across two faces of the stone (figure 6.14).

As well as the two major groupings of cupmarkings – those on rock

FIGURE 6.9. Ballymeanoch, Mid Argyll, stone settings.

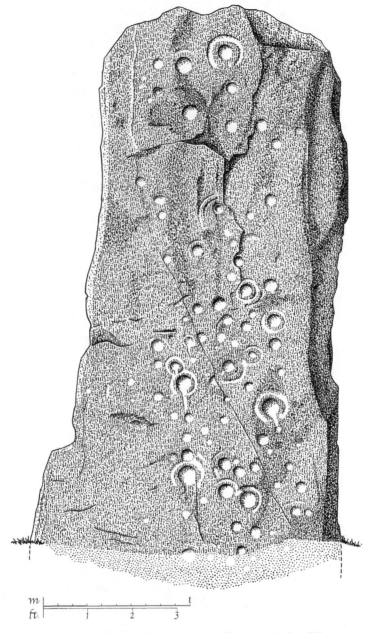

FIGURE 6.10. Ballymeanoch, Mid Argyll, decorated standing stone (scale 1:25).

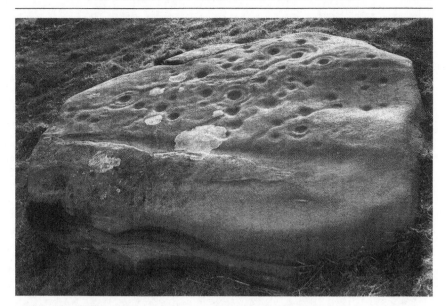

FIGURE 6.11. Auchalick Wood, Cowal, cup-and-ring marked boulder.

FIGURE 6.12. Cairnbaan, Mid Argyll, cup-and-ring marked rocksheet.

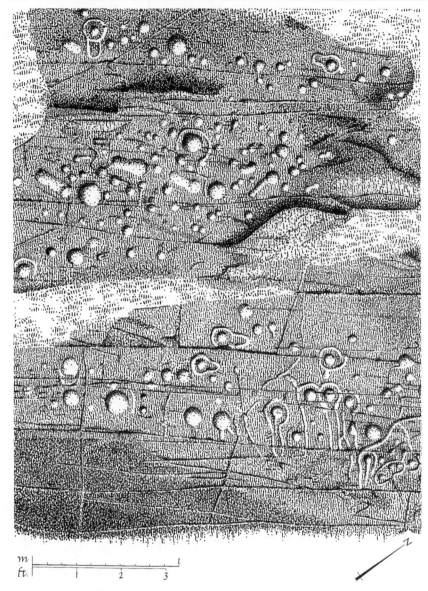

FIGURE 6.13. Kilmichael Glassary, Mid Argyll, cup-and-ring marked rocksheet (scale 1:25).

FIGURE 6.14. Temple Wood, Mid Argyll, double spiral on the stone circle.

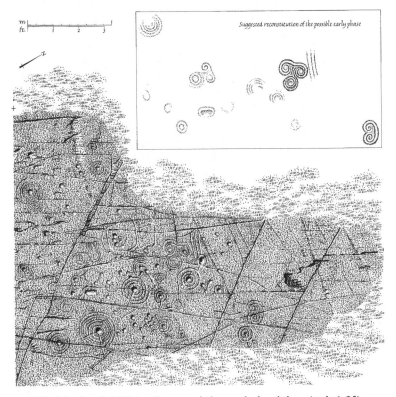

FIGURE 6.15. Achnabreck, Mid Argyll, cup-and-ring marked rocksheet (scale 1:25).

FIGURE 6.16. Cairnbaan, Mid Argyll, cup-and-ring marked rocksheet (scale 1:25).

outcrops or boulders, and those associated with neolithic monuments – there is a third context in which what are probably neolithic cup-and-ring marked stones occur. There is a small number of stones which have been moved from their original position and have either been reused in a later monument or have been identified as stray finds. In many cases they appear to have been removed from their original context in antiquity, as part of the deliberate dismantling or destruction of a neolithic monument. This phenomenon is widely attested from Brittany to Scotland during the neolithic period, and the deliberate demolition of the northern stone circle at Temple Wood (Scott, J. G. 1989) provides a good example from Argyll. It is possible to speculate that it is from contexts such as this that the ring and cup-and-ring marked stones found in the Bronze Age cairns in Kilmartin may originally have come (figures 6.21a and 23). The excavation of the stone circle at Balbirnie, Fife, demonstrated the reuse of several decorated stones, one cut-down to form the side-slab of a cist; another was a packing stone within a pit in which a cist had been constructed, and all had probably featured in an earlier phase (Ritchie 1974). That the Kilmartin stones have been reused, there is little doubt; the Nether Largie North capstone has been overcut by the later decoration, and other examples of decorated stones reused as cist slabs from beyond Argyll have clearly been broken before being inserted into their new positions. While many of the reused cupmarked stones may have formed part of the structure of neolithic monuments – the Nether Largie North capstone may initially have been part of a standing stone – it is possible that some may originally have served a different purpose, such as the cupmarked slab found in the burial chamber in the Dalladies long barrow in Kincardine (Piggott, S. 1972), and have come from, as yet, unrecognised types of neolithic contexts.

Although plain and guttered cups, cups with one or more rings, and grooves are by far the most common motifs used by the neolithic carvers, the repertoire is, in fact, much wider and includes: spirals (figure 6.14), peltas (figure 6.15), stars (figure 6.3 and 17), ringed stars (figures 6.3, 16–17), rosettes (figure 6.18), parallel grooves (figure 6.18–19), and uncupped rings (figure 6.23). All these motifs are found in the Kilmartin area, but they are relatively rare elsewhere in Argyll. Like the cupmarks themselves, these motifs occur in different proportions in most of the areas of the Atlantic seaways – from Galicia in Spain, to Brittany and Ireland – where this style of decoration, sometimes referred to as Passage Grave Art, is found (Shee-Twohig 1981).

A feature of cup-and-ring decoration which, somewhat surprisingly, has only relatively recently been recognised is that, on stylistic grounds, on some of the larger decorated rock-sheets, the carvings appear to have been carried out by more than one hand and were probably executed over a considerable period of time. At Achnabreck 1 (figure 6.15) a group of carvings on the highest point of the outcrop is partially overlain by a later series of markings (RCAHMS 1988, 87–98, no.113). On the same outcrop it is possible to identify different styles of carving, which suggests the presence of more than one carver (strictly-speaking the technique was picking or pecking). An even more

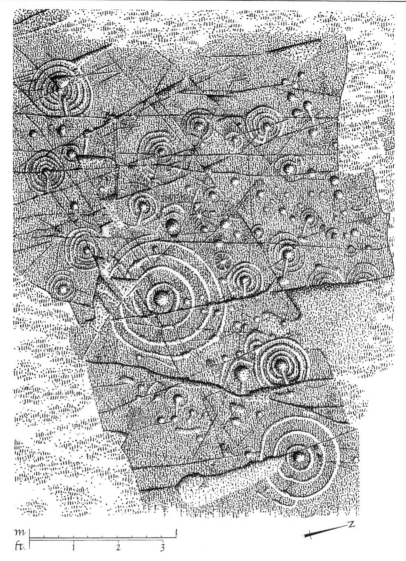

FIGURE 6.17. Poltalloch, Mid Argyll, cup-and-ring marked rocksheet (scale 1:25).

striking example of this can be seen at Ballygowan (figure 6.20) where, at the eastern edge of the decorated surface, a relatively poorly-executed cup with two rings has been added to an otherwise homogeneous group of markings (RCAHMS 1988, 102–3, no.123).

　　None of the cup or cup-and-ring markings in Argyll has been dated, and their contexts normally make direct dating difficult. The oldest known Scottish cup-markings were found within the burial chamber of a long barrow at Dalladies, Kincardine, which has been dated to the fourth millennium BC

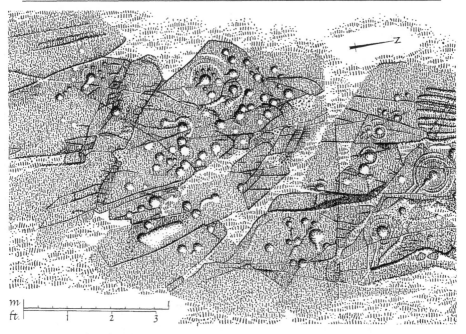

FIGURE 6.18. Ormaig, Mid Argyll, decorated rocksheet (scale 1:25).

(Piggott, S. 1972). This simple cupmarked slab probably represents an early stage in the development of the cupmarking tradition, but there is every possibility that some of the Argyll examples are of equally early date. Although cupmarked slabs are found in Bronze Age and later contexts, there is no direct evidence that they were still being carved as late as the second millennium BC. It is therefore likely that the majority of the cup and cup-and-ring markings were produced in the thousand years or so between about 3500 BC and the appearance of Beaker pottery in the second half of the third millennium BC.

FIGURE 6.19. Ormaig, Mid Argyll, decorated rocksheet.

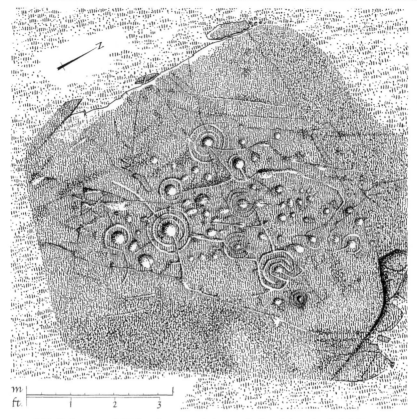

FIGURE 6.20. Ballygowan, Mid Argyll, cup-and-ring marked rocksheet (scale 1:25).

DECORATION IN THE EARLY BRONZE AGE

The apparent demise of the cup-and-ring mark tradition in the middle of the third millennium BC coincides with the beginning of Bronze Age rock art, the latest of the rock carving styles to be found in Argyll. As the name implies, this style dates from the Bronze Age, in particular, from its opening phase, i.e. from about 2500 BC to 1800 BC. Examples of Bronze Age rock art are found thinly scattered throughout Britain, and the unusual concentration of finds in the Kilmartin valley and its environs, the only part of Argyll in which this style of carving has been found, further emphasises the special nature of the neolithic and Bronze Age archaeology of that area.

In one sense, the use of decorated stone surfaces in the Bronze Age is more complex than that found in the preceding period. For not only were stones carved in new styles, but also decorated slabs removed from neolithic contexts were incorporated into Bronze Age monuments. The reasons for this reuse of earlier material is poorly understood, and it is uncertain whether it

FIGURE 6.21. Nether Largie North, Mid Argyll; a, cup-and-ring marked and axe decorated cover-slab from the central cist beneath the round cairn; b, axe decorated end-slab from the central cist beneath the round cairn (scale 1:15).

represents the deliberate desecration of neolithic monuments or a continued veneration of the earlier tradition.

Whereas cup-and-ring markings were placed in public, or at least semi-public, settings, namely on display on natural rock surfaces and stone monuments, Bronze Age carvings are exclusively found with burials, either in flat cemeteries or under cairns. Their recurrent association with individuals in cists or burials suggests that the decoration is private and is clearly connected with death or the after-life, in much the same way as grave-goods accompanying the body.

Bronze Age decoration is most commonly found on the end-slabs and

FIGURE 6.22. Ri Cruin, Mid Argyll: axe-decorated end-slab from a cist beneath the round cairn (scale 1:15).

cover-stones of cists (figures 6.21–2) or on the stone settings associated with less elaborate burials (e.g. figure 6.23, Nether Largie Mid, RCAHMS 1988, 67–8, no.67). There are two decorated side-slabs – Kilbride (Campbell and Ritchie 1984; RCAHMS 1988, 79, no.98) (figure 6.24) and Badden (RCAHMS 1988, 75, no.81) (figure 6.25), but at Badden the carving may be of earlier date. The Bronze Age decoration is always placed on the inner face of the slab; this is also the case for the majority of the reused cupmarkings, but at

FIGURE 6.23. Nether Largie North, Mid Argyll, ring-marked slab associated with a burial beneath the round cairn (scale 1:15).

FIGURE 6.24. Kilbride, Mid Argyll: axe-decorated side-slab from a cist.

least one example (Poltalloch, RCAHMS 1988, 80–3, no.104.2, grave 4) has cups on both faces of an end-slab.

Bronze Age decoration is characterised by the use of naturalistic motifs, by far the most common being a representation of an unhafted copper or bronze flat axe. These may occur in groups of two (figures 6.21b, 24) or more (figure 6.21a, 22), and the designs may have been carefully executed (figure 6.21) or only roughly carved (figure 6.24). A more enigmatic motif (figure 6.26) was found on the end-slab of a cist which lay immediately outside the kerb of the cairn at Ri Cruin (RCAHMS 1988, 72–4, no.76). It has been interpreted as either a hafted bronze halberd with attached pennants or as a boat (following Scandinavian examples). If it is a hafted halberd, it contrasts with the plain axes and is more akin to the hafted neolithic stone axes seen on standing stones and in chambered tombs in Brittany.

The use of the axe motif in a funerary context raises a number of interesting questions. Flat axes are a characteristic find of the Early Bronze Age. However, they are rarely found in association with burials and are most frequently recorded either as stray finds or as part of a bronze hoard. Conversely, copper/bronze daggers were relatively frequently buried as grave-goods, but they have not been recorded as a rock art motif in Scotland. The use of representations of unhafted axes must imply some special meaning, now lost to us, but one which may also be reflected in the unhafted condition of many of the axes discovered in hoards or as stray finds. In some cases, these may

FIGURE 6.25. Badden, Mid Argyll: decorated side-slab from a cist (scale 1:15).

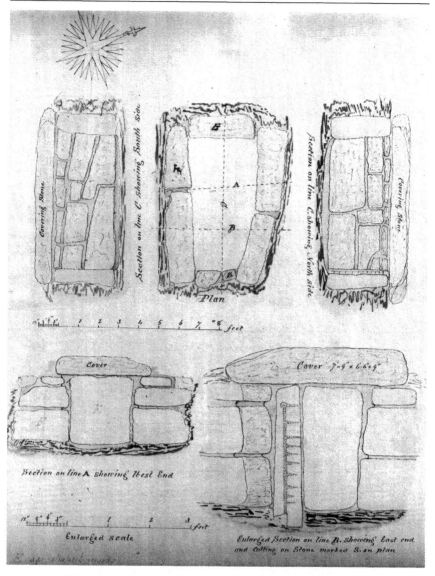

FIGURE 6.26. Ri Cruin, Mid Argyll: plan and section of a cist beneath the cairn, showing the decorated slab.

represent some form of ritual activity, rather than simply being founder's hoards.

In addition to the representational motifs discussed above, there is a number of slabs found in Bronze Age contexts which bear angular geometric designs (figures 6.25, 27). The origins of these slabs are unknown but, like the cupmark stones from cists, they may be neolithic in date and in reuse. The best known of these stones is the Badden Slab (figure 6.25); it had formed

FIGURE 6.27. Carn Ban, Mid Argyll: decorated slab found inside a cist beneath the round cairn (scale 1:15).

the side-slab of a Bronze Age cist. It is decorated with a double row of lozenge motifs and has clearly been reused, the decoration having been overcut to accommodate rebates for the end-slabs of the cist. Such cavalier treatment of the decoration is reminiscent of the superimposition of flat axes on the cup-marked cist-cover at Nether Largie North (figure 6.21a), and may similarly indicate that the carving is of neolithic date. A fragment of another slab with lozenge designs was found inserted as a grave-good, into a cist in a cairn at Carn Ban, Cairnbaan (figure 6.27), a short distance to the west of Badden; here, too, the decoration was not complete and the stone appears to have been reused (RCAHMS 1988, 57, no.36).

Richard Bradley (1993, 63–5) has drawn attention to the dichotomy, in the neolithic period, between the positioning of cupmarkings and angular decoration, with the cupmarks and related motifs being associated with the open air or exterior of monuments, while angular carving, such as that found at Badden and Carn Ban, is more frequently found within monuments. In Argyll, stones carved in the angular style are not associated with neolithic monuments, but have been found either as stray finds or in cists, in the latter case probably reused. Thus the tradition of the use of angular decoration within a monument appears to continue into the Bronze Age and is associated with the deliberate reuse, often in defaced form, of the earlier outward-looking cupmark style.

LATER MARKINGS

In addition to the neolithic and Bronze Age rock carvings described above, there are several other carvings which have in the past been attributed to the prehistoric period, but which are probably of much later date: the 'devil's hand' at Kilneuair (Campbell and Sandeman 1962, 37); the two left hands at Barnakill (Morris, R. W. B. 1977, 60); and the Glen Domhain deer (Morris, R. W. B. 1977, 85). All are described in RCAHMS 1992 (187, no.81; 525, no.279; and 528, no.283 respectively).

7 Forts, Duns, Brochs and Crannogs: Iron Age Settlements in Argyll

D. W. Harding

Argyll is exceptionally rich in field monuments of the later prehistoric and early historic periods. The *Inventories* of the Royal Commission on Ancient and Historical Monuments of Scotland, representing the state of knowledge between about 1960, when the Commission's fieldwork programme began, and 1988, when the last of the relevant *Inventories* was published, list nearly five hundred sites, broadly categorised as forts, brochs, duns, crannogs and hut-circles. Given this wealth of surviving evidence, it is surprising that a greater research effort has not been directed at the fundamental, but still largely unresolved, questions regarding the dating, function and social and economic roles of these several classes, and their wider relationships within the context of Iron Age settlement in Atlantic Scotland and beyond.

An examination of the overall distribution of field monuments in Argyll (figure 7.1) shows particular concentrations of forts and duns around the coast of Kintyre, in north Knapdale and the coastal regions of Lorn, with a marked paucity of sites in North Argyll and the Cowal peninsula. On the islands, the distribution is likewise variable, with eastern Mull and most of Jura largely devoid of sites. The distribution is plainly determined by the prevailing topography, with virtually no sites above the 600 ft contour, and most sites favouring locally-defensible positions within reasonable proximity to lower-lying coastal land. It is reasonable to suppose that climatically the warmer, wet lowlands would be preferable for settlement than the cooler, wet foothills and uplands, while the coastal lowlands would offer greater potential in terms of agriculture and the exploitation of marine resources. Excavation of forts and duns has yielded basic evidence for the products of stock-rearing and cereal cultivation, and there is accumulating evidence that some duns may have been focal points within an agricultural landscape (Nieke 1990, 139). Though in terms of modern land-use much of Argyll (Bibby et al. 1982)

FIGURE 7.1. Distribution of forts, brochs, duns and crannogs in Argyll, Bute and Arran.

is currently designated as suitable only for improved grassland or rough grazing, Alcock and Alcock (1987, 137) have rightly stressed that such assessments are based upon modern farming practice, and plainly, from extensive evidence of pre-improvement agriculture, are not indicative of the potential under earlier agricultural regimes.

In Kintyre (presumed from Ptolemy's *Geographia* of the second century AD to be the territory of the *Epidii*), the largely coastal distribution of duns is particularly marked. Sites classified by the RCAHMS as forts may occupy higher ground than those classified as duns; 30 per cent of forts are at a greater height than the highest of the duns. These include the very few that are located above the 600 ft contour, notably Knock Scalbart, Ballywilline and Ranachan Hill, at very nearly 700 ft dominating a series of summits north of the Laggan, which divides the Mull from the upland spine of Kintyre. It is perhaps surprising that Knock Scalbert and Largiemore (at around 550 ft in the same chain of forts) are among the few forts in Argyll which contain evidence of occupation in the form of hut-stances, though we need not infer that these prominent locations were necessarily intended for permanent rather than seasonal or tactical occupation.

FORTS

The very heterogeneous character of the Argyll forts may, nonetheless, advise caution. In terms of area enclosed, structural morphology and topographical location, there are many variations which could reflect differences in date, or social and economic function. Most are small in area, but some are barely larger than the larger duns. Among the larger forts, Dun Ormidale in Lorn encloses 3 hectares, but its surviving defences are relatively slight and there are no traces of internal structures. Cnoc Araich in Kintyre, enclosing 2.5 hectares, has multivallate defences, presumably to compensate for its lack of natural defences, but equally has no evidence of internal occupation. Both have attracted the description of 'minor *oppida*', but there is no archaeological evidence at present apart from their relative size to justify their status. The term *oppidum* has also been applied to The Doon, Drumadoon, Arran, a headland fort of some 5 hectares, where the remains of houses were once reported but are not now visible. Also on Arran, Cnoc Ballygowan, enclosing about 3 hectares, has been classified as an unfinished fort. In absolute terms, of course, these sites are minute compared to the protohistoric *oppida* of continental Europe, which can enclose areas well in excess of 100 hectares, and, in the absence of any evidence for their political, economic or social function, the term is misleading and should be abandoned.

As regards the layout of forts, multiple defences or partial outworks are not uncommon, though it is not always clear whether these were the product of a unitary design or of several different periods of building activity. Ranachan Hill is a case in point, where the small, neatly-coursed stonework of the inner-most enclosure contrasts with the massive and irregularly-laid facing-stones of the outworks; this has led to the suggestion that the former was a later work altogether (Feachem 1966, 84). At Balloch Hill, on the other hand, surface survey had suggested that the two principal ramparts were the result of successive episodes of building (RCAHMS 1971, 66, no.158), where subsequent excavations (Peltenburg 1982) argued that the inner enclosure and outworks were integral to the design of the fort from the outset of its Iron Age occupation in the second half of the first millennium BC, before the site reverted to an open settlement in its final phase. The Balloch sequence serves as a timely warning against the temptation to construct generalised models of site development, in the case of Argyll from larger to smaller enclosures, or forts to later duns, which, though perhaps valid for individual sites, need not be universally applicable. Equally, we should be wary of applying models derived from other regions, such as the Borders, or the chronology associated with them, to regions where the political, economic or social determinants of settlement may have been quite different.

If absolute height was not a major factor in the siting of the majority of forts and duns, natural defensibility within the local terrain evidently was. Both were frequently located on rocky summits, knolls, spurs, or took advantage of precipitous ridges or promontories, while smaller duns may occupy even more precipitous stacks. Some ridge forts, like The Torr, Shielfoot, or even Dun Mac Sniachan, are so constricted in parts of their interior that it is difficult to see what justified the effort of extending the defensive enclosure, while certain stack duns, like Dun Fhinn, must have presented extreme problems of access, and not just to those whom they were designed to keep out. Though none of these locations is demonstrably favoured in one period rather than another, it is noteworthy that Dun Fhinn, which is significantly overlooked from the landward side, and Kildonan dun, whose rocky knoll on the shore of Kilbrannan Sound is similarly though less immediately overlooked, have both yielded convincing evidence of first millennium AD occupation. Elsewhere in Atlantic Scotland sites with a similar seaward aspect, overlooked from the landward side, as at Dun Grugaig on Skye or Caisteal a'Mhorair, North Tolsta, Lewis, may be similarly late in date, and need not be bracketed with cliff-edge duns of the later prehistoric period.

One class of fort, for which an early historic dating is generally accepted, is the nuclear fort, characterised not only by its layout of citadel with multiple annexes, but also by the fact that the latter may be disposed on a series of terraces below the citadel summit. Since the class was initially recognised (Stevenson, R. B. K. 1949) evidence has accumulated for regarding nuclear forts, whether unitary or cumulative constructions, as a distinctive Dark-Age development, and not a later adaptation of early Iron Age fortifications, as once proposed (Feachem 1966). The type-site in Argyll is, of course, Dunadd, for which there is no evidence whatsoever of earlier occupation. If such key sites are regarded as major royal strongholds, Alcock has argued that others of lesser, but still royal, status might be inferred as potential candidates; he has proposed Dun a'Chrannag, Dun a'Choin Dhuibh and Dun Chonallaich in Mid Argyll (Alcock, Alcock and Driscoll 1989). Among putative smaller nuclear forts, it should be noted that Little Dunagoil on Bute has yielded evidence of earlier occupation in the form of Late Bronze Age and Iron Age artefacts (Marshall, D. N. 1964). There is always the risk of mis-identification, of course (the re-dating, confirmed by radiocarbon and thermoluminescence of the Dunion, Roxburghshire, once regarded as a nuclear fort, to the closing centuries BC and early centuries AD (Rideout, Owen and Halpin 1992) is a case in point), but there would seem to be a case for targeted research excavation of this group of Argyll forts.

The most recent summary of research on the fortifications of Argyll has been that of Dr Margaret Nieke (1990), which derived substantially from that writer's analysis of settlement patterns of the first millennium AD in the Atlantic province (1984). For the general class of forts, with the notable exception of nuclear and related forts, for which an early historic date is not in contention, Nieke cites the evidence of Balloch Hill (Peltenburg 1982), Eilean an Duin (Nieke and Boyd 1987) and Duntroon (Christison et al. 1905) in support of their construction and occupation in the later first millennium BC. Notwithstanding the limited sample of adequately-excavated examples, and the very considerable diversity of sites currently included in the class, which constrains extrapolation to the series as a whole, this conclusion is unlikely to excite dissent, on the basis of the presently-available evidence. We should not, however, constrain our consideration of the date of forts within the conflicting claims of the later prehistoric and early historic periods. Elsewhere the origin of fortified settlements can be traced back to the later Bronze Age at least, and there is no *a priori* reason why the movement towards enclosure should have been retarded in Atlantic Scotland. Again, the evidence of Bute is pertinent. Notwithstanding the inadequacies of older excavations, there is an abundance of material evidence from Dunagoil, Bute (Mann 1915; 1925; Marshall, J. N. 1915) for occupation, if not the fortification of the hill, in the later Bronze Age, including mould fragments indicative of bronze working. Dunagoil also yielded a La Tène Ic brooch, ring-headed pins and other material of undoubted Iron Age date, and this, together with suggestions that there may have been structural modifications to the defences, points to a multi-period occupation of the site.

DUNS

The dating of the smaller duns is, however, more controversial, as Nieke acknowledges. Alcock asserted the case for assigning these sites to an early historic horizon, on the not unsubstantial grounds that, of around a dozen excavated examples, only one had produced evidence for occupation in the first millennium BC (Alcock and Alcock 1987, 131). We should be clear that Alcock does not discount the possibility, as yet not well documented archaeologically, that some Argyll duns originated and were occupied in the first millennium BC; but more emphatically he is not prepared to regard the evidence of early historic occupation as simply reuse of pre-existing sites. For the purposes of his assessment of the settlement hierarchy of Dál Riata, of course, this distinction is immaterial. But from the point of view of a prehistorian, it is puzzling that so little evidence for earlier occupation has so far been forthcoming, given the emerging pattern elsewhere in Atlantic Scotland, which is indicative of a long sequence of occupation of comparable sites from the later prehistoric into the early historic period.

Three factors may have a bearing upon this dilemma. First, Argyll duns are a very heterogeneous collection of monuments, which even on subjective inspection admit to a variety of ground-plans and topographical locations, and, if we subscribe to the Commission system of classification, some significant variation in area enclosed. For the Argyll *Inventories*, the Commission adopted a distinction of convenience between fort and dun in which the latter was defined as 'a comparatively small defensive structure with a disproportionately thick drystone wall, usually but not always sub-circular or oval on plan, and enclosing an area not exceeding about 375 sq. m. (4000 sq. ft.); it would thus normally hold only a single family group' (RCAHMS 1971, 18; see also Maxwell 1969). Once this distinction had been adopted in the Kintyre *Inventory*, consistency clearly required that it be retained for subsequent volumes, and it would be surprising if, after more than twenty years' fieldwork and six further volumes, the classification did not show a number of anomalies. First, as is inevitable with any arbitrary division of this kind, there are sites which morphologically are virtually indistinguishable, but which fall on either side of the borderline. Thus Dun Breac, Ardvergnish, Mull is classified as a fort, whereas Dunan an t'Seasgain, Gigha, Ballycastle, Luing and Cnoc na Sroine, Mull are treated as duns (Harding 1984, figure 11.6). Indeed, several other smaller forts of oval or pear-shaped plan with single entrance, and enclosing only a slightly greater area, show similar layout and construction, like the later fort at Largiemore or the inner enclosure at Balloch Hill in Kintyre, of which the last has been shown to have had later prehistoric occupation (Peltenburg 1982). Second, there is a marked disparity of sites even within the dun classification. It has been argued elsewhere (Harding 1984) that a distinction might be drawn between those circular or sub-circular duns which approximate in size to brochs, and which potentially could have been roofed dwellings (figure 7.2), and those somewhat larger dun-enclosures which are not dissimilar in plan from some of the smaller forts (figure 7.3), for which a different function and context should be argued. Even within the category of potentially-roofed duns Alcock has rightly pointed out that some oval (or indeed sub-rectangular) structures could have supported a hipped ridged roof rather than a conical one (Alcock and Alcock 1987, 133). Even if sites like Dun Fhinn, with its sub-rectangular ground-plan, or Kildonan, more debatably, with its sub-triangular layout, were capable of being roofed, they stand apart from the circular dun-house model represented by Rahoy. Domestic building-plans in Britain in the later prehistoric period, in contrast to those of Continental Europe beyond the Atlantic fringes, are almost invariably circular. Of the dozen excavated duns in Argyll, therefore, Rahoy is one of the few from which one might have expected evidence of occupation in the first millennium BC, an expectation which was, of course, borne out by Childe's excavation (Childe and Thorneycroft 1938a). The problem, therefore, until we can refine the current classification of duns, is to target sites that might reasonably be expected to yield evidence of first millennium BC occupation, and not to draw

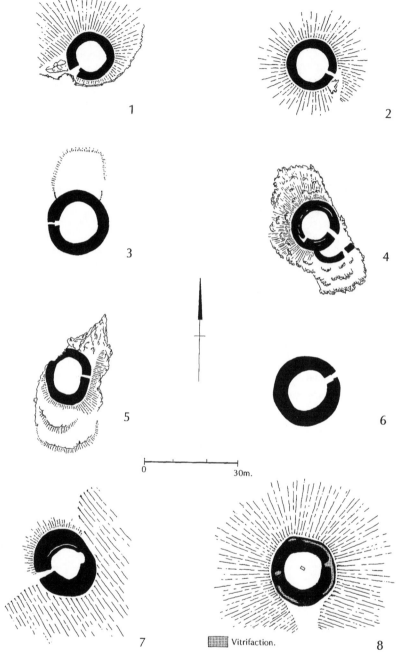

FIGURE 7.2. Dun Houses (with *Inventory of Argyll* volume and article number): 1. Dun Leigh, Lorn (*2*, no.175); 2. Tom a Chaisteil, Lorn (*2*, no.194); 3. Borgadel Water, Kintyre (*1*, no.187); 4. An Sean Dun, Mull (*3*, no.177); 5. Cnoc a' Chaisteal, Lergychoiniebeag (*6*, no.286); 6. Caisteal Suidhe Chennaidh (*2*, no.159); 7. Dun Ballymeanoch, Mid Argyll (*6*, no.273); 8. Rahoy, Morvern (*3*, no.222).

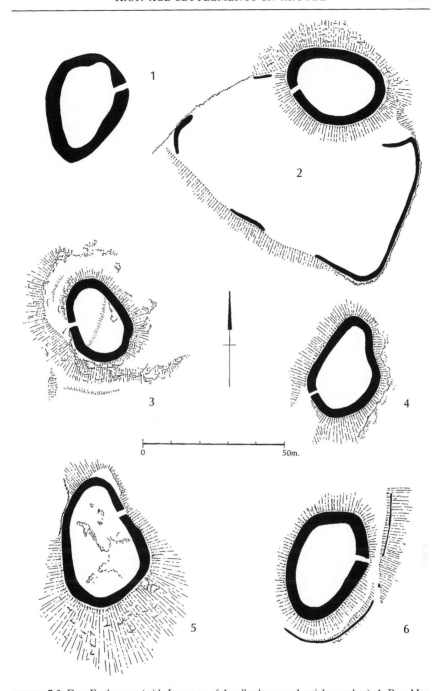

FIGURE 7.3. Dun Enclosures (with *Inventory of Argyll* volume and article number): 1. Barr Mor, Lorn (*2*, no.158); 2. Cnoc na Sroine, Mull, inner enclosure (*3*, no.182); 3. Barr Iola, Cowal (*6*, no.277); 4. Dunan an t-Seasgain, Gigha (*1*, no.194); 5. Dun Breac, Ardvergnish, Mull (*3*, no.132); 6. Ballycastle, Luing (*2*, no.155).

inferences from specific and possibly untypical sites across the group as a whole.

A second factor which may have militated against the recognition of later prehistoric foundations among the duns of Argyll stems from the relative paucity of diagnostic material finds for this period in Atlantic Scotland. Rahoy's early date is clinched by the iron socketed axe and bronze La Tène Ic brooch, though how closely such exotic items can define the occupation of a site is very much open to debate (Clarke 1971). Most of the regular material remains from Iron Age settlements in Atlantic Scotland – beads, spindle-whorls, hammer-stones, whetstones and the like, and even pottery (Topping 1987) – are not amenable to close dating, and, until some reliably-excavated and independently-dated sequences become available, are likely to remain so. It is instructive to note that in several instances (of forts as well as duns) a dating from the first or second centuries AD has been tentatively advanced (but not earlier) on the basis of beads or the occasional sherd of Samian, and in the absence of types which are diagnostically earlier, or more radiocarbon dates, we can only proceed with due caution on the basis of what evidence is available. Yet we have the example of the Milton Loch crannog (Guido 1974) as a salutary warning against a dependency upon such finds as indicators of the primary occupation of a site.

The third factor which may have obscured the potential for earlier occupation of duns is not unrelated to the last. There is increasing evidence from other regions of Atlantic Scotland for a protracted, but not necessarily continuous, sequence of occupation from as early as the middle of the first millennium BC well into the first millennium AD. In some circumstances, like the Howe in Orkney or Berie in west Lewis, the successive phases are reasonably well-defined stratigraphically. In others, like the older classic site at Jarlshof on Shetland, the sequence was defined by a spatial shift around the site. But there are other circumstances in which later reoccupation will have largely obliterated, or at least obscured the earlier occupation, and in the case of older excavations, where the potential for multi-period occupation was not always sufficiently appreciated, the result may be a misreading of the time-span of occupation represented. An instance of the latter is the site of Dun Cuier on Barra (Young, 1956), a site which the excavator regarded as essentially single-period, and assigned to the 5th–7th centuries AD, but which now, as Armit has effectively argued (1988, 81; 1990b, 55–7), can be seen to include a secondary, circular structure of first millennium AD date within the walls of an earlier broch or galleried dun (figure 7.4.3). *Pace* MacKie later in this volume the internal occupation associated with the hearth at Dun Cuier is not demonstrably primary. It is associated with the inner wall which, if regarded as secondary, as its asymmetrical relationship to the galleried dun would suggest, would have obliterated or obscured the primary occupation deposits precisely because the successive phases of occupation are both founded on or close to bedrock. As such, it parallels the rebuilding of Pictish-period structures within the

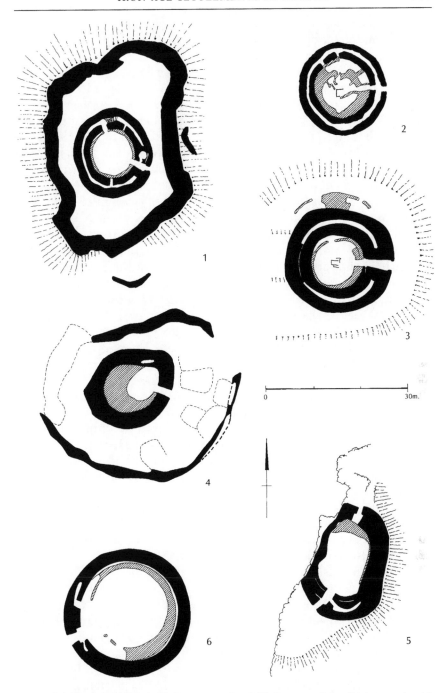

FIGURE 7.4. Brochs and Duns with later occupation (with *Inventory of Argyll* volume and article number where appropriate): 1. Dun Mor Vaul, Tiree (*3*, no.167); 2. Berie, Lewis; 3. Dun Cuier, Barra; 4. Dun Ibrig Tiree (*3*, no.210); 5. Druim an Duin, Mid Argyll (*6*, no.293); 6. Ardifuir, Mid Argyll (*6*, no.270).

tumbled broch walls at Berie (figure 7.4.2), though without the same degree of structural complexity.

With these analogies in mind, we are bound to ask whether the same phenomenon might not be a feature of the duns of Argyll. The most obvious candidate for reconsideration in this regard must be Ardifuir in Mid Argyll (figure 7.4.6). Circular on plan, the dun itself encloses an area 19 m in diameter, thus posing problems in terms of its potential superstructure. It otherwise, however, displays several of the architectural characteristics of a complex Atlantic roundhouse of later prehistoric date, namely door-checks and sill-stone in the entrance passage, a guard cell leading off that passage, a gallery with intramural stair and a scarcement around the inner wall-face. What is clear, however, and what appears to have been recognised by the 1904 excavators, though sometimes disregarded subsequently, is that Ardifuir had more than one phase of occupation. Within the enclosure was a penannular structure, 15 m in diameter, composed of edge-set slabs, with some interspersed horizontal drystone coursing, revetted into earth and rubble between it and the dun walls, in a fashion which is closely reminiscent of the principal cell of the 'Pictish' period re-occupation of the Berie broch in Lewis. Hamilton (1968, 115) seems to have regarded this as an example of a drystone fort with internal range of lean-to buildings, based on the model which he had proposed for Clickhimin. The fact that this structure, however, is eccentrically disposed in relation to the plan of the dun, a relationship mirrored in the secondary phase at Dun Cuier, argues against its having been integral to the original occupation. Though the artefactual assemblage from Ardifuir certainly includes material of indisputably early historic date, therefore, in the absence of reliable stratigraphic evidence for the context of these finds, we cannot be sure that the dun itself belongs to this horizon. Hence, in any assessment of the hierarchy of structures of the early historic period in Argyll, it might be safer to focus on the secondary roundhouse at Ardifuir rather than on the dun itself.

We have noted the apparent similarity of construction between the secondary occupation at Ardifuir and the 'Pictish period' structures at Berie. Further examples of edge-set slab construction could be cited from the Pictish and Norse settlement at Buckquoy on Orkney (Ritchie, A. 1977) and elsewhere, but it would be a mistake to assume that this building technique was necessarily diagnostic of later periods. Edge-set slabs with horizontal coursing was in evidence at Cnip, Lewis, in a post-wheelhouse phase of occupation which showed no evidence of a break in material culture, and more recent excavations at Berie (1993) have shown the same technique in a post-wheelhouse, pre-Pictish phase of occupation. Indeed, the same technique defines the walls of a hut-circle of uncertain, but possibly prehistoric, date at Ardnave, Islay (RCAHMS 1984, 127–9, no.241). The technique is plainly suited to structures whose foundations are revetted either into sand or into the collapsed rubble of earlier buildings, and as such may be typical without being diagnostic of any given period.

There are several other instances in Argyll of duns which show clear evidence of secondary reuse, though in one instance at least (Piggott, C. M. 1949) this could have been the result of comparatively recent activity. In two instances, however, the balance of probabilities favours reuse in antiquity. At Dun Ibrig, Tiree (figure 7.4.4), the collapsed rubble of an oval dun has been revetted with a stone facing to create a smaller oval structure, utilising the pre-existing dun entrance. At Druim an Duin, Knapdale (figure 7.4.5), the secondary wall was in evidence only across the northern sector of the oval dun, blocking the northern of its two original entrances. The excavator makes only passing reference to this feature (Christison et al. 1905); it is important, nonetheless, since it casts doubt over the question whether the small finds from the excavation, including part of a rotary quern, are necessarily indicative of the date of the primary dun (Alcock and Alcock 1987, 131).

A further, well-documented example of secondary occupation within the walls of a complex Atlantic roundhouse is the circular structure which abuts the inner face of the inner broch wall at Dun Mor Vaul, Tiree (figure 7.4.1), blocking off two of the broch's three gallery entrances. The excavator tentatively suggested that this secondary structure could have been a wheelhouse, whilst acknowledging that there was no evidence of the radial piers characteristic of that type, and that the site lay outwith the known Hebridean distribution of wheelhouses (MacKie 1974, 49). We shall have occasion to review the Dun Mor Vaul sequence in due course; for the present this example simply serves to underline the regularity with which monumental drystone roundhouses in the Atlantic west were re-used for less pretentious domestic structures.

The relative dating of forts and duns has sometimes been inferred from sites where the two classes of structure apparently occur in sequence. The most convincing of these is Dun Skeig in Kintyre (figure 7.5.2). Three structural phases are represented, of which the earliest, represented by a fort wall which encloses the summit of the hill, is not only overlain by the secondary, oval dun at its south-west end, but also has been severely robbed, presumably for the construction of the later duns. The secondary dun, the interior of which occupies a slight hollow curiously below the level of the adjacent ridge to the north, is also distinguished by its substantially vitrified wall-core. The final phase is represented by a smaller, circular dun at the north-east end of the summit, where the line of the original fort wall may have been renovated as an outwork to the dun. This structure has door rebates within its entrance passage, and walls which are certainly thick enough to have accommodated galleries, though it would require excavation to show whether such existed. Its late status within the sequence is argued by the apparent inclusion of re-used vitrified material within its walls, though it is possible that the surviving structure itself represents some modification of its original form. The sequence of construction is rather less obvious at The Torr, Shielfoot (figure 7.5.3), where the main fort (ia) and dun (ii) are both heavily vitrified,

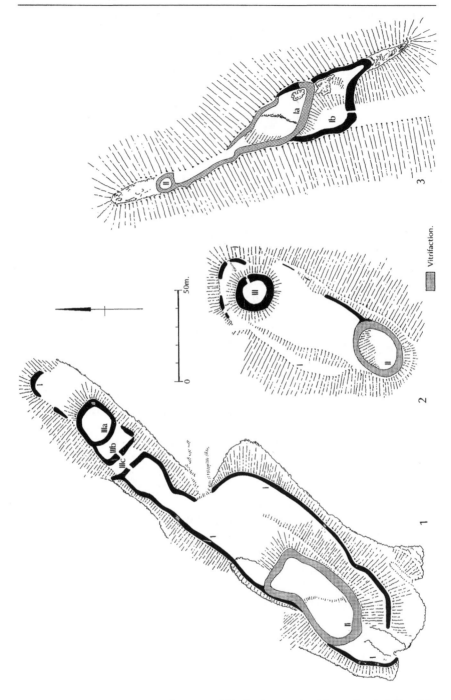

FIGURE 7.5. Site Sequences (with *Inventory of Argyll* volume and article numbers): 1. Dun Mac Sniachan, Benderloch, Lorn (*2*, no.136); 2. Dun Skeig, Kintyre (*1*, no.165); 3. The Torr, Shielfoot, (*3*, no.160).

in contrast to the supposed annexe (1b) which is not. The extraordinarily narrow, elongated extension from main fort to dun in any event suggests that the structural sequence may have been more complex than is apparent from field-survey. Finally, there is a complex sequence of forts and dun at Dun Mac Sniachan, Benderloch (figure 7.5.1). Here again the earliest fort was the largest, encompassing the entire ridge with a single wall which shows traces of vitrification in places. Overlying this enclosure at the south-west end of the ridge is a smaller, heavily-vitrified fort, which excavation in the late nineteenth century suggested may have had more than one building phase. Material remains from that excavation, including metalwork of Roman date, though not strictly associated with either phase of construction, suggests an occupation in the early first millennium AD. Reliance upon exotic imports of this kind, however, is a highly contentious issue (Clarke 1971). Also secondary to the early fort is a smaller dun at the north-east end of the ridge, the plan and layout of which, with outworks, does not immediately demand comparison with smaller dun houses. In all three instances, there is good reason for regarding the larger forts as primary within the site-sequence, and the smaller, circular duns as secondary. But even these sites might have had a more complex structural history than is evident from field-survey alone. In any event, we should not extrapolate from individual sites a general model in which all such forts are early and all variants of dun are late, any more than we can now regard all wheelhouses as later than brochs on the basis of a classic site-sequence like Jarlshof.

It would be pertinent to question whether the presence of vitrifaction itself affords any indication of date. Vitrifaction, whether in the walls of a small, circular dun-house like Rahoy or in the ramparts of a larger fort like Dun Mac Sniachan, implies the use of a timber framework in their construction. Timber-lacing is certainly a characteristic building technique of the earlier Iron Age in Britain, from the seventh or sixth centuries BC, and from the later Bronze Age in Europe. But it is by no means diagnostic of an early date, as the vitrified examples at the Mote of Mark, Kirkcudbrightshire, and Green Castle, Portknockie in Banffshire, clearly demonstrate. Whether an individual site shows traces of vitrifaction depends on whether its walls were fired, and to what extent. If we believed that vitrifaction was a deliberate device designed to produce a stronger defensive wall, and characteristic of some particular region or cultural group, then its occurrence might have chronological significance. In reality, experimental research (Childe and Thorneycroft 1938b; Ralston 1986) has shown that vitrifaction is extremely hard to achieve, and is likely only to be partially effected, as is evident on a number of sites. Far from strengthening the walls, its effect is destructive, and this rules out any notion of its having been a deliberate construction technique. Given the problems experienced experimentally in firing such walls, let alone sustaining the necessary temperature to achieve vitrifaction, it seems likely that vitrifaction results from the systematic razing of a site after capture. Finally, vitrifaction is not a uniquely Scottish phenomenon but one which is quite widespread in Continental Europe (Ralston 1981). In sum, it cannot of itself be regarded as diagnostic of any specific period or cultural group, and there is therefore no compelling reason for regarding its occurrence in Argyll, whether in small dun-houses or larger forts, as a result of diffusion from regions further east (MacKie 1976).

One reason for the assumption that a significant proportion of duns must have originated in later prehistoric times is the fact that their distribution in Atlantic Scotland complements that of brochs, which, even on the conventional chronology, would have been assigned to a span between the first century BC and the opening centuries AD. As a result of research in Orkney over the past fifteen years, the antecedents of brochs can now be traced there well back into the mid-first millennium BC (for a current assessment, see Armit 1990a; Harding 1990). This is bound to strengthen still further the enquiry into dun origins in the west, not least because some, at any rate, share several of the architectural traits displayed by brochs, including intra-mural cells or galleries, scarcement, door rebates in the entrance passage and so forth. The principal differences are that dun-houses are less regular in plan, and their walls are less thick, proportionate to their overall diameter, compared to brochs. Neither of these factors precludes their functioning as roofed, domestic structures, though it seems improbable that they could have attained the height or the defensive capacity of the broch towers. They also display features which are not characteristic of brochs. The most distinctive of these, of course, is the incorporation of a timber framework within the wall, the element which provides the catalyst for vitrifaction, and one which duns have in common with a number of forts. Only a limited number of sites display evidence for this technique of construction, which, unless the wall was burnt, is unlikely to be detected without excavation. But it has prompted a distinction between duns with timber-framed walls and those with apparently solid stone-built walls, with the inference that the latter might be regarded as later in date. Among the latter, another construction technique has been remarked, namely the use of internal revetments or medial wall-faces, apparently designed to strengthen the wall core and to prevent it slumping, which might argue for a greater wall-height than is sometimes assumed. In general, this technique is not shared with forts in Argyll, though cognate systems of internal rampart revetment are known on later prehistoric fortifications elsewhere in Britain and abroad. Experience in the Outer Hebrides has shown that even duns, the walls of which appear superficially to be solid, may after some initial removal of collapsed rubble prove to have galleries; where the walls are sufficiently thick to have accommodated such a feature, it may therefore be difficult to distinguish between an internal revetment and one face of an intra-mural gallery.

Notwithstanding some differences in architectural form and function from the developed broch towers of the north and north-west, there seems to be a strong case for regarding dun-houses in Argyll as a regional variation within the distribution of Atlantic roundhouses of the later prehistoric period.

Variation in structural form may well reflect differences in social, political or economic function, and it is worth noting in this regard that there are many more forts in Argyll than are found in those regions where the distribution of brochs is densest. With the exception of defended coastal promontory sites, fortified enclosures are comparatively rare in these regions. In Argyll, therefore, we may be observing not just a regional variation in architectural tradition, but a difference in social hierarchy reflected in the variation of settlement types. It should be remarked that, even within the distribution zone of brochs, there are distinctive regional groupings, such as the nuclear series of the north, represented by Gurness, Lingro and Midhowe on Orkney. If we can accept that the external occupation of these sites at least overlapped with that of the broch towers (Hedges 1987), then clearly a different social order is here represented than that which typifies the brochs of the western Highlands and Islands.

BROCHS

Brochs, as conventionally defined, are represented in Argyll, though mostly on the islands of the Inner Hebrides. Several, like Dun Bhororaig on Islay, Tirefour Castle, Lismore (figure 7.6.2), Dun nan Gall and Ardnacross, Mull, and Dun Mor Vaul, Tiree (figure 7.6.1) display a combination of classic broch features, including intramural galleries, scarcements, guard cells, doorrebates and bar-holes in the entrance passage, while others less well-preserved may equally conceal such elements of their construction. The majority also have the additional protection of outworks, either a complete outer wall circuit or cross-walls barring access along a steep-sided ridge. The class of enclosed broch is also represented on Skye at Dun Boreraig (figure 7.6.3), Dun Colbost (figure 7.6.5), Dun Hallin (figure 7.6.4) and Dun Suledale. Whilst we cannot be certain without excavation that the outworks were in all cases contemporary with the broch occupation, the pattern is nonetheless sufficiently recurrent to regard this as a regular form of broch settlement in the Inner Hebrides. Outworks of both variants also protect galleried dun-houses, as at Dun Aisgain, Mull (figure 7.7.4), Dun Chroisprig, Islay (figure 7.7.3) and Dun Rostan (figure 7.7.6), overlooking Loch Sween, and several apparently solid-walled dun-houses on Mull and Tiree. In such cases, classification might more meaningfully be based upon the total layout of the settlement than upon the particular architectural features which the house itself apparently displays. What activities were assigned to the enclosed area outwith the broch walls is uncertain, since only at Dun Mor Vaul has excavation addressed this issue. Here, in addition to quantities of domestic débris, curved settings of stonework suggest external buildings (MacKie 1974, fig.5), but it was still unclear to which phase of occupation these belonged.

As the only broch in our region which has been excavated in modern times, Dun Mor Vaul is plainly crucial to an understanding of this important class of field monument. The excavation of 1962–4 was primarily concerned with

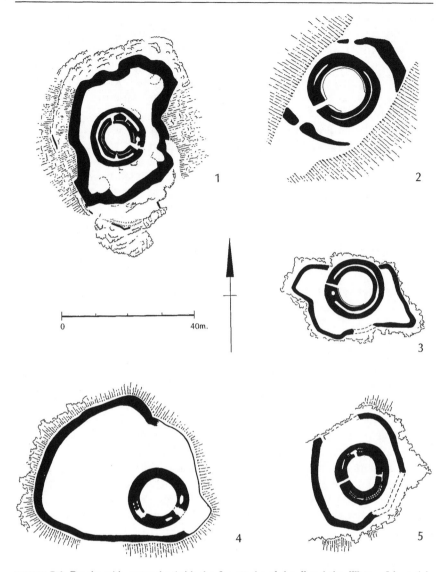

FIGURE 7.6. Brochs with outworks (with the *Inventories of Argyll* and the *Western Isles* article numbers): 1. Dun Mor Vaul, Tiree (*3*, no.167); 2. Tirefour Castle, Lismore (*2*, no.147); 3. Dun Boreraig, Skye (no.505); 4. Dun Hallin, Skye (no.509); 5. Dun Colbost, Skye (no.506).

the clarification of the occupational sequence of the site, and the dating and use of its successive phases. The internal stratigraphy of the broch occupation is complex and might be subject to debate in detail, but the main outline of the sequence seems reasonably secure. The earliest, pre-broch phases produced some evidence for timber structures, together with pottery of the distinctive 'Vaul ware'. Dating of this phase depends upon two radiocarbon dates

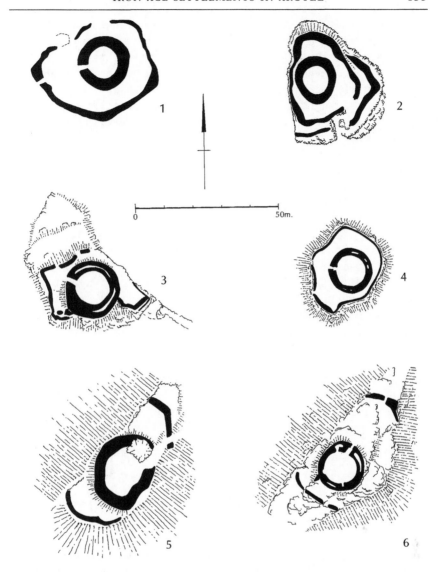

FIGURE 7.7. Duns with outworks (with *Inventory of Argyll* volume and article number): 1. Dun Hanais, Tiree (*3*, no.206); 2. Dun Heanish, Tiree (*3*, no.208); 3. Dun Chroisprig, Islay (*5*, no.208); 4. Dun Aisgain, Mull (*3*, no.186); 5. Camaslaich, Seil (*2*, no.160); 6. Dun Rostan, Mid Argyll (*6*, no.315).

(GaK–1092, 400bc ± 110 from context *Epsilon 2* and GaK–1098, 445bc ± 90 from context *Eta 2*), which would be consistent with an initial prebroch occupation as early as the mid-first millennium BC. In fact, context *Eta 2* is described as a 'mixed layer of earth, ash and stones ... which merged imperceptibly with the widespread broch floor above' which also yielded the upper stone of a discoid rotary quern, not apparently intrusive from the floor

level above, but 'resting nearly' on the floor of the wattle-and-daub hut below
(MacKie 1974, 39). The introduction of rotary querns may now be regarded
as an innovation of the last two centuries BC, but even allowing for calibration
at the two sigma level, this is hardly within the range of the GaK 1098 date,
which must therefore be regarded as incompatible with its associated material.
The construction of the broch itself was assigned by the excavator to the first
century BC or AD on the basis of the material assemblage, which included
pottery of the Clettraval style, and further radiocarbon dates from various
contexts related to the broch and its subsequent occupation, two of which
were discounted as anomalous. In fact, the reliability of the entire series of
radiocarbon dates from Vaul has been questioned, in the light of apparent dis-
crepancies involving Gakushin dates for sites elsewhere (Lane 1990, 113;
Ashmore *infra*).

In fact, MacKie's dating of the broch was very largely determined by his
conviction that it was the product of southern migrants of the first century
BC or shortly thereafter interacting with the native community. The latter continued to produce Vaul ware, while the intrusive overlords were responsible
for the introduction of Clettraval ware, in which everted rim pottery acquired
arcaded ornament, supposedly derived from later Iron Age styles of Wessex.
Whatever evidence can be marshalled for long-distance contacts with Atlantic
Iron Age communities, few prehistorians would now accept the need for
migrants from southern England as a catalyst for the appearance of brochs,
and in particular the notion of a refugee movement in the first century BC has
for too long constrained our understanding of broch origins. In any event,
the direct equation of pots and people, as commonly invoked up to the 1960s,
would now be regarded as simplistic, which is not to say that pottery is not
an important index of culture. But the cameo of native and newcomer,
crouching at opposite ends of the broch gallery, each with his own distinctive
and exclusive style of pottery, seems a trifle extravagant even by the standards
of the genre.

A further key issue is highlighted by the excavation of Dun Mor Vaul, that
of the broch's function. For its initial occupation, MacKie adduced a series
of arguments in favour of its use as a temporary refuge in times of crisis for
a sizeable community; only in the subsequent phase did he see the broch as
the permanent residence of a single family unit. The case rests upon several
factors, of which the absence of a fixed hearth from the earlier occupation
was seen as crucial. One problem with this interpretation, as MacKie
acknowledges, is that it pre-supposes habitations elsewhere, for which at
present there is no evidence. The evidence is hardly conclusive either way,
and we may question the probability that such monumental structures were
built simply for the purposes of temporary occupation. Nonetheless, the issue
needs to be addressed, since if MacKie's view is accepted, it implies a
significant shift in the social organisation of settlement during the broch's lifetime.

CRANNOGS

A class of field monument of which there are several examples in Argyll is the crannog, a settlement on an artificial or sometimes reinforced natural island located in shallow water by the margins of inland lochs. A number of those recorded in the *Inventories* are demonstrably of medieval or later date, but equally it is clear that some, here as in other parts of Scotland, were occupied in the later prehistoric and early historic periods (Barber and Crone 1993). Though the size of the crannog platform may vary, those for which a date in the later first millennium BC or early first millennium AD may be inferred appear to have supported only a single circular house of timber and thatch construction, and hence may be presumed to have sustained a single extended family unit. They may thus be regarded as the equivalent of dun-houses among contemporary land-based sites.

Of around fifty crannogs and related sites in Argyll, only one, at Loch Glashan, Mid Argyll, has been excavated in modern times, and that proved to have been occupied in the second half of the first millennium AD. A site which yielded evidence of earlier occupation is one of two crannogs investigated by Munro in 1890 in Lochan Dughaill, Clachan, Kintyre (figure 7.8.1). The material assemblage, which included two whetstones, a perforated stone disc, part of a cannel-coal bracelet and a small crucible, is hardly diagnostic chronologically, though none of these need be out of context in the opening centuries AD. The form of construction of the principal house, comprising concentric post-circles with radially-disposed timbers resting on the foundations of the crannog, can be matched on crannogs of later prehistoric to Dark-Age date. The fact that such sites were constructed and occupied from at least the middle of the first millennium BC, however, has now been established beyond doubt by radiocarbon dating, notably by a series of dates from sites in Loch Tay (Morrison 1985, 24). Within our area, a crannog off Ederline in Loch Awe yielded a date of 370bc ± 45 (UB−2415) from the heartwood of a substantial timber recovered during underwater survey in 1972 (RCAHMS 1988, 205, no.352.4).

The objective of the Loch Awe survey (and of a parallel exercise in Loch Tay) was not simply to increase the number of known crannogs, but to study their relationship to the local landscape. Certain factors clearly determine the location of crannogs, which are commonly sited in relatively shallow water, as far offshore as practicable before the loch bed shelves steeply away to the loch bottom. Where the shoreline plunges precipitately into deep water, plainly crannog construction is impractical. Even given a suitable foundation, however, it is unlikely that a crannog will be sited where it would face a long wave fetch down the loch. Allowing for these considerations, Morrison recognised a positive relationship between the occurrence of crannogs and the availability of agricultural land. He further remarked that, where usable arable land was not associated with a crannog, because of the practical constraints referred to above, duns or dun-names suggested a complementary

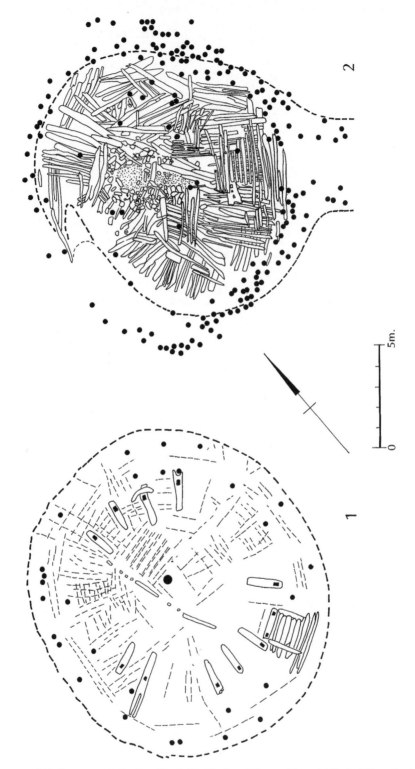

FIGURE 7.8. Crannogs: 1. Lochan Dughaill, Clachan, Kintyre (*1*, no.241); 2. Milton Loch, Kirkcudbrightshire.

distribution of land-based settlement (Morrison 1985, 74–80). Whatever the status or function of individual crannogs, therefore, there are grounds for believing that their economy was dependent in some measure upon the exploitation of the local agricultural potential.

Social considerations

Finally, we should address again the vexed question of the social and political role of forts, duns and crannogs. Most recent discussions have been based upon the premise that the majority of duns and crannogs (though not yet demonstrably forts other than nuclear forts) were built or occupied in the early historic period. The case for regarding strongholds such as Dunadd and Dunollie as royal centres of Dál Riata seems archaeologically well-supported, but the identification of sites which might equate with the rank of free farmers, still less any intermediate class of nobles, who in the chain of clientship might stand between them and the king, is much more problematic. Alcock and Nieke have underlined the lack of correlation between the number of surviving duns in different parts of Argyll and the considerably greater number of households recorded in the tenth-century administrative survey of Dál Riata, the *Senchus Fer nAlban* (Nieke 1983; Alcock and Alcock 1987, 135f), a problem which can only be exacerbated if the case advanced above is accepted, that the number of duns and crannogs which belong to the later prehistoric period has been underestimated.

Nieke has argued nonetheless that duns and crannogs represent a very considerable investment of labour and resources in their construction, and that their occupants must therefore have been of higher social status in order to command such resources. Relatively high-status artefacts from such sites would appear to endorse this argument (Nieke 1990, 140), though only for their later first millennium AD occupation. Marshalling the resources of a community doubtless did require a higher social authority, but does it follow that those who could command resources only used them to their own benefit, or would not this be one of the functions of the client relationship? Once built, a dun if adequately maintained should have had a life-span of many generations, with implications in terms of the inheritance of assets and obligations. On balance, it seems probable that the smaller duns, or dunhouses, were occupied by single, extended family units of free but not noble status, whose livelihood was dependent upon the agricultural resources of the areas in which they were located. Given the investment of effort in their construction, and the absence of any complementary group of settlements, it seems likely that most were intended for permanent, rather than seasonal or emergency occupation. Notwithstanding the particular case that has been advanced for Dun Mor Vaul, it seems reasonable to adduce the same arguments for the permanent occupation of brochs.

Assuming the existence of an intermediate class of noble status, our present inability to assign to it a distinctive sub-group of field monuments could result from two factors. Either the superior status of this group was expressed in a form other than the type of dun it occupied, or archaeological research has failed to recognise the diagnostic features of superior-status duns. Alcock and Alcock (1987, 134f) pointed tentatively to the 29 per cent of duns which were accompanied by outworks as one potential category for superior status, with room to house subordinates in the extra-mural enclosure. We have noted above that outworks can also distinguish some western brochs, including Dun Mor Vaul, and whilst the evidence for extra-mural settlement remains very slight by comparison with some Orcadian brochs, the possibility of more complex settlement of Argyll brochs and duns is one that would certainly warrant testing by excavation.

Many problems remain to be addressed by future research regarding the later prehistoric and early historic field-monuments of Argyll. The vexed issue of dating can only be resolved by excavation, but this needs to be undertaken as part of a broader strategy aimed at understanding not just the occupational sequences of individual, and possibly unrepresentative sites, but how the different classes of monument relate to each other and to the developing landscape pattern as a whole. This might then permit a better assessment of the economic, political and social roles and relationships between groups of sites within the settlement hierarchy. An essential pre-requisite, however, is a more critical analysis of the various classes of monument represented in the region, and it is for this initial objective that the *Inventories* of the RCAHMS must form an invaluable foundation.

8   Dun Mor Vaul Revisited: Fact and Theory in the Reappraisal of the Scottish Atlantic Iron Age

Euan W. MacKie

THE MIDDLE IRON AGE IN ARGYLL

The period from approximately 100 BC to AD 300 in Atlantic Scotland is conveniently known as the middle Iron Age and is well defined by the predominantly new material culture which appears with the hollow-walled brochs and allied sites, and which is distinct – both stratigraphically and in terms of its contents – from that of the preceding early Iron Age horizon and that of the succeeding late Iron Age (MacKie 1965a, 118, fig.6; 1971, 65, fig.7; 1995b, 100). Unfortunately the material cultures concerned have so far been mainly found in the broch province; the Iron Age sites of mainland Argyll rarely yield many artefacts at any period. In broad terms the middle Iron Age horizon is defined (except in Caithness and Sutherland) by the appearance of large quantities of finely made pottery, often decorated, in a variety of local styles and by a rich array of new artefacts of stone and bone. Also new are bronze ornaments like spiral finger-rings and penannular brooches and a variety of glass beads including the characteristic small annular yellow bead and the larger 'Meare spiral', usually of translucent glass with an inlaid yellow spiral. Disc-shaped rotary querns, probably adjustable (MacKie 1986, 5–11), also appear and mark a striking technological advance over the beehive and bun-shaped querns of the southern mainland. Iron tools are not often found, but the remarkable array recovered from inside the violently destroyed Leckie broch in Stirlingshire (MacKie 1978; 1982; 1986, 16) suggests that this period saw a substantial advance in this area of technology also.

A number of sites of this period have produced Roman fragments, which should not have started to occur among the tribes of the Highlands and Islands before their first appearance in southern Scotland with the invading army

141

under Agricola in the late first century AD. At several broch sites where the stratigraphy is reasonably clear, like Dun Mor Vaul and Crosskirk, the Roman fragments do not appear until some time after the first middle Iron Age deposits have been accumulating. This is the main reason for suggesting that the start of this period should be set not later than the first century BC.

In mainland Argyll there is a dearth not only of systematically excavated Iron Age sites with clear stratigraphies but also of much in the way of finds from those which have been explored. The suggestion that timber-framed (vitrified) hillforts belong to an early Iron Age period, when only saddle querns were in use, goes back to the excavations of the Duntroon fort in Mid Argyll in 1904 (Christison et al. 1905; RCAHMS 1988, 164–5, no.257). The contrast is marked with the three other sites explored at the time – the duns of Ardifuir and Druim an Duin and the nucleated hilltop stronghold of Dunadd. The latter site proved to belong to the Early Historic period, contemporary with, and sharing many fine bone artefacts and discoid rotary querns with, the late Iron Age period in regions without such historical records further west and north, and more recent excavations have confirmed this (Lane 1984).

The two duns mentioned yielded few finds, but probably enough to place their origins in the middle Iron Age; for example those from Druim an Duin included a rotary quern and those from Ardifuir a fragment of second-century Roman Samian pottery (RCAHMS 1988, 180–2, 271–2, nos 293 and 270). The only Mid Argyll site that has been radiocarbon-dated failed to reveal any artefacts, Eilean an Duin (RCAHMS 1988, 166, no.258). Further south in Kintyre second-century material has been recovered from several duns like Kildalloig, Dun Fhinn and Kildonan Bay, Kintyre (RCAHMS 1971, 19, pl.7, D, E and F; 87–8, no.219, 83–4, no.203, 88–9 no.220); each of these excavated duns was also evidently in use for several centuries, into the late Iron Age or even into early Medieval times. Kildalloig also yielded one of the 'type fossils' of the middle Iron Age period, a bronze spiral finger-ring. Nevertheless there is a tendency to place many if not most of the Argyllshire duns into the late Iron Age (Nieke 1983).

In striking contrast to the meagre results obtained from these mainland excavated Iron Age sites is the single systematically explored broch in Argyll, Dun Mor Vaul on the island of Tiree (figure 8.1) (MacKie 1974; RCAHMS 1980, 92–4, no.167). Here not only was a deep stratigraphical sequence found, but each occupation layer had large quantities of pottery and other artefacts, while a series of radiocarbon dates tied down the various site phases reasonably accurately. Paradoxically, although the quantity and variety of the information obtained from this site are enormous, and the potential for using it to make unusually detailed inferences about the technology and social structure of the inhabitants correspondingly great, and even though the excavations have been published in detail since 1974, the Dun Mor Vaul report has attracted more criticism than constructive comment. It is the primary purpose of this chapter to ask why this has happened.

FIGURE 8.1. Dun Mor Vaul, Tiree.

BACKGROUND TO THE TIREE EXCAVATIONS

Early in April 1964, the third of three seasons of work at the broch site at Dun Mor Vaul came to an end. Eighteen months later papers in *Antiquity* and the *Proceedings of the Prehistoric Society* signalled the progress of this new phase of research into the Iron Age cultures of maritime, or Atlantic Scotland by publishing accounts of its preliminary conclusions, an important pillar of which was this first stratigraphical excavation ever of a Hebridean broch (MacKie 1965a; 1965b). Ten years after the work finished, it was published in detail (MacKie 1974). This excavation, together with surface fieldwork carried out in most areas of Atlantic Scotland between 1962 and 1964, and three other excavations conducted between 1965 and 1968, provided a mass of evidence which allowed the author to construct a new picture of the origin and development of the broch- and wheelhouse-building cultures of the Scottish Iron Age (MacKie 1965a and b; 1971). The main points of this have recently been summarised again (MacKie 1992; 1995b). Part of the reason for the present paper is that the author senses that the significance of the mass of well-documented information obtained from this site – superior to anything published previously, with the exception of Jarlshof and Clickhimin, Shetland (Hamilton 1956 and 1968) – has not been fully appreciated, and has even been misunderstood, by some of the more recent contributors to the field. As a result, some modern syntheses have omitted important data.

Background to the argument

The excavation of Dun Mor Vaul still stands alone in the west of Scotland in providing a record of a more or less continuous sequence of occupation deposits from about the middle of the first millennium BC until approximately AD 300 (with some suggestions of a sporadic later Norse activity); during this long period a broch was built at a clearly defined point in the stratigraphical sequence. Two other brochs, Dun Vulan in South Uist and Loch na Berie in Lewis, are in process of exploration and should eventually produce comparable data, while Howe, Orkney, has also been completely excavated (Smith, B. 1994). The Tiree broch was the first prehistoric site in Scotland to which radiocarbon dating was systematically applied and, for all these reasons, remains a fundamental pillar of any reconstruction of the nature and development of the Iron Age cultures in the far west, and indeed in Atlantic Scotland as a whole.

Over the last ten years, however, several papers have appeared which have tried to show that various important aspects of the site have been mis-interpreted. To some extent of course this kind of re-appraisal of major excavated sites is inevitable as knowledge accumulates and ideas alter, and one or two examples are given later of how the excavator now thinks he may have been mistaken about some aspects of the site and its finds. Yet some of the criticism discussed here goes well beyond that, by maintaining that the excavator misinterpreted the dating and stratigraphy of the site because of preconceived ideas, that he distorted some of the evidence and, further, that he produced a report that is inadequate because it does not allow one to compare the actual evidence with the various competing hypotheses about it.

The following sections deal with four important areas of the report about which such doubts have been raised. These are firstly the stratigraphy of the site, secondly the nature of the Iron Age pottery styles found and their inter-relationships, thirdly the radiocarbon dating of the site sequence and fourthly the social conclusions drawn from all this evidence. The question of the origin of various elements in the middle Iron Age material culture – and in particular of whether any parts of it were exotic – is not addressed here.

Structure and layout of the report

It seems advisable first to outline the structure of the report, even though it is clearly explained in its *Introduction*, in order to put the various published comments in context. It may well be asked why it is necessary to explain all this again here since the report itself can easily be consulted. The reason is that fundamental misunderstandings about the site, presumably based on reading the report, have been published. When the author came across the words, 'The excavation report does not permit one to choose between these rival hypotheses with any confidence' (Armit 1991, 210), he realised that either he had failed to describe the evidence from the site adequately or that something else had gone badly wrong. Could the report really be so incomprehensible and inadequate, despite all the efforts made to lay it out systematically and logically, to explain in detail the methods of reasoning and to separate fact from theory? Or have Armit and Lane, as well as others to a lesser degree, just not bothered to study it properly despite making firm pronouncements on its contents and failings (Armit, 1990; 1991; Lane 1987).

The author's guiding principle was to keep the description of what was found on the site distinct from the conclusions built on this data and the hierarchical structure of the report reflects this, as does the considerable detail given about the finds and their stratigraphical contexts. Thus *Part 1* is an account of what was found and it consists, first, of a description of the broch itself and its outer wall, followed by accounts of the stratified sequences of layers found inside and outside it; each of these latter sections describes a specific part of the site. These stratigraphies are of course the key to the interpretation of the site and the great majority of the successions were clear and unambiguous. There are of course a large number of plans and section drawings of the features found.

Thus most of *Part 1* consists of descriptions of superimposed layers and occupation floors, each of which has a list of the artefacts and samples that were respectively found in and taken from it. Each of these basic units of excavation was known as a *Bag*, that is all or part of a natural layer, but never knowingly from more than one, found in an arbitrary area – a trench or inside part of the broch. It was given a number and also an unique four-letter code; the latter was written on the objects and the Bags are all listed in numerical order, with their equivalent Contexts and Phases, in *Appendix K*.

Subsequently all the Bags which proved to be from a single natural layer, known as a Context, were grouped under the Greek letter code allocated to it. In the final stage of the analysis the Contexts themselves were where possible grouped into major site Phases. All this, it must be stressed, was based on the observed site stratigraphy and not on any preconceived ideas about what might be found.

Each of the Small Finds (potsherds and other artefacts deemed worth measuring in precisely) is described and illustrated in stratigraphical order of Contexts, and also has a code which links with the artefact appendix at the end of the report (described below). Thus the bronze spiral finger-ring found in layer 2 of the intra-mural gallery is mentioned under Context *Beta-1* (DMV, 27) and not only has with it the figure and plate number of its drawing and photograph but also the code '7/P', which refers to the table of artefact distribution (DMV, 116, fig.10). Square 7/P on the table contains a '1' signifying that only one bronze ring was found in *Beta*, and the same code leads one to the appropriate section in the Artefact Appendices where a detailed description of the ring is given. Of course scanning column 7 will also show what other spiral finger-rings were found and where (there were none), while row P will show what other material came from *Beta*, the wind-blown earth found in the intra-mural gallery of the broch.

Likewise the large amount of pottery found is mentioned briefly in the same way in the various Contexts in *Part 1*, but the illustrated sherds are described in detail in *Appendix C* where the numbering is linked directly to the drawings. The finds drawings themselves are unusual in that everything important found in a given Context is shown together, and the contents of the Contexts themselves are shown mainly in stratigraphical order. This contrasts with the usual system of showing finds by type, but it was hoped that this information could be almost as easily gained from the *Appendices*, while the manner of arranging the illustrations has the advantage of directly reflecting what was found with what in the ground.

Thus the primary excavated data is presented in *Part I* and in the *Appendices*. *Part II* consists of discussions and analyses, and these are themselves arranged in an hierarchical order. First comes a discussion of how the two major stratigraphical sequences, in the broch itself and in the outer court, were built up and how their various components were linked together. This was quite a complex operation which took a long time to work out (long after the fieldwork had finished) and the reasoning is shown pictorially in figure 8.2. Here each of the five main sequences is shown as a column with any physical connections between them indicated; thus one can see for example that no such links were found between the two separate sequences inside the broch and that in the outer court, the correlations being inferred from indirect evidence. Uncertainties are indicated by question marks. Gaps in the columns show where it is assumed, after reviewing the evidence from the whole site, that a pause in the accumulation of layers took place. This is a pictorial and more primitive form of the diagrammatic matrix devised by Harris some years later (1979 and 1989).

Only after this laborious stratigraphical analysis were the major phases of the site's history deduced, and these are indicated on the same diagram, the left side showing 'major events' and the right side the numbers of the Phases. With the latter the eight radiocarbon dates are marked at their appropriate stratigraphical levels and the layers in which Roman material was found are indicated. All this last stage of reasoning is described in detail in section II/11 'The major phases of the site's occupation', while the evidence for the absolute chronology of the site is summarised separately in section II/12. Only after all this comes section II/13, a discussion of 'The site in its wider context', and this of course is the part of the report that is most open to modification in the light of later research.

With the benefit of hindsight it can be seen that there were two flaws in the way this excavation was conducted and therefore in the resulting report (apart from any of the conclusions about the 'wider context' which have to be modified because of subsequent discoveries). The first was the failure to carry out systematic sieving of the occupation deposits; it was thought that painstaking trowelling would retrieve all important artefacts, but experiences at Leckie broch showed later that water-sieving revealed many missed by this method and that a very few were even missed then. The second problem arises from the fact that the radiocarbon dates were undertaken at a relatively early stage in the development of the technique and are not so precise as those produced now. Nor is the simple calibration used then adequate by modern standards (Topping 1987, 73). In addition doubts have been raised about the reliability of early dates from the Gakushin University laboratory in Japan (apparently those with numbers below GaK–3000) which provided several of

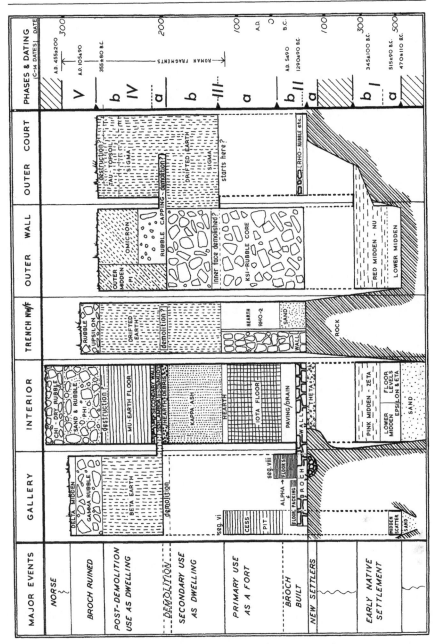

FIGURE 8.2. Diagrammatic representation of the five main stratigraphies found at Dun Mor Vaul, integrated into the major site Phases and with points of contact indicated. The radiocarbon dates are shown 'raw' but in terms of the now abandoned best half life rather than the Libby figure (DMV, 67, fig.9).

the dates from Dun Mor Vaul (Lane 1990, 113). This problem will be considered below.

THE STRATIGRAPHY OF DUN MOR VAUL

Before discussing the reservations that have been published about the stratigraphy of the site, it will be useful to summarise the interpretation of the layers found which is given in the report. It should be stressed that this inferred site sequence stands entirely on its own and does not depend at all on the radiocarbon dates.

Phases 1a and 1b: the lowest midden layers found, resting on sterile subsoil, were allocated to a pre-broch era, Phase 1b. One of these (Context *Nu*) ran under the outer wall of the broch and the other (*Zeta*) was found in the central court, under the primary broch floor and within a deep cleft in the rocky knoll on which the broch stands. Below that at one point was an early floor level with a broken pot (Phase 1a, *Epsilon-1*) on top of an old ground surface resting on sterile sand; the latter also appeared in other parts of the interior (*Eta-1*). With one exception only sherds of Vaul and Dunagoil ware were found in these pre-broch layers which seem likely, from the radiocarbon dates obtained (table 8.5), to fall somewhere between the eighth and the first centuries BC.

Phase 2b: this was marked by the construction of the broch on top of the levelled-off earlier deposits; for example the top of the Phase 1b midden (*Zeta*) was sharp and clean with no sign of an old turf line and seemed to have been cut away (DMV, 147 and fig.7, section 1). A strip of peripheral paving, extending about 2 m out from the inner wall-face, was laid on the new flat surface of the central court and around about three-quarters of the interior (a raised rocky surface occupied the other quarter; DMV, fig.3). Unequivocal broch construction layers (Contexts *Alpha-1, -3* and *-4*) were found in the ground-level mural gallery, resting on clean rock, and they yielded both the pre-broch Vaul ware and the entirely new Everted Rim ware. There was also an occupation deposit, full of potsherds and animal bones, of the same period in another part of the gallery (*Alpha-2*). These are still the only closed deposits known of material which were almost certainly laid down during the period of a few months during which a broch tower was being built. Two radiocarbon dates were obtained from samples from these deposits (table 8.5). There were slightly lower and earlier mixed earth layers with the new material culture (*Theta* and *Eta-2*), which were allocated to Phase 2a, presumably starting not long before the broch was built.

Phase 3a: the whole of the central court was covered by a thick occupation deposit (Context *Iota*) which overlay both the earlier Phase 1 middens and the primary peripheral paving of the broch. A fragment of second-century

FIGURE 8.3. The broch entrance passage showing the door frame in the background and the lintelled drain in the floor. The latter leads to the water tank, one lintel of which can be seen in the floor (scale in feet).

Roman glass was found at the top of this layer which also contained very large quantities of pottery (both Vaul ware and Everted Rim ware), animal bones and other artefacts. The whole deposit was pale in colour, unlike most Iron Age occupation layers which tend to be dark grey because of organic refuse. A cess pit in one section of the basal mural gallery seems to have been in use in this Phase and doubtless explains the relative cleanliness of the *Iota* deposits, despite much bone refuse; there was also a water tank and overflow drain in the central court, but no central hearth (figures 8.3–4).

Phase 3b: a thin layer of red and black ash (Context *Kappa*) covered the *Iota* layer and was directly linked with a large rectangular stone hearth which had been laid on top (figure 8.4). This had four whale vertebra post-sockets beside it which evidently supported some kind of framework over the fire.

Phase 4: the presumed high broch hollow wall was largely dismantled at this point, almost down to the lintels of the ground level gallery, which were

FIGURE 8.4. The central hearth of Phase 3b with the excavated Phase 3a water tank, unlintelled in the foreground. The section has cut away the near end of the hearth, showing that it rests on the *Iota* floor deposits of Phase 3a, with no sign of an earlier hearth underneath (scale in feet).

removed. This allowed fine, wind-blown earth to drift into the open gallery (Context *Beta*) and also, for a short time, into the central court while this was unroofed (Phase 4a). A low-roofed roundhouse with a new wall facing was then built inside the broch and a distinctive occupation layer of dark earth (Context *Mu*) accumulated inside it; no central hearth was found, although there was a small stone fireplace against the sw wall (DMV, fig.8). The *Beta* earth deposits in the gallery could be linked to this stage of the central court sequence through two of the gallery doors. The blowing earth may have been a new development, perhaps indicating intensive tilling of the ground nearby. Almost the whole of the dark grey earth deposits in the outer court (Contexts *Sigma* and *Tau*) seem to belong to this phase, for which one radiocarbon date was obtained (table 8.5).

Phase 5: there were one or two equivocal signs of a final destruction of the roundhouse inside the reduced broch but the material from the final phase of occupation almost all came from the top layer in the mural gallery – rubble from the collapsing wall (Context *Gamma*) which rested on the wind-blown earth; in one section of the gallery there was some fine earth with many sherds on top of this rubble (Context *Delta*). The pottery included a very high percentage of native Vaul ware, in sharp contrast to that from the top of the deposits in the outer court.

Norse phase: one disarticulated human burial, probably Norse, was found in the rubble of the central court and was radiocarbon dated to the eighth or ninth centuries; a small deposit of Norse artefacts including a composite bone comb came from a high level in the mural gallery. There was also a partial skeleton, of unknown but possibly recent date, on top of the *Gamma* deposits.

Doubts about the pre-broch horizon

The identification of the pre-broch occupation at Dun Mor Vaul (Phases 1a and 1b) and its material culture are of crucial importance for the understanding of the development of the early and middle Iron Age cultures of the western islands of Scotland. The significance of the discovery is such that it is only to be expected that the conclusion should initially be questioned and the report studied to discover whether the evidence for the pre-broch occupation and its dating is convincing. Armit questioned the hypothesis and concluded that it was mistaken, and that the Phase 1 deposits inside the broch were in fact primary broch material:

> MacKie postulates that the first three [radiocarbon] dates [that is the samples from Phase 1 deposits] related to pre-roundhouse [Armit's term for the broch] occupation although the sections and plans do not support this and the absence of convincing structures associated with Phases 1a and 1b means that we cannot rule out the possibility that those levels were the primary roundhouse occupation levels (DMV, 74). MacKie's failure to consider this possibility appears to derive from his belief that the roundhouse would have had a level floor while the early deposits lie deep in a cleft; evidence from many other roundhouse sites does not warrant this assumption. An alternative and opposite view suggests that MacKie's floor levels were construction levels and that his secondary occupation was in fact primary occupation (Nieke 1984, 172). The excavation report does not permit one to choose between these hypotheses with any confidence. (Armit 1991, 210)

An explanation for this scepticism as expressed in the first hypothesis (that there was no pre-broch horizon) may be available. Armit has argued elsewhere that the new evidence from Orkney and the Outer Hebrides means that there is now no reason to restrict hollow-walled brochs to a relatively narrow time span beginning in the first century BC (Armit 1990c), and he evidently believes therefore that Dun Mor Vaul could have been built much earlier than the excavator concluded. The inferences about which deposit in the central court was the primary broch floor level depended, however, on the stratigraphy of the site, not on assumptions, and the details of this stratigraphy should have been discussed in detail before an alternative interpretation was offered. If the lowest occupation level was in fact a primary broch deposit the tower could well be somewhat older than the report proposed and the distinction between broch pottery and aboriginal pottery would be lost. This hypothesis has obvious attractions to anyone proposing a strictly non-diffusionist explanation for the evolution of the Scottish Atlantic Iron Age cultures (Armit 1990b; Hedges 1987; 1990), and a non-hierarchical interpretation of the societies concerned, but it can only be sustained by distorting the evidence.

As already explained, the first layer in the central court which was allocated to the broch period (*Iota*) lay on top of the levelled-off earlier midden inside the rocky cleft which was deduced to be pre-broch; it also lay on top of the peripheral stone paving at the base of the inner face of the wall, a standard feature of the primary floors of hollow-walled brochs which is usually found resting on subsoil, for example at Leckie (MacKie 1982, fig.5 and pl.2). This *Iota* stratum contained abundant sherds of Everted Rim pottery, which the older levels did not, and this new ware also occurred in the *primary* floor packing resting directly on clean rock inside the ground level mural gallery (Context *Alpha*). These two basic points are consistently glossed over by critics of the Dun Mor Vaul sequence, presumably because they are inexplicable in the alternative scenarios so far offered.

Another fundamental point ignored by Armit is that the allocation of the lowest occupation deposits under the broch to a pre-broch period is also supported by the discovery of an exactly similar midden underlying the outer wall of the tower. This deposit (Context *Nu*) was similar in appearance and texture, also lay on the underlying rock and also yielded only Vaul and Dunagoil ware sherds with not a trace of Everted Rim pottery. Moreover the radiocarbon dates both for this midden and the Phase 1a deposits under the broch were substantially older than those obtained for the Phase 2, 3 and 4 levels. Yet none of this is mentioned and the 'proof' of the excavator's misinterpretation is his alleged assumption about level floors and the sweeping and unsubstantiated implication that plenty of other 'roundhouse' floors were not level, presumably in the sense that they similarly included deep, unfilled rocky clefts.

Incredulity is the only possible reaction to this last assertion. Every primary floor so far exposed by skilled excavation in a hollow-walled broch like Dun Mor Vaul has proved to be more or less level, with a strip of peripheral paving about 2 m wide round the outside and a substantial stone hearth in the middle, on the same level; around the inner edge of the paving there are usually traces of a ring of post-holes which are thought to have supported the raised floor of a wooden roundhouse, its outer edge resting on the level stone ledge or scarcement in the inner wall-face. Examples include Clickhimin (Hamilton

1968, fig.8, section AA') and probably Jarlshof (Hamilton 1956, 44–8 and fig.22), both in Shetland, Crosskirk in Caithness (without post-holes, Fairhurst 1984, 56–61, Ills 23 and 28), Dun Troddan in western Inverness-shire (the first site to reveal such a ring of posts, Curle 1921, 90–2, figs 3 and 5), and Leckie in Stirlingshire (MacKie 1982, fig.5). Although the primary floor levels in Midhowe and Gurness in Orkney (Callander and Grant 1934; Hedges 1987, 34f) were hardly exposed they appear to have been fairly level (apart from containing wells) and, judging from the photographs, the situation inside Howe is the same (Smith, B. 1994, Ill.29).

Occasionally such sites are built on gently sloping, fairly even rock surfaces, but in such cases the lowest floors either follow the rock or are on top of levelled-up packing. One broch with a markedly sloping rock floor is Caisteal Grugaig in western Inverness-shire (Graham 1949, 15, fig.3), but no-one knows whether the nineteenth-century clearance removed any levelled-up internal floor deposits. The situation in the semibroch (non-circular broch-like structure) Dun an Ruigh Ruaidh in Wester Ross is similar, and here the primary floor did follow the sloping subsoil (MacKie 1980, fig.8). Dun Ardtreck in Skye, by contrast, had a levelled-up primary floor on top of the sloping rock (MacKie 1975, pl.5d). To the author's knowledge no hollow-walled broch has been found in which the primary floor contains a substantial, unfilled and uncovered, dangerously steep-sided cleft in the rock, and he would be most interested to see Armit's list of these. To make such a suggestion moreover implies a lack of awareness of the nature of the multi-storeyed wooden roundhouse contained within hollow-walled brochs (MacKie 1995b, 153).

This rather cavalier and one-sided treatment of the complex stratigraphical data from Dun Mor Vaul recalls a recent attempted re-interpretation of Dun Cuier on Barra in the Outer Hebrides (Armit 1988). Here the gallery-walled dun was reinterpreted as a broch and therefore re-dated to the middle Iron Age despite the presence inside it of a *primary* occupation level on rock which contained only *late* Iron Age material (including composite bone combs) and which was simply not discussed. The argument was repeated (Armit 1990b, 55–9) despite the mistake having been pointed out earlier (MacKie 1988), though this time with a better discussion of the late bone pins and combs. Lane repeats the idea (1990, 122), 'Unfortunately Young did not recognise the complexity of the site and it seems that stratigraphy, if present, was not recognised.' In fact it was observed and described, but both Armit and Lane seem to find it difficult *a priori* to accept what was found. In view of comments earlier in this volume it can only be repeated that Alison Young clearly described the late Iron Age horizon as resting on clean sand which was directly on rock. One cannot legitimately re-date a site by assuming a completely vanished occupation layer. There was a final horizon on top of Hearth 2, with featureless coarse pottery, which could belong to the supposed secondary internal wallface.

Was the broch built as a farmhouse?

The question of the apparent absence of a central hearth inside Dun Mor Vaul in Phase 3a (the primary occupation) is intriguing, and this leads to a consideration of the second alternative hypothesis about the nature of the interior deposits. At the time of the excavations, the author had no reason to doubt that the broch had no central hearth in Phase 3a, especially as one of the cross sections cut into the lower deposits removed about 40 cm from its east corner and found nothing below it except the primary *Iota* floor deposits (DMV, fig.4). This led directly to the hypothesis that in its primary phase of use Dun Mor Vaul was not the exclusive residence of a single family or lineage, but was the kind of stronghold which could be used as a refuge for the whole local community in times of danger.

Since that time it has become clear that such a situation is unique among the well-excavated brochs; at Leckie, for example, there were four large central hearths on top of each other, the lowest resting on rock (MacKie 1982, 61–4, pl.3 and figs 5 and 6), and the same seems to have been found (under more primitive conditions of excavation) at Dun Troddan (Curle 1921, 89–90, fig.5). A central hearth is likely to be present in both Midhowe and Gurness in Orkney (MacKie 1995b) and was found on the primary sloping floor in Dun an Ruigh Ruaidh in Wester Ross (MacKie 1980, 39–44, fig.4, pls 5a and 5b) as well as in at least one of the early Iron Age stone roundhouses of Orkney (Hedges 1987, 1, figs 1.7 and 1.8, pl.1.5). This makes the situation at Dun Mor Vaul highly unusual, and with the benefit of hindsight, it is clear that the whole of the visible hearth there should have been removed to make sure that there was no earlier one below it. This could still be done; the central court is empty, the walls turfed over and in good order and the rectangular hearth is immediately below the modern turf floor.

There is also now a strong theoretical commitment, based on good evidence (MacKie 1987), to the 'broch equals farmhouse' concept and therefore a disposition among some to challenge any evidence which, for example, appears to support the older concept of 'broch equals stronghold'. A central hearth is usually taken to be a reliable sign that a structure was the domestic residence of a single family or lineage, so one would perhaps expect all the 'broch farmhouses' to have had one from the start. In 1981 Barrett argued strongly that the old view of brochs as forts was wrong and that we should return to the neglected hypothesis of Sir Lindsay Scott who made out a strong case that they were primarily farmhouses (Scott, Sir L.1947). Ironically other new evidence persuaded the author soon afterwards that Barrett was quite right about this and a new scenario with Scott's basic hypothesis (though not his inferences about the structure of brochs) as its foundation was offered (MacKie 1988b).

Barrett also objected to the concept of 'secondary' structures inside and around brochs, arguing that this is a misunderstanding of the excavated evidence. This appears to be another straightforward deduction from the belief that the old view is clearly mistaken; this is that the hollow-walled towers were originally forts, with clear interiors and uncluttered by external domestic dwellings (Barrett 1981, 212).

Dr Margaret Nieke's thesis (1984) was also quoted by Armit in support of his alternative view about the significance of the lower strata inside Dun Mor Vaul broch. Since her unpublished idea has been used in print it may reasonably be quoted here. The section is in fact part of a long and useful discussion on the site (172–5), which is also designed to show that the idea of the broch having been a refuge in Phase 3a is mistaken. This could of course be a straightforward exercise in deduction, saying in effect that 'our superior knowledge about brochs now makes it clear that they were low-walled farmhouses; therefore any excavated evidence that suggests that any broch, and Dun Mor Vaul in particular, was ever a tall tower-like refuge must be wrong.' Although the discussion is detailed and fair on the whole, it is difficult, because of this presupposition, for Nieke and those who argue like her to distinguish between plausible and implausible reinterpretations; they all seem plausible because they fit the new general theory.

A good example is the rather strained attempt to prove that the fragmentary hearths found in the outer court could represent permanent occupation in an early stage in the broch's history, thus nullifying the 'broch equals refuge' hypothesis. 'The subsequent construction of a central hearth within the broch then marks a reorganisation of activity space within both the broch and the outer court. This could be associated with changing attitudes towards food preparation and the processes and individuals involved in it.' (Nieke 1984, 172). Leaving aside the unusual reasoning which implies that a sociological speculation can be advanced as an argument against a concrete aspect of a site's stratigraphy, no account is taken here of the stratigraphy of the outer court, which strongly suggests that all the grey earth deposits there, and the hearths within them, post-dated the dilapidation of the outer wall and therefore belong to Phase 4 (DMV, fig.7, section 2).

Likewise the existence of a water tank at the beginning of the site's use, and its conversion to a rubbish pit later on (before Phase 4a and the demolition of the broch), tends to support the idea that Dun Mor Vaul was a refuge in Phase 3a and a residence in Phase 3b. Nieke argues against such a distinction, not implausibly (asking for example why no ash apparently fell into it in Phase 3b from the adjacent hearth), and suggests that it was a water tank throughout Phase 3. This is perfectly possible, though one must still find a period before Phase 4a for it to be used as a dry rubbish pit, apparently for some time. Here the alternative view strains the evidence more than the 'official' one.

Nieke does not show complete objectivity in her discussion of the dating of the end of Phase 3 by a fragment of Roman glass (Nieke 1984, 173): 'The sherd itself is extremely small (c. 0.6 × 0.3 cm). This being the case it must be questionable to what extent such a small sherd can be accurately dated and whether it could not have been moved through archaeological deposits with great ease (for example by worm action).' It may be suggested that these arguments are not entirely suitable for a formal academic thesis. The first statement denigrates the expertise of the glass specialists concerned (DMV, 148f), yet without showing equivalent expertise, while the second should surely not have been made without establishing first whether worms can in fact exist in the earth floor of a roofed and inhabited roundhouse. They certainly could not have existed later since, after abandonment, the earth floor was covered, first with sand and rubble and later with dry rubble.

However the main line of argument concerns the *Iota* floor deposits of Phase 3a. The report itself suggests that the lower part of this layer represents a levelling of the interior, but that, because the upper parts overlie the broch peripheral paving, they represent several later such depositions to the floor, apparently over a long period of use (DMV, 42). Nieke suggests that the hearth and its ash spread represent the primary domestic use and that everything before the hearth must be material dumped in the court. The primary arguments against this are fourfold. First the peripheral paving is most unlikely to have been laid and then immediately buried. The second point concerns the freshness of the occupation material in *Iota* and the paleness of the deposits themselves. Almost none of vast quantities of bones and potsherds were in the least worn or weathered; the bones are clean and fresh-looking and the majority of the potsherds have clean, freshly broken edges; several clusters of sherds were found which had been further broken *in situ* (DMV, pl.IX B). Third, there were also level spreads of peat ash and charcoal which looked like the remains of small temporary fires rather than dumped material (DMV, 42). Fourth,and even more important, the proportions of the various pottery styles found at the site were quite different in this Phase 3a deposit than in those of the unequivocal construction deposits of Phase 2b, a few feet away in the mural gallery; if the *Iota* floor had been material dumped during the construction of the broch one would perhaps expect the proportion of Everted Rim ware to be similarly high to that in the basal layers of the gallery.

The upper part of the *Iota* layer in particular did not look like a random collection of earth and assorted occupation débris scraped up from ground surfaces outside and brought in. The paleness of the deposits and the presence of sand and gravel (DMV, 42) suggest that beach deposits were brought in at the start of Phase 3a to even off the interior in line with the peripheral paving, but this of course cannot explain the quantities of fresh-looking pottery, artefacts and animal bones (not to mention the peat ash and charcoal spreads) which filled it. At intervals further spreads of beach material were doubtless brought in and spread about to cover up these bones and sherds and also, gradually, the peripheral paving. The steady accumulation of the occupation layer on top of this paving is well known from other brochs.

Finally, and as indicated in the report, the presence of the cess pit in the base of one deep section of the intra-mural gallery goes far to explain the continued cleanliness of the Phase 3a deposit; those of Phase 4 immediately above the ash layer of 3b were dark grey, the pit having fallen into disuse (DMV, fig.6, section vi). What is more, a distinct turf line or old ground surface was observed on top of the cess pit deposit (shown in the section referred to) and under the wind-blown earth layer which accumulated on top of it. This strongly implies that the cess pit fell into disuse, and that the top of the deposit dried and hardened, some time before the broch was partly dismantled at the start of Phase 4, thus allowing earth to blow in and cover it. Again this hiatus after the use of the cess pit exactly fits the view that it was used in Phase 3a and not in 3b, which might have lasted quite a long time.

In terms of the precise nature of the Phase 3a occupation, however, the situation at Dun Mor Vaul is still not entirely clear, and there could be a small central hearth at the base of the *Iota* deposits exactly under the surviving part of the large one on top of that layer. Yet, if there is one, it might be expected that a second widespread though thin layer of peat ash would have been observed lower down than the *Kappa* deposit and linked with that earlier hearth, but no such stratum was observed in the cut sections or in the trowelled areas. Also the presence of up to 30 cm (more in places) of *Iota* floor under the hearth (DMV, figs 7, no.1, and 8, section along F) surely implies that any such earlier hearth was buried, unless replaced more than once.

A third point is that the top of the rectangular hearth was at the same level as, and formed a continuous surface with, the lintels covering the water tank (DMV, pl.III A); these were assumed to be a primary feature because the overflow drain, in a rocky groove under the pebbled floor of the entrance passage, can hardly be other than primary. If there was an earlier hearth one would perhaps expect the level of that to match the tank and the rectangular hearth to have been higher.

Some Hebridean brochs, presumably the earlier ones if the author's scheme of typological development is valid (MacKie 1992, figs 1–4), could have been built primarily not as fortified family dwellings but have become such later. This does not mean that we have to go back to the 'broch means fort' hypothesis; the evidence for brochs being intimately linked with specific tracts of arable land is far too strong for that (Anderson, J. 1883, 205f; Scott, Sir L. 1947; Fojut 1982). They could each have been the nucleus of a small, sub-tribal territory, built and owned by the dominant lineage in the area, the equivalent to the member families of the *fine* or clan gentry in late Medieval Scotland (MacKie 1987, 12–16; 1995a, 66), but arranged in a slightly different way to the majority of brochs. They could have been planned at first to accommodate large numbers of people for short periods of time, though doubtless lived in by the tribal gentry for the rest of the time.

Significant support for this idea comes from the Dun Ardtreck semibroch on Skye which also failed to reveal a large central hearth in the primary interior deposits, which were shallow and which rested directly on fairly smooth rock. This situation contrasted sharply with the structurally very similar Dun an Ruigh Ruaidh in Wester Ross which revealed a large primary central hearth (MacKie 1980, pls 5a and 5b). It is true that the whole of the interior of Dun Ardtreck was not excavated, but if a hearth remains in the unexplored area it must be unique in being well off centre (MacKie 1975, pl.5D). It must be relevant too that Dun Ardtreck produced a very similar Hebridean Iron Age material culture to that found at Dun Mor Vaul, and that Dun an Ruigh Ruaidh failed to produce this characteristic assemblage. It will surely be enlightening to know the nature of the primary floor inside the Loch na Berie broch in Lewis (Harding and Armit 1990, 94).

There are still some odd things about the sequence of occupations inside the Tiree broch. The absence of a clear central hearth in Phase 4b for example makes one wonder whether such a feature has always to be characteristic of a roundhouse occupied by a single family, and therefore whether Dun Mor Vaul in Phase 3a might have been such an ordinary dwelling after all, even without a central fireplace. Yet central hearths are so common that it seems more likely that there was something unusual about both Phases 3a and 4b. Indeed the nature of the Phase 4b deposits could be said also to reinforce the picture in the report of Phase 3a as a period of intense occupation without a central hearth.

An internal roundhouse?

There is one further aspect of the nature of the building in Phase 3a which needs to be reviewed, particularly since it was not discussed in much detail in the excavation report (DMV, 83) and has been ignored in subsequent commentaries on the site. One of the most important features of a hollow-walled broch is what might be called the multi-storeyed wooden roundhouse which, it has been suspected for a long time, was built inside it. The raised floor was ring-shaped, like a balcony, with the outer edge resting on the stone scarcement that is a universal feature of the inner wall-faces of brochs; the inner edge was attached to a ring of massive posts perhaps 2 m out from the wall and the sockets for these have been found in nearly all well-excavated hollow-walled brochs (MacKie 1995b, 153). Half a century ago Graham (1948, 68–70; 1949, 14–19) showed how the pattern of the openings in the inner wall-faces of brochs supported this view of the wooden structure resting on the scarcement and was against the hypothesis of a lean-to roof (Curle 1921, 90–2).

Only one large post-hole which may have been part of a ring was noticed inside Dun Mor Vaul despite the existence of a ledge scarcement about 1.8 m above the primary floor. Of the other comparable sites excavated by the author only Dun Ardtreck on Skye similarly failed to reveal signs of the internal ring of posts, though here the wall was too ruined for a scarcement to be preserved and the primary floor deposits were quite thin and rested on fairly smooth rock (MacKie 1975, pl.5d). Post-sockets may thus have been impracticable there. Dun an Ruigh Ruaidh, resting on boulder clay, had a scarcement and revealed an oval of massive post-holes, as did the Leckie broch in Stirlingshire, although at the latter site the wall was ruined to below scarcement level.

It is true that at the time the Tiree broch was being excavated the author had not appreciated the importance of the ring of posts in revealing the wooden elements in the architecture of hollow-walled brochs, despite having read Graham's article and Curle's report on Dun Troddan. Thus the post-holes may have been missed, a supposition supported by the fact that a very clear one turned up in the right position when a section was being drawn (DMV, fig.8, section along F). The large charred post-stump was probably discovered too early, and was in any case too close to the centre, to have formed part of such a ring (DMV, fig.8, pre-broch levels, SF no.492); however it did not appear to be in its original position. The fact that the primary *Iota* floor deposits were relatively pale and clean may also explain the failure to notice post-holes, particularly as the layer immediately on top (the *Kappa* ash deposit) was also quite pale. In most of the other sites mentioned the floor deposits were dark and tended to fill the emptied post-holes, and this made them easier to spot.

All that can be said about Dun Mor Vaul with certainty is that it seems likely from general considerations, and from the discovery of one hole in a section at the right distance from the wall, that very probably there was a ring of posts supporting a raised annular wooden floor resting on the scarcement in Phases 2b and 3a. It certainly cannot be shown that there was not. If there was, the wooden roundhouse may well have been dismantled in Phase 3B, when the large hearth was inserted. Fairly large areas of the reddish ash spread from this fireplace were exposed and carefully trowelled, and it seems unlikely that post-holes in this would have been missed, especially as the layer im-mediately above was dark. The roundhouse was certainly out of the way by Phase 4a when the upper works of the broch tower were taken down.

The existence of an internal wooden roundhouse in Phases 2b and 3a would appear to make unlikely for a quite different reason the alternative scenarios about the level of the primary broch floor already discussed.

Distorted stratigraphical evidence?

In his 1987 paper Lane disputed the evidence assembled by the author in favour of a period of close contact, at the start of the broch-building epoch, between on the one hand the western Atlantic Province of Scotland and, on the other, southern England and Brittany. One of the clearest signs of such contact could be the 'Wessex bowl', what appears to be a Hebridean copy of a type of 'eyebrow-ornamented' bowl widely used in southern England in the pre-Roman Iron Age (DMV, pl.XII B; MacKie 1969, pl.V C). This is not the place to review the meaning of these apparently exotic artefacts and here the author intends only to comment on one aspect of Lane's criticism of this idea. It is worth quoting the paragraph in full because it is clear that to Lane this idea is an example of a flawed archaeological approach in which 'an attempt to recognise them' (English migrants in the Hebrides) 'has resulted in a distortion of the' (Hebridean) 'archaeological record' (1987, 63):

> This vessel is made in local fabric by local methods. It was made with
> an Everted Rim which was then trimmed off. Decoration consists of

one very faint channelled arch repeated round the shoulder of the pot. In size it is quite comparable to other vessels at Dun Mor Vaul ... It is however much smaller than the Wessex 'prototypes' ... Thus it is only its simple decoration, and a superficial resemblance to a bead-rim bowl, that allows any differentiation from the rest of the assemblage. *MacKie is forced to postulate* that a vessel was made and fired, and then had its rim removed, as a momento [*sic*] of the Wessex homeland (1971, 46). This vessel was found in a context thought to indicate a date near the end of the primary broch floor deposit, the same deposit with Roman glass dated 160–250 AD ... *MacKie has to argue* that the vessel pre-dates the broch in order to relate it to Wessex material of the first or second century BC and thus to date early in the presumed evolution of Clettraval ware ... *Again the argument can only be maintained by doing violence to the site stratigraphy*. With Clarke (1970, 220) I must express doubt at this interpretation. (Lane 1987, 59; emphases added)

Two points can be made immediately. First, the author was not 'forced to postulate' anything; this extraordinary and unique little pot clearly stands out from the rest of the Everted Rim assemblage and requires an explanation, and the one devised fits the evidence neatly; it may turn out to be wrong, but it was not forced. With a diameter of 3.8 in, it is in fact not similar in size to other local vessels, being right at the lower end of the range for Everted Rim pots. If it is a copy of a Wessex bowl, it is of course a miniature version.

Second, no straining of the dating evidence occurred. The broken bowl was in a thin part of the *Iota* layer of Phase 3a, but it was not possible to know at what stage in the accumulation of that layer it was broken; the fact that the group of sherds was in a compact heap suggests a late stage, but the fact that it was in a sheltered position at the foot of the broch wall could mean that it was much earlier. Neither is it possible to know how old the pot was when it was broken; it could easily have been made in the first century BC and thus be far older than the piece of Roman glass on top of the *Iota* layer which Lane seems to think is a decisive counter argument. It seems elementary archaeological reasoning to infer that an early object can be in a later layer without 'doing violence to the site stratigraphy'.

THE POTTERY STYLES AND SEQUENCE

The published evidence from Dun Mor Vaul appears to support important social inferences which have relevance for broch studies in general. One of the most significant of these is the sharp distinction drawn between the 'native' *Vaul ware*, consisting of two distinct vessel-types (small vases and larger barrel-shaped urns) and found in all the strata from the pre-broch deposits, and the darker, more globular *Everted Rim* jars, which appear in quantity on the site just before the broch was built. The two classes of pottery differ in every way – in form, colour, texture, hardness and in decoration – and they

FIGURE 8.5. Sherds of *Vaul ware* from Phases 3 and 4 (scale 1:4).

remain distinct even though they co-existed in every deposit from Phase 2a onwards (DMV, figs 12–19). The pattern of the fluctuating proportions of the two types from phase to phase also made sense in terms of the pottery styles belonging to two distinct population groups, or social classes, one being the aborigines of the island and the other a dominant class which arrived or emerged at the time the broch was built (DMV, 160). Examples of the pottery styles are illustrated in figures 8.5–7.

Lane rightly points out that the perceived significance of the pottery sequence built up at Dun Mor Vaul may well have to be changed as more such sequences, dated by radiocarbon, are built up in the Western Isles,

FIGURE 8.6. Reconstructed Vaul ware urn from Phase 3a.

FIGURE 8.7. Everted Rim ware sherds from Phases 3 and 4.

though none has yet been published (1990, 111). He is also correct in saying that the various 'styles' of pottery described by the author were not defined as closely as they might have been in objective terms, that is through a statistical comparison of their sizes, diameters, decorative techniques and so on. They were defined by eye as they were discovered simply because the vast majority of the rim, base and decorated wall sherds seemed to fall into the categories described which were distinguishable through their colour, texture, form and decoration. This point is pursued below.

Anyone wishing to challenge the published conclusions about the pottery sequence at Dun Mor Vaul might have been expected to undertake an extensive re-examination and re-analysis of the sherds from the site which, since their excavation, have been stored by stratigraphical context in the Hunterian Museum with just such fresh work in mind; Lane however felt able to undertake his brief but bold reassessment without such a detailed first hand study (1987, 58; 1990, 111). He raised two specific doubts: first that there was a clear distinction between the two main classes of pottery defined (that is the Everted Rim broch pottery and the two incised-line decorated Vaul vessels) and, second, that the 'aboriginal' Vaul ware was much older than the broch – not in terms of stratigraphy, but rather of the radiocarbon dates, a point discussed below. However this kind of discussion rapidly starts to go round in circles without hard data from which to compile some statistics, and to supply these the author has undertaken a limited new study from the mass of information in the report.

A careful reading of the excavation report shows that some of Lane's points are invalid. For example he states that 'Everted Rim ware, Cordoned Everted Rim Ware and Clettraval Ware are only distinguished by the addition of single decorative traits (firstly, cordons and, secondly, "channelled arch" decoration)' (Lane 1990, 111). The terminology used in one part of the report was misleading in this respect since all these three 'wares' are in fact sub-varieties of Everted Rim ware. The part concerned is the diagram of Hebridean pottery styles and their suggested time spans where the three sub-varieties of Everted Rim ware are labelled 'ware' at the tops of the columns concerned (DMV, fig.20). However the three major styles of pottery are described in detail and clearly distinguished, that is *Vaul ware*, the native pottery, appearing in two distinct vessel forms, which is present from the beginning of the occupation of the site; *Everted Rim ware* in its various decorative types, which, with one exception, appears only in Phase 2a and later levels and as a single vessel form, the jar; and *Dunagoil ware*, which has links with mainland hillfort pottery (DMV, 157) and also goes back to Phase 1a. The simple statistical comparison of the frequency of these three radically different types of pottery – also makes this clear (DMV, table on p.162).

Moreover Lane's arguments can sometimes become confused:

> In the site report Vaul Ware and the Everted Rim Wares were reported as having distinct colours and fabrics ... Subsequent work on the Dun Mor Vaul pottery suggested that a high percentage of the Everted Rim Wares had organic inclusions (personal communication F. Murray), but no such correlations of inclusions or 'fabric' has been demonstrated elsewhere. In any case, organic or 'grass tempering' is not chronologically or culturally specific. (Lane 1990, 112).

One does not have to be a specialist in the Hebridean Iron Age to be able to spot the *non sequiturs* employed in this argument, which is presented as if it is another demonstration of the fallaciousness of the author's scheme. The author made no reference to 'organic tempering' in his discussion of the pottery styles from Dun Mor Vaul, relying on other criteria to distinguish them, so cannot be criticised on these grounds. In any case if it is true that Everted Rim ware has such tempering and the other styles do not then this would add to, not subtract from, the evidence for the distinctiveness of this pottery tradition at the site! No 'subsequent work' was done on the pottery collection in the Hunterian Museum; the person mentioned was employed under a Manpower Services Commission scheme to catalogue the site collection in detail on special cards and no other written report on the pottery was requested or submitted to the author.

Lane also objects to the difficulty of dating the Dunagoil ware (which he admits is a distinct style) from the inclusions of large gravel in its fabric, but no such attempt at dating was made by the author; the ware was *defined* by being plain and having these gravel inclusions (DMV, 157). The entire argument presented by the author for the different pottery styles at Dun Mor Vaul and their dating depends *solely* on the material from that site and on the stratigraphical contexts there in which the various styles were found.

Just as irrelevant is the statement '... there is no published evidence to show such coherent groups throughout a wider geographical area' (Lane 1990, 112). Even if this were true, it is unlikely to affect the Tiree evidence, which stands by itself. In fact clear examples of the Clettraval sub-style of Everted Rim ware have been found in various sites in the Outer Hebrides (including the type site, Scott, Sir L. 1948), at Dun Ardtreck in Skye and as far south as

Dun Cul Bhuirg on Iona (Ritchie and Lane 1980; RCAHMS 1982, 30–1). Also a clear example of a Vaul ware vase rim sherd, sharply contrasting with the local pottery, was found at Crosskirk broch, Caithness (Fairhurst 1984, Ill.67, no.549) and incised-line decorated pottery, not dissimilar from Vaul ware, occurs in the middle Iron Age (Phase 7) levels at Howe, Orkney (Smith, B. 1994, Ills 146–9). Likewise the late Bronze Age levels at Jarlshof in Shetland have yielded examples of what look like plain Vaul ware urns (Hamilton 1956, 30, fig.15), including one with characteristic incised geometric decoration.

It seems to be necessary to reaffirm that there is an absolute distinction both in form and decoration between the three wares. Applied waist cordons are, with a handful of exceptions, always found on Everted Rim jars, as is curvilinear channelled decoration. Incised decoration in geometric patterns is only found on Vaul ware vases and urns. An additional fundamental point, not noticed or ignored by Lane, is that the bases of the two groups are consistently different. Both vessel types of Vaul ware, as well as the Dunagoil urns, *always* have footed bases which are almost invariably quite flat on both surfaces (DMV, figs 11–19); the Everted Rim jars not only lack such a foot, but the interior surface of the base is usually slightly dome-shaped on top and occasionally slightly concave below, giving the *omphalos* shape characteristic of southern Iron Age pottery styles with their origins in Hallstatt beaten bronze vessels (Harding 1974, 139). This will become clear if the many detailed drawings are studied.

A further important technical difference lies in manufacturing techniques. Many Everted Rim jar sherds show the overlapping joins of the ring-building process clearly; it was by this technique, for example, that the base was made as a separate piece and the first wall section added to it (e.g. DMV, pl.XII C and fig.12, no.97). Likewise the rim section was often made separately, the everted lip being made by folding the clay over inwards. In all such cases the lower edge of the upper strip was split circumferentially and the rounded upper edge of the part below was fitted into this gap and the join smoothed down – the 'tongue and groove' method. Very few Vaul ware sherds, either vases or urns, were found which show such evidence of ring-building in the wall and rim. On the other hand the bases of these seem to have been formed as separate plates and the overlapping joint with the side can sometimes be seen, but in a simple overlap rather than the tongue and groove. These vessels look as if they have been formed from a block of clay, perhaps, in view of their symmetry, on some form of slow wheel.

A new statistical analysis of the pottery by size

In view of the criticisms referred to it seemed appropriate to collect some further information about the four main vessel types found at the site in order to try to devise an independent test for their genuineness. Table 8.1 shows the results of a study of the diameters and rim angles of 167 of the sherds illustrated in the excavation report and identified into the three main wares (one with two vessel forms) on the basis of the descriptions published there. The aim of the exercise was to find out whether there are further aspects of the size and shape of the pots which are specific to the ware, or whether the published classifications become blurred when the sherds are analysed in this way.

style	no.	average diameter	average rim angle
EVERTED RIM JARS	64	7.45 ± 2.04	56.0 ± 9.5
VAUL WARE VASES	39	4.85 ± 1.2	63.6 ± 7.8
VAUL WARE URNS	56	8.26 ± 1.82	121.2 ± 13.7
DUNAGOIL URNS	8	11.04 ± 3.03	122.3 ± 15.6

Table 8.1 Results of the measurements of the diameters and rim angles of 167 illustrated pots from Dun Mor Vaul in inches.

A copy of the full table of results has been deposited in the National Monuments Record of Scotland, together with an explanation of how the measurements were taken. Figure 8.8 shows the results in diagrammatic form with the ranges of pot diameters shown as standard deviations. The *area* under each curve represents how the measured sample would be distributed around the mean or average figure of the vessel diameters (the centre line) if it accurately reflects the nature of the total pot population. The curves extend to three standard deviations (*sigma (s)* values) on either side of the mean and

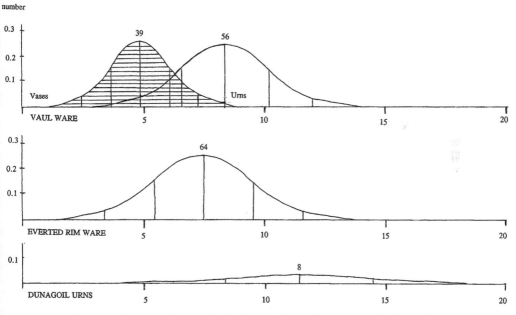

FIGURE 8.8. Statistics of rim diameters for the four vessel types found among the three main wares at Dun Mor Vaul. Horizontal scales in inches.

these are shown by the vertical lines; thus the diameters of 68.3 per cent of the ideal population fall between 1*s* on either side of the mean, 95.3 per cent between ± 2*s* and almost 99.8 per cent between ± 3*s*. The steeper the curve (i.e. the smaller the *s*-value) the more tightly clustered the diameters are about the mean. The height of the top of each curve is determined by the size of the population measured (written next to it) and the *s*-value; thus the curve for the Vaul vases is higher than that of the Vaul urns despite the smaller sample measured because the *s*-value for the former is smaller, the pots being less variable in their size. By contrast the curve for the Dunagoil urns is very flat both because so few could be included in the study, and also because even those few vary considerably in size; we therefore have only an approximate idea of how a larger population would be distributed.

These simple statistics seem to reinforce the published classification of the pottery. The strongest criticism by Lane is that there is no perceptible difference between the Vaul vases with their out-turned lips and the Everted Rim jars with their more sharply angled rims, although, as already noted, this proposition can only be maintained by avoiding any mention of the almost universal correlation of different types of clay (texture and colour), decoration and form of base with the two vessel types. However we can now see from the new data that the two kinds of pots are different in terms of their sizes and rim angles also. Vaul vases are markedly smaller than the Everted Rim jars, their mean diameter of 4.85 inches (12.3 cm) being not much over half of that of the latter. Moreover the spread of these measurements, as shown by the *s*-value, is also much less (figure 8.8); in other words the diameters of these little pots fall between a much narrower range, and much lower down the size scale, than do those of the jars, and one might conclude that they were designed to be drinking vessels to be held in both hands, or occasionally in one if very small. Vaul urns, being barrel-shaped, are easily separated out from the rest by their rim angles but their use as storage jars, or perhaps as pots for semi-liquid food on the table (porridge, stews and so on), seems to be confirmed by the larger size of the mouths; the average is close to that of the Everted Rim jars but the size range is somewhat smaller, though not so small as that of the vases. The few gritty Dunagoil urns are distinctly larger on the whole but the average rim angle is about the same and they should surely be storage pots.

The rim diameters alone support the idea that Vaul vases and urns had different functions, a conclusion which amplifies what is already fairly clear from the shape of the vessels. Consideration of the curves shows that at least 68.3 per cent of the mouth sizes of the ideal population of each occupy mutually exclusive size ranges, and this is well explained by the functions suggested earlier.

By contrast, the mouth sizes of the Everted Rim jars are not only on average much larger than those of the Vaul vases, but they also cover a much wider range of sizes, almost exactly spanning those of the two forms of Vaul ware vessels; the mean diameter falls between those of the two older native vessel types (figure 8.8). This suggests that the jars were used for more than one purpose, the larger ones perhaps for storage and for holding food on the table and the smaller ones no doubt serving as mugs. This new style of pottery of the broch builders evidently provided in one form a complete range of vessels, covering all the uses for which the two pot types of the older Vaul ware were made. Its makers not only introduced an entirely different kind of pottery, but also a quite different social tradition in which a single vessel served for every purpose, varying only in size. One could hardly have a clearer confirmation of the distinctiveness of the two ceramic traditions and of the domestic traditions which they were manufactured to serve.

Of course the standard deviation diagram, being a mathematical construct, suggests a wider spread of rim diameters in the ideal complete population of pots than was actually found or is indeed likely from practical considerations. It seems rather improbable for example that even one Vaul vase or Everted Rim jar in a thousand would be only 1.5 inches in diameter. The actual ranges of sizes found were: Vaul vases 2.5 to 8.0 inches, Vaul urns 5.0 to 13.0 inches and Everted Rim jars 4.0 to 12.0 inches.

It may also be noted that the average angle that the turned-out rims of Vaul vases makes with the plane of the mouth is about 8° steeper (closer to the vertical) than that of the jars; this too fits with the conception that the jars are descended ultimately from direct copies of the riveted bronze vessels of the Continental Hallstatt tradition with their sharply angled out-turned rims and concave or *omphalos* bases. The Vaul vases by contrast probably had their more gently curved lips designed for easy drinking. It is true that the standard deviations of both angle figures are large (the angle of the rims fluctuate over a wide range) and that there is therefore probably no statistical difference between the two groups. It has to be remembered however that the angle the Vaul vase rims make with the horizontal plane is certainly underestimated in this study; being mainly S-shaped the part next to the lip is almost always shallower than that immediately below and if the average curvature was taken a more vertical lip would result. The Everted Rim jars on the other hand tend to have fairly straight lips which usually make a fairly sharp angle with the body.

Is Everted Rim ware really absent from Phase 1?

Both Lane and Topping have expressed doubts that Everted Rim pottery only arrived on the site in Phase 2a, despite the author's assertions that no sherds of it were discovered in undisturbed Phase 1 deposits (DMV, 160). If this were true it would of course cast doubt of another kind on the assumption that Everted Rim ware was the pottery of the broch-builders and Vaul ware was that of the aboriginal population of Tiree. The table of pottery in the report (DMV, 162) is the evidence cited because it shows that 6 per cent of the sherds in the Phase 1b contexts (*Zeta* and *Nu*) were of Everted Rim ware; table 8.2 for Phase 1 repeats and amplifies this, showing a very small quantity of Everted Rim ware among the predominant Vaul and Dunagoil sherds.

	VAUL WARE	DUNAGOIL WARE	EVERTED RIM WARE
Phase 1: Pre-broch			
Phase 1a (*Epsilon*)	93.24	6.76	0.0
(51 sherds)			
Phase 1b (*Zeta*)	85.36	12.20	2.44
(41 sherds)			
Phase 1b (*Nu*)	86.25	10.00	3.75
(80 sherds)			
Phase 1, all deposits	88.37	8.14	3.49
(172 sherds)			
Phase 2: Immediately pre-broch and broch construction			
Phase 2a (*Eta*)	79.17	0.0	20.83
(24 sherds)			
Phase 2a (*Theta*)	80.00	3.33	16.67
(30 sherds)			
Phase 2a, all deposits	80.43	1.05	18.52
(54 sherds)			
Phase 2b (*Alpha*)	30.06	1.23	68.71
(163 sherds)			
Phase 3: Primary occupation			
Phase 3a (*Iota*)	66.88	4.79	28.33
(480 sherds)			
Phase 3b (*Kappa*)	43.75	1.79	54.46
(112 sherds)			
Phase 4: Secondary occupation			
Phase 4b (*Mu-2*)	33.86	0.79	65.35
(86 sherds)			
Phase 4b (*Beta*)	36.27	1.04	62.69
(193 sherds)			
Phase 4 inside broch	33.86	0.79	65.35
(254 sherds)			
Phase 4: Outer Court: secondary occupation			
Phase 4 (*Sigma*)	24.96	0.0	75.04
(605 sherds)			
Phase 4 (*Tau*)	16.60	0.38	83.02
(265 sherds)			
Phase 4 Outer Court	22.41	0.11	77.48
(870 sherds)			
Phase 5: Post broch			
Phase 5 (*Gamma* and *Chi*)	68.85	0.90	30.25
(443 sherds)			
Phase 5, late (*Delta*)	86.48	8.11	5.41
(37 sherds)			
Phase 5 (all deposits)	77.66	4.51	17.83
(480 sherds)			

Table 8.2 Frequency of the three major pottery styles at Dun Mor Vaul as percentages layer by layer in five phases.

Part of the explanation for this is that at one point an inexperienced excavator mixed up the material from the *Iota* broch floor and the *Zeta* midden below it. The report hints at this on p.38, explaining that the material from this part of the trench was found before the significance of the midden deposit was realised. Another example was a sherd found in the deposits of the ealiest pre-broch habitation (*Epsilon -1*). 'One Everted Rim sherd of totally different ware was almost certainly derived from a much higher level and mixed ... by an inexperienced excavator' (DMV, 38). Topping draws attention to this sherd and claims that the author ignored its significance, but fails to mention the circumstances of the find given in the report (Topping 1988, 80). Table 8.2, based on a new count of diagnostic sherds from Phases 1, 2a and 5, shows a tiny proportion of possible Everted Rim sherds in all the Phase 1 deposits. None were unequivocally diagnostic, and bearing in mind that a few sherds at the boundaries of layers could have been put in the wrong tray during the excavations, the evidence of this site is just not strong enough to contradict the overall impression, which is that only Vaul and Dunagoil ware were on the site before Phase 2a.

There was however one low level in the SE quadrant of the broch interior, well below the horizon of the broch peripheral paving and resting on the underlying sterile sand, which did produce some anomalous material, including one large and indisputable Everted Rim sherd (DMV, fig.12, no.90). These deposits (*Eta-1* and *-2*) have never been fully understood, mainly because of the apparent conjunction between the upper stone of a large discoid rotary quern and an adjacent heap of charred barley dated by radiocarbon to the fifth century BC; at the time of writing of the report it seemed impossible that such a quern could be older than about the first century BC.

Essentially an old living floor was found at the base of the occupation deposits in the SE Quadrant – a thin layer of black trampled sand resting on lighter grey sand at a depth of about 0.5 ft. (Context *Eta-1*: DMV, 39). Many fragments of fired clay daub, with clear impressions of wattling, were found on this floor and in the deposits immediately above (*Eta-2*), and the quern was lying, flat and upright, almost directly on it, though without its lower stone. The barley was close by and at the same level as the quern (DMV, fig.8, 'pre-broch levels'). Also close by and at a similar level in the *Eta-2* deposits was a large Everted Rim sherd with unique decoration of two prominently zig-zagged applied cordons, one in the angle of the rim (DMV fig.12, no.90). Among the sherds resting on the floor level were two base sherds of unequivocal Everted Rim jars which were not illustrated in the report and, higher up, two cordoned wall sherds from normal Everted Rim jars (DMV, fig.12, nos 93 and 95). All this material was of course stratified below the *Iota* floor deposits of Phase 3a. As is explained in the report:

> Originally it was thought that the absence of fragments of daub from the unequivocal pre-broch deposits, as well as the presence of the cordoned neck-band sherd, and the rotary quern, argued that this wattle-and-daub hut only just antedated the broch itself. However the

dating of the grain sample, found just above the lowest floor level here,
to 445 ± 90 bc, compares well with that of roots below the earliest pre-
broch midden (400 ± 110 bc) and contrasts strikingly with the date for
the primary broch period (ad 60 ± 90). There can be no doubt that the
wattle and daub structure must belong to the earliest phase of occupation of the site: the C-14 date for the grain presumably dates its
destruction by fire quite accurately (Appendix M). (DMV, 70)

The belief that the radiocarbon measurement accurately dated this structure clearly caused the author some uncertainty as to how to interpret the rest
of the evidence from the SE Quadrant, which had seemed reasonably unequivocal up to that point. This is seen in the two paragraphs following the
one quoted where various attempts are made to reconcile the presence at the
same level, and close together, of a fifth-century BC structure and of middle
Iron Age artefacts. After reviewing the evidence again it now seems possible
that the author's faith in the cereal grain date was misguided, though understandable at the time, and it is this date which distorted his final interpretation
of the low levels in the SE Quadrant. Topping points out that dates from
samples grown in a single year are in fact less reliable than others, not more
so as was thought twenty years ago. The *Eta-1* floor with its wattle-and-daub
structure and the deposits immediately above it now seem best explained in
the way they were originally, that is as evidence of the presence on the site of
a small group just before the broch was built – in Phase 2a at the start of
the middle Iron Age and not in Phase 1 in the early Iron Age. Quite probably
the habitation floor here was an old turf line which had been re-exposed
by digging down through Phase 1 deposits. The evidence (in the many fragments of baked daub) for a fierce fire on the site (entirely absent from
unequivocal Phase 1 levels) would then match that found in the *Theta*
deposits on the raised rocky area in the NW Quadrant (incinerated Everted
Rim sherds and the charred stump of a post); these last have always been
allocated to Phase 2a. The rotary quern of course fits far better into the later
context.

It may be objected of course that the date for the grain is accurate and is
the crucial evidence for dating 'middle Iron Age' artefacts like Everted Rim
ware and rotary querns back several centuries earlier to the early Iron Age.
This would make it easier to argue for an extension of the broch period back
to that earlier period also. The apparent discovery of a rotary quern in the
early Iron Age levels at Howe in Orkney may bear on this problem (Smith,
B. 1994, 206). Against this idea, however, is the evidence from Clickhimin
in Shetland, where several elements of the middle Iron Age material culture
were associated with the ring-fort, but not rotary querns (Hamilton 1968,
45–96).

Nevertheless, whatever the absolute date of the wattle-and-daub hut in the
SE Quadrant, the deposits were quite distinct from the undisturbed Phase 1
deposits nearby and there is very little doubt that, at Dun Mor Vaul at least,

there was a long period in the early Iron Age when incision-decorated Vaul ware and the gritty Dunagoil ware alone were in use and that Everted Rim ware appeared much later.

Pottery analysis at Staffordshire University

A neutron activation analysis of sherds from a number of Iron Age sites in the Western Isles, including Dun Mor Vaul, failed to yield any evidence for or against either the existence of various distinct styles of pottery, or for the idea that some pottery may have been imported (Topping 1986). In November 1994 twenty sherds from Dun Mor Vaul were analysed in the Department of Ceramic Technology in the University of Staffordshire in Stoke-on-Trent, as part of a student dissertation (Gair 1995). The sherds involved were badly damaged in the process. The questions asked of the analysts were in two categories. In the first place any information about the methods used to fire pottery on Tiree in the Iron Age would be welcome, as would any about the way the vessels were made. In the second place it was hoped to produce some independent technological evidence concerning the reality or otherwise of the three major wares; it was also hoped to detect any changes over time that might have occurred in manufacturing methods. To this end examples of the three main wares – plain wall sherds – and from three widely separated periods of the site's occupation, were chosen for analysis.

PHASE	VAUL WARE	DUNAGOIL WARE	EVERTED RIM WARE
Phase 1 (c.700–300 BC)			
Context *Nu*	(1) DMHP	(4) 376.DMHP	—
	(2) DMKK	(5) part 376?	—
	(3) DMHP?	—	—
Phase 2b (c.late 1st century BC or early 1st century AD)			
Context *Alpha*	(6) DMLL.15	(9) no No. now	(10) DMFR
	(7) DMGJ	—	(11) DMGJ
	(8) DMFR	—	(12) DMGP
Phase 4b (3rd century AD?)			
Context *Tau*	(13) DMDN.12	(16) DMAV	(18) DMAF
	(14) DMDN	(17) DMDT	(19) DMAV
	(15) DMES	—	(20) DMDT

Table 8.3 The sherds submitted for analysis to the University of Staffordshire.

Two main kinds of analysis were performed, namely mineralogical and thermal. *Petrographic analyses* consist of studying, with polarised light microscopy, the mineral components of the sherds, which can be those of the clay from which the pot was made and also any tempering material added during the manufacturing process. A study, for example, of the grain sizes present in the clay can give clues to the source of the clay and clues to the

methods of manufacture can also be obtained. The method involves examination of thin sections of the pottery which, prior to cutting and grinding, had to be resin impregnated. *Thermal analyses* consist in reheating the
sherds in various ways and this data can reveal, for example, the temperatures
reached during the original firing. Thermogravimetry (T.G.) measures
weight changes in the sample while it is being continuously heated, Differ-
ential Thermal Analysis (D.T.A.) measures the energy changes in a sample
while heated compared with a standard, and Dilatometry measures linear
shrinkage of the sherds after firing.

Results

Distinction between wares. In terms of the basic question being addressed
here, namely whether there is any independent scientific evidence for the
fundamental distinction between Vaul ware and Everted Rim ware, only one
analysis, petrographic, produced clear-cut results. Because Tiree is formed
of very old Lewisian gneiss (Whittow 1977, 252f) any clays formed on the
island will contain grains of these rocks, which broadly divide up into four
main types, namely *Acid, Intermediate, Basic* and *Ultrabasic*. The division is
based on the kinds of minerals which are present and in particular on the
feldspars; silica is an important component of the various kinds of feldspars
and Gair's diagram shows how the percentage of silica present gives an indication of which of the four main kinds of igneous rock is present (Gair 1995,
table before p.33).

When the twenty sherds are classified in terms of which of these four types
of rock is present a reasonably clear result appears (table 8.4). The ten sherds
diagnosed as Vaul ware generally contain Intermediate rocks with a tendency
to be towards the high silica Acid end of the classification table. Only one
sherd (no.7) contained Basic, Doleritic material. On the other hand the four
gritty Dunagoil ware sherds all contain Basic rocks with lower silica content,
except for no.16 which is Intermediate, and the classification of this last was
not certain. The five Everted Rim sherds all contain Basic rocks except for
one (no.10) which has Intermediate; there are no Acid igneous rocks and
the mineralogical characteristics are similar in general to those of Dunagoil
ware.

WARE	ROCK TYPE			
	Acid	*Intermediate*	*Basic*	*Ultrabasic*
Vaul ware	2	7	1	—
Dunagoil ware	—	1	3	—
Everted Rim ware	—	1	4	—

*Table 8.4 Occurrence in terms of their rock inclusions of the three main wares identified
among 19 sherds from Dun Mor Vaul (after Gair 1995, 63).*

'The above results suggest that Vaul ware could have been manufactured from different clay deposits than the other pottery as the other igneous rocks present contain more siliceous materials' (Gair 1995, 64).

Firing temperatures. The presence of, and alteration of, certain minerals in sherds give clues about the firing processes used in the Iron Age. For example the study of the quartz grains present in sherd no.2 (Vaul ware) suggests that the firing temperature rose above 573°C. On the other hand the presence of unaltered micas in many sherds, and of the muscovite form in no.15 (Vaul ware), suggests that the firing temperatures were not high. Muscovite for example is not present in rocks heated above 625–715°C. On the other hand it is suggested that post-burial conditions could sometimes encourage re-hydration and therefore conversion of the post-fired minerals to their original form. More research would have to be done in this area.

Again common hornblende is converted to basaltic hornblende on heating to above 800°C. The analytical techniques could not demonstrate conclusively that basaltic hornblende was present among the sherds, but yellow and green hornblendes (common) were present in sherds 13 and 15, suggesting again that firing temperatures were relatively low.

Origin of tempering. It is well known that temper was often added to the clay before moulding into vessels to avoid cracking during firing, and crushed sherds and rocks were often used. It can often be hard to decide whether mineral grains present were in the clay naturally or were added by the potter. The fact that many of the quartz grains observed in the Dun Mor Vaul sherds were angular suggests that these were deliberately added by the Tiree potters since any such grains present naturally in clays formed by sedimentation in water would tend to be rounded. On the other hand in heavily glaciated areas such as the highlands of Scotland and the Hebrides one would expect the presence of boulder clays which, from the nature of their formation, could well include small angular mineral grains. This particular problem of temper-ing could presumably be solved by identifying and analysing some clay deposits on Tiree and finding out whether they are sedimentary or boulder clays.

Origin of clays. In general, studies of the minerals present in the Tiree sherds show that they match very well the local Lewisian rocks and suggest that all the pottery analysed was probably made from clays on the island (a con-clusion already reached by Topping in 1987 on the basic of neutron activation analysis).

Pottery statistics and social class

Having re-emphasised with old stratigraphical information, and with new statistical and analytical data, the validity of the original division of the Dun Mor Vaul pottery into three main styles, falling broadly into 'native' and 'broch builders' pottery, and having also confirmed with the same new evidence that the broch-builders and the older native population had distinct social customs in terms of their table pottery, it may be useful to point out again how much valuable information was gained by plotting the frequency of these styles through the five main phases of the site's occupation (DMV, 157–65, fig.21 and table on p.162). When these dramatic fluctuations (table 8.2) were compared with the history of the site as inferred from the stratigraphy interesting social inferences could be made (DMV, 164f).

The details of these inferences are given in the report, but they are potentially so important for the understanding of broch society that some are mentioned again briefly here. That Vaul ware belonged to an aboriginal population that had been living on the island since long before the broch was built, and that Everted Rim ware is closely associated with the broch builders is shown not only by the absence of the latter from the Phase 1 pre-broch levels, but also by the sudden drop in the proportion of Everted Rim ware in Phase 5, at the end of the site's occupation. The broch was then in ruins and squatters (who are likely to have been mainly of native stock) left refuse in and on top of the rubble in the basal mural gallery. This is particularly evident in the only occupation deposit of that period – Context *Delta* on top of the *Gamma* rubble in segment v of the gallery (DMV, 34). The pottery from that earth deposit immediately under the turf was entirely of Vaul ware vases and urns (apart from two cordoned wall sherds) and confirms in a most convincing manner that Everted Rim ware had completely gone out of use on this site by Phase 5. In the report it was not separated out from the *Gamma* deposits, the pottery from which contained about a quarter of Everted Rim ware, but it is here for the first time (table 8.2).

Likewise three of the four major broch-occupation horizons (Phases 2b to 4b) show proportions of about two-fifths Vaul ware to three-fifths Everted Rim ware. The exception is Phase 3a, the primary broch occupation floor, where in sharp contrast Vaul ware makes up almost three-quarters of the total. This is well explained if in its first phase of use the broch tower was used as a refuge for the whole community in times of danger and if the majority of that community, or clan, were of aboriginal stock. The ruling group who built the tower were, it is suggested, of different origins and using different pottery, reflecting a social organisation which can also be inferred from quite different evidence (MacKie 1995a, 665). This group's pottery was dominant on the site while the tower was being built and also in later Phases, from 3b to 4b, when the broch seems to have been converted into a family residence.

The more detailed table of the pottery found in different parts of the site in Phase 4 make this contrast between broch builders' and aboriginal pottery even clearer (table 8.2). The extensive earth deposits in the outer court (*Sigma* and *Tau*) were inferred from stratigraphical evidence to belong to Phase 4 (and probably to 3b also), that is to the period of secondary occupation when the site seems to have been converted into a farm for the ruling group and (except in 3b) when the tower was much reduced in height. That the outer wall was also dilapidated at this time is clearly shown by the way the *Sigma* earth deposits rest against its exposed and much reduced wall core on the inside, the built face having gone (DMV, fig.7, section 2). Topping tries to show that the *Tau* deposits could be somewhat earlier (1987, 74) but the stratigraphy contradicts this.

Everted Rim ware is overwhelmingly predominant in the outer court deposits, particularly in the 15 cm immediately below the turf line (context *Tau*), that is just before the abandonment of the site, and the contrast between this situation and the predominance of Vaul ware in the abandonment levels of the ruined broch – and especially in the *Delta* deposit – a few feet away could not be more striking. As described (DMV, 89) one has the impression of an abrupt cessation of activity in this flourishing Iron Age farm and of the simultaneous disappearance of most of the people who used Everted Rim ware. The author wondered whether an explanation for this might be found in the exploits of the legendary Irish hero Labhraidh Loingseach (Meyer 1913, 40, paras 21 and 44; MacKie and MacAoidh 1969, 281) who (in Medieval Gaelic):

> *Ort ocht turu tire Iath, ort iathu Idrech,*
> *ort ocht scuru Scithach, selaig sluagu Siblech.*

> 'He smote eight towers on Tiree, he destroyed the land of Idrech,
> he laid waste eight strongholds of the men of Skye, he devastated
>   the people of Siblech.'

THE RADIOCARBON DATES

As noted Dun Mor Vaul was the first Scottish Iron Age site to be dated absolutely by stratified organic samples measured for their radiocarbon content and, of the nine dates obtained, six were entirely consistent with the stratigraphy (DMV, 228–31; table 4). Of the other three, two conflicted wildly both with the majority and with the stratigraphy while the third (from the sample of charred grain already discussed) would be a perfectly good Phase 1 date except that the disc quern close by has inevitably thrown some doubt on it.

However, as both Lane (1987, 58) and Topping (1987) have pointed out, most of the Dun Mor Vaul dates were obtained in the mid and late 1960s and have rather large standard deviations by modern standards; also the calibration used in the report is now inadequate. It is therefore possible that the Phase 1 samples might be too old, but equally, however, they might be too young, and there is no way of telling which other than by assessing them against the site stratigraphy and against any appropriate independent archaeological dating evidence, such as Roman material. For example it seems unlikely to be entirely coincidental that the two otherwise plausible dates from, respectively, a deposit just before and from one a little later than the time of Roman contact were good matches; these were ad 60 ± 90 for Phase 2b and ad 160 ± 90 for Phase 5 (table 8.5, nos 5 and 6). Likewise the two dates from the Norse period were reasonable matches (table 8.5, nos 8 and 9).

Armit sees no reason *a priori* to restrict the age of the hollow-walled brochs to the first century BC and later; Dun Mor Vaul could therefore have been built much earlier than the excavator concluded. Unfortunately this idea is justified with several misleading statements, as discussed above (Armit 1991, 210). Yet it is clearly explained, both in Appendix M and in the section on site chronology (DMV, 92–5; 228–31), that every organic sample chosen for possible radiocarbon dating was collected precisely because its stratigraphical position was as clear and unequivocal as possible. The three samples thought in the report to date Phase 1 (table 8.5, nos 1–3) were of course associated with the deposits previously allocated to that Phase on stratigraphical grounds. One was obtained from roots from the old ground surface under the lowest midden (*Epsilon-2*) in the undisturbed NE Quadrant of the broch interior. The other was from animal bones in the midden sealed below the outer wall (Context *Nu-2*) and is likewise stratigraphically reliable. In view of what was said earlier the third date, from a sample of charred grain, cannot

THE DUN MOR VAUL ^{14}C DATES

Lab. no.	Raw date & material	Corrected date 68.2% confidence	95.4% confidence	Site Phase & context
1. GaK–1092	2350 ± 110 bp roots	800 BC (1.00) 250 BC	800 BC (1.00) 150 BC	Phase 1a *Epsilon–2*
2. GaK–1225	2230 ± 100 bp animal bones	400 BC (1.00) 170 BC	800 BC (0.02) 700 BC 550 BC (0.98) AD 1	Phase 1b *Nu–2*
3. GaK–1098	2395 ± 90 bp charred grain	760 BC (0.28) 680 BC 660 BC (0.06) 630 BC 600 BC (0.03) 580 BC 550 BC (0.64) 390 BC	800 BC (1.00) 250 BC	Phase 2a *Eta–2*
4. GaK–1096	3145 ± 90 bp charcoal	1530 BC (1.00) 1310 BC	1700 (1.0) 1150 BC	Phase 2b *Alpha–4*
5. GaK–1097	1890 ± 90 bp charcoal	AD 10 (1.00) AD 230	110 BC (1.00) AD 340	Phase 2b *Alpha–2*
6. GaK–1521	2240 ± 80 bp charcoal	400 BC (0.30) 340 BC 320 BC (0.70) 200 BC	520 BC (1.00) 90 BC	Phase 4b *Tau*
7. GaK–1099	1790 ± 90 bp charcoal	AD 120 (1.00) AD 340	AD 20 (1.00) AD 430	Phase 5 *Gamma–6*
8. GaK–1520	1460 ± 200 bp bone	AD 340 (1.00) AD 780	AD 100 (1.00) AD 1000	Norse
9. GX–3426	1145 ± 155 bp human bone	AD 690 (1.00) AD 1020	AD 600 (1.00) AD 1250	Norse? final use of interior

Table 8.5 Probability distributions of the nine ^{14}C dates from Dun Mor Vaul. The 1 and 2 Sigma time spans – corrected according to the Stuiver and Kra tables (Radiocarbon 1986) – are indicated. The numbers in brackets add up to 1.00 in each entry and show the probability of the date falling within the time span concerned; for example for GaK–1521 there are two separate 1 sigma spans and there is a 30% probability that the real age falls between 400 and 340 BC and a 70% probability that it falls between 320 and 200 BC.

now be ascribed to undisturbed deposits of Phase 1; it seems more likely to be much later, perhaps belonging to Phase 2a, just before the broch was built. As Topping points out, organic samples which have grown in a single year, like grain, are less, not more, reliable than other kinds because of the unquantifiable effects of sunspot activity. He gives the time span of this dated sample at 785–215 BC in real years, presumably before any allowance is made for sunspot activity (Topping 1987). Whether elements of the middle Iron Age, including the discoid rotary quern, could have arrived in the Western Isles as early as the third century BC seems doubtful to the author at present.

Only two dates were obtained for the secondary occupations, in Phases 4b (late) and 5 (table 8.5, nos 6 and 7) and they were similarly linked to specific deposits within, or linked to, the structures. Even so the date for Phase 4b seems to be about half a millennium too old.

The two dates linked to Phase 2b, the construction of the broch (table 8.5, nos 4 and 5), were from primary clay floor packing inside the mural gallery and resting *on rock*, and which accumulated *after* the broch wall had been built up to at least a few feet in height (Contexts *Alpha-2* and *Alpha-4*: DMV, fig.6, vii and viii). Although one of these was a millennium too old, the context of the sample itself was impeccable. Yet Armit goes on to say that the excavator's 'interpretation is based on the assumption that the floor level which he identified was the original one' (1991c, 210). As noted, the two radiocarbon dates for the building of the broch came from the intra-mural gallery, not the floor of the central court, thus Armit's point is both sweeping and inaccurate.

Lane too has commented adversely on the value of the radiocarbon dates from Dun Mor Vaul in terms of building up an absolute chronology for the site and, therefore, also for the pottery styles (1990 113–15, Ill.7.2). Yet in saying 'Since two of the Dun Mor Vaul dates were rejected as archaeologically unacceptable … and the remainder only accepted because they were not incompatible with the excavator's views, I believe it is a mistake to rely on the Dun Mor Vaul dates', he too shows that disregard of precise factual detail in favour of a high sounding generalisation which, it is not too much of an exaggeration to say, has been the bane of many writers on the Scottish Atlantic Iron Age over the last fifteen years. The two originally rejected dates (table 8.5, nos 4 and 6) were not 'archaeologically' but 'stratigraphically unacceptable'; they conflicted with the rest of the dates from the same site only in their *stratigraphical* contexts. By contrast, in its original use (Piggott, S. 1959), the phrase meant in effect 'the dates must be rejected because they do not fit with the archaeological dating evidence available before radiocarbon tests were applied.' The rest of the dates were accepted not because they favoured the author's views (he had no firm views on what the absolute dating of the Phase 1 occupation at Vaul was likely to be before the dates came in), but because they broadly verified the order of the site Phases previously deduced from the stratigraphy.

It is also necessary to address the generalised cloud of doubt which Lane has attempted to throw over the Dun Mor Vaul radiocarbon dates because all but one were performed at the Gakushin laboratory in Japan, about the early performance of which there *may* be some uncertainty (Lane 1987, 58). Such doubts could be legitimate, but at present the author has no way of knowing if this is so. However, it is irresponsible to fail to mention in this context the point already alluded to – that the stratigraphically acceptable dates for Phases 2b and 5 correlate extremely well with the presence of second-century Roman fragments in all the layers between Phase 3a (late) and 5 (table 8.5, nos 5 and 7). How can one by implication condemn the Phase 1 dates as suspect because they cannot be corroborated by Roman artefact dating – while being forced to admit that the others seem accurate for the same reason? In the same way the Gakushin date for the Norse horizon at the site is a reasonably good match, especially when calibrated, with the Geochron date for a similar late layer, though both do have large standard deviations.

Topping analyses more dispassionately the problem of recalibrating the radiocarbon dates from Dun Mor Vaul and other Hebridean sites (1987, table 1), although the calibration he uses has in fact been superseded (Lane 1990, 115, Ill.7.2). The essential point is that the time spans for most of the dates are somewhat longer when the dates are converted into calendar years, though sometimes not by very much (table 8.5). It may be pointed out too that both Topping and Lane give a slightly misleading impression of the inaccuracy of radiocarbon dates in the Iron Age after they have been calibrated by quoting only the total two standard deviation time spans as if the dates concerned could fall anywhere within them. Comments like 'The recalibration gives them all a much wider real year equivalent than was originally perceived ...' (Topping 1987, 74) tend to confirm this impression. Yet it is important to stress that the uncertainty of each date is still in the form of a standard deviation, and that therefore there are still two in three chances that it falls within the 1 sigma span.

Concerning date no.3, for the charred grain from Phase 2a, this still presents a problem in view of the apparently clear association between the grain and a disc-shaped rotary quern. At present such an early date for a quern of this type seems improbable (MacKie 1995b), but it may be that it is in fact providing an important clue, and that elements of middle Iron Age material culture, including disc querns, were in the Western Isles a century or two earlier than the first century BC.

CONCLUSIONS

Chronology

In a recent paper Armit (1991) distinguishes 'five levels of chronology' in the area but, quite remarkably, omits any discussion of stratigraphy which should be the foundation of archaeological relative dating. The basis for our understanding of the development of the settlements and defences of the Atlantic province from the end of the Bronze Age until the Pictish period and beyond is the sequence of material cultures built up from the evidence of site strati-graphies. This has been outlined twice by the author in terms of 'Stages' (1965, fig.6, modified in 1971, fig.7), but it now seems easier to combine them into broader periods called the early, middle and late Iron Ages. An important task is clearly to define the date of the boundaries between these phases as closely as possible, and it is here of course that radiocarbon dates are important.

In the case of Dun Mor Vaul, five major phases of occupation were dis-tinguished, but before the application of radiocarbon dating the absolute dates of these phases were, with one exception, vague. Phase 1 seemed likely to be early Iron Age, but no characteristic artefacts were found except for one minia-ture, red-slipped Everted Rim jar (DMV, fig.13, no.113). Phase 2 likewise had no datable material except a bronze wire ring-headed pin of a kind that turned out to be present in Phase 1 as well, and was therefore of no chronological value for this purpose. The exception was provided by the presence of second-century Roman material in layers from late Phase 3a to Phase 5 which seemed to tie down that part of the site's occupation quite neatly to between about AD 100 and 300. This seemed to be confirmed by the absence of late Iron Age (Stage v) material from the site, it having been found stratified above middle Iron Age levels at the wheelhouse site of A Cheardach Mhor in South Uist (Young and Richardson 1960) and found in quantity without a clear earlier occupation at Dun Cuier on Barra (Young 1956). When radiocarbon dates were obtained they seemed to fit into this scenario quite well.

The part of the chronological scheme advanced in the report that has some-times been misunderstood is that concerning the date of the construction of the broch in Phase 2, which also seemed to coincide with the start of the middle Iron Age, or to have occurred very soon after it. This was refined to the middle of the first century BC purely on circumstantial historical evidence, based on the assumption that most of the 'exotic' objects found in the middle Iron Age material culture had south English links and that political events in the south at that time could have stimulated 'refugees' to come north and galvanise the local cultures. It is perfectly possible of course that that this scenario is based on mistaken assumptions (Alcock, L. 1984, 15) and that the mid first century BC date for Phase 2 at Dun Mor Vaul cannot therefore be reliable; the relevant radiocarbon date is far too imprecise to provide a check. What is important to remember, however, is that the failure of that particular chronological argument (if it has failed) will have no effect at all on the relative chronology of the site or on the reasonably accurate absolute dating of Phases 3b to 5, or on the development of the pottery styles and other artefacts throughout the site's history.

Objectivity and deduction

This paper is not intended as another episode in a 'notable rearguard action' by the author (Armit 1990b, 46) to defend his ideas of the 1960s against the supposed march of progress. Obviously things are bound to change in any field of archaeology as new evidence emerges and new ideas are put forward, and the author hopes he has demonstrated a sufficient capacity to undergo a complete change of mind over something fundamental when the evidence demands it (1986, 12) to deserve a reasonable hearing when he thinks the evidence does not warrant a revolution in thinking, for example over the recent attempt to re-interpret the broch of Gurness in Orkney (MacKie 1995b).

As explained elsewhere (MacKie 1992, 117) the author's primary concern is that the hard archaeological evidence be given absolute priority, even when – indeed particularly when – a powerful new idea or approach seems to make all old views redundant. Yet in writings on the Scottish Atlantic Iron Age of Scotland over the last fifteen years it has not always been obvious that this has happened; by contrast what has often been apparent is the deductive or 'theory first' approach in which a proper understanding of the archaeological evidence is believed to be possible only when the correct theoretical assumptions are made (Barrett 1981, 205). During the last quarter of a century our ideas of the causes of social change in prehistory have changed dramatically to the extent that even mildly diffusionist explanations seem inherently unfashionable (Lane 1987, 47) and various explanations based on local development seem far more plausible. Such events are commonplace in the history of science and learning and on the whole have a constructive effect. However it can happen that some practitioners find the new ideology a useful excuse for rejecting all older interpretations without actually assessing the data properly; it is all too easy to assume that the new theory means the old evidence has to be wrong, and this seems to have happened occasionally in research into some areas of the Atlantic Iron Age. The evidence for this mental attitude, which might be called 'naive deduction', has been reviewed for one particular excavated site and unfortunately seems strong. Occasionally things get out of hand and actual distortions of previously published views, or even of published evidence, result, but the author prefers to think that this is an unconscious result of a flawed theoretical approach.

9 Early Christian Archaeology in Argyll

Ian Fisher

The most distinctive and widespread field-remains of the Irish settlement in Scottish Dál Riata are those of the early church. The earliest extant church-buildings in the area are of twelfth-century date, but many churchyards and burial-grounds have ancient origins. The wider area of Irish settlement con-tained five documented monasteries (of which two are in Argyll); numerous smaller enclosed sites of monastic or eremitic type; many small rural chapels of drystone or clay-mortared construction; and a corpus of about 450 carved stones ranging from simple cross-inscribed grave-markers to great free-standing crosses, of which 300 are in Argyll. The Early Christian archaeology of the region is closely linked with that of other Atlantic areas of Britain and Ireland, but its principal monastic centre of Iona is comparable in scale, complexity and archaeological potential with the greatest monasteries of midland Ireland. Continuing research on the archaeological and historical problems of Argyll has been illuminated by recent Irish field-surveys and catalogues of sculpture, and detailed studies of Irish and Welsh historical, literary and legal sources (e.g. Lacy 1983; Harbison 1992; Kelly 1988; Davies 1982).

Nevertheless the area had its own distinctive character, with close contacts with Pictland and Northumbria. The upstanding and excavated remains on Iona give it a special place in the archaeology of Irish monasticism, while the Latin *Life* of its founder Colm Cille or Columba (d.597), by his successor Adomnán (d.704), is one of the most precious and informative documents of the early Irish church (Anderson and Anderson 1991; Sharpe 1995). The crosses of the monastery stand at the beginning of the great series of Irish stone crosses, and their artistic character strengthens the historical arguments for the production there of that most celebrated of insular gospel-books, the Book of Kells (Fisher 1994).

STATE OF RESEARCH

In addition to the Royal Commission's survey of the field-archaeology and sculpture of Argyll (RCAHMS 1971–92), its regional context is being examined in a study of pre-1200 sculpture in the remainder of western Scotland (Fisher forthcoming). Excavation has been limited to valuable but for the most part small-scale work, mainly on rescue sites, at Iona, and to a few small sites such as Ardnadam and St Ninian's Point, Bute (Rennie 1984; Aitken 1955). Except at Iona aerial photography has so far made a limited contribution, and the rugged terrain and extensive bracken-cover limit its potential. Topographical and environmental research, particularly the study of peat-bogs and coastal dunes and machair, are becoming increasingly important for this period (e.g. Barber 1981, 368–75).

Place-name studies are of great value for the location and understanding of early ecclesiastical sites. Attention has already been given to names including the word *Annat*, 'an old (abandoned) church', which shows interesting variations from its use in Ireland (Macdonald 1973a), and of which several examples are recorded in Argyll (e.g. RCAHMS 1975, 22, 98, 115, 120–1, nos 214, 219, 233–4). Other elements which merit further study include *disirt*, 'hermitage'; *cladh* and *reilig*, 'burial-place', and *teampull*, 'church'. Many ecclesiastical sites, extant or vanished, have names in 'Kil-' (Gaelic *Cill*, 'church', or 'burial-ground'), often compounded with a personal name. Little work has been done in the thorny field of dedications since Watson's major publication of 1926. Dedications to the major saints of Dál Riata, Columba of Iona, Moluag of Lismore, and Maelrubha of Applecross, are widespread, but the most numerous dedications, usually anglicised as 'Kilbride', are to the Irish female saint *Bríd* or Brigid.

MONASTERIES

The field-remains in Argyll, as well as the principal historical sources, are predominantly monastic in character. Major monasteries are documented on the islands of Iona and Lismore, as well as dependencies of Iona such as those on Tiree and the unidentified *Hinba*. Surviving remains indicate that there was also a significant monastic settlement on Eileach an Naoimh in the Garvellach Isles. The Western Isles were ideal for those seeking 'a desert place in the ocean' (Anderson and Anderson 1991), and there are a number of enclosed sites of eremitic character, extending beyond Argyll to the distant outlier of North Rona, which closely resemble those of the west coast of Ireland. The major foundations were not merely 'island monasteries' but, in the case of Iona at least, 'archipelago monasteries', as were other Columban houses such as Lindisfarne and Inishbofin. Except for the drystone double-beehive cell on Eileach an Naoimh, however, no upstanding stone structures earlier than the twelfth century have been identified with certainty. Excavation at Iona confirms the evidence of Adomnán that, as in Aidan's Northumbria, most buildings were of timber, *more Scottorum* ('after the fashion of the Irish'), and this may account for the total lack of visible structures at sites such as Cladh a' Bhile, Ellary (RCAHMS 1992, 53–4, no.20).

IONA

The monastery of Iona (RCAHMS 1982, 12–21, 31–49, no.3) was founded in 563 by Columba (Colm Cille), an Irish monk of royal lineage, who was also the founder of celebrated Irish houses such as Durrow. By the seventh century Columban monasteries had been established in Pictland, and in the 630s a mission led by Aidan undertook the conversion of Northumbria. Abbot Adomnán (679–704) was an eminent scholar and ecclesiastical statesman, and he and his successors made frequent visits to their monasteries in Ireland, and sometimes to Northumbria. The continuing prestige of Iona brought great men such as Niall Frossach (d.778), king of the Cenél nEogain, and Artgal son of Cathal, king of Connaught (d.791), in 'pilgrimage and penitence' to spend their last years there. The monastery suffered repeated Norse raids in the ninth century, but it is likely that its authority over the Columban *paruchia* or family of monasteries was only transferred to Kells in the second half of that century (Herbert 1988, 68–77).

The view from Dùn Í, the highest summit of the island, embraces the Hebrides from Islay to Rum and Skye, and out to Coll and Tiree, as well as the distant mainland of Argyll. Adomnán records constant voyaging in skin-covered or wooden boats, with Columba himself visiting Skye and Ardnamurchan, as well as Ireland and the Inverness area of Pictland. Large timbers for buildings and boat-building were transported in the late seventh century from the mainland, a distance of at least 75 km, and the massive slabs of schist required for St John's and St Martin's Crosses were brought a similar distance from the Loch Sween area in the following century. Despite the recorded drownings of monks of Iona and of Applecross 'in the depth of the sea' (Anderson 1922, i, 236), the island was ideally placed for its regional and international roles, yet safely removed from the centres of political power and warfare in Dál Riata.

Iona measures only 5.5 km from north to south by 2.5 km in greatest width and 1.5 km across the low-lying central belt, yet it includes a great variety of terrain in its 800 hectares. There is abundant rough grazing for cattle, which have always been important in the island's economy. Midden material from the monastic site shows that cattle of prime age were regularly used for food, but the paucity of sheep bones confirms the negative evidence of Adomnán. Other natural resources attested in the middens include red deer, numerous varieties of fish, and seals, which as well as providing meat and oil may have been valued for their skins.

Pollen-analysis of deposits from the monastic area indicates that cereals were being grown on the eastern plain in the seventh and eighth centuries (Barber 1981, 347f). However, it is clear from Adomnán's account that the

FIGURE 9.1. Port na Curaich, Port an Fhir-bhréighe, Iona, cairns.

main cultivation-area in Columban times was the 'little western plain' or *campulus occidentalis*, which still retains its equivalent Gaelic designation, 'the Machair'. Its light soil was susceptible to spring and early summer droughts, one of which, in the 680s, was ended by a miraculous downpour following a monastic procession to Columba's *colliculus angelorum*, the (natural) mound of Sithean ('Fairy Hill'), bearing relics of the saint including books written in his own hand. Here and elsewhere in the Hebrides, however, the abundant supplies of seaweed as natural fertiliser compensated for the lightness of the soil, and the machair remained in tillage until the nineteenth century.

Port na Curaich, a small bay at the extreme south end of Iona, is the traditional site of Columba's arrival from Ireland in 563, and a series of cairns on the adjacent shingle beach may witness to pilgrimage in the medieval period or even earlier (figure 9.1) (RCAHMS 1982, 257, no.19). The monastery itself (ibid., 31–49, no.3) was laid out on the eastern plain that slopes gently to the Sound of Iona and is traversed by Sruth a' Mhuilinn. This 'mill stream' flows out of the Lochan Mór, a loch below the south slope of Dùn Í, which before drainage in the eighteenth century measured about 8 hectares and which is bounded on the south-west by an ancient earthwork *tochar* or causeway. In early times, when other valleys to the south-west were occupied by lochs, this was probably one of the best means of access to the cultivated area on the west coast. The south-west part of the monastic enclosure included a rocky hillock, Cnoc nan Càrnan, whose eastern cliff may have sheltered the oak and ash trees represented in the pollen record from the earliest monastic phase. A smaller outcrop, Tòrr an Aba, situated immediately west of the medieval abbey, may be the eminence from which Columba pronounced his final blessing on the monastery, and it was marked by a cross, probably of medieval date, which like others in the literary and archaeological record had a millstone for its (surviving) base. The eastern edge of the monastic area was marked by a steeper fall to a rough foreshore littered with erratic granite

FIGURE 9.2. Iona, *vallum* in the foreground, the medieval Abbey at the centre, Tòrr an Aba is to the right of the Abbey, and St Oran's Chapel and graveyard are just behind Tòrr an Aba.

boulders, but sheltering several small 'ports', tiny sandy beaches or narrow gullies into which a currach or small boat could be drawn.

Adomnán's Life of Columba is one of the principal literary sources for the lay-out of early Irish monasteries, describing a wide range of domestic buildings and workshops, churches and oratories, burial-places, crosses and open spaces, all surrounded by the *vallum monasterii*, the 'rampart of the monastery' (Macdonald 1984). Parts of the vallum at Iona, to the north-west and west, are massive upstanding earthworks associated with partly-infilled ditches (figure 9.2), while elsewhere the lines of buried ditches (and other artificial disturbances) have been identified by aerial photography or by variations in the magnetism and resistivity of the soil. The earthworks of the Columban monastery enclosed an area of eight hectares or more and were of great complexity. Recent excavation has indicated the possibility that part of the western vallum is of pre-Columban date (McCormick 1989; Ashmore, *infra* pp.281–2), and the obvious overlapping lines or internal divisions reflect the growth so vividly described in the preface to the ninth-century *Martyr-ology of Oengus* (Stokes 1905, 26), whereby:

> '*The cells that have been taken by pairs and by trios,*
> *they are Romes with multitudes, with hundreds, thousands*'

At Iona, the multiple and, in some places, overlapping enclosures are the physical manifestations of the expansion from Columba's initial settlement of 563 to the monastery of two centuries later, which politically and artistically was one of the greatest centres of the Irish church. It is likely that the enclosed area reached its greatest extent, some 360 m from north to south and 200 m to 300 m from east to west, in or shortly before the eighth century.

The most detailed excavation of the vallum (Barber 1981), conducted by John Barber for the Scottish Office in 1979 in advance of burial-ground extension, examined a 15 m length of ditch, about 5 m wide and 3 m deep, which ran north-west to south-east immediately outside the north-east boundary-wall of the burial-ground, Reilig Odhráin. At the north-west the ditch terminated in a causeway (later followed by a medieval boulder-paved road), beyond which it presumably continued south-west to meet the eastern cliff of Cnoc nan Càrnan below an upstanding earthen rampart. Peat began to form to a substantial depth in the ditch as soon as it was completed, prob-ably early in the seventh century, and by the eighth century it was a wide but shallow feature which may by then have marked the boundary of the burial-ground. Surviving plant-remains indicate that it was bounded by a hedge containing elder, hawthorn and holly which, if a later poem 'attributed' to Columba is to be believed, was a possible source of ink (Murphy 1956, 70f). The question of whether a rampart was associated with this ditch, and if so whether it lay to north or south of it, is a contentious one, but the writer be-lieves that the ditch was the south boundary of the monastery in the seventh century. Geophysical evidence shows that it continued east across the adjacent field, and that a curving ditch to the south enclosed an annexe including Reilig Odhráin. The same survey indicates a presumably later arrangement with an annexe (whose ditch was excavated in the grounds of the St Columba Hotel in 1974) attached to another buried ditch running north-west to south-east across the field. The continuation of this last ditch north-west across Reilig Odhráin would reach the cliff-face of Cnoc nan Càrnan at the same point as the early seventh-century ditch, below the earth-work on the higher level, and this alignment coincides with a massive granite cross-base in Reilig Odhráin which may have marked an entrance through the vallum.

The peat that formed in the lower part of the excavated seventh-century ditch contained quantities of worked wood, waste cores from the manufac-ture of alder-wood bowls on a pole-lathe, and leatherwork including shoes with decorative vents and tongues identical to those shown in the Books of Durrow and Mulling. This waste material suggests that workshops for these crafts were situated close to the ditch in the first half of the seventh century, while evidence of metal- and glass-working was identified in 1979 in a pit a few metres north of it. Other craft-material, including moulds for glass studs (Reece 1981, 24f), was found about 90 m to the north, close to a small lime-kiln, but no associated workshop structures have been identified in either area.

The worked wood from the ditch includes a pole with a withy twisted round it and a square-section oak timber, 1.1 m in length and grooved on two faces, which was probably used as a vertical post with timber panels or wickerwork slotted into it. These finds, and the excavated remains of buildings, fully support the evidence of Bede and Adomnán that timber was the normal material of Irish monastic buildings. In the area north of the excavated ditch the west end of a circular or round-ended building was identified in 1979. Its inner ring of post-holes, whose timbers had been renewed more than once, measured about 13 m across, while an outer ring containing slighter posts showed no signs of re-use and had presumably held a verandah or buttresses. While circular stone buildings are common in small monastic settlements in western Ireland and Scotland, timber ones are rare, although smaller ones have been excavated in secular contexts such as Deer Park Farms (Co. Antrim) and Moynagh Lough Crannog (Co. Meath). This structure invites comparison with the *monasterium rotundum* mentioned by Adomnán as exist-ing at Durrow in Columba's time. Material from a pit underlying the build-ing suggests a date later than the middle of the seventh century, and it evidently remained in use for a considerable period. A short distance to the west, and just south of Tòrr an Aba, a trench for one wall of what was pre-sumably a rectangular building, about 10 m in length and with adjacent buttress-pits, was identified in 1959. It is not known whether any dating-evidence was recovered, but it has been suggested that the building-technique was the same as that of 'style IV' at the Northumbrian royal palace of Yeaver-ing (Northumberland), with continuous vertically-set planks in a trench about 0.3 m wide (Hope-Taylor 1977, 237f). Both of these buildings seem appropriate for the communal structures, such as the refectory and guest-house, mentioned by Adomnán, or the *magna domus* for which timber was imported from the mainland in his own time. A much simpler style of timber-construction was excavated in 1957 on the summit of Tòrr an Aba, where a stone setting incorporating a ring of charcoal was identified as the burnt re-mains of a wicker-built hut (Fowler 1988). Further evidence of timber build-ing was identified in 1967 under the medieval bakehouse west of the abbey, in the form of a mass of post-holes, but once again dating was uncertain and no individual building-plans could be identified (Reece 1981). Excavation in other areas, including east of the abbey, has shown hearths and other evidence of occupation, but no buildings have been recognised (ibid.; Haggarty 1988).

Adomnán seems to indicate a single church (*ecclesia, oratorium*) in Columba's monastery, large enough to contain the monks and with an attached chamber or *exedra*. The area immediately west of the medieval abbey church was evidently a major liturgical focus in the eighth century and later, marked by St John's and St Matthew's Crosses, and it is probable that an early church underlies the medieval nave, although it is impossible to say whether the building of Columba's time occupied that position. The medieval church and the eighth-century crosses are orientated about 23° south of east, and this suggests that the crosses were associated with a church large enough to follow the slope of the site rather than run obliquely across it. It may be assumed that by the eighth century the principal church on Iona would have rivalled the scale and elaboration of that at Kildare as described by Cogitosus (Radford 1977). Close to the north-west angle of the nave, and separated from St John's Cross by a small enclosure containing early graveslabs, there is a tiny chapel, rebuilt in 1962 on its original wall-footings. Measuring only 3.2 m by 2.2 m internally and with projecting buttresses or antae flanking the narrow west doorway, it is to be compared with the very smallest Irish oratories, such as those on Skellig Michael (Co. Kerry), and with that on North Rona, rather than with chapels elsewhere in Argyll. Excavation outside its south wall found no trace of a timber predecessor, but the retention of this humble structure indicates its great antiquity and sanctity. Indeed, the traveller Martin Martin in the last decade of the seventeenth century reported that 'in a little cell lies Columbus's tomb ... This gave me occasion to cite the distich, asserting that Columbus was buried in Ireland, at which the natives of Iona seemed very much displeased, and affirmed that the Irish who said so were impudent liars' (Martin 1934, 287f). It is possible that the chapel and St John's Cross indeed mark the site of the original burial-place from which Columba's remains were translated, probably in the second half of the eighth century (Fisher 1994, 46f).

The question of burial-grounds on Iona in the Columban period suffers, as on many Irish sites, from the continuing use of Reilig Odhráin for burial up to the present, and the lack of visible remains at the several other burial-places remembered in local tradition. As indicated above, the probable alignment of the vallum in the eighth century appears to bisect Reilig Odhráin (whose present enclosure dates only from the eighteenth century except on the north), and it may have developed in or after that period as a site for aristocratic lay burials, a function which it retained until the end of the medieval period. The monastic cemetery, which presumably included Columba's grave, marked by the stone that he had used as a pillow, may well have been in the area west of the medieval abbey, where several burials have been identified. The major crosses in this area are likely to have been visited during processions, and Adomnán mentions a cross marking an incident in the last days of Columba's life, which in his own time still stood in a millstone base beside a roadway. It is probable that an early path followed the shingle ridge on which a medieval cobbled road was laid out, running south-west from the abbey to Reilig Odhráin and crossing the original causeway through the excavated vallum ditch. The probable location of a major cross (perhaps St Oran's) beside a subsequent vallum gateway about 30 m further south has already been mentioned. The shingle ridge carrying the medieval road is still liable to collect surface-water after heavy rainfall, and in this and other excavated areas there were numerous stone-built drains of Early Christian and later date.

LISMORE AND OTHER MONASTIC SITES

Lismore 'in Alba' (Scotland) was founded by Moluag, a contemporary of Columba who died in 592, and the names of later abbots are recorded. Continuing veneration for the monastic site of Kilmoluag led to the erection there of the medieval cathedral of Argyll, partially preserved as the parish church (RCAHMS 1975, 156–63, no.267). The monastic site is for the most part open, but field-survey has so far been unrewarding except for the identification of a possible enclosure preserved in vanished or extant field-boundaries (Macdonald 1973b). The most precious relic of the monastery is the *Bachall Mór*, the crosier of the saint, which remains on the island in the care of the head of the Livingstone family, the 'baron of Bachuil'.

Adomnán and the Irish annals refer frequently to Tiree with its monastery of *Campus Luinge* or *Magh Luinge* ('the plain of Luinge'), an important daughter-house of Iona, and foundations by other monks. Both of the medieval parish churches of the island, at Kirkapoll and Soroby (RCAHMS 1980, 153–8, 166–70, nos 310, 327) were dedicated to Columba, and both preserve early sculpture, while the enclosed site at Ceann a' Mhara (*infra*; RCAHMS 1980, 165–6, no.325) may be an associated hermitage.

The most substantial undocumented site of monastic character in Argyll is on Eileach an Naoimh (RCAHMS 1984, 170–82, no.354) in the Garvellach Isles, an area having strong traditional associations with St Brendan 'the Navigator', of Clonfert. Like some western Irish sites the approach is by a series of terraces, the highest one being an enclosure which is partly cut into the hill-side. The monastic area has been much affected by medieval ecclesiastical use and later agrarian buildings, including a barn and corn-drying kiln, but two notable early features are preserved on the periphery of the site. On a prominent knoll to the south there is 'Eithne's Grave', a small stone-revetted circular enclosure containing an early cross-marked stone. Close to the shore, and far enough from the agrarian area to have escaped stone-robbing, there is a double-beehive cell of Irish type, whose corbelled roof-construction is well preserved (figure 9.3).

The founders of two of the other monasteries of Dál Riata are well documented, Donnan of Eigg who was martyred with his community by unknown attackers in 617, and Maelrubha, a monk of Bangor (Co. Down) who left Ireland in 671 and founded Applecross (*Apurcrosan*) two years later. Although Kildonnan on Eigg is, like Lismore, largely free from later development, no traces of the monastic enclosure have been identified (Macdonald 1973b). The main evidence of continuing monastic life is provided, as at Applecross, by carved stones, some of which have interesting Pictish connections (Fisher forthcoming). The area adjoining the churchyard at the head of Applecross Bay had been heavily trenched for land drainage even before it was afforested

FIGURE 9.3. Eileach an Naoimh, Garvellachs, bee-hive cells from south-east.

in the late 1960s, and even aerial photography can do little to reconstruct the extent of this house, on the borders of the Pictish area, with its unique late foundation-date. The final documented monastery, at Kingarth on Bute, is associated with the shadowy figure of St Blane. Extensive but inadequately recorded excavations in the 1890s (Anderson, J. 1900; plans in NMRS) identified a straggling enclosure-wall, now rebuilt, to the north of the Romanesque parish church, and remains of structures to the south-west of the terraced burial-ground. These buildings are not dateable, but the area produced a wider range of motif-pieces than any other Scottish site, some of them on re-used roofing-slates.

SMALL MONASTERIES AND EREMITIC SITES

Throughout the area there is a considerable number of enclosed sites, often containing remains of chapels and hut-circles or stances, and in some cases carved stones, which closely resemble sites in such areas as the Dingle and Iveragh peninsulas in Co. Kerry (Cuppage 1986; Fanning 1981; Henry 1957). Some of these may be classified as small monasteries, but others are in situations so remote, inaccessible, or lacking in any hinterland that they may reasonably be described as communal hermitages or 'eremitic monasteries' (Thomas, C. 1971, 44–7).

A classic model for the relationship of different grades of monastic site is provided in Adomnán's account of Virgno or Fergnae, an Irish monk who passed his latter years in the dependent monastery of *Hinba*, some of them 'in isolation in the place of the anchorites in *Muirbolc Már*' (Sharpe 1995, 230). The 'head of the hermitage' is documented in 1164 on Iona itself, where the fragmentary site of Cladh an Disirt, the 'burial-ground of the hermitage' (RCAHMS 1982, 242–3, no.7) is situated 400 m north-east of the abbey. Archaeological evidence suggests a similar relationship on Canna, where a monastery of some consequence is indicated by crosses and other sculpture from the site of a medieval church dedicated to Columba at A' Chill, the main settlement-area of the island (Fisher forthcoming). On a rock-platform at the foot of steep cliffs some 4 km to the west there is the enclosed site of Sgòr nam Ban-naomha, with a 2 m-thick wall almost 40 m in diameter (Dunbar and Fisher 1973). Its difficulty of access suggests that it was occupied by anchorites, perhaps accompanied by lay-penitents living under strict discipline as depicted by Adomnán. The ultimate 'desert place in the ocean' was the tiny island of North Rona (Nisbet and Gailey 1960), 70 km from the nearest habitable land, with its small oval enclosure and a slab-lintelled oratory and simple crosses which resemble those of such Irish sites as Skellig Michael.

The position of small enclosed sites in Argyll within this hierarchy is more difficult to define, since they do not share the inaccessibility of those just described. Several of them are, like Iona, insulated but close to areas of secular settlement for which they probably supplied pastoral care. An outstanding example is Cladh a' Bhearnaig, Kerrera (RCAHMS 1975, 119–20, no.232), facing the major Early Historic fortification of Dunollie across the mouth of Oban harbour. Its curvilinear enclosure, 60 m in diameter, is the largest among sites of this type in western Scotland, and it is divided into two unequal parts by a curving wall as in many Irish examples. Nave Island, with its small enclosure containing a thirteenth-century chapel re-used for kelp processing, is one kilometre offshore from the Ardnave peninsula of Islay, an area of intensive early settlement. A cross-fragment identified during the survey of the site in 1981 (RCAHMS 1984, 225–8, no.383) is closely related to the eighth-century cross at Kilnave (ibid., 219–22, no.374), which may mark a focus for lay worship served from the island.

St Patrick's Temple, Ceann a' Mhara, Tiree (RCAHMS 1980, 165–6, no.325), is an irregular enclosed site on the shore below low cliffs in one of the most rugged parts of that low-lying island. Although the chapel itself is a lime-mortared medieval structure, and the name is also of late character, the enclosure contains hut-platforms and cross-marked stones of early type. It is tempting to suppose that this was an eremitic offshoot of one of the larger monasteries on Tiree itself, or directly of Iona, which is visible from the site. Eilean Mór (RCAHMS 1992, 66–74, no.33), lying in the 'MacCormac Isles' at the mouth of Loch Sween, may be associated with the Leinster saint Abbán Moccu Corbmaic (Maclean 1983), as was the mainland church of Keills or 'Kilvickocharmick' (RCAHMS 1992, 83–93, no.45) with its ninth-century cross. The enclosed site on Eilean Mór, close to a natural harbour, contains a medieval chapel and a slab-like cross of probable tenth-century date (figure 9.4), but it has also produced grave-markers of much earlier character (figure 9.5). A small cave among cliffs in the south part of the island, now entered by an opening in the roof but originally almost completely dark, bears

FIGURE 9.4. Eilean Mór, Loch Sween, cross.

on the east wall a rock-cut Chi-Rho cross and a marigold, both of early type, and it may be identified as a place for ascetic meditation. The hermit tradition was revived here in the late medieval period, for a cross of about 1400 was set up as a sea-mark by 'John, priest and hermit of this island' and his patroness, the wife of the Lord of the Isles. Post-Reformation evidence shows that the chaplain here was also responsible for a nearby site of eremitic character, St Columba's Cave on the shore of Loch Caolisport (RCAHMS 1992, 200–1, no.94), which again bears early rock-cut crosses above a medieval altar. St Ciaran's Cave, on the foreshore of the south-east coast of Kintyre (RCAHMS 1971, 145–7, no.298), contains a boulder carved with an elaborate marigold. Similar coastal caves, with numerous crosses which may testify to later pilgrimage to places of ascetic retreat, are found in the Ross of Mull at the Nuns' Cave, Carsaig and at Scoor (RCAHMS 1980, 159, 166–7, nos 318, 326). A remarkable example of this pattern is seen at St Molaise's Cave on Holy Island, Arran, where a group of small knife-cut crosses appears

FIGURE 9.5. Inverneill House, Mid Argyll, cross-marked stone, probably from Eilean Mór.

to be associated with adjacent Norse runic inscriptions that date from the Norwegian royal expedition of 1263 (Fisher forthcoming).

THE LAITY

The difficulties of identifying the provision made for the lay population are well illustrated by the Scottish contribution to a recent symposium on Pastoral Care (Blair and Sharpe 1992), which had to concentrate on religious houses, while giving due attention to secular patronage. For the Columban period one can extrapolate from Adomnán and from Bede's account of the enthusiastic evangelising of Irish missionaries in Northumbria, but no archaeological picture emerges. The most prominent lay group in Adomnán are those penitents who spent years under strict monastic discipline, in some cases no doubt in the small eremitic sites which have been described above.

The sculpture of the area shows little evidence of the aristocratic patronage that is so obvious in Pictish sculpture, with its constant depictions of riders and hunting scenes. The Kilnave Cross on Islay, however, stands close to an area of early settlement, and may mark a centre of lay worship, perhaps served from the enclosed site on the nearby Nave Island (*supra* p.191). Many of the medieval churches and chapels throughout the area occupy ancient sites, usually with names in 'Cill-', but it is not known whether they originated as monasteries or as secular burial-grounds.

There are remains of a number of early drystone or clay-mortared rural chapels, standing in very small burial-grounds, which are particularly common on Islay (RCAHMS 1984, fig.26; 1992, fig.6). One of the smallest examples, at Duisker in Islay, measured about 3.8 m by 2.8 m internally and had a doorway in the (liturgical) west wall, while that at Gleann na Gaoith' in the same island measured 5 m by 2.9 m and had a north doorway. Their chronology is uncertain, although most are likely to belong to the Christian Norse period, from the tenth century onwards, rather than to the Columban one. The walls of the small chapel identified below St Ronan's Church, Iona, in 1992 (O'Sullivan 1994), and that at St Ninian's Point, Bute (Aitken 1955), overlay Christian burials, but neither produced evidence for close dating, nor for timber predecessors. Further excavation and comparison with the Manx keills, which relate to a better-documented settlement-pattern, may establish the role of these small chapels, but it must always be remembered that these were the sites that did not thrive. Only investigation of the medieval church-sites can hope to build up a comprehensive picture of secular worship before the late twelfth century.

Adomnán offers some glimpses of popular religion, of the type common among Celtic peoples, and the Reformation has not entirely eliminated such traces, notably in the veneration paid to holy wells. In some cases these are associated with carved stones, notably at Kilmory Oib, Mid Argyll (RCAHMS 1992, 172–3, no.78). The evidence for pilgrimage to places on Iona and to certain caves has been mentioned, and the subject deserves further study in the light of the abundant Irish evidence. At Sgòr nam Ban-naomha, the ruined huts were used as 'beds' in which the sick were laid, and offerings of rounded stones were placed on an 'altar' which has recently produced fragments of an eighth-century graveslab (Somerville 1899; Fisher forthcoming). The rotation of stones, to produce good fortune or a favourable wind, is attested at Iona and other sites, and has parallels at Inismurray and other Irish sites.

BURIALS

Few early burials preserving skeletal material have been identified, but some interesting burial-practices are known, including the circular 'special grave' enclosure on Eileach an Naoimh (*supra*). The use of white quartz pebbles is a continuing feature of many burial-grounds, and one which can be traced back to the Neolithic period (RCAHMS 1975, 57, no.78; Mitchell 1884; O'Sullivan 1994, 358f). A small number of slab-lined long-cists, comparable to the Manx 'lintel-graves', have been found on Mull (RCAHMS 1980, 138, no.286) and elsewhere, but most burials appear to have been in simple un-lined pits, and unoriented examples are known (Rennie 1984; Reece 1981; Aitken 1955). Literary references include the supposed burial of the Pictish king Bridei son of Bile at Iona in a log coffin (Anderson 1961, 96f; Clancy and Márkus 1995, 166f), perhaps similar to those excavated at Whithorn, and the erection of Columba's stone pillow as a marker beside his grave (Anderson and Anderson 1991, 224f). It is obvious that many of the carved stones described below were grave-markers, or perhaps cemetery markers, but Iona has almost a monopoly of large graveslabs, a few of them inscribed. Separate areas for the burial of women were in use until about 1760 at Iona Nunnery, and also until a late date at St Blane's, Kingarth, and the custom is well known in Ireland (O'Sullivan 1994; Hamlin and Foley 1983).

SCULPTURE

There is a great variety of sculpture ranging from small simple stones similar to those found on Irish eremitic sites, in places as remote as North Rona and St Kilda, to some of the largest and most elaborate of Irish High Crosses (Fisher forthcoming). The difference in the character of patronage from that in Pictland has been noted above, and led to a predominance of simple carvings. The ascetic way of life did not encourage elaborate commemoration and long-lasting professional schools of carving, and even at Iona, that most literate of communities, very few stones bear inscriptions. Many of these simple carvings, such as the recently discovered pillar bearing a 'pedestalled cross' at Bagh na h-Uamha, Rum, nonetheless offer possibilities for icono-graphic and stylistic comparisons with material in Ireland, Man and further afield. One topographical comparison which links Ireland with western and eastern Scotland is the carving of a cross at a landing-place, exemplified by a rock-cut Chi-Rho on the Isle of Raasay, a tau-cross on Tory Island (a Columban site off the Donegal coast), and a cross cut on a massive boulder at Lybster (Caithness). Wayside crosses at Iona and elsewhere (RCAHMS 1980, 137, no.167; 1992, 209, no.105) established a precedent which was followed by MacLean's Cross on Iona and other late medieval crosses in the West High-land area. Boundary-crosses are frequently mentioned in folk-tradition, and the clearest examples of this are at Kilchoman, Islay (RCAHMS 1984, 196–7, no.366. 1, 2).

The sign of the cross was in everyday use in Columba's monastery for bless-ing practical objects (e.g. Sharpe 1995, 166f, 177f), and an interesting appli-cation of this is the cross-marked quernstone from Dunadd (Campbell, E. 1987; RCAHMS 1992, 526). It was also in universal use for sanctifying places of worship and burial, and on individual grave-markers. In several cases crosses were carved on prehistoric standing-stones, and a small cross was in-cised on a façade-stone of a chambered cairn near Kilfinan (RCAHMS 1980, 126–7, no.263; 1984, 162, no.328; 1992, 50, no.11 and 210, no.107). Almost all of the total of about 450 pre-Romanesque carved stones from western Scotland bear incised or relief crosses, and many are of cruciform shape. Moreover, these forms are often combined, or a simple type repeated, as on many of the stones at Cladh a' Bhile, Ellary (figure 9.6) (RCAHMS 1992,

53–61, no.20). An interesting exception is the stone at Lochgoilhead (ibid., 194, no.87.1), bearing an incomplete alphabet and an ogam inscription. Other ogam inscriptions are those on a small stone bearing the Irish name *Cron(a)n* from a cist-burial at Poltalloch (ibid., 199, no.91), and the indecipherable examples on a rock-outcrop at Dunadd and on a pillar-stone on Gigha (ibid., 526–7, no.281; RCAHMS 1971, 96–7, no.244).

The collection of about one hundred carved stones on Iona (RCAHMS 1982, 179–219, no.6.1–108) contains examples of most of the types found in the area, ranging from small grave-markers with the simplest of incised crosses to some of the largest of Irish high crosses. While some stones display Scandinavian influence, and the simpler ones cannot be readily dated, it is likely that a high proportion of them are of seventh- and eighth-century date, and it would be interesting to compare the collection with large Irish ones such as Clonmacnoise if the later stones at each site could be separated out. Many of the simple stones resemble those found at small monastic sites, hermitages and burial-grounds, but there are also a number of large recumbent graveslabs, mostly bearing ringed crosses, of a type that does not occur elsewhere in the West Highlands and only rarely in western Ireland. Seven of these graveslabs bear Irish names or inscriptions, mostly using the formulae *OR(OIT) DO X* or *OR(OIT) AR ANMAIN X* ('A prayer for [Fergus; Loingsechan; Mael-Phadraig]'; 'a prayer for the soul of [Eogan; Flann]'). Latin appears only on the earliest of the inscribed stones, a wedge-shaped gravemarker which is incribed on the top edge *LAPIS ECHODI* ('the stone of Echoid'). However, the small number of inscriptions in one of the most literate of Irish monasteries, and the amateur character of the lettering and design of most of the carved stones, suggest that personal commemoration was a low priority in eighth-century Iona, in contrast to the splendour of the high crosses. The stone of Echoid, whose name is represented in modern Irish *O hEochaidh* ('Haughey'), is probably of the seventh century and bears a simple but elegant compass-drawn Chi-Rho cross. The difference between its ornament and that of St John's Cross is comparable with the gulf between the early psalter known as the Cathach and the Book of Kells, but the contrast in both cases was one of function as well as chronology.

Of the remaining groups of carvings in Argyll, the largest is that at Cladh a' Bhile, Ellary (figure 9.6) (RCAHMS 1992, 53–61, no.20). Most of the thirty stones are modest in scale and bear crosses of simple basic design but elaborated by repetition or the addition of pellets and crosslets. The largest is a pillar bearing an ornamented equal-armed cross and a large hexafoil or marigold, the most elaborate Scottish example of a motif favoured in Gaul and Ireland, which is also found at St Ciaran's Cave (*supra*) and on a smaller pillar at Cumbrae. The equal-armed cross has similarities to Merovingian manuscripts of the early eighth century, and the absence of ringed crosses from a collection of this size strongly suggests that the site was abandoned during that century. Apart from Ellary, Knapdale is rich in other early stones, with some neatly-incised crosses decorated with groups of three dots and prob-

FIGURE 9.6. Cladh a' Bhile, Ellary, Mid Argyll, burial-ground and Early Christian stones.

ably associated with Eilean Mór, and a large pedestalled cross on a rock-outcrop at Daltote. The cross-slab standing beside the holy well at Kilmory Oib (*supra* p.194) shows a double-transomed cross flanked by doves or peacocks, a favourite motif in Mediterranean art. Another carving with wide cultural links is the human-headed and fish-tailed cruciform stone from Riasg Buidhe, now in the grounds of Colonsay House (RCAHMS 1984, 256–8, no.389), which may have been influenced by pilgrim flasks from the Holy Land, showing the head of Christ above the cross.

Sculpture in peripheral areas, including Dumbartonshire and the islands of the Clyde, shares many of the features found in that of Argyll (Fisher forthcoming). The groups of stones on Bute, Cumbrae and Inchmarnock show a strongly Irish style at first, but are later influenced by the Scandinavian taste of the adjacent mainland. At Applecross there are several fragments, perhaps all from the same large cross-slab, showing competent but somewhat mechanical interlace and spiral-work having Pictish connections and perhaps of the early ninth century. The collection on Canna ranges from the simplest of grave-markers to two crosses, both with remarkable iconography, and the smaller group of carvings on Eigg shows similar variety. Carved stones on Skye and the mainland north of Applecross are few and simple, while most of those on the Outer Isles are probably of the period of Scandinavian settlement. This area also includes Pictish symbol-stones on Raasay, three in northern Skye, at Gairloch, Inverewe, and on Pabbay (Barra) and Benbecula. However, simple stones of purely Irish type are found on the two most remote islands of the area, St Kilda and North Rona.

The major crosses of Iona, St Oran's, St John's and St Martin's, were described by the writer in 1982 as 'an early and experimental group, and not derived from any established tradition of stone-carving' (RCAHMS 1982, 18), and there is no reason to alter this judgement. Adomnán mentions three crosses on Iona in or soon after Columba's lifetime, one of them standing in a millstone, but these were presumably of timber, like the one erected by the Iona-educated Oswald before the battle of Heavenfield *c*.635. Despite this long tradition, which by the eighth century is likely to have produced timber crosses of considerable scale and ornamental elaboration, the decision to produce monumental crosses in stone, equalling the largest Northumbrian ones in height and far exceeding them in span, was a bold one in an area where there was no tradition of stone architecture and where memorial stones were of the simplest character. The close relationships between the individual crosses are established by shared motifs, notably snake-and-boss and a specific pattern of spiral ornament, but their great differences in design and ornamental treatment show the constraints imposed by the shortage of suitable stone for carving, and the difficulties faced by the stonecarvers (presumably imported from an area with a longer tradition and better sources of stone) in identifying and exploiting this material. Certain stylistic features, such as the lack of framing in the figure-carving on the west face of St Martin's Cross, may indicate a link with Pictland, but for the most part the carvers would be mere executants, working under the direction of monks with their own traditions of manuscript- and metalwork-design which are very obvious in the ornamental repertoire of the crosses.

Geologically and structurally the earliest of the group is the ringless St Oran's Cross (RCAHMS 1982, 192–7, no.6.80), three massive but incomplete pieces of coarse mica-schist from Mull fitted together by mortice-and-tenon joints cut into a horizontal arm 1.99 m across. It has large rounded armpits, and its ornament combines snake-and-boss and interlinked bossed spirals, of surprising sophistication in such intractable material, with small figure-scenes or paired beasts in the constrictions around the cross-head. The carving of the Virgin and Child between two angels, at the top of the one surviving face of the cross-shaft, has many analogies with the illustration in the Book of Kells.

St John's Cross (figure 9.7) (RCAHMS 1982, 197–204, no.6.82), whose damaged but magnificent original stonework was returned to Iona in 1990 for display in the Abbey Museum, measured at least 5.3 m in height and 2.17 m in span, the widest cross in these islands except for the one at Ray in north Donegal. In its final form it comprised four main pieces (one of them now lost), and four ring-segments, all linked by mortice-and-tenon joints. The shaft and cross-head, which was jointed behind its bossed centre, are of green chlorite-schist from the distant Argyll mainland, and the top of the upper arm and the ring-fragment are of mica-schist from the Ross of Mull. On the basis of visible damage to the base of the cross, the structural inefficiency of its construction, and the way in which these joints cut across panels of complex ornament, it was suggested in 1982 that the pieces of local mica-schist were additions to an original ringless cross, which probably began with a single joint at the centre of the cross-head. In this form, and with its double-curved arms, it would have resembled (but with a much greater span) such Northumbrian crosses as that at Ruthwell. Whether or not the designer was

FIGURE 9.7. St John's Cross, Iona.

consciously emulating Northumbrian models, his ornamental language was purely Irish. In the new technology of stone-carving, however, Iona lacked the experience or the materials to realise the ambitions of the abbot who commissioned St John's Cross, and it is likely that it was damaged in an early fall. The repairs described above may thus have created for the first time in stone one of the world's most celebrated monumental forms, the 'Celtic' ringed cross.

The ornamental repertoire of St John's Cross is an extension of that of St Oran's, with many varieties of snake-and-boss, and spiral ornament which includes parallels for that on the Chi-Rho page of the Book of Kells. The main influence on this three-dimensional style is that of metalwork, seen in the multitude of small interlinked spirals and the granule-like pellets in the 'bird's-nest' bosses, while the cruciform groups of large bosses, repeated on all of the Iona crosses, resemble those on Irish shrines. The most significant parallels are with the snake-and-boss ornament of St John's Cross, where lizard-like creatures are attacked by fierce dragon-heads attached to snakes' bodies which spiral out of the principal bosses. This motif is closely paralleled in the gilt-bronze plaques now at St Germain-en-Laye, which have been convincingly identified as the finials of a great house-shaped shrine, other fragments of which were found in a ninth-century grave at Gausel in western Norway (Hunt 1956). In considering a context for the dispersal of these high-quality pieces, we may note the poem by Walafrid Strabo (d.849) on the Iona monk Blathmac, who was martyred by 'Danes' in 825 after refusing to divulge the hiding-place of 'the precious metals wherein lie the holy bones of St Columba' (Anderson 1922, i, 263–5). The close links of the St Germain/Gausel finials with the Book of Kells and with the panel of snake-and-boss ornament on the great Pictish cross-slab at Nigg make an Iona provenance likely. While the shrines of other Columban saints, notably Adomnán, may also have remained on Iona for part of the ninth century, these artistic links suggest that the snake-and-boss motif was associated with Columba himself, who intervened to save his companions from the attacks of monsters, and whose final blessing of his island secured its people and cattle from the venom of snakes 'so long as its inhabitants keep Christ's commands'. The inspiration for the creation of the crosses and of the Book of Kells may have been the enshrinement of Columba's relics, in advance of their circuits round Ireland in 753 and 767.

The Kildalton Cross, on Islay, and St Martin's Cross, on Iona, which were both designed with monolithic rings and still stand in their original positions, have many points of ornamental and iconographic interest. At Kildalton (figure 9.8) (RCAHMS 1984, 206–12, no.367.1), where the abstract ornament shows astonishing virtuosity in intractable local epidiorite, the Virgin and Child with two angels occupy the top of the east face of the shaft, as on St Oran's Cross, and the representation is a simplified version of that carving. Other small figure scenes, confined to the same face, depict David and the Lion, Abraham's sacrifice of Isaac, and what appears to be Cain slaying Abel, a complex series of theological symbols of eucharist and salvation. St Martin's

FIGURE 9.8. Kildalton Cross, Islay.

Cross (figure 9.9), 4.3 m high but only 1.19 m in span, places the Virgin and Child in the centre of the west face of the cross-head, above an Old Testament series (Daniel, Abraham and Isaac, and David as harper with another musician). The placing of these Virgin and Child panels in dominant positions on three of the crosses of the Iona group is consistent with the special role accorded to Mary in the Columban *paruchia* from the seventh century onwards. The hymn *Cantemus in Omni Die* (Clancy and Márkus 1995, 177–92) by the Iona monk and canon-law scholar, Cú-chuimne (d.747), with its references to the liturgical praise of *Maria de tribu Iude* (Mary from the tribe of Judah), seems particularly apposite to St Martin's Cross, with its

FIGURE 9.9. St Martin's Cross, Iona.

FIGURE 9.10. Kilfinan, Cowal, carved stone.

image of Christ and His Mother set above the most significant figures in their genealogy, and facing an ancient processional way.

The second half of the eighth century marked the zenith of sculpture in Dál Riata, but crosses and cross-slabs continued to be produced on Iona and elsewhere through the succeeding centuries. St Matthew's Cross (RCAHMS 1982, 208–11, no.6.84), which until 1994 stood immediately west of Iona abbey church, is closely linked by the iconography of its Adam and Eve scene to the Broken Cross at Kells (Harbison 1992, 2, fig.328), while its proportions as reconstructed from early graphic sources match those of Irish crosses of the late ninth and early tenth centuries. Perhaps at this period there was a fashion in the Irish Sea area for cross-slabs, presumably influenced by the earlier Pictish type. Among the outstanding examples of this vogue are the slabs at Fahan, Co. Donegal (Lacy 1983, 268f), and that at Ardchattan (RCAHMS 1975, 110–11, no.217.1) which has some links with Manx carvings of the tenth century. The Ardchattan slab is also related to the slab-like cross on Eilean Mór (figure 9.4) (RCAHMS 1992, 70–2, no.33.3), with its ill-proportioned rider and broad interlace. A cross-slab at Kilfinan (figure 9.10) (ibid., 107–8, no.61.3) bears coarse snake-and-boss ornament, closer in style to that of some Irish crosses than to those of Iona, while a tall slab on Sanda (RCAHMS 1971, 151–2, no.301.1) has regular rows of small bosses, reminiscent of such late Pictish cross-slabs as the Shandwick stone. By the late tenth century, however, some carvings were blending Irish and Scandinavian taste in ornament, and cross-slabs at Iona and Kilbar (Barra) also bore Old Norse runic memorial inscriptions.

10 The Norse in Argyll

Marilyn M. Brown

The first impact of the Norse on Argyll is dramatic, datable and destructive. The *Annals of Innisfallen* record, under the year 795, the devastation of Iona (Anderson, A. O. 1922, i, 256). Other sources tell of raids around the coasts of Britain from Lindisfarne to Dorset (Anderson, A. O. 1922, i, 255–7; Plummer 1892, 54–7). Argyll was drawn into the great movement of wealth and people that has been called the Viking Age, and its history cannot be treated in isolation from events in Scandinavia and Western Europe (Sawyer 1982).

Were it not for the presence of the major monastic site of Iona, little detail would be known from literary sources of events in Argyll and the western seaboard of Scotland in the years prior to the advent of the first raiders from Scandinavia. Chronicles tell of the succession and deaths of kings and nobles, battles of Picts and Scots, and the burning of Dumbarton in 870 (Macquarrie 1994, 29f). They reflect the interests of the chronicle writers, whose accounts are probably based on material first assembled at Iona: the adoption of the monastic life at Iona by kings, their pilgrimages to and burial on Iona. The close links between Ireland and the islands and coastlands of Argyll (both inhabited by *Scotti*), certainly go back to the traditional migration of Fergus Mor and his sons from Dál Riata (the coastal area of present day County Antrim), to what is now Argyll (Nieke and Duncan 1988). They are well attested from the movements of clerics and kings between the Irish kingdoms and Iona. The kin-based nature of the society of Scottish Dál Riata is described in the *Senchus Fer nAlban*, 'History of the Men of Scotland', a tenth-century compilation incorporating material of the mid-seventh century (Bannerman 1974). It provides a survey of the inhabitants of Argyll in terms of houses; the Cenel nOegusa, who occupied Islay, consisted of 430 houses, the Cenel nGabrain (Jura, Kintyre, Cowal, Arran and Bute) 420 houses, while the Cenel Loairn (Lorn, Coll, Tiree, Colonsay, Mull and North Argyll) had 560 houses. Every twenty houses had to provide, for the king's service, two seven-benched boats, which probably required twenty-eight oarsmen. That the provision of military aid to the ruler in Argyll took the form of naval service stresses the importance of sea travel to the inhabitants of the Southern Hebrides and mainland Argyll, and the necessity of maintaining control over what is, from the modern viewpoint, a scattered collection of settlements in an area of islands and deeply indented coastlines, where communications by land might face considerable natural obstacles.

Since its foundation, Iona had been a centre where the wealth of many generations had been concentrated in the form of church ornaments, shrines, vestments and decorated book covers. It was not, of course, the only monastic house in Argyll, although it is the only one whose plundering by Norse raiders is recorded. Documentary sources mention monasteries at Ailech (possibly Eileach an Naoimh), on Tiree, on Hinba (possibly Jura), at Cella Diuni, near Loch Awe, on the unidentified Elena Insula (Anderson and Anderson 1961, 286–9) on Lismore (Anderson, A. O. 1922, i, 19, 95), while the presence of the elaborate ringed cross at Kildalton, Islay, and the remains on Nave Island, off the north coast of Islay (RCAHMS 1984, 27), suggest the existence of other monastic settlements, unrecorded in the surviving sources. Whether any of these (with the possible exception of the house founded by St Moluag on Lismore) survived until the period of the Viking incursions is uncertain, although the dating of the sculpture at Kildalton and Nave Island to the second half of the eighth century and the eighth century respectively indicates ecclesiastical activity on these sites in the immediately preceding period. The position of monasteries as repositories of ecclesiastical wealth (they may in addition have served as places of safe-keeping for the possessions of the laity and indeed for food storage) made them prime targets for piratical attacks (Lucas 1967). Only the monastic houses with the strongest tradition, the most powerful relics and the greatest wealth were able to survive as religious communities.

The links with Ireland had been constantly maintained since the time of Columba, and it was to that island that the community of St Columba looked initially for a refuge from Norse raiding, to an inland site at Kells, County Meath. The land was acquired in 804, after a 'burning' had been recorded at Iona in 802, and the new monastery was built between 807 and 814 (Anderson, A. O. 1922, i, 258–60). The abbot of Kells continued to bear the title of Abbot of Iona.

Since the publication of P. H. Sawyer's illuminating and provocative survey of the Scandinavian impact on Europe, *The Age of the Vikings*, in 1962, much attention has been paid (among other subjects) to supporting or disproving his proposition that the monastic chroniclers, who provide most of the information on which any account of the Viking raids must be based, were prone to exaggerate the violence and destructive nature, as well as the scale, of the incursions, both because they were direct and indirect sufferers, and because they wished to draw a moral conclusion about God's wrath on an undeserving people and the need for repentance. While Sawyer was more concerned with the major attacks in France and England, it is important to examine the impact of the Viking incursions in Argyll and the islands, using all the forms of evidence available. Iona and its satellite monasteries in Scotland had been spared the intermittent raiding arising from the identification of Irish monasteries with secular families and kingdoms, attacks which seem to have spared valuables of a sacred character (Lucas 1967, 180). Iona was completely undefended and seems to have had no provision for defence. The devastation of 795 was followed by the burning of 802, while in 806 sixty-eight members of the community of Iona were killed (Anderson, A. O. 1922, i, 258). This disaster was followed by the departure of Cellach, the abbot of Iona, to Kells and the establishment of the monastery on a new site (Anderson, A. O. 1922, i, 259). Cellach resigned the abbacy in 814 and returned to Iona, dying there in the following year (Anderson, A. O. 1922, i, 259). The next attack on Iona is recorded under the year 825 when Blathmac, an Irish prince and former warrior, who had charge of the community there, was killed by raiders (Anderson, A. O. 1922, i, 263–5). The event formed the subject of a poem composed at the abbey of Reichenau, in southern Germany, by Walafrid Strabo, who was abbot there from 838–49, based on information, it must be presumed, provided by Irish monks. While the poem contains traditional elements, appropriate to accounts of martyrdoms, such as the saint's foreknowledge of and eagerness for death, it provides some details of an actual raid. There had obviously been some advance warning of the attack; the shrine of St Columba had been concealed in the ground under a thick layer of turf, and Blathmac had time to propose that the weaker members of the community should seek safety in flight, using their knowledge of the local terrain to escape, while the more resolute brethren remained to be killed. The raiders are described as 'rushing through the open buildings ... slaying with mad savagery the rest of the associates', before demanding from Blathmac the whereabouts of the shrine. After he had told them that he had no knowledge of its place of concealment and would not have told them even if he had such knowledge, he was killed. The 'fierce soldier' then began to dig for the treasure, but with no success. Blathmac was buried on Iona and became a source of miracles, and Strabo records, writing within twenty-five years of the murder, that there 'the Lord is worshipped reverently with fitting honour'. A sufficient number of people survived to give an account of the death of Blathmac and to preserve the knowledge of the hiding place of the shrine. The thieves wanted the 'precious metals' which enclosed the bones of St Columba. There is no suggestion here of captives being taken to be ransomed or sold as slaves, only of speedy and somewhat disorganised looting. The determination of the community to continue to occupy Iona stands out.

Although the various surviving annals record successive raids on the islands and coasts of Britain, relatively little is made of the native response. Only a devoted minority would deliberately seek or welcome death at the hands of the pagan invaders. The *Senchus fer nAlban* (Bannerman 1974, 147) describes a possibly ideal system of raising men for military service, a system which could, theoretically, call out some 2000 men. The accounts preserved in religious houses may give too passive a picture of the ideal religious house; the sixty-eight members of the community of Iona killed in 806 may have been fighting back (Lucas 1967, 178f), but there is no record of organised secular opposition to the Norsemen on the island. It is at the period of the most intensive Viking raids that the Scottish line of the kings of Dál Riata was establishing itself in the kingship of Fortriu, the area of central Scotland around Forteviot in Perthshire, and as rulers of both Picts and Scots. It has been suggested that it was the major incursions on the traditional Dalriadic regions that impelled the Scottish rulers to establish themselves in the Pictish heartlands by what may have been a combination of inheritance and conquest (Smyth 1984, 180; Broun 1994). It is not until 836, according to the *Annals of the Four Masters* (a seventeenth-century compilation, which harmonised the different dates from various early sources, possibly incorrectly), that Godfrey, son of Fergus, lord of Oriel (or Airgialla, the south-west part of Irish Dál Riata) came to reinforce Scottish Dál Riata at the bidding of Kenneth, son of Alpin (Anderson, A. O. 1922, i, 267; Bannerman 1974, 117f; O'Cuiv 1988). Kenneth MacAlpin was not, at this date, king of a united kingdom of Picts and Scots, although it is possible he or his father may have governed Dál Riata on behalf of Eoghanan, who was king of both peoples (Anderson, M. O. 1982,111f). Eoghanan, together with his brother 'and others ... almost without number' (Anderson, A. O. 1922, i, 268), died in battle in 839 against a Norse fleet which is recorded as sailing northwards after destroying Leinster and Brega, presumably towards the coasts of Dál Riata. With the advent of this fleet of sixty-five ships, the invasions into western Scotland achieved a different scale of organisation, and possibly of size. Against it the army led by the king of both Picts and Scots was spectacularly unsuccessful.

In the mid-ninth century it may be possible to recognise a new phase in the Norse incursions in Argyll. Gofraidh mac Fergusa or Geoffrey, son of Fergus, appears to have a first name of Scandinavian origin (Gothfrith) and an Irish patronymic (Sellar 1966; Crawford, B. E. 1987, 47). He is called the leader of the Airgialla (Anderson, A. O. 1922, i, 267), a subgroup of the Dalriadic Scots and may, on the basis of his name, have been born of an Irish father and a Norse mother. By 853, when his death is recorded in the *Annals of the Four Masters*, he is called lord of the *Innsi Gall* (Anderson, A. O. 1922, i, 284), or the islands of the foreigners, presumably the Hebrides. The political developments that lay behind his change of position from a leader of a Dalriadic sept to the ruler of a territory, explicitly described as alien, are unrecorded. Co-operation with the Norse incomers in settling and raiding may have been the chosen course of the inhabitants of the islands and coastal Argyll.

The Norse presence in Argyll would be recognised archaeologically, even in the absence of documentary sources, by the presence of burials accompanied by objects of distinctively Scandinavian character (Grieg 1940, 29–63; Andersen 1995). These burials, found on the islands of Coll and Tiree, Mull, Colonsay and Oronsay, Islay and Gigha (with only questionable evidence for burials on the mainland), are divided approximately equally, where sufficient evidence survives to allow an identification, between men and women (Fell 1984, 130; Jesch 1991, 19f). The burials of children with grave-goods has not been recorded in Argyll (Batey et al. 1993). No burials accompanied by grave-goods have been recognised in Argyll belonging to a period later than the Bronze Age, and the resumption of this custom marks a major change in religious practice. These burials contain objects that are similar to those in graves found near Dublin, in the Isle of Man, the Outer Hebrides, the rest of the Inner Hebrides, Orkney, Shetland, Iceland and the Scandinavian homelands (Grieg 1940; Jansson 1981), although the grave deposits possess individual characteristics.

The burials belong to the ninth and tenth centuries. Close dating based on the objects found in the graves poses considerable difficulties (Petersen 1919; 1928) and earlier attempts to provide narrow brackets based on typology of brooches and weapons in Scandinavian contexts have been modified (Wilson 1976a, 397; Graham-Campbell 1980, 27f and 67f), but the evidence points to the presence of settlers in the islands not many years later than the raids of the earlier ninth century. The form of the burials is most closely paralleled (outside the Hebrides and the Isle of Man), in the Scandinavian homeland, in western Norway (Brøgger 1929, 121f), the area from which, according to later literary and historical sources (Anderson, A. O. 1922, i, 322–4; Arbman 1961, 51f), the majority of the early raiders and settlers came. It is also the area where the discovery of decorative metalwork of insular origin, gained through raiding or trading, in Viking-period graves is most common (Wamers 1985, 51–4).

The graves of thirteen individuals have been certainly identified, and there is a similar number of possible burials where the nature of the remains or the reliability of the account prevents any certain conclusion. Where the information is available, all but one of the burials were found in an area of sand-hills, with sand blow being the principal reason for the discovery of the site. Although the presence of burials in sand dunes may indicate the preference of Norse settlers for farming on the easily drained machair land, it may be that the distribution pattern seriously misrepresents burial sites and settlements. The absence of burials from Jura may indicate that the settlement, suggested by place-name evidence, took place after pagan burial rites had ceased, or that interments were made in an area where they have not been exposed by the weather in recent times.

All the burials in Argyll have been found by chance (although the presence of upright stones at Machrins, Colonsay, led to the excavation of the settlement and the subsequent discovery of the grave (Ritchie 1981). Not one has been identified from the surviving surface remains, although it is likely that some at least formed locally prominent monuments at the time of the funerals.

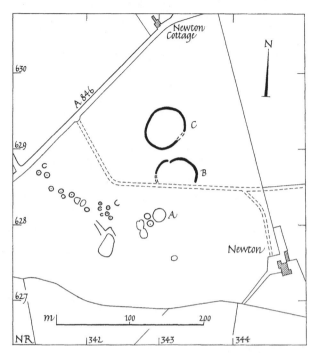

FIGURE 10.1. Newton, Islay, cropmarkings showing ring-ditches and enclosures.

The male burial found at Ballinaby in Islay in 1932 (Edwards 1934) had been placed in a natural sand mound, as was that at Machrins on Colonsay (McNeill 1892). Others may have been similarly positioned, but insufficient evidence survives, either because of changes in the landscape or the lack of detail recorded at the time of the earlier discoveries. Only a small proportion, between 15 and 20 per cent, of the much larger number of graves known in Norway, had been placed under mounds (Solberg 1985), and these cairns appear to have indicated the graves of important members of the community. Upright stones may have marked the summit of the mounds, as the excavator at Carn a' Bharraich believed (McNeill 1891). The brooches, belonging to a female burial, discovered at Ballinaby in 1788 (Anderson, J. 1880, 71) came from under the largest standing stone on Islay, a choice of burial place that may reflect a recognition of the importance of that site, whether religious or secular, to earlier inhabitants of the island, or at least the desire for a prominent memorial above a grave. A local tradition records the burial of Godfred Crovan, king of Man, under the standing stone at Carragh Bhan on the Oa in Islay (Anderson, A. O. 1922, ii, 98; Lamont 1966, 16). The majority of burials under cairns or barrows (there are relatively few barrows or earthen mounds in Argyll) have been conventionally assigned to the early prehistoric period. However, recent fieldwork and aerial reconnaissance have pointed to

FIGURE 10.2. Newton, Islay, aerial photograph showing ring-ditches and central pits.

the existence of a group of round and square ditched barrows, which probably belong to the early and mid first millennium AD in Scotland (Alcock, E. 1992). The excavation at Newton on Islay (McCullagh 1989; superseding RCAHMS 1984, 55, no.31) of three circular ditched features, which were visible as part of a larger cropmark complex on aerial photographs (figure 10.1–2), may provide evidence of the funerary practices on the island prior to the establishment of the burial enclosures associated with *kil*-names; these are often round or oval in plan and may contain the sites of chapels, which are in some cases of later date. The ring-ditches at Newton are between 5 m and 7 m in internal diameter with rectangular pits set centrally, some 2 m in length, aligned east and west, of a suitable depth to accommodate an extended inhumation; no skeletal remains or grave-goods were found. The excavator concluded that a Bronze Age date was unlikely for these features and would associate the cemetery with the period of Dalriadic settlement on Islay. Such a burial tradition, with the raising of low mounds over graves, although discontinued for several centuries, might provide a familiar background for the early Norse settlers in the Inner Hebrides.

The construction of the graves by the Norse took two main forms – the stone-lined grave such as those found at Ballinaby, Islay (Edwards 1934), and Machrins, Colonsay (Ritchie 1981) and the burial chamber or enclosure. The stone-lined grave or long cist closely resembles those found widely in Scotland belonging to the mid first millennium AD, where no church building has been recognised immediately adjacent to the burials (Alcock, E. 1992). The type continues into the medieval period, and examples have been noted in churchyards. The other, the stone grave enclosure, the most elaborate of which is found at Kiloran Bay, Colonsay (Anderson, J. 1907a), while it resembles in some ways burials of high status in Norway and Denmark, is peculiar to the islands of Scotland (Shetelig 1945, 31).

Only one burial, that at Machrins, Colonsay, was discovered during a modern excavation, and in only one other instance, the finds made at Ballinaby, Islay, in 1788–9 by a naval ship's crew, close to the standing stone, has the discovery been made deliberately (RCAHMS 1984, 149, no.294, 4). All but one of the burials were found in sand dunes suffering from erosion: the circumstances surrounding the discovery of the two oval brooches, indicative of the grave of a woman, near the distillery at Newton, Islay, in 1845 (Anderson, J. 1880, 71f; Campbell, J. F. 1862, lxxiii) are unknown, but may date from building works there. It seems unlikely that the burials and finds recorded to date represent a fair statistical sample of the Norse graves in Argyll. Even in the nineteenth century the element of chance in recording finds is remarkable, as, for example, when J. F. Campbell remarks, in a letter about lending the brooches from Newton (figure 10.3) for exhibition in the National Museum of Antiquities in Edinburgh, that he had seen two similar brooches from Mull (Anderson, J. 1880, 72), thus providing the only record of a Viking burial on that island. The noting of burials with rich multiple grave-goods may also distort the pattern. The distribution of known burials does not match that of Norse-derived place-names in the islands, which, however, probably reflects a later phase of Norse settlement and influence. It has been suggested that the burials on Islay, Colonsay, Oronsay, Tiree and Coll are those of raiders or traders who had a temporary residence. This theory views the islands of the coast of Argyll as small, poor and unlikely to support a society that could furnish the rich burials that have been recorded as chance discoveries (Eldjarn 1984, 7f). It is a theory that derives to some extent from looking at small scale distribution maps showing the islands of the Inner Hebrides disappearing under the symbols of Norse burials, not realising either their position on the routes between Scandinavia, the Orkneys and Ireland and in particular Dublin, or the agricultural resource represented by these low-lying and fertile islands, and possibly from not considering the peculiar position and status of those who are likely to have been the first generation of settlers of Norse origin in Argyll.

Some evidence for the economy and society within the islands known to

FIGURE 10.3. Newton, Islay, oval brooch.

the Norse settlers in the ninth and tenth centuries, the period to which all the graves can be assigned, can be gained from an examination of the burials and their accompanying grave-goods. One of the first points to be noted is that the settlers, though moving into lands that had been Christian for centuries, did not adopt the prevailing custom of burial in a defined cemetery, in consecrated ground, but retained a choice of burial site similar to that in Scandinavia. This suggests that at least some of the settlers felt sufficiently alien, as colonists, from the inhabitants of the islands to flout a strong custom, and that they were sufficiently powerful to be able to do so. There are no records of discoveries of burials in known ecclesiastical burial grounds, accompanied by finds of Scandinavian character, such as are known from certain English churchyards (e.g. Grieg 1940, 4, 18f), extensively in the Isle of Man (Grieg 1940, 4, 22–6) and from that of St Cuthbert's churchyard, near Kirkcudbright (Grieg 1940, 2, 13). The presence of very crudely incised crosses on two of the slabs of the enclosure at Kiloran Bay, Colonsay, might suggest a related attitude to Christianity (Anderson, J. 1907a, 443). However, the picture of the situation in the Hebrides might develop with further excavation and discoveries. The excavations at Peel Castle, in the Isle of Man, during the years after 1982 revealed Norse pagan graves, both male and female, with a similar construction – a long cist – and on the same alignment as earlier Christian graves related to an earlier Christian chapel or keeil (Youngs, Clark and Barry 1985, 210f; 1986, 180f; 1987, 174, and 1988, 293f). It is notable that there is no clear evidence for cremation connected with any of the graves found in Argyll. It was a rite practised contemporaneously with inhumation in Scandinavia; there are a few instances elsewhere, including northern England, the best example being Ingleby in Derbyshire (Richards et al. 1995); the elaborate tomb on the Ile de Groix, a small island off the south coast of Brittany, where a substantial boat and its fittings, including twenty shield bosses, were burnt and covered by a cairn (Du Chatellier and Le Pontois 1909). There might be practical reasons for this in the Hebrides, given the amount of fuel necessary for a successful cremation; reluctance to sacrifice

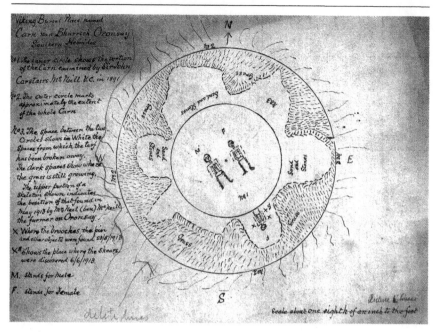

FIGURE 10.4. Carn a'Bharraich, Oronsay, Symington Grieve's sketch plan of 1913.

a sizeable boat or the lack of timber on the islands might be relevant factors. The custom in Argyll, on the existing evidence, appears to have been for an individual burial place, the choice of which was possibly influenced by the pre-existence of a mound or cairn of natural or artificial origin, which provided a marker for the grave, or a standing stone which would bear witness to the religious, but non-Christian nature, of the site. It may have been envisaged that cemeteries would be formed around these burials, but a rapid adoption of native custom led to burial in Christian enclosures.

Carn a' Bharraich, Oronsay, contains the remains of three bodies, the largest number of persons buried in one place (figure 10.4) (McNeill 1891; Grieve 1914); the burials are associated with what are believed to be some of the earliest Norse objects in Scotland. The mound, about 4 feet (1.22 m) in height, lies above the beach on the east side of the island in an area of sand-dunes, a little more than a kilometre from Oronsay Priory. The name attached to it, distinguishing it from the mounds generally referred to as *Sithean*, 'fairy mound', and probably to be translated as Cairn of the Barra Men, might suggest one of the many burials near the shore of those who have been drowned at sea. It was thought by the discoverer of the burials in 1891 to have had two thin slabs, about 4 feet 6 inches (1.37 m) and 4 feet (1.22 m) high, placed erect on its summit, and there were many slabs of schist in its makeup. The mound had been much damaged by erosion, and it was not possible to say whether any of the three bodies were deposited at the same time. Two inhumations were noted in 1891; the bodies had been laid side by side with the

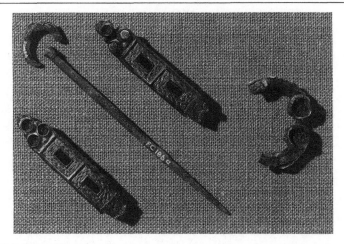

FIGURE 10.5. Carn a'Bharraich, Oronsay, brooches formed from strap-ends, brooch and ringed pin found in 1891 (scale 1:2).

heads NNW. The more easterly skeleton, thought to be that of a woman of considerable age, was accompanied by two beads, one of serpentine and the other of amber, and had, adhering to the left collar bone, a brooch which had been made from the hinge-plate of a shrine of insular workmanship; a similar brooch was recovered after further investigation (figure 10.5). The brooches were of gilded bronze decorated with interlace, each with one triangular terminal containing settings for three amber studs; the main panels divided into two rectangular fields with provision for securing a leather strap at the rear by means of rivets; the other end was formed by one half of a hinge. The brooches closely resemble the strap holders on the house-shaped Monymusk reliquary (Duns 1881) and probably came from a similar object or possibly another form of shrine, such as a book shrine, designed to be carried securely in its casing around the bearer's neck. This is one of the clearest examples in Scotland of material derived from the looting of a religious house, and its adaptation to secular use.

Iron pins were attached to the strap holders in order to form brooches, which were worn instead of the usual oval brooches to hold the over tunic of a Norse woman in place. The rusting of the pin has preserved part of a circular cord which was looped around the catch and under the point of the pin, as well as part of the material of the garment to which it was attached. These brooches were accompanied possibly by a brooch which held the cloak in position. This was a pseudo-penannular bronze brooch with settings for now vanished stones marking the terminals. The brooch may be of Scottish or Irish manu-facture and the use of an exotic foreign artefact for the third brooch in the set was a feature of Norse fashion (Roesdahl 1991, 37; Fanning 1988). A bronze ringed pin would have held together the neck of the shirt. The brooches and pin were an essential part of a woman's dress, rather than items specifically laid in the grave. By her side lay the skeleton of a man, again reported as being

FIGURE 10.6. Carn a'Bharraich, Oronsay, oval brooches and pin found in 1913 (scale 1:2).

of considerable age, accompanied at the time of the investigation only by an iron knife blade, near the right thighbone, and a ring made from a limpet shell. In the north part of the mound a bed of charcoal was found containing boat-rivets, pieces of bronze and a stone-sinker of steatite with a well-drilled hole by which a rope could be attached, which may have been a sounding line. The evidence points to the burning of a boat as part of the funerary rites. In Scandinavia it would be usual for the burning of a boat to accompany the cremation of the body, the vessel itself presumably providing much of the fuel necessary. The number of rivets found is not recorded, but about 300 rivets were recovered from the excavation of a boat burial at Knoc y Doonee on the Isle of Man (Kermode 1930). The discovery of a third burial from Carn a' Bharraich was not made until 1913, when erosion uncovered a skull, and subsequent investigations revealed a burial lying with its head to the north, accompanied by two bronze brooches, a bronze ringed pin (figure 10.6), a bone needle case (figure 10.7) and a pair of iron shears. Examination of the skull suggested that the woman was 'beyond middle life' (Grieve 1914, 276). Traces of the cord which connected the brooches, as well as the material to which they were attached, are preserved by the corrosion of the iron pins. The relationship between the three burials as conjectured in the sketch plan made in 1913 (figure 10.4) strongly suggests that there were two primary burials, whose deposition was at least planned at the same time, with a third inserted later into the edge of the mound. Although there are no other certain burials of Norse date on Oronsay, there are some finds from Lochan Cille Mhoire where teeth and iron rivets were identified as belonging to a Viking burial in 1891

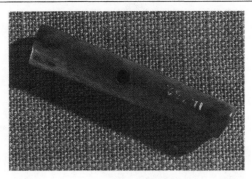

FIGURE 10.7. Carn a'Bharraich, Oronsay, needle-case found in 1913 (scale 1:2).

(RCAHMS 1984, 152, no.299), and at Druim Arstail (RCAHMS 1984, 150 no.297) where there was an inhumation within a stone enclosure in a sand mound, reminiscent of the burials at Kiloran Bay, Colonsay, and Ballinaby, Islay.

The other main group of burials in Argyll (which has sometimes been referred to as a cemetery) is that discovered over many years at Ballinaby on Islay. The circumstances of their recording, the form of the graves and the nature of the grave-goods provide a fair illustration of the range of Norse burials on Islay. At least four burials have been recorded from Ballinaby, and it is likely that another one or possibly two should be added to this total. The burials lie within an area of sand-dunes near the west coast of the Rhinns of Islay, adjacent to fertile arable land. The earliest possible find is a sword illustrated by Pennant (1790, i, pl.xliv) as coming from Islay, and may have been unearthed at Ballinaby, where Pennant was a guest of the owner. The first certain finds emerged in May 1788 when two oval brooches were presented to the Society of Antiquaries of Scotland, appearing in their list of acquisitions (*Archaeologia Scotica*, 3 (1831), Appendix, ii, 68) (figure 10.8); they were said to have been found under a large standing stone at Ballinaby, possibly the one that still stands 4.9 m in height, or perhaps the one mentioned by Pennant (1790, i, 257) during his visit to Ballinaby in 1722, as equidistant from the other two, which has now disappeared, possibly as a result of over-enthusiastic searching for Norse material. It would be pleasant to think of Pennant's conversation as providing a stimulus that brought these Ballinaby brooches into the Society's collections and public record. Their discovery, however, appears to have encouraged further interest in the area. The author of the description of the parish of Kilchoman in the *New Statistical Account* published in 1845 (*NSA*, 7, Argyll, 650) records that, 'Above forty years ago, Captain Burgess of the *Savage* Sloop of War, with a party of his crew, dug up part of the sandhill near it [the tallest standing stone], where they found one or two swords, a pike head and many human bones. These arms they carried away: the ground has since lain undisturbed'. Examination of Lieutenant Burgess' log in the Public Record Office suggests that his

FIGURE 10.8. Ballinaby, Islay, oval brooches presented to the Society of Antiquaries of Scotland in 1778 (scale 1:2). The back view shows the impression of fabric.

excavation at Ballinaby took place at the beginning of August 1788 when he was 'employed in sundries'.

In 1877 the OS surveyors recorded the discovery of a double burial in a sand-dune some 400 m to the west of the standing stone (Name Book, Argyll, 33, p.105); a fuller record was made by Joseph Anderson (Anderson, J.1880). The skeletons lay a short distance apart with their heads to the east, at a depth of 0.4 m, in an enclosure formed of stones set on edge. The female burial was accompanied by two oval brooches, twelve beads which probably hung between the brooches, a silver pin with a filigree decorated head and a knitted silver wire chain (figures 10.9–10) (Graham-Campbell 1995, 130). In addition to the items related to personal dress, the body was accompanied by a glass linen smoother, a bronze needle case containing a needle, a bronze ladle reminiscent of Irish liturgical vessels (figure 10.11) (O'Floinn 1983), bronze mounts decorated with repoussé ornament from an unidentified object, possibly for mounting on leather over wood (figure 10.12), a mount with a curved edge, perhaps from a drinking horn, and teeth from an iron heckle for combing flax (although in the original account it was associated with the male burial because it was thought to be part of a helmet). The other skeleton was found with a sword in its scabbard (figure 10.13), a shield boss and grip (figure 10.14), an iron spearhead, a ferrule containing the remains of a wooden shaft, two axes, an adze, a hammer and tongs for smithing, as well as fragments of a cauldron and what may have been the terminal of a drinking horn (figure 10.15). The description by the finder of the discovery

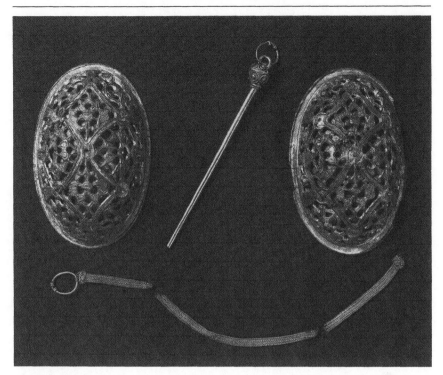

FIGURE 10.9. Ballinaby, Islay, two oval brooches, silver pin and silver wire chain (scale 1:2).

FIGURE 10.10. Ballinaby, Islay, glass linen smoother and beads.

FIGURE 10.11. Ballinaby, Islay, bronze ladle, and detail of compass decoration on the handle.

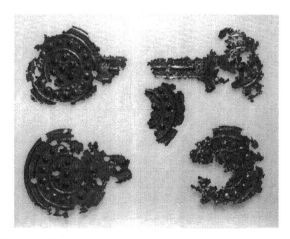

FIGURE 10.12. Ballinaby, Islay, bronze mounts with repoussé ornament.

FIGURE 10.13. Ballinaby, Islay,
sword in its scabbard (scale 1:10).

FIGURE 10.14. Ballinaby,
Islay, shield boss and grip
(scale 1:2).

FIGURE 10.15. Ballinaby, Islay, iron tools (scale 1:4).

FIGURE 10.16. Ballinaby, Islay, sword (scale 1:10).

FIGURE 10.17. Ballinaby, Islay, buckle and ringed pin (scale 1:2).

in 1877 of this double burial, again made as a consequence of erosion, states that 'a line of stones formed a sort of enclosure round each of the skeletons'. This suggests a divided enclosure with each burial having its own defined area, with the further possible implication that, although the burials were laid out in close relation to each other, they may not have been strictly contemporary.

The latest burial to be uncovered at Ballinaby, which lay about 360 m to the west of the double grave, was discovered in 1932 (Edwards 1934). The skeleton lay fully extended in a cist formed of upright slabs, aligned ENE and WSW, with the head at the WSW end; it was found at a depth of about 0.45 m below the surface of the eroding sand-dune. The body was accompanied by a sword (figure 10.16), gilded bronze buckle with a zoomorphic tongue and a ringed pin (figure 10.17), a shield boss, an axe and fragments of an iron sickle or knife. Examination of the skeleton revealed that it belonged to an individual of 'advanced years'.

The other two burials known from Islay were female burials; that from Newton (Anderson, J. 1880, 71f; Campbell, J. F. 1862, i, lxxiii) was found in a gravel bank in 1845, accompanied by two oval brooches, an amber bead and some fragments of iron; the other from Cruach Mhor near the west shore of Loch Indaal was found in a dispersed state in an area of deflating sand dunes as a result of surface collection over several years. Only the fragments

FIGURE 10.18. Sockton, Co. Durham, representations of Norse warriors.

of the two oval brooches can be attributed to a burial with any certainty, but the presence of amber and jet-like beads, a bronze buckle, a steatite spindle whorl, an iron buckle and a possible iron weaving batten among the finds might belong to a Norse settlement, though it would seem more probable that some at least are to be associated with the grave (Gordon 1990). Pottery from the neolithic to the medieval period has been collected in this area.

This recital of the circumstances surrounding the recording of eight identifiable Norse burials from Islay gives some indication of how partial our surviving accounts may be. Four male and four female burials are known; the identification of female graves may be rendered easier because of the ready recognition of the characteristic oval brooches (Randsborg 1980, 126), while graves containing iron weapons and tools which are subject to more rapid decay are less certainly identified. The representation of a standing figure from Sockburn, Co. Durham, gives a clear picture of male dress of the period (figure 10.18). Three of the female graves are known only because of the survival of the brooches, or a record of them, with little information about their original context.

The most elaborate of the burials known from Argyll is that from Kiloran Bay on the north-west coast of Colonsay (Anderson, J. 1907a). It was discovered in 1882 in sand dunes about 200 m from the sea, in an enclosure measuring some 4.65 m by 3.1 m overall according to the published account, although slightly smaller according to the manuscript plan (figure 10.19). The enclosure, which lay east and west, was formed of upright stone slabs, two of which were marked with a crudely incised cross (figure 10.20). The sand within the enclosure was full of boat rivets, evidence for the burial of a boat and an indication that the boat was of approximately the same dimensions as the enclosure. It is not known whether the boat was placed upright within the enclosure, or, as seems rather more likely from the position of the body, inverted over the enclosure like a roof. This variety of boat burial, although rarer than that in which the boat contained the burial deposit, is known from Norway and Denmark (Shetelig 1954, 94f). The body lay in a crouched position in the south-west corner of the enclosure; this is an unusual arrangement for a Norse inhumation, where the body would more normally be placed fully extended. What is not mentioned in the account of the

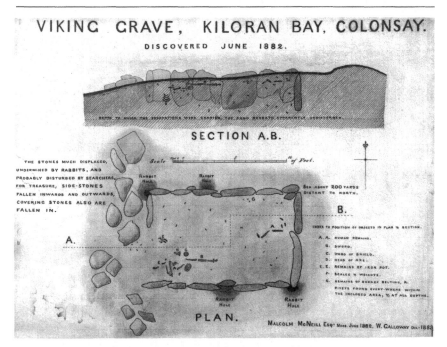

FIGURE 10.19. Kiloran Bay, Colonsay, plan by Malcolm McNeill, 1882, and William Galloway, 1883.

FIGURE 10.20. Kiloran Bay, Colonsay, cross-marked slab (scale 1:10).

FIGURE 10.21. Kiloran Bay, Colonsay, sword hilt and axe (scale 1:4).

discovery (written from the excavator's notes some twenty-five years later), but is indicated on the plan and on the section drawing, is a second group of apparently human remains lying in a central position at the east end of the grave, with at least three long bones and some smaller bones shown at a distance of some 2.1 m from the other skeleton and about 0.6 m from the horse harness which lay close to the north side of the enclosure. The bones do not resemble those of a dog, which would be the most probable animal to be buried in a grave also containing a horse. The information on the plan indicated disturbance of the enclosure by rabbits and possible disturbance by 'searchers for treasure', but it seems unlikely that a group including large and small human bones would have been removed to such a distance from the original interment. It seems likely that there was a second body within the enclosure, presumably since it was accompanied by no grave-goods, it had a lower status than the primary interment, but lack of evidence makes it difficult to compare profitably with the grave from Ballateare, Jurby, on the Isle of Man (Bersu and Wilson 1966) where a secondary burial was interpreted as a sacrifice designed to accompany the dead man into the after life. Other examples are known from Scandinavian graves (Foote and Wilson 1970, 411f; Randsborg 1980, 133f).

The crouched body lay close to an iron sword, a spearhead, an axe, a shield-boss, fragments of an iron pot, a silver pin (Graham-Campbell 1995, 31), four bronze studs and a bronze balance with seven decorated weights (figures 10.21–3). Outside the enclosure on the east lay the skeleton of a horse (Kavanagh 1988), accompanied by an iron girth-buckle; one of its hind legs had been struck by at least one heavy blow. Some time after the end of the excavation, three Northumbrian copper stycas were found on the surface of the loose sand (figure 10.24). The two that can be identified were issued under Eanred I (808–41) and Wigmund, Archbishop of York (831–54); the coins have been pierced for suspension, presumably for use as amulets, and are not to be regarded as current coins; they provide only a *terminus post quem* for the

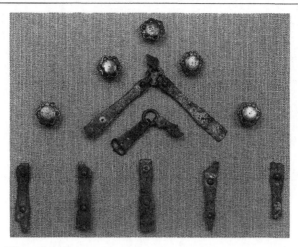

FIGURE 10.22. Kiloran Bay, Colonsay, harness mounts (scale 1:4).

burial. The two slabs, crudely incised with crosses, one forming part of the west end of the enclosure and the other situated at the east, raise the question of the relationship between pagan burials and Christianity in the ninth century on Colonsay. The crosses are far from prominent, and as a statement of belief (or even of acknowledgement of the power of the Christian religion) would have an extremely muted impact. It is possible to speculate that they may relate to the probable second burial in the enclosure.

The other well-recorded Norse burial discovered on Colonsay (Ritchie 1981), the only one to be discovered as the result of modern excavation, was at Machrins where erosion had exposed the remains of a small settlement. An oval-shaped long cist was discovered some 14 m to the ESE of the settlement, aligned NE and SW, containing the remains of a flexed body that had been buried on its side; the upper part of the body had not survived, but the head would have lain at the SW end of the cist, as in the cist burial at Ballinaby (Edwards 1934). It was accompanied by the skeleton of a small dog, as well as a ringed pin, a fragment of decorated bronze and fragments of an iron knife (figure 10.25). None of the objects is sufficiently diagnostic, nor did sufficient skeletal material survive to establish whether the burial was male or female. The radiocarbon date obtained indicated a span of AD 684–1014 (GU–1114). At least one other burial of Norse date is known from the area of Machrins (McNeill 1892, 61f; Anderson, J. 1907a, 441; Loder 1935, 31); in 1891 a burial was discovered in the sand-dunes accompanied by an iron sword, the fragment of a shield, a penannular brooch, iron pot, axehead, spear, rivets, an amber bead, a bronze pin and fragments of horse harness, again suggesting an animal sacrifice in reality or ritual. Other possible burials on Colonsay are known from Ardskenish (Anderson, J. 1907, 441f), where a bronze buckle not unlike that from the female grave at Kneep, Lewis (Welander et al. 1987), and two ringed pins have survived, from Cnoc nan Gall (Ritchie 1981, 263,

FIGURE 10.23. Kiloran Bay, Colonsay, balance and weights.

278f), where, in addition to a human and equine tooth, a small number of iron clench nails, which may have come from a boat, have been preserved (Eldjarn 1984, 8), and from Traigh nam Barc (McNeill 1910, 30f), where the discovery of a burial in a stone coffin, with a much decayed iron sword close by, may be a male burial of the Norse period. The local tradition of a

FIGURE 10.24. Kiloran Bay, Colonsay, Northumbrian coins (scale 2:1).

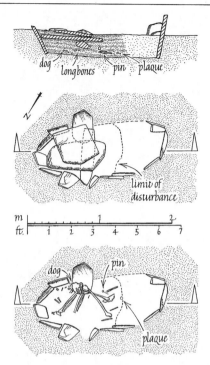

FIGURE 10.25. Machrins, Colonsay, excavation plan.

battle on the site may suggest the discovery of other burials there. In contrast to the situation on Islay, it is only male graves that can be identified with any certainty, although the finds at Ardskenish and the later discovery at Machrins might belong to either a male or female burial.

The other islands have relatively few recorded Norse graves; on Gigha a 'square box of stone', covered by large boulders was found in a sand pit (Anderson, R. S. G. 1939, 17); it contained a bronze balance, three lead weights and a lead spindle whorl, presumably re-used as a weight, which recalls the balance found at Kiloran Bay, Colonsay. It probably represents a male burial, although no human remains were recorded, and it might possibly have been a hoard; evidence from Birka, a major trading centre in Sweden, reveals the presence of scales and weights in women's graves also (Stalsberg 1991). Burials from Cornaigbeg, Tiree (*Stat Acct.*, 10 (1794), 402; Anderson, J. 1874, 554), are reported to have been accompanied by iron swords, some of which had hilts decorated with silver, shields, a spearhead and horse bones; none of these survive. These finds would suggest Norse male burials, while the unlocated female burial from Tiree is known only from a pair of oval brooches and a bronze pin (Anderson, J. 1874, 554). The discovery of an inhumation burial associated with an iron spearhead at Grishipoll on Coll, possibly suggesting a Norse context (Ritchie and Crawford 1978,

94f), reflects the most common association in Norway, a burial with a single weapon (Solberg 1985). Mull has produced evidence of only one burial, a pair of oval brooches, now lost and recorded only casually (Anderson, J. 1880, 72).

All the certain finds of Norse burials in Argyll have come from the islands, and there are only very doubtful references to boat graves near the coast at Cul na Croise, Goirten Bay, Ardnamurchan (Lethbridge 1925) and Oban (Shetelig 1954, 75), which might point to settlement on the mainland. A spearhead, recorded as accompanying a burial in a cist near Kilmartin (*NSA*, vii, Argyll, 560), and two swords recorded from a mound on Kerrera (*Discovery and Excavation in Scotland 1965*, 9) may be of Norse date. There is evidence for the burial of some fourteen individuals, accompanied by grave-goods of distinctively Norse character, and a similar number of cases where finds do not survive to allow proper consideration of the question. The chance nature both of discoveries and of their recording has been stressed and it is unlikely that the graves provide a representative sample. They do, however, provide some material evidence for the nature of Norse settlement in Argyll. Of the fourteen burials, seven belong to women, who were buried dressed, in characteristically Norse clothing and wearing ornaments of Norse design, suggesting permanent settlement on the islands off the coast of Argyll. Attempts to deduce information about the economic conditions of the early Norse settlers in Argyll from the contents of surviving graves are liable to be limited in scope, not only by the very small sample available, but by the particular religious and cultural nature of the deposits. What is known of the beliefs of the inhabitants of the Scandinavian lands about life after death, prior to their conversion to Christianity, comes mainly from other sources, particularly from the sagas (Foote and Wilson 1970, 387–414). It is indeterminate and uncodified; possible destinations were the shadowy underworld of Hel and the fighting and feasting of Valhalla: what was desirable was a superior version of earthly life. The belief that in the afterworld the dead were united with those to whom they were attached emerges both from literary sources and from the evidence of burial sites. What also emerges from literary sources is the importance of a man's good name, the reputation that will live after him in the memory of later generations (Roesdahl 1991, 62f).

The burial of weapons in male graves in the islands of Argyll provides the most certain means of identifying the graves; all of the better recorded graves there contain more than one weapon, while in Norway, where a much larger sample of Norse graves is available, some two-thirds of male graves have only one weapon, with the axe being the most common choice, followed by the spear and the sword (Solberg 1985); the majority of graves containing only an axe or a spear had no visible marker. The definite male graves in Argyll would all fall into the highest of three classes of burial, identified in Norway, which have been associated with different social groups recognised in Scandinavian law codes (Foote and Wilson 1970; Randsborg 1980, 126). In Norway, the graves of older women are associated with richer grave-goods

(Dommasnes 1991). However, the settlers in Argyll, whose graves have been discovered, are likely to have belonged to the first generation of a group or family of settlers, who died while the influence of the traditions of their home-land was at its strongest and before the local custom of unaccompanied in-terment in burial grounds was adopted. Those buried in these conditions were successful settlers, who may also have been successful pirates or traders with a personally acquired surplus of goods. The traditions of inheritance, of what goods passed by right to the heirs, and which could be disposed of at the will of the owner, are unknown, but must have influenced the choice of grave-goods. The evidence of the graves would point to a relatively rich society with disposable wealth, in a position to engage in trade or gift-exchange (Samson 1991). The choice of grave-goods in addition to weapons may point to econ-omic traditions. The burial at Kiloran Bay had, as well as sword, spear, axe and shield, a fine set of scales and weights, pointing to trade or exchange of goods with the need to measure small quantities of silver, and a cauldron, presumably an indication of the ability to grant hospitality. The male burial at Ballinaby was accompanied by, in addition to weapons, a cauldron and a drinking horn, tools for smithing and possibly for woodworking, providing evidence for the practice of these crafts, so necessary, among other appli-cations, for shipbuilding. Local custom may have influenced the burial deposits; graves on Islay contain no evidence for boat burial, and there is, as yet, no evidence for animal sacrifice there, such as has been uncovered on Colonsay and Tiree.

Of the 4629 burials of Norse date recognised in Norway only 18 per cent were those of women, although women's graves form a higher pro-portion of the total in the western coastal areas of Norway, the traditional area from which the majority of the settlers in the Scottish islands came. The objects buried in the double grave at Ballinaby indicate a similar social status to that of the male burial, with tools for the production and care of linen, as well as exotic objects, like the bronze ladle and the repoussé mounts. The impression given is that this is the burial of the mistress of a substantial household. As in the case of the male graves, it is not known what criteria governed the deposition of property in the graves. In the majority of cases (Cruach Mhor providing a possible exception) the surviving finds indicate that women were buried with their jewellery and objects associated with dress.

The graves in Argyll can be attributed to the later ninth and tenth centuries, although the shrine mounts from Carn a'Bharraich and the brooch from Machrins date from the eighth century or earlier. The oval brooches of Berdal type from Carn a'Bharraich possibly belong to the second half of the ninth century (Graham-Campbell 1980, 27); the brooches from the 1788 find at Ballinaby probably belong to the tenth century, but little can be dated precisely within this period.

No settlement remains which can be definitely attributed to the Norse period have been recognised in Argyll, although they have been searched for over many years (Alcock and Alcock 1987). This situation, it must be said, also applies to the succeeding medieval period where only ecclesiastical sites or secular sites of high status can be identified from surface remains. Sub-rectangular or sub-oval structures such as those on Drimore on South Uist (MacLaren 1974) or from the Braaid on the Isle of Man, where a number of defended promontory sites also contain rectangular buildings of Norse date (Cubbon 1983, 18), have not been discovered. The excavation at Machrins (Ritchie 1981) uncovered a settlement consisting of four single-roomed structures, square on plan with rounded corners, with walls of upright slabs set into shallow grooves in the sand; three of these houses had hearths. The flimsy nature of the stone work would suggest a seasonal use of the site; walls and roof would be constructed of turf and timber with no substantial upright posts. The buildings are best compared with those associated with secondary occupation of the wheelhouse at A Cheardach Mhor (Young and Richardson 1960). The animal bone from one of the houses yielded a radiocarbon date with a span of AD 709–1020 (GU–1115). The date raises the question of whether the settlement has Scottish or Norse associations; the presence of a Norse burial close by might imply a Norse relationship, while the buildings probably belong to a native tradition, although their slight nature makes their attribution to any cultural tradition difficult, and the small finds are in-sufficiently diagnostic. There is no evidence here that would elucidate the re-lationship between the native inhabitants of the island and the Norse incomers (Ritchie, A. 1993, 25–7). Structures such as those from the Norse period at the Udal on North Uist (Crawford and Switsur 1977, 131; Crawford, I. A. 1981), have not been recognised, nor have buildings such as those best known from the Bay of Birsay (Ritchie, A. 1977; Morris, C. D. 1985, 216–21; 1993), or Pool, on Sanday (Hunter et al. 1993), or Westness on Rousay (Kaland 1993), all in Orkney, although further excavations in eroding sand dunes might well change this apparent void (Batey 1987, 46–58). Long stone-lined hearths of a Norse type, not visibly associated with buildings or floors, have been noted near Garvard on Colonsay (where a bronze pin of late tenth-century date was found close by), and near Druim Arstail on Oronsay (Ritchie 1981, 268).

While the situation in Argyll cannot be directly compared with that in Iceland, where the Norse, many of whom are believed to have come from, or by way of, the Western Isles (Sawyer 1971, 212), began laying out farms in virgin territory, it may be noted that burials tend to be discovered at a distance of about 400 m from the primary farmstead. It is probable that some of the finds of material belonging to the later part of the first millennium AD within forts and duns in Argyll constructed at an earlier period may be related to settlement, temporary or possibly more permanent, by the Norse raiders or settlers, but no structures that can plausibly be attributed to Scandinavian tradition have been identified. There is no evidence for the mechanism by which the Norse took possession of land in the Hebrides (Morris, C. D. 1977; Crawford, I. A. 1981), beyond that of later landholding and fiscal organisation

(Johnston 1995). With the adoption of Christianity or of Christian burial customs, the source of the most direct evidence of Norse settlement in Argyll ceases. The linguistic influence of Norse on Argyll place-names has been permanent, although it is far from uniform across the region (Nicolaisen 1969; 1982). It must be presumed that the inhabitants of the southern islands of Argyll were speaking a Celtic tongue, probably the early form of Gaelic, originating with the immigration from Ireland, when the first Norse settlers arrived, and that they were speaking a later form of the Gaelic language when the Isles became part of the Scottish kingdom in 1266 (Fellows-Jensen 1984; Andersen 1991; Johnston 1995). The Celtic and Norse tongues never formed a recognisable dialect, although some words of Norse origin have been adopted into Gaelic. Whether Old Norse ever completely replaced an earlier Celtic tongue in any of the islands of the southern Inner Hebrides is unknown, but the volume of place-names of Norse origin, particularly on Coll and Tiree, where it has been estimated at 50 per cent, Norse to Gaelic, against 30 per cent for Islay, and 15 per cent for Mull and Lismore (Thomas 1882; Scott, Sir L. 1954, 189: Johnston 1995, 111f), suggests a thorough renaming by the Norse settlers and traders. Many of the names refer to natural features, in particular valleys (the element *dalr* 'dale' was adapted into Gaelic), but also to coastal headlands and inlets. The significance of these topographical names is difficult to assess (Fraser 1995, 92f). The more useful evidence for the extent of Scandinavian settlement, as opposed to a 'sphere of influence' (Nicolaisen 1982, 108) would appear to come from place-names containing habitative elements, which often in Islay takes the form '-bus', derived from the Old Norse *bolstathr*, barley farm, as in Persabus or Lurabus, or '-poll', as it appears in Tiree and Coll, in Kirkapoll or Crossapoll. These elements are believed to belong to a secondary stage of Norse settlement (Nicolaisen 1969; Andersen 1991), but they are perhaps most usefully considered in the context of local place-name studies concerned with agricultural changes and developments. There are relatively few names of Norse origin in Colonsay, Oronsay, Gigha, or on the mainland of Argyll, and the majority of these relate to natural features, such as Inverlussa in Knapdale which contains the element *laks-a*, 'salmon river', although Soroba on the Craignish peninsula has been identified as a settlement name ending in *-baer* (Andersen 1991, 143). There has been much discussion of the question of the usefulness of Norse place-names as an indication of the extent and density of settlement, but given the converse influence of Gaelic over the intervening centuries, their survival argues for a well-established pattern of Norse landholding in Islay, Coll and Tiree, while a name such as Conisby (on the Rhinns of Islay) from Old Norse *Konnungsbaer* ('king's village') raises the question of the organisation of the kingdom of the Sudreys.

The political developments in Argyll, which are known mainly from later sources, written to serve the purposes of Irish kings of the eleventh century, are obscure, but the islands seem to have provided the base for a group of warriors called the '*Gall-Gaedhil*' or 'foreign Gaels', described as Scots and foster children of the Norsemen (Smyth 1977, 115). Their leader was known as Ketil the White and their defeat by a Norse army, led by Olaf of Dublin, is recorded in 857 (Anderson, A. O. 1922, 286). The identification of Ketil the White with a character in a later saga, Ketil Flatnose, has been suggested (Smyth 1977, 118–26; Crawford, B. E. 1995, 106), but must remain un-proven. His history and that of his family is bound up with the events in the Hebrides. His daughter, Aud, is recorded as marrying the king of Dublin, Olaf (Smyth 1984, 156); he defeated Ketil the White, and may have been the same Olaf who is recorded in the chronicles as raiding the land of the Picts and successfully laying siege to the fortress of the Britons at Dumbarton in 870, taking captives and rich plunder (Anderson, A. O. 1922, i, 301f). The political relations between the Irish, Norse and the *Gall-Gaedhil* are far from straightforward and it is unlikely that the position in the Hebrides was other than unstable (Lucas 1966; Broun 1994). Although Argyll seems to lie in the path of Viking movements between Ireland and the mainland of Scotland, conditions permitted the choice of Iona as burial place of Kenneth MacAlpin in 859 (Anderson, A. O. 1922, i, 289). The situation in the islands would appear to have been fluid, with movement of people between Scandinavia, Caithness and Ireland, and in the later ninth century, to Iceland. Aud, daughter of Ketil Flatnose, emigrated to Iceland (Smyth 1984, 160–6), accompanied by members of her family, friends, slaves and treasure. The influences to which the Norse settlers in the Hebrides were exposed, accord-ing to the convincing accounts of later writers, included Christianity; Aud is said to have erected crosses and to have chosen to be buried below high water mark, because she did not wish to lie in unconsecrated ground. A relative, Helgi the Lean, was a Christian, but worshipped Thor in times of crisis. Christianity appears to have virtually died out among the settlers, once they returned to a strongly Scandinavian milieu in Iceland (Anderson, A. O. 1922, i, 342f). The settlers who remained in the islands of Argyll were, however, living in a Christian country and had adopted Christianity, however super-ficially. Evidence for a blending of cultures in this sphere does not appear in the archaeological record until the late tenth or early eleventh century, in the form of a runic-inscribed graveslab commemorating Kali, son of Olvir, who was buried on Iona (RCAHMS 1982, 190, no.6, 69); other examples of such a fusion are the tenth-century cross, decorated with plaitwork, which was found on Iona, but which may have originated in the Isle of Man (RCAHMS 1982, 212–13, no.6, 95; Liestol 1983), the rune-inscribed slab, probably of the late tenth or early eleventh century, from Inchmarnock, Bute (Black 1890), and the late eleventh-century slab from Doid Mhairi near Port Ellen on Islay, where the cross is accompanied by foliage ornament in the Norse 'Ringerike' style (RCAHMS 1984,170, no.351).

The initial impact of the Norse came with their raids on wealthy monastic houses, but the profitable disposal of loot requires a trading network, and the presence of scales on Gigha and at Kiloran Bay, Colonsay, illustrates this aspect of Viking economic life. The weights are decorated with mounts of

Anglo-Saxon, Irish and Scottish origin with the enamelled examples drawing their ultimate design from Arabic script (Graham-Campbell 1980, 88f). The extent of trade is difficult to assess; it would appear that artefactual evidence for earlier direct contacts by sea between Argyll and the continent ceases around 700 (Lane 1994; Campbell, E. 1996, 86–9). Without the presence of suitable diagnostic goods such as pottery, it is difficult to estimate the volume of traffic (Wilson 1976a, 110f; Crawford, B. E. 1987, 134f; Kruse 1993). The islands of the Inner Hebrides lay on the western sea routes, and in particular on the route to Ireland and Dublin, and settlement there might provide the opportunity not only to trade north and south, but to exact tolls on others. Ireland might also provide the timber for the construction of ships; one of the wrecks discovered at Skuldelev, near Roskilde in Denmark, a narrow, fast vessel, designed to carry up to fifty men, and suitable for raiding rather than trading, was, on the evidence of dendrochronology, constructed of timber from Ireland (Roesdahl 1991, 86). One discovery which may illuminate the dangers of the narrow seaways between the islands is the gold arm-ring of tenth-century date, found in the Sound of Islay, which possibly came from a wreck (Graham-Campbell 1983), although, since a similar find was made in the English Channel, a ritual deposit has been suggested (Graham-Campbell 1995, 61). While towns were established in Ireland by the Norse (Bradley, J. 1988), through the impetus of their maritime enter-prise, there is no indication of any trading centre in the southern Hebrides. The most probable exports from the islands would be fish, farming surpluses, barley (Islay and Tiree were particularly fertile), cattle, and products derived from cattle, while slaves formed a source of revenue. In 986 the *Annals of Ulster* record that 'when the Danes came to the shore of Dalriata in three ships 140 of them were killed and others sold as slaves' (Anderson, A. O. 1922, i, 489). The distinction between trading and raiding may at times have been a fine one, but there is evidence that the two activities were carried out in different types of ships and by different classes of men (Smyth 1984, 143f). The possession of treasure itself conferred the ability to be ostentatiously generous, a much admired quality among the Norse of this period, accord-ing to references in the later sagas (Vestergaard 1991, 99), and one which would raise the status of a leader and enable him to forge useful alliances.

While the presence of a silver coinage would facilitate a trading economy, in the context of Argyll it is probably more useful to see the hoards as readily portable individual wealth (Graham-Campbell 1982; Kruse 1993, 187), per-haps as a source for silver jewellery (Gaimster 1991); no finds of single coins are known from the tenth century. A hoard containing more than a hundred Anglo-Saxon coins, in addition to a Kufic dirhem and some pieces of silver, was deposited near Machrie in Islay about 975 (Scott, W. H. 1854); two possible finds from Tiree, deposited about the same time, may have had a similar composition, while hoards are known from Iona, deposited about 986, and Inchkenneth, an island off the coast of Mull, about 998–1002, as well as one from Kilmartin on the mainland of Argyll (*NSA*, 7, Argyll, 560). The coins come mainly from Anglo-Saxon England, but also from the Norse kingdom of York and Dublin, from Normandy, and from France, as well as the one Kufic coin. The inclusion in the hoards of silver ingots as well as gold and silver ornaments suggests that the coin was assembled as bullion rather than being current coin in a fully coin-issuing economy. The non-recovery of hoards in the 970–80s would indicate a period of unrest in the islands, perhaps reflecting that in Ireland (Graham-Campbell 1976). The deposition of the large hoard from Iona has been associated with a raid on Christmas night 986, when the abbot and fifteen of the elders of the church were killed (Stevenson, R. B. K. 1951; RCAHMS 1982, 21, 48). However, the kings of the line of Kenneth MacAlpin continued to choose Iona as their burial place, in spite of the apparent lack of security, maintaining a cultural link between the ruling house of Scotland and the western seaboard. The themes of the raiding of Iona, royal burials and strife in the Hebrides and the mainland of Argyll continue through the tenth and eleventh centuries. It has been suggested that the movement from Iona to Kells marked a break in the identification of the ruling house of Dál Riata with the Columban community, but religious life was maintained on Iona, and the movement of Columban relics to Dunkeld in 848 by Abbot Indrechtach was far from ending the involvement of the Scottish crown with the Columban church, rather marking the political extension of Gaelic kingship (Broun 1994) and a confirmation of the power of the saint (Airlie 1994).

In 980 the Norse king of Dublin and former king of the Scandinavians in York, Olaf Cuaran, went on a pilgrimage to Iona where he died. With this symbolic reconciliation between the former Viking raider and the monastery of Iona, a new phase in the history of the Norse in Argyll may perhaps be recognised, moving gradually towards the establishment of the kingdom of Man and the Isles and the later medieval lordship of the Isles, partaking of a mixed Norse and Celtic heritage.

It is perhaps inappropriate to conclude on such a peaceful note; a notably violent raid on Iona took place in 986 and three years later Godfrey, son of Harold, King of the Hebrides, was killed by the men of Dál Riata, raiding continuing through the islands (Anderson, A. O. 1922, i, 489f, 494). It might be more fitting to end, as the chapter began, with account of a Norwegian attack on the monastery of Iona, the last one recorded, which took place in 1210, while the Isles were still under the overlordship of the Norwegian crown, when 'both Birchlegs and Croziers sailed with twelve ships upon piracy out among the western lands. And they plundered in the neighbouring islands, because the kings in the islands had civil war among themselves. They pillaged the holy island, which Norwegians have always held sacred; then they fell out and parted. And so their men were slain in various places' (Anderson, A. O. 1922, ii, 379).

11 Radiocarbon Dates from Archaeological Sites in Argyll and Arran

Patrick Ashmore

Before radiocarbon dating, archaeologists judged the similarity in date of things from their similarity in form. This 'typological' dating pulled all similar looking things of similar purpose together chronologically. Taken to extremes it produced estimates of time that were far too short. For instance, Stuart Piggott's otherwise estimable *The Neolithic Cultures of the British Isles* (1954) had the Neolithic starting in Britain about 2500 BC and ending about 1500 BC. That period was nearly a thousand years too short as well as between 1500 and 1000 years too late.

Radiocarbon dating, on the other hand, tends to spread events that belong in the same period apart, because of the errors attached to measurements of radioactivity. A few mildly aberrant dates could (given the absolutely small number of dates) make it seem that a phenomenon like the shell mounds of Oronsay lasted for centuries longer than it actually did. Unfortunately, if it be accepted that the typological method of dating is unreliable, there is no independent way of checking the validity of radiocarbon dates. Throwing away seemingly extreme dates (for instance the earliest and the latest dates for the shell mounds), is theoretically unjustifiable when the sample of dated sites is as small as it is, and the nature of hunter-gatherer settlement is so little understood. Other protocols for rejecting dates have been developed by a wide variety of archaeologists. Frequently, for instance, singleton dates are rejected. The view has been taken here that Scottish archaeology is still very much in an exploratory phase as far as dating is concerned, and thus even those dates about which one should probably be wary have been included (with suitable health warnings).

The chronological summary that follows is based on the generalisation that the radiocarbon dates are mainly, albeit only broadly, right. Until many more sites have been dated, by radiocarbon or other techniques such as dendro-

236

chronology or thermoluminescence, there is no way of assessing where or how important the exceptions to this generalisation are. That there are exceptions is quite certain.

What the chronological summary and tables below make clear is that neat divisions, like the Palaeolithic, Mesolithic and Neolithic, and the Bronze and Iron Ages, are misleading. Even allowing for the tendency of radiocarbon dating to spread out events, the tables suggest that people did particular things according to ancient tradition in one part of the area long after those in other parts had accepted new ideas about those specific aspects of their culture (although quite probably the two groups kept pace in changing yet other aspects of their way of life). Nevertheless, divisions are useful in providing a structure to what otherwise often seems an unwieldy mass of information, and the chronological tables have been split into patently arbitrary 500-year chunks, and the descriptive narrative into broad periods based on collections of those chunks.

The boundaries used in the descriptive narrative are at the start of the 500-year blocks; the first dates for settlement in western Scotland, at about 7500 BC; the first dates for the building of major structures by farmers, at about 4000 BC; the first beakers, at about 2500 BC; and the appearance of fortifications, at about 500 BC.

There is no evidence that the centuries surrounding these dates saw the incoming of large groups of new people (not even at the beginning, at 7500 BC), nor dramatic changes in the way of life. However, they do correspond roughly to the old divisions into the Mesolithic, Neolithic, Bronze Age and Iron Age, and may thus aid the transition in thinking from the old divisions to true chronology.

DESCRIPTIVE NARRATIVE

7500 to 4000 BC: The sites dated between about 7500 and 5500 BC probably do not include the earliest settlement in Argyll, for the earliest dated settlement in Scotland (at Kinloch, Rum) is not far to the north and seems to have begun about 7500 BC. There is a considerable variety of types among the dated sites, which suggests that hunters and foragers exploited a wide range of environments. It is perhaps due merely to chance that between about 5500 and 5000 BC the only dated sites are on Oronsay. In the next 500-year period there was use of the cave at Ulva, and the midden at Risga, but in the 500 years before the conventional start of the Neolithic in Scotland, at 4000 BC, the only dated sites (the date from Machrie Moor is probably from old wood or aberrant) are again on Oronsay. Not too much should be made of this, since the sample represented by the excavated sites is small and heavily biased towards the Oronsay middens.

4000 to 2500 BC: In the 500-year period after 4000 BC, people seem still to have been active on what had been hunter-gatherer sites. However, types of site generally attributed to farmers rather than hunters and gatherers came into use, and at Ulva the dated pit contained cereal grains, suggesting farming nearby. That said, at Port Charlotte only what seem to be ritual activities preceding the building of the chambered cairn can be attributed to this period, not use of the tomb for burials, while the fire in the forecourt of the chambered cairn at Monamore could be earlier than burials in the tomb. The pits with early pottery at Machrie Moor are very interesting since similar pits have been found at several sites in Scotland where ritual centres were to develop. The small settlement at Ardnadam is, very broadly, comparable to other small Neolithic settlements with houses built of stone, turf and timber. The date from Temple Wood is thought by the excavator to relate to the early timber setting there. It is from a piece of oak charcoal that may have been from the heart of an old tree, so the setting could be younger. That said, it does seem from the site at Pitglassie in Aberdeenshire that circular settings with vertical stones or timbers may be quite as early as this. The exciting possibility that the timber setting at Temple Wood belongs before 3500 BC, rather than somewhere between 3000 and 2000 BC, should not be rejected. The dated sites of the latter half of the fourth millennium include shell middens and use of the tomb chamber at Port Charlotte, and a putatively Neolithic house at Dunloskin Wood. Monamore seems to have gone out of use within a few centuries of 3000, and the important ritual centre at Machrie Moor was probably built around then for the dates for the timber rings there cluster around 3000. Even after 3000 BC there are signs of a hunter-gatherer way of life, along with Neolithic houses and settlements. However, the sites dated do not include shell mounds or caves; they are open sites on Jura that may as easily represent visits by farmers as by hunter-gatherers. The date obtained from the Gakashuin laboratory for the settlement at Townhead has been regarded as too late by some authors, and it is worth presaging the comments about GaK dates below, that the errors attached to dates produced by that laboratory (at least for sites on islands in the Pacific) seem to have been unusually prone to larger than normal errors.

2500 to 500 BC: The 500-year period after 2500 BC saw some considerable changes but also signs of continuity. Fields (their soil containing Beaker sherds) covered the site of the timber rings at Machrie Moor, although the rings were not forgotten. Extraordinarily their exact sites were later to be used for stone circles built of rounded boulders. The Beaker grave at Sorisdale has the earliest date of any Beaker burial in Scotland. The burnt mounds on Machrie Moor, Arran and at Borraichill Mor, Islay, are very early examples of the type. They may imply cooking during hunting or herding, for neither seems to represent a communal cook-house, nor a sweat-house. The house at Ardnave continues a Neolithic tradition of houses with straight sides and round corners. Food Vessels such as those found at Ardnave may be closely related to some late Neolithic wares. Between 2000 and 1500 BC settlement continued at Ardnave, and middens accumulated at Kilellan. A round house at Tormore on Arran had thick turf walls lined with wattle; Beaker pottery was found in it. The burial ritual on Islay seems to have been inhumation, while on the mainland it seems to have been cremation, and disposition in small cairns. Basal peat near field walls at Achnacree and the ox yoke in peat from Loch Nell reflect prior agricultural activity. The story between 1500 and 1000 BC seems to be very similar, apart perhaps from the date for primary occupation at Dun Mor Vaul (which may in part reflect an unusually large error in dating, since it was provided by the GaK laboratory). A post-built structure on a platform at Kilellan may have been a house. Between 1000 and 500 BC settlement continued or recommenced at Achnasavil, Auchategan, Kilellan and Cul a'Bhaile. Settlement began at Balloch Hill, which was fortified towards the end of this period or the beginning of the next. Evidence of swallowing up of fields by peat continues to appear at Achnacree. The general burial rite seems to have been cremation and disposal in small cairns. However, bodies were placed in MacArthur Cave, Oban; perhaps a new expression of a very ancient tradition, or a chance survival of a more widespread practice.

500 BC to AD 1000 and later: In this period nearly all the dates are associated with fortified (or about to be fortified) sites: Balloch Hill, Dunadd, Dun Mor Vaul and Eilean an Duin, although there are also dates for undefended settlement at Kilellan and for cremation at Claggan. Even one of the two first dates from Iona, which fall in the second half of this period, may immediately precede rampart building. Most of the dates between AD 500 and 1000 come from the settlement and ecclesiastical sites on Iona and the fort on Dunadd; but there are also a few dates for undefended settlement and inhumation on the islands, and a platform of uncertain purpose at Colintraive. The last date from Dunadd falls well after AD 1000, but has a fairly large error attached to it. The few subsequent dates for artificial structures are of limited interest or significance.

MORE ON ERRORS

The accuracy of radiocarbon dates has increased considerably over the past decade, during which international studies initiated by the Scottish laboratories (International Study Group 1982, 619) have helped dating facilities to ensure consistent and reliable results. The 1982 study showed that two of the twenty laboratories compared in the study had true errors over four times those quoted, four had true errors over twice those quoted, while eight had errors between those quoted and twice those quoted and four had errors less than those quoted. The advice of the study group was that errors could vary over time at any given laboratory, and that the errors quoted by liquid scintillation laboratories should be multiplied by between 1.2 and 3.0, depending on what errors had been allowed for in the quoted error (International Study Group 1982, 622, Table 3). Dr M. Stenhouse of the Glasgow laboratory (GU numbers) recommended in 1982 that all the errors he had quoted for GU numbers below GU–1500 should be multiplied by 1.4 and if, after that, they were less than ±110, they should be read as ±110 (Stenhouse, M. J. pers. comm.). Professor M. G. L. Baillie of the Palaeoecology Centre at Queen's University Belfast studied several sets of dates from the early 1980s including a large set obtained at the GU laboratory. He concluded that the errors quoted for these dates should be multiplied by 2.6 (Baillie 1990, 366). In fact the dates had been obtained by a research student using machinery other than that used for standard dates at the time, and Baillie's conclusions do not apply to dates supplied to archaeological customers in the early 1980s. They do, probably, give a good impression of the errors which should be applied to dates obtained a few years earlier; but, frustratingly, it is not possible to say to which dates this larger error factor of 2.6 should be applied. Quite separately, comparisons of GaK dates for sites in the Pacific with those obtained by other laboratories have suggested that the errors which should have been attached to GaK dates were very considerably higher than those quoted by the laboratory (Spriggs and Anderson 1993).

However, there is no widely agreed basis for attaching any particular correction factor to any particular date (apart from those GU dates covered by Dr Stenhouse's advice). Some laboratories seem often to have quoted mainly or only the 'counting error' attributable to the random nature of radioactive disintegration of carbon 14. They did not include some or all of the several other sources of possible error in their measurements. Some of the true errors associated with these early assays may be systematic. That is to say, all the dates produced by the laboratory may have been consistently too old (or too young) by decades. Other errors may have been random, but larger than allowed for by the laboratory in quoting the date.

It seems very likely indeed that the errors attached to the dates produced by many laboratories (but not all) before about 1982 (and in particular those produced in the 1970s) should be increased substantially if they are to be comparable with errors quoted today. In the tables more realistic errors have been indicated in the last but one column. However, because there is no widespread agreement on how to provide a more accurate error assessment, the errors originally quoted by the laboratories have been used for calibrating the dates.

THE ARRANGEMENT OF THE TABLES

The tables are arranged in half-millennium blocks. The dates are more likely to belong in the blocks to which they have been assigned than to any other block. However, dates near the beginning of a block are almost as likely to belong in the previous block. Dates near the end of a block are almost as likely to belong in the next block.

The columns are as follows:

Site name	The name of the site.
Submitter / bibref	The name of the submitter or a bibliographic reference. The reference may be to the site rather than to the individual date. PREPUB means that the site has not yet been published. References to PREPUB dates here should not be cited without the permission of the project director.
National Grid Ref.	A six-figure National Grid Reference.
Calibrated date (Intcal93)	The radiocarbon date, exactly as quoted by the laboratory, converted into a calendar date range using the programme CALIB 3.03 using the intercept method (Stuiver and Reimer 1993). The figures quoted are for a range within which there is a 95 per cent chance that the true date lies. The first number is at the oldest end of the range. The number or numbers inside the brackets are what the central radiocarbon date converts to. The last number is at the youngest end of the range.
Context, taphonomy and comments	A mixture of comments from the original submission and from subsequent consideration. As used here, *taphonomy* means 'how the datable material in the sample used for dating got to where it was found on the archaeological site'.
Material dated	A simple division into charcoal, shell, human bone etc.
Labcode	The unique code quoted by the laboratory. Each consists of a laboratory identifier and a date number. For instance, GU–1000 means date number 1000 from GU (Glasgow University, now housed at the Scottish Universities Research Reactor Centre).
Age BP	The raw radiocarbon 'date'. BP means before AD 1950.
Sort Age	Since marine shell dates have to have 400 radiocarbon 'years' (these have been approximated to the canonical 405 radiocarbon 'years') subtracted from them before calibration using Intcal 93, this column is adjusted accordingly.
Error	This is the error as originally quoted by the laboratory – and it is sometimes smaller than it would be were all possible sources of laboratory measurement error included in it.
Error (pref.)	More realistic values for the errors have been indicated. It must be emphasised that this is not a scientific exercise, but a rough guide. These expanded errors have not been used in calibrating the dates, and it is up to the reader to make allowance.

Note that increasing the estimate of random error does not change the central date produced by calibration. It is also still more likely that the true date lies close to the quoted central date (say, within a hundred-year block centred on the quoted date) than that it lies in any other hundred-year block. However, increasing the error estimate means that it is relatively more likely that the true date will fall in one of the nearby hundred-year blocks.

d13C   This is a measure of how much the living organism differentiated between two isotopes of carbon, and it allows an estimate of how differently the organism treated ordinary and radioactive carbon. It should be about −20 for human or animal bone, −25 to −26 for charcoal, −28 to 29 for peat and 0 for marine shell.

Since this chapter was written, articles by J. van der Plicht and F. G. McCormac ('A note on Calibration Curves' *Radiocarbon*, *37, 3* 963–4) and J. van der Plicht, E. Jansma and H. Kars (The 'Amsterdam Castle: A Case Study of Wiggle Matching and the Proper calibration Curve' *Radiocarbon*, *37, 3* 965–8) have made it seem more likely than before that the 1993 calibration curve used here is less accurate in some places than the 1986 calibration curve. Some calibration estimates may thus be less good than they might be by 18 radiocarbon years.

The matter of what calibration curve to use should be settled in 1997 at the radiocarbon conference in Groningen. Note, however, that the result will be to shift a few dates from one half millennium box to the next; but the relative position of the dates will not change and for all the dates quoted here, for practical purposes, the extra error will be swallowed up by other errors associated with the dates.

Site name	Submitter/ bibref	National Grid Ref.	Calibrated date (Intcal93)	Context, taphonomy and comments	Material dated	Labcode	Age BP	Sort Age	Error	Error (pref)	d13C
DATES BETWEEN ABOUT 7500 BC AND 7000 BC											
Druimvargie, Oban	Bonsall et al. 1995	NM857296	7533 (7423) 7067	Bone artefact from midden.	animal bone	OxA–4608	8340	8340	80	80	
Lussa 1, Jura	Mercer 1980	NR645874	7961 (7234, 7221, 7202, 7179, 7143, 7118, 7098) 6264	Charcoal from base of NE of 3 small rings of stones. See also SRR–159 (7963 ±200 BP).	wood	SRR–160	8194	8194	350	490	
DATES BETWEEN ABOUT 7000 BC AND 6500 BC											
Lussa 1, Jura	Mercer 1980	NR645874	7193 (6993, 6961, 6931, 6929, 6863, 6845, 6773) 6545	Mixed charcoal from two of three small stone rings. See also SRR–160 (8194 ±350 BP).	charcoal	SRR–159	7963	7963	200	280	
Druimvargie, Oban	Bonsall et al. 1995	NM857296	7032 (6645) 6478	Bone artefact from midden.	animal bone	OxA–4609	7890	7890	80	80	
Cnoc Sligeach, Oronsay	Jardine and Jardine 1983	NR358880	7193 (6601) 6253	Inner part of shells of Ostrea edulis, Patella spp., Arctica islandica and Littorina spp. within storm beach gravel deposit in CS73/11. See also Birm–463m (7210 ±130).	shell	Birm–463i	8220	7820	170	240	–0.1
Druimvargie, Oban	Bonsall and Smith 1989	NM857296	7001 (6598) 6474	Bone uniserial barbed point from midden in rock shelter.	bone	OxA–1948	7810	7810	90	90	

Site name	Submitter/ bibref	National Grid Ref.	Calibrated date (Intcal93)	Context, taphonomy and comments	Material dated	Labcode	Age BP	Sort Age	Error	Error (pref)	d13C
DATES BETWEEN ABOUT 7000 BC AND 6500 BC (continued)											
Newton, Islay	McCullagh 1991	NR341628	7000 (6596) 6425	Hazelnuts from F436, basal layer in F35, Area 2, a subrectangular depression full of microliths, hazelnuts and charcoal interpreted as a dwelling place or a flint working area.	hazelnut	GU–1954	7805	7805	90	90	–24.4
Ulva Cave	Bonsall et al. 1994	NM431384	7043 (6595, 6573, 6569) 6252	Black soil from the lowermost Holocene deposit, with marine shells in hollow in Pleistocene surface. The d13C value implies little contamination with carbon from marine shells and the calibration used here assumes no marine effect.	soil humic acid	GU–2704	7800	7800	160	160	–26.4
Newton, Islay	McCullagh 1989	NR343627	7256 (6546) 6070	F408, uppermost layer in F35, Area 2, a subrectangular depression full of microliths, hazelnuts and charcoal, interpreted as a dwelling place or a flint working area.	hazelnut	GU–1953	7765	7765	225	225	–25.3
DATES BETWEEN ABOUT 6500 BC AND 6000 BC											
Staosnaig, Colonsay	Mithen PREPUB	NR397934	6991 (6475) 6266	Bulked sample of charred hazelnut shell fragments lying immediately adjacent to each other within fill 17 of feature 24, a large stone-lined pit in an area of hearths and pits.	charred hazelnut		7720	7720	110	110	

DATES BETWEEN ABOUT 6500 BC AND 6000 BC (continued)

Site name	Submitter/ bibref	National Grid Ref.	Calibrated date (Intcal93)	Context, taphonomy and comments	Material dated	Labcode	Age BP	Sort Age	Error	Error (pref)	d13C
Ulva Cave	Bonsall et al. 1992	NM431384	6599 (6458) 6370	Shell from the basal layer of midden in area C.	shell	GU-2600	8060	7660	70	70	0.5
Coulererach, Islay	Mithen PREPUB	NR208652	6466 (6376) 6179	Charcoal from occupation horizon (trench 1) associated with dense narrow blade artefact scatter and sealed below 1.75 m of peat. Charcoal fragment removed from monolith in laboratory. Abrasion pattern on charcoal fragment suggested it derived from a hearth.	charcoal	OxA-4924	7530	7530	80	80	−26.4
North Carn, Jura	Mercer 1972	NR685939	6412 (6211) 6042	Charcoal from base of small sunken L-shaped setting, perhaps a hearth and seat.	charcoal	SRR-161	7414	7414	80	110	
Lon Mor, Oban	Bonsall et al. 1993	NM853283	6369 (6184) 6045	A charred hazelnut from a midden 30–40 cm below modern ground surface, in sandy loam soil, containing numerous lithic artefacts (including microliths) and common charcoal fragments.	charred hazelnut	AA-8793	7385	7385	60	60	−25.0
Bolsay Farm, Islay	Mithen PREPUB	NR225572	6381 (6102, 6099, 6045) 5771	Bulked sample of charcoal fragments from fill of feature cut 26 fill 16. This feature was sealed by in situ occupation deposits and colluvium.	charcoal	Q-3219	7250	7250	145	145	

Site name	Submitter/ bibref	National Grid Ref.	Calibrated date (Intcal93)	Context, taphonomy and comments	Material dated	Labcode	Age BP	Sort Age	Error	Error (pref)	d13C
DATES BETWEEN ABOUT 6500 BC AND 6000 BC (continued)											
Cnoc Coig, Oronsay	Mellars 1987	NR360885	6369 (6008) 5723	Shell from a midden; same shell as Birm–326Y (7290 ±120) and Birm–326Z (7240 ±200).	shell (inner)	Birm–326X	7610	7210	150	210	
DATES BETWEEN ABOUT 6000 BC AND 5500 BC											
Glean Mor, Islay	Mithen PREPUB	NR239577	6176 (5956) 5685	Charcoal fragment from occupation horizon immediately above and within iron pan in heavily podsolized soil, sealed 50 cm peat. Charcoal associated with a very dense microlithic assemblage. AMS. Same context as *Beta* 32237.	charcoal	*Beta* 32238	7100	7100	125	125	
Cnoc Coig, Oronsay	Mellars 1987	NR360885	5968 (5710) 5526	Shell from a midden; Same shell as Birm–326X (7610 ±150) and Birm–326Z (7240 ±200).	shell (middle)	Birm–326Y	7290	6890	120	170	
Cnoc Coig, Oronsay	Mellars 1987	NR360885	6043 (5679) 5340	Shell from a midden; same shell as Birm–326Y (7290 ±120) and Birm–326X (7610 ±150).	shell (outer)	Birm–326Z	7240	6840	200	280	
Cnoc Sligeach, Oronsay	Jardine and Jardine 1983	NR358880	5947 (5661, 5647, 5639) 5443	Middle part of shells of *Ostrea edulis*, *Patella* spp., *Arctica islandica* and *Littorina* spp. within storm beach gravel deposit in CS73/11. See also Birm–463i; (8220 ±170).	shell	Birm–463m	7210	6810	130	180	–1.2

Site name	Submitter/ bibref	National Grid Ref.	Calibrated date (Intcal93)	Context, taphonomy and comments	Material dated	Labcode	Age BP	Sort Age	Error	Error (pref)	d13C
DATES BETWEEN ABOUT 6000 BC AND 5500 BC (continued)											
Rockside, Islay	Mithen PREPUB	NR221638	5706 (5633) 5590	Charcoal from occupation horizon (context 2 trench 1). This is a very humic horizon containing an unabraded microlithic assemblage sealed by c.1.5 m of colluvium. AMS Context below that of Beta 37625 (3980 ±150 BP) and Beta 37626 (3420 ±70 BP).	charcoal	Beta–37624	6800	6800	40	40	
Seal Cottage, Oronsay	Jardine, W. G.	NR361885	5950 (5621) 5389	Same shell as two other Birm–326 dates: 6850 ± 120 and 6800 ± 200.	shell (inner)	Birm–326i	7180	6780	150	210	
MacArthur Cave, Oban	Bonsall and Smith 1989	NM859304	5693 (5583) 5441	Antler biserial barbed point from midden.	antler	OxA–1949	6700	6700	80	80	
DATES BETWEEN ABOUT 5500 BC AND 5000 BC											
Cnoc Sligeach, Oronsay	Jardine and Jardine 1983	NR358880	5674 (5437) 5081	Inner part of valve of *Arctica islandica* within occupation layer in CS73/11. See also Birm–464m (6840 ±160).	shell	Birm–464i	6910	6510	160	225	0.2
Seal Cottage, Oronsay	Jardine, W. G.	NR361885	5580 (5420, 5402, 5379, 5356, 5345) 5141	Shell from midden. Same shell as two other Birm–326 dates: 6800 ± 200 and 7180 ± 150.	shell (middle)	Birm–326m	6850	6450	120	170	
Cnoc Sligeach, Oronsay	Jardine and Jardine 1983	NR358880	5668 (5415, 5406, 5376, 5361, 5340) 4942	Middle part of valve of *Arctica islandica* within occupation layer in CS73/11. See also Birm–464i (6910 ±160).	shell	Birm–464m	6840	6440	190	265	0.2

Site name	Submitter/bibref	National Grid Ref.	Calibrated date (Intcal93)	Context, taphonomy and comments	Material dated	Labcode	Age BP	Sort Age	Error	Error (pref)	d13C
DATES BETWEEN ABOUT 5500 BC AND 5000 BC (continued)											
Seal Cottage, Oronsay	Jardine, W. G.	NR361885	5634 (5320) 4863	Shell from midden: Same shell as two other Birm–326 dates: 6850 ±120 and 7180 ±150.	shell (outer)	Birm–3260	6800	6400	200	280	
Caisteal nan Gillean, Oronsay	Mellars 1987	NR359879	5275 (5201, 5176, 5136) 4927	Charcoal from the base of midden layer 4, trench C.	charcoal	Q–3008	6190	6190	80	80	
Caisteal nan Gillean, Oronsay	Mellars 1987	NR359879	5250 (5051) 4836	Charcoal from the base of midden layer 4, trench C.	charcoal	Q–3007	6120	6120	80	80	
DATES BETWEEN ABOUT 5000 BC AND 4500 BC											
Caisteal nan Gillean, Oronsay	Mellars 1987	NR359879	5196 (4932) 4780	Charcoal from the top of midden layer 4, trench C.	charcoal	Q–3009	6035	6035	70	70	
Risga	Bonsal and Smith 1990, 360	NM610600	5198 (4905, 4872, 4865) 4711	Red deer antler mattock in shell midden.	antler	OxA–2023	6000	6000	90	90	
Cnoc Sligeach, Oronsay	Jardine and Jardine 1983	NR358880	5260 (4902, 4876, 4854) 4495	Middle part of shells of *Patella* spp., within storm beach gravel deposit in CS73/11. See also Birm–462i (5850 ±140).	shell	Birm–462m	6390	5990	160	225	–1.5
Risga	Bonsall and Smith 1992	NM610600	4907 (4773) 4571	Red deer antler artefact in shell midden.	antler	OxA–3737	5875	5875	65	65	

Site name	Submitter/ bibref	National Grid Ref.	Calibrated date (Intcal93)	Context, taphonomy and comments	Material dated	Labcode	Age BP	Sort Age	Error	Error (pref)	d13C
DATES BETWEEN ABOUT 5000 BC AND 4500 BC (continued)											
Priory Midden, Oronsay	Mellars 1987	NR346889	4896 (4770) 4604	Charcoal from shell midden layer 19 with red deer antler.	charcoal	Q-3001	5870	5870	50	110	
Kilpatrick, Arran	Barber, J. PREPUB	NR908266	4918 (4770) 4539	16/03/318 Charcoal from old ground surface under the primary barrow, thought to be of Neolithic date.	charcoal	GU-1561	5870	5870	75	75	-26.5
Priory Midden, Oronsay	Mellars 1987	NR346889	4800 (4714) 4540	Charcoal from shell midden layer 19 with red deer antler mattock.	charcoal	Q-3000	5825	5825	50	110	
Cnoc Sligeach, Oronsay	Mellars 1987	NR372890	5048 (4587) 4245	Bone from shell midden.	bone	GX1-904	5755	5755	180	250	
Ulva Cave	Bonsall and Smith 1992	NM431384	4780 (4581) 4457	Limpet scoop in upper part of midden in area C.	red deer antler	OxA-3738	5750	5750	70	70	-23.6
Priory Midden, Oronsay	Mellars 1987	NR346889	4712 (4539) 4458	Charcoal from shell midden layer 18.	charcoal	Q-3002	5717	5717	50	110	
Ulva Cave	Bonsall et al. 1992	NM431384	4717 (4518) 4360	Top layer of midden in area C.	shell	GU-2602	6090	5690	70	70	0.6
Cnoc Coig, Oronsay	Mellars 1987	NR360885	4685 (4502) 4361	Charcoal from below shell midden.	charcoal	Q-3006	5675	5675	60	60	
DATES BETWEEN ABOUT 4500 BC AND 4000 BC											
Cnoc Coig, Oronsay	Mellars 1987	NR360885	4672 (4466) 4353	Charcoal from below shell midden.	charcoal	Q-3005	5650	5650	60	60	

DATES BETWEEN ABOUT 4500 BC AND 4000 BC (continued)

Site name	Submitter/ bibref	National Grid Ref.	Calibrated date (Intcal93)	Context, taphonomy and comments	Material dated	Labcode	Age BP	Sort Age	Error	Error (pref)	d13C
Cnoc Coig, Oronsay	Mellars 1987	NR360885	4690 (4465) 4340	Charcoal from trench E unit 8, lower shell midden with red deer antler mattock.	charcoal	Q-1353	5645	5645	80	110	
Cnoc Sligeach, Oronsay	Jardine and Jardine 1983	NR358880	4788 (4457) 4090	Inner part of valve of *Pecten maximus* within occupation layer in CS73/11. See also Birm–465m (5900 ±150). Associated with a barbed point.	shell	Birm–465i	6010	5610	150	210	–1.3
Cnoc Coig, Oronsay	Mellars 1987	NR360885	4711 (4356) 4008	Charcoal from trench E unit 6, lower shell midden with red deer antler mattock.	charcoal	Q-1354	5535	5535	140	195	
Priory Midden, Oronsay	Mellars 1987	NR346889	4458 (4348) 4252	Charcoal from shell midden layer 9/10.	charcoal	Q-3003	5510	5510	50	110	
Cnoc Sligeach, Oronsay	Jardine and Jardine 1983	NR358880	4687 (4345) 3985	Valve of *Pecten maximus* within occupation layer in CS73/11. See also Birm–465i (6010 ±150). Associated with a barbed point.	shell	Birm–465m	5900	5500	150	210	–2.2
Machrie Moor, Arran	Haggarty 1991	NR912324	4465 (4345) 4262	Mixed charcoal from a pit with plain Neolithic pottery, a flint knife and other flints. This date may be 'too old'. See GU–2321 (4820 ± 50 BP) from a nearby pit with very similar potsherds.	charcoal	GU–2320	5500	5500	70	70	–25.6

DATES BETWEEN ABOUT 4500 BC AND 4000 BC (continued)

Site name	Submitter/ bibref	National Grid Ref.	Calibrated date (Intcal93)	Context, taphonomy and comments	Material dated	Labcode	Age BP	Sort Age	Error	Error (pref)	d13C
Cnoc Coig, Oronsay	Mellars 1987	NR360885	4445 (4344) 4257	Charcoal from trench E, unit 2, upper shell midden with red deer antler mattock.	charcoal	Q–1351	5495	5495	75	110	
Caisteal nan Gillean, Oronsay	Jardine and Jardine 1983	NR359879	4463 (4342) 4163	Patella shells in midden. See also SRR1458a (4750 ± 180 BP).	shell	SRR–1458b	5890	5490	70	110	0.9
Caisteal nan Gillean, Oronsay	Mellars 1987	NR359879	4453 (4341) 4238	Charcoal from midden layer 3, trench C.	charcoal	Q–3010	5485	5485	50	50	
Priory Midden, Oronsay	Mellars 1987	NR346889	4448 (4337) 4230	Charcoal from shell midden layer 7.	charcoal	Q–3004	5470	5470	50	110	
Caisteal nan Gillean 2, Oronsay	Mellars 1987	NR359879	4454 (4334) 4151	Charcoal from lower midden.	charcoal	Q–1355	5460	5460	65	110	
Caisteal nan Gillean, Oronsay	Mellars 1987	NR359879	4361 (4331) 4162	Charcoal from midden layer 3, trench C.	charcoal	Q–3011	5450	5450	50	50	
Caisteal nan Gillean 2, Oronsay	Mellars 1987	NR359879	4546 (4331) 3973	Charcoal from basal midden.	charcoal	Birm–347	5450	5450	140	195	

Site name	Submitter/ bibref	National Grid Ref.	Calibrated date (Intcal93)	Context, taphonomy and comments	Material dated	Labcode	Age BP	Sort Age	Error	Error (pref)	Error d13C
DATES BETWEEN ABOUT 4500 BC AND 4000 BC (continued)											
Cnoc Sligeach, Oronsay	Jardine and Jardine 1983	NR358880	4546 (4331) 3973	Middle part of shells of *Patella* spp., within storm beach gravel deposit in CS73/11. See also Birm–462m (6390 ± 160).	shell	Birm–462i	5850	5450	140	195	–1.5
Caisteal nan Gillean 2, Oronsay	Mellars 1987	NR359879	4946 (4331) 3639	Shell from basal midden.	shell	Birm–348	5850	5450	310	435	
Cnoc Coig, Oronsay	Mellars 1987	NR360885	4520 (4323, 4281, 4262) 3973	Charcoal from trench E unit 3, upper shell midden with red deer antler mattock.	charcoal	Q–1352	5430	5430	130	180	
Cnoc Sligeach, Oronsay	Mellars 1987	NR369888	4548 (4317, 4291, 4256) 4009	Charcoal from shell midden trench B layer 7.	charcoal	BM–670	5416	5416	159	220	
Caisteal nan Gillean 2, Oronsay	Mellars 1987	NR359879	4456 (4220, 4195, 4151, 4111, 4107) 3799	Shell from lower shell midden.	shell	Birm–348B	5720	5320	140	195	
DATES BETWEEN ABOUT 4000 BC AND 3500 BC											
Cardingmill Bay, Oban	Bonsall and Smith 1992	NM847293	4229 (3981) 3791	Antler artefact from lower part (xv) of shell midden.	antler	Ox–A3740	5190	5190	85	85	

Site name	Submitter/ bibref	National Grid Ref.	Calibrated date (Intcal93)	Context, taphonomy and comments	Material dated	Labcode	Age BP	Sort Age	Error	Error (pref)	d13C
DATES BETWEEN ABOUT 4000 BC AND 3500 BC (continued)											
Caisteal nan Gillean 2, Oronsay	Mellars 1987	NR359879	4331 (3973) 3662	Shell from lower shell midden.	shell	Birm-348C	5570	5170	140	195	
Caisteal nan Gillean 2, Oronsay	Mellars 1987	NR359879	4354 (3965) 3535	Charcoal from trench B, layer 3, upper shell midden.	charcoal	Birm-346	5150	5150	380	530	
Monamore, Arran	MacKie 1964	NS017288	4222 (3950) 3662	Hearth in forecourt under blocking of chambered cairn.	charcoal	Q-675	5110	5110	110	155	
Cardingmill Bay, Oban	Connock et al. 1993	NM847293	3970 (3930, 3875, 3808) 3713	Charcoal from upper layer of early shell midden in fissure in cliff face.	charcoal	GU-2796	5060	5060	50	50	−25.6
Glenbatrick Waterhole, Jura	Mercer 1974	NR518798	4338 (3901, 3882, 3802) 3361	Charcoal from trough.	charcoal	GX-2564	5045	5045	215	300	
Cardingmill Bay, Oban	Connock et al. 1993	NM847293	3962 (3898, 3885, 3800) 3704	Shell from upper layer of early shell midden in fissure in cliff face.	shell	GU-2899	5440	5040	50	50	0.56
Temple Wood, Kilmartin	Scott, J. G. 1989	NR826978	4313 (3794) 3371	Charcoal from stone hole 8 of dismantled circle to north of main circle, 50 cm below ground surface; which may be heartwood from earlier timber circle? The stone hole was almost certainly back-filled in ancient times and since then apparently not been disturbed.	charcoal	GU-1296	5025	5025	190	190	−25

DATES BETWEEN ABOUT 4000 BC AND 3500 BC (continued)

Site name	Submitter/ bibref	National Grid Ref.	Calibrated date (Intcal93)	Context, taphonomy and comments	Material dated	Labcode	Age BP	Sort Age	Error	Error (pref)	d13C
Port Charlotte, Islay	Harrington and Pierpoint 1980	NR248576	3986 (3792) 3641 mean of 3 dates is 3779 (3663) 3542	Carbonised hazelnut shells and charcoal from occupation layer, with animal bones and flints under chambered cairn. Same level as HAR-2836 (4660 ± 90 BP) and HAR-3486 (4940 ± 70 BP). There is no significant difference between the 3 dates, whose mean is 4890 ± 50.	charred hazelnut and charcoal	HAR-3487	5020	5020	90	90	−26.3
Cardingmill Bay, Oban	Connock et al. 1993	NM 84742935	3958 (3787) 3661	Shell from lower layer of early shell midden in fissure in cliff face.	shell	GU-2898	5410	5010	60	60	0.95
Ulva Cave	Bonsall 1994	NR346889	3951 (3777) 3649	Charcoal from lower infill of pit containing charcoal, charred cereal grains and marine shells.	charcoal	GU-2707	4990	4990	60	60	−25.4
Cardingmill Bay, Oban	Connock et al. 1993	NM847293	3939 (3772) 3653	Charcoal from lower layer of shell midden in fissure in cliff face.	charcoal	GU-2797	4980	4980	50	50	−25.8
Newton, Islay	McCullagh 1989	NR341628	3941 (3759 3736, 3725) 3642	Charcoal from Pit F3, a small pit with charcoal Neolithic pottery, cut by possible fence lines, which were in turn earlier than pit F4 dated by GU-1951 (4880 ± 60 BP).	charcoal	GU-1952	4965	4965	60	60	−27.4

DATES BETWEEN ABOUT 4000 BC AND 3500 BC (continued)

Site name	Submitter/ bibref	National Grid Ref.	Calibrated date (Intcal93)	Context, taphonomy and comments	Material dated	Labcode	Age BP	Sort Age	Error	Error (pref)	d13C
Port Charlotte, Islay	Harrington and Pierpoint	NR248576	3939 (3705) 3547 mean of 3 dates is 3779 (3663) 3542	Carbonised hazelnut shells and charcoal from occupation layer with animal bones and flints under chambered cairn. Same level as HAR–2836 (4660 ± 90 BP) and HAR–3487 (5020 ± 90 BP). There is no significant difference between the 3 dates, whose mean is 4890 ± 50 BP.	charred hazelnut and charcoal	HAR–3486	4940	4940	70		–26.4
Newton, Islay	McCullagh 1991	NR341628	3783 (3656) 3530	Context 4 in Pit F4, a large pit, possibly the socket for a single massive post, cutting possible fence lines, which were in turn later than pit F3 dated by GU–1952 (4965 ± 60 BP).	charcoal	GU–1951	4880	4880	60		–26.3
Machrie Moor, Arran	Haggarty 1991	NR912324	3700 (3636) 3386	Mixed charcoal from pits with bits of six plain Neolithic pots. See also GU–2320 (5500 ± 70 BP) from which came very similar potsherds.	charcoal	GU–2321	4820	4820	50	50	–25.5
Machrie Moor, Arran	Haggarty 1991	NR912324	3709 (3622, 3576, 3535) 3353	Oak charcoal in pit cutting early ditch terminal: another such pit contained plain Neolithic pottery.	charcoal	GU–2315	4770	4770	90	90	–26.4
Cardingmill Bay, Oban	Bonsall and Smith 1992	NM847293	3691 (3621, 3580, 3533) 3367	Bone artefact from upper part (XIV) of shell midden.	bone	OxA–3739	4765	4765	65	65	

Site name	Submitter/ bibref	National Grid Ref.	Calibrated date (Intcal93)	Context, taphonomy and comments	Material dated	Labcode	Age BP	Sort Age	Error	Error (pref)	d13C
DATES BETWEEN ABOUT 4000 BC AND 3500 BC (continued)											
Caisteal nan Gillean, Oronsay	Jardine and Jardine 1983	NR359879	3950 (3616, 3591, 3525) 2928	Wood charcoal in midden. See also SRR–1458b (5890 ± 70 BP).	charcoal	SRR–1458a	4750	4750	180		–26
Ardnadam, Cowal	Rennie 1984	NS163791	3699 (3613, 3600, 3519) 3342	Charcoal from the lowest hearth of a small sub-rectangular structure, No.5, middle to late in the sequence of a small settlement, with Neolithic pottery close by.	charcoal	GU–1549	4740	4740	90		
Dunloskin Wood, Cowal	Rennie forthcoming	NS166785	3794 (3510, 3396, 3388) 3037	Charcoal from the hearth of either a 9.5 m round house, or possibly an oval turf house, on a platform. See also GU–2064 (4570 ± 150 BP) from same context.	charcoal	GU–2063	4725	4725	150	150	
Port Charlotte, Islay	Harrington and Pierpoint 1990	NR248576	3645 (3506, 3408, 3385) 3345 mean of two dates is 3511 (3365) 3127	From chamber of chambered cairn according to a letter of 13 Oct 1980. Probably from charcoal. See also HAR–2084. There is no significant difference between the two dates, whose mean is 4625 ± 50 BP.	charcoal	HAR–2406	4710	4710	70	70	
DATES BETWEEN ABOUT 3500 BC AND 3000 BC											
Cnoc Sligeach, Oronsay	Jardine and Jardine 1983	NR358880	3623 (3496, 3461, 3377) 3345	Wood charcoal within occupation layer in CS73/11. See also Birm–464i (6910 ± 160).	charcoal	SRR–1457	4670	4670	50	110	–24.1

DATES BETWEEN ABOUT 3500 BC AND 3000 BC (continued)

Site name	Submitter/ bibref	National Grid Ref.	Calibrated date (Intcal93)	Context, taphonomy and comments	Material dated	Labcode	Age BP	Sort Age	Error	Error (pref)	d13C
Port Charlotte, Islay	Harrington and Pierpoint	NR248576	3642 (3493, 3467, 3374) 3100 mean of 3 dates is 3779 (3663) 3542	Carbonised hazelnut shells and charcoal from occupation layer, with animal bones and flints under chambered cairn. Same level as HAR-3487 (5020 ± 90 BP) and HAR-3486 (4940 ± 70 BP). There is no significant difference between the 3 dates, whose mean is 4890 ± 50 BP.	charcoal and nuts	HAR-2836	4660	4660	90	90	-25.2
Achnasavil, Kintyre	Carter and Tipping 1992; Siggins and Carter 1993	NR791386	3614 (3370) 3147	Charcoal layer sealed by colluvium; part of a scatter of pits and postholes dug into a mid-Flandrian river terrace.	charcoal	GU-3072	4640	4640	50	50	-27.4
Lussa River, Jura	Mercer 1971	NR642868	3692 (3363) 2917	Charcoal among occupation material at the fringe of a hardpan rich in charred material. Charred hazelnuts and acorns were found above this hardpan. See also (BM-555, 4200 ± 100 BP).	charcoal	BM-556	4620	4620	140	195	
Cnoc Sligeach Oronsay	Mellars 1987	NR372890	3895 (3362) 2708	Shell from shell midden.	shell	GX-1903	5015	4615	210	295	
Dunloskin Wood, Cowal	Rennie forthcoming	NS166785	3650 (3346) 2887	Charcoal from the hearth of either a 9.5 m round house or possibly an oval turf house, on a platform. See also GU-2063 (4725 ± 150 BP) from same context.	charcoal	GU-2064	4570	4570	150	150	

Site name	Submitter/ bibref	National Grid Ref.	Calibrated date (Intcal93)	Context, taphonomy and comments	Material dated	Labcode	Age BP	Sort Age	Error	Error (pref)	d13C
DATES BETWEEN ABOUT 3500 BC AND 3000 BC (continued)											
Port Charlotte, Islay	Harrington and Pierpoint	NR248576	3499 (3336) 2929 mean of two dates is 3511 (3365) 3127	Charcoal from a fire on the old ground surface, lit against a large side stone in the second part of the main chamber of the chambered cairn. See also HAR–2406; the mean of these two dates from the chamber is 4625 ± 50 BP.	charcoal	HAR–2084	4540	4540	70	70	–26.0
Machrie Moor, Arran	Haggarty 1991	NR912324	3347 (3253, 3248, 3098) 2923 (weighted mean of this and GU–2325 is c.3330 (3080, 3064, 3041) 2920)	Mixed charcoal from postholes of main timber ring. See also GU–325 (3980 ±180 BP from pure oak) with which this date is compatible. Grooved Ware was found in a posthole of this ring.	charcoal	GU–2316	4470	4470	50	50	–26.0
DATES BETWEEN ABOUT 3000 BC AND 2500 BC											
Auchategan, Glendaruel	Marshall, D. N. 1978	NS002843	3254 (2884) 2500	Charcoal from a hearth of Period 2 of Neolithic occupation in a house or settlement of small houses of indeterminate plan.	charcoal	I–4705	4250	4250	110	110	
Glenbatrick Waterhole, Jura	Mercer 1974	NR518798	3500 (2878) 2144	Charcoal from a supposed cooking pit.	charcoal	GX–2563	4225	4225	230	230	

DATES BETWEEN ABOUT 3000 BC AND 2500 BC (continued)

Site name	Submitter/ bibref	National Grid Ref.	Calibrated date (Intcal93)	Context, taphonomy and comments	Material dated	Labcode	Age BP	Sort Age	Error	Error (pref)	d13C
Lussa River, Jura	Mercer 1971	NR642868	3029 (2873, 2798, 2780, 2711, 2709) 2485	Charcoal from amongst occupation material in a hardpan rich in charred material. Charred hazelnuts and acorns were found above this hardpan. See also BM-556 (4620 ±140 BP).	charcoal	BM-555	4200	4200	100	100	
Monamore, Arran	MacKie 1964	NS017288	3033 (2871, 2801, 2775, 2715, 2706) 2466	Top of thick layer of deposits in forecourt of chambered cairn.	charcoal	Q-676	4190	4190	110	155	
Machrie Moor, Arran	Barber, J. PREPUB	NR912323	2886 (2586) 2362	Hazel and oak charcoal from site 1 MM86 posthole F1326 of phase 2, a post hole of the outer ring.	charcoal	GU-2324	4080	4080	90	90	-25.8
Townhead, Rothesay, Bute		NS083643	3496 (2582) 1748	Charcoal from a hearth associated with plain Neolithic pottery. Pottery specialists suggest that this date is several centuries too late. See note on GaK dates.	charcoal	GaK-1714	4070	4070	100	300	

DATES BETWEEN ABOUT 2500 BC AND 2000 BC

Site name	Submitter/ bibref	National Grid Ref.	Calibrated date (Intcal93)	Context, taphonomy and comments	Material dated	Labcode	Age BP	Sort Age	Error	Error (pref)	d13C
Rockside, Islay	Mithen PREPUB	NR221638	2890 (2468) 2034	Charcoal from colluvium deposit (context 9, trench 1) containing high density of microlithic artefacts. Context above that of *Beta* 37624 (6800 ±40 BP) and *Beta* 37626 (3420 ±70 BP).	charcoal	*Beta-* 37625	3980	3980	150	150	-25

DATES BETWEEN ABOUT 2500 BC AND 2000 BC (continued)

Site name	Submitter/ bibref	National Grid Ref.	Calibrated date (Intcal93)	Context, taphonomy and comments	Material dated	Labcode	Age BP	Sort Age	Error	Error (pref)	d13C
Machrie Moor, Arran	Haggarty 1991	NR912324	2917 (2468) 1953 (weighted mean of this and GU-2325 is c.3330 (3080, 3064, 3041) 2920)	Pure oak from a posthole of the main timber ring. See also GU-2316 (4470 ± 50 BP) from mixed charcoal, with which this date is compatible.	charcoal	GU-2325	3980	3980 weighted mean of this and GU-2316 is 4435 ±47	180	180	–26.1
Machrie North, Arran	Barber, J. PREPUB		2852 (2451, 2429, 2403) 2036	Charcoal (and cremated bone) with Beaker burial in cist.	charcoal	GU-1565	3905	3905	110	110	–25
Sorisdale, Coll	Ritchie and Crawford 1978	NM272638	2468 (2394, 2383, 2342) 2197	Collagen from femora of semi-articulated skeleton buried with all-over-corded Beaker in a pit.	human bone	BM-1413	3884	3884	46	65	
Machrie North, Arran	Barber, J. PREPUB	NR900348	2467 (2328) 2144	The sample of hazel and alder came from F30, the lower fill of pit F19 with abundant pottery and carbonised plant remains characteristic of crop cleaning or processing waste, which indicates that this deposit consists of domestic refuse and that the charcoal is unlikely to have been of significant age before deposition. The pit lay below the leached horizon of the overall podsolic profile and it cut an earlier hillwash deposit, which itself sealed a sub rectangular structure.	charcoal	GU-3527	3870	3870	50	50	–28.1

DATES BETWEEN ABOUT 2500 BC AND 2000 BC (continued)

Site name	Submitter/ bibref	National Grid Ref.	Calibrated date (Intcal93)	Context, taphonomy and comments	Material dated	Labcode	Age BP	Sort Age	Error	Error (pref)	d13C
Machrie North, Arran	Lehane 1990	NR899343 or 904346 acc. GU database	2476 (2315) 2057	Burnt mound.	charcoal	GU–1567	3860	3860	65	65	–25
Achnasavil, Kintyre	Carter and Tipping 1992; Siggins and Carter 1993	NR791386	2466 (2289) 2057	Charcoal in the lower fill of pit among a scatter of pits and postholes dug into a mid-Flandrian river terrace.	charcoal	GU–3070	3850	3850	60	60	–27.2
Achnasavil, Kintyre	Carter and Tipping 1992; Siggins and Carter 1993	NR791386	2464 (2285) 2048	Charcoal in the lower fill of pit among a scatter of pits and postholes dug into a mid-Flandrian river terrace.	charcoal	GU–3071	3840	3840	60	60	–26.7
Machrie Moor, Arran	Haggarty 1991	NR912324	2577 (2285) 1952 mean of 3 dates is 2291 (2194, 2154, 2148) 2045 in next period	Stake from field fences succeeding timber circles and preceding stone circles. See also GU–2319 (3770 ± 50 BP) and GU–2317 (3780 ± 50 NP).	charcoal	GU–2322	3840	3840	110	110	–26.1
Kilpatrick, Arran	Barber, J. PREPUB		2461 (2283) 2049	Layer of brown earth underlying cairn and overlying earlier unexcavated monument.	charcoal	GU–1177	3835	3835	55	110	–25

DATES BETWEEN ABOUT 2500 BC AND 2000 BC (continued)

Site name	Submitter / bibref	National Grid Ref.	Calibrated date (Intcal93)	Context, taphonomy and comments	Material dated	Labcode	Age BP	Sort Age	Error	Error (pref)	d13C
Machrie North, Arran	Barber, J. PREPUB	NR899343	2463 (2279, 2217, 2209) 2039	Burnt mound; mound 8, see also GU–1569 (380 ± 65 BP).	charcoal	GU–1566	3825	3825	65	65	–22.5
Kilpatrick, Arran	Barber, J. PREPUB	NR908266	2455 (2197) 1984	Charcoal from old ground surface under a secondary cairn containing two cists.	charcoal	GU–1562	3790	3790	65	65	–26.2
Distillery Cave, Oban	Saville and Hallen 1994	NM859301	2451 (2193, 2155, 2148) 1984	Antler spatula.	antler	OxA–4509	3780	3780	60	60	–23.9
Machrie Moor, Arran	Haggarty 1991	NR912324	2394 (2193, 2155, 2148) 2034 mean of 3 dates is 2291 (2194, 2154, 2148) 2045 in next period	Possible hearth associated with field fences succeeding timber circles and preceding stone circles. See also GU–2319 (3770 ± 50 BP) and GU–2322 (3940 ± 50 BP).	charcoal	GU–2317	3780 mean of 3 dates is 3781 ± 34	3780	50	50	–25.7
Machrie Moor, Arran	Haggarty 1991	NR912324	2330 (2190, 2160, 2145) 1988 mean of 3 dates is 2291 (2194, 2154, 2148) 2045 in next period	Stake from irregular pit associated with fence lines succeeding timber circles and preceding stone circles. See also GU–2317 (3780 ± 50 BP) and GU–2322 (3840 ± 50 BP).	charcoal	GU–2319	3770	3370	50	50	–26.3

Site name	Submitter/bibref	National Grid Ref.	Calibrated date (Intcal93)	Context, taphonomy and comments	Material dated	Labcode	Age BP	Sort Age	Error	Error (pref)	d13C
DATES BETWEEN ABOUT 2500 BC AND 2000 BC (continued)											
Borichill Mhor, Islay	Barber, J. 1990	NR307652	2272 (2166, 2087, 2040) 1913	Charcoal from body of a horse-shoe shaped burnt mound.	charcoal	GU–1465	3695	3695	60	110	–25.5
Ardnave, Islay	Ritchie and Welfare 1983	NR289745	2273 (2090, 2037) 1889	Mostly alder from floor of house in period 2.	charcoal	GU–1440	3687	3687	60	110	–24.4
Ardnave, Islay	Ritchie and Welfare 1983	NR289745	2274 (2035) 1884	Mostly oak from hearth sealed by wall of period 2 house.	charcoal	GU–1439	3680	3680	65	110	–25.4
Ardnave, Islay	Ritchie and Welfare 1983	NR289745	2192 (2022, 2000, 1983) 1826	Mostly alder from floor level within main wall.	charcoal	GU–1442	3655	3655	60	110	–25.3
DATES BETWEEN ABOUT 2000 BC AND 1500 BC											
Ardnave, Islay	Ritchie and Welfare 1983	NR289745	2194 (1944) 1739	Hazel charcoal on old ground surface immediately below wall of house of period 2.	charcoal	GU–1371	3610	3610	85	115	–24.6
Upper Largie, Kilmartin	Mercer and Rideout 1987	NR832993	2137 (1932) 1743	Charcoal from the fill and packing soil of a cist and cist pit on a gravel terrace.	charcoal	GU–1978	3595	3595	70	70	–26.1
Kilellan, Islay	Ritchie, A. forthcoming	NR286721	2130 (1926) 1748	Birch, alder, willow and *pomoideae* from a domestic refuse midden deposit, undisturbed and sealed by disturbed midden.	charcoal	GU–3517	3590	3590	60	60	–26.5

DATES BETWEEN ABOUT 2000 BC AND 1500 BC (continued)

Site name	Submitter/ bibref	National Grid Ref.	Calibrated date (Intcal93)	Context, taphonomy and comments	Material dated	Labcode	Age BP	Sort Age	Error	Error (pref)	d13C
North Carn, Jura	Mercer 1972	NR685939	2131 (1917) 1743	Charcoal from the Main Area above gravels burying the Mesolithic occupation traces (see SRR-161, 7414 ±80 BP) and below peat.	charcoal	SRR-162	3584	3584	65	110	-25.7
Machrie Moor, Arran	Barber, J. PREPUB		2036 (1911) 1752	Alder, hazel, pomoideae and oak charcoal from bulk sieving of Site XI, layer MM85, F413 with ard marks in it.	charcoal	GU-2318	3580	3580	50	50	
Bolsay Farm, Islay	Mithen PREPUB	NR225572	2092 (1877, 1834, 1822, 1795, 1787) 1643	Charcoal fragments from context 3 recovered from 1993 test pit when sampling site. Associated with a very high density of microliths.	charcoal	Beta-3535?	3525	3525	80	80	
Kentraw, Islay	Ritchie 1987	NR267629	1946 (1872, 1840, 1811, 1808, 1781) 1685	Bone from one of 4–6 inhumations in a clay-luted cist with a food vessel, a flint and a decorated miniature pot.	human bone	GU-2189	3510	3510	50	50	-20.6
Tormore, Arran	Barber, J. PREPUB		1942 (1854, 1849, 1768) 1642	From bank of earliest hut with AOC Beaker sherds.	charcoal	GU-1176	3485	3485	60	110	-25
Ardnave, Islay	Ritchie and Welfare 1983	NR289745	2132 (1758) 1513	Mostly alder from hearth within main wall.	charcoal	GU-1441	3480	3480	120	170	-24.6
Loch Nell, Lorn	Sheridan, A. National Museums of Scotland		1937 (1737, 1714, 1701) 1517	A wooden ox yoke found in a bog.	wood	OxA-3541	3430	3430	85	85	

DATES BETWEEN ABOUT 2000 BC AND 1500 BC (continued)

Site name	Submitter/ bibref	National Grid Ref.	Calibrated date (Intcal93)	Context, taphonomy and comments	Material dated	Labcode	Age BP	Sort Age	Error	Error (pref)	d13C
Ardnave, Islay	Ritchie and Welfare 1983	NR289745	1971 (1735, 1718, 1693) 1466	Mostly alder and birch from an old ground surface near the house.	charcoal	GU–1444	3425	3425	100	140	–25.3
Rockside, Islay	Mithen PREPUB	NR221638	1915 (1734, 1721, 1689) 1517	Charcoal from stabilised horizon of soil formation containing micro-lithic assemblage (context 8 trench I) AMS date. Context below Beta–37625 (3980 ±150) and above Beta–37624 (6800 ±40 BP).	charcoal	Beta–37626	3420	3420	80	80	
Machrie North, Arran	Lehane 1990	NR917336	1975 (1685) 1426	Burnt mound.	charcoal	GU–1568	3405	3405	115	115	–25
Glean Mor, Islay	Mithen PREPUB	NR239577	1896 (1680) 1449	Charcoal fragment from occupation horizon immediately above and within iron pan in heavily podsolized soil, sealed by c. 50 cm of peat. Charcoal associated with a very dense microlithic assemblage. AMS. Same context as Beta–32238 (7100 ±125).	charcoal	Beta–32237	3390	3390	90	90	
Balloch Hill, Kintyre	Peltenburg 1982	NR677176	1870 (1671, 1664, 1636) 1460	Charcoal from a cremation under a small mound, with two bucket urns, decorated miniature vessel, charred pine or spruce wooden dish, flints and rough pendant.	charcoal	HAR–1902	3360	3360	70	70	

DATES BETWEEN ABOUT 2000 BC AND 1500 BC (continued)

Site name	Submitter/ bibref	National Grid Ref.	Calibrated date (Intcal93)	Context, taphonomy and comments	Material dated	Labcode	Age BP	Sort Age	Error	Error (pref)	d13C
Traigh Bhan, Islay	Ritchie and Stevenson 1982	NR215700	1876 (1613) 1409	Bones of a disturbed inhumation in cist 2 (of 3), which also contained a burial with a food vessel (see GU-1379 (3005 ±105 BP).	human bone	GU-1378	3330	3330	95	130	-21.8
Ardnave, Islay	Ritchie and Welfare 1983	NR289745	1856 (1609, 1551, 1548) 1421	Mainly cattle bone from upper floor levels of period 2 house.	animal bone	GU-1274	3325	3325	80	110	-20
Achnacree, Black Crofts, Connel	Ritchie, A. et al. 1974	NM923329	1731 (1596, 1569, 1529) 1448	An organic layer of soils immediately under a field wall.	soil	SRR-219	3309	3309	50	110	
Acharn, Morvern	Ritchie, A. et al. 1975	NM703507	1676 (1519) 1415	Charcoal with a cremation with small bone pin-head or bead in a pit near Cairn 1.	charcoal	SRR-594	3264	3264	55	110	-27.3
Ardnave, Islay	Ritchie and Welfare 1983	NR289745	1749 (1511) 1212	Charcoal from a hearth beside a secondary occupation level sealed by a sand flow.	charcoal	GU-1272	3230	3230	120	170	-25
Temple Wood, Kilmartin	Scott, J. G. 1989	NR826978	1739 (1509, 1472, 1468) 1230	The oak charcoal was sealed below apparently infilled brown soil forming part of the cairn material overlying pit cremation E within stone circle.	charcoal	GU-1300	3225	3225	105	145	-25
Tormore, Arran	Barber, J. PREPUB		1679 (1509, 1472, 1468) 1313	Below earliest habitation on site.	charcoal	GU-1175	3225	3225	80	112	-25

DATES BETWEEN ABOUT 1500 BC AND 1000 BC

Site name	Submitter/ bibref	National Grid Ref.	Calibrated date (Intcal93)	Context, taphonomy and comments	Material dated	Labcode	Age BP	Sort Age	Error	Error (pref)	d13C
Cul a'Bhaile, Jura	Stevenson, J. B. 1984	NR549726	1676 (1498, 1482, 1455) 1307	Alder charcoal from the internal slot of the period 2 round house; probably residual and too early by 200 years.	charcoal	GU–1384	3214	3214	80	110	26.5
Traigh Bhan, Islay	Ritchie and Stevenson 1982	NR215700	1743 (1494, 1486, 1450) 1138	Mixed bones of two individuals in cist 2 (of 3).	human bone	GU–1380	3210	3210	120	170	–22.4
Dun Mor Vaul, Tiree	MacKie 1974	NM042492	1610 (1412) 1136	Primary floor in gallery of phase 2b.		GaK–1096	3145	3145	90	270	
Kilpatrick, Arran	Barber, J. PREPUB		1673 (1389, 1334, 1327) 938	Charcoal from the post holes of the structure on an unenclosed house platform.	charcoal	GU–1623	3095	3095	135	135	–25
Temple Wood, Kilmartin	Scott, J. G. 1989	NR826978	1515 (1384, 1340, 1323) 1117	Alder charcoal including piece of diameter c. 0.2 m from stakehole to E of cremation deposit of burial E.	charcoal	GU–1529	3085	3085	80	80	–24.2
Temple Wood, Kilmartin	Scott, J. G. 1989	NR826978	1519 (1300, 1276, 1269) 938	Oak charcoal with a little hazel on old ground surface (gravel subsoil with clay patches) beneath 20 cm cobble spread within nw quadrant of southern stone circle. (Quoted as 3055 ±110 d13C –25 in publication).	charcoal	GU–1527	3045	3045	110	110	–25.6
Temple Wood, Kilmartin	Scott, J. G. 1989	NR826978	1416 (1294, 1284, 1268) 1119	Oak charcoal sealed beneath a stone slab forming part of the revetment surrounding the circular stone setting round cist D in the centre of the stone circle.	charcoal	GU–1297	3040	3040	55	110	–25

DATES BETWEEN ABOUT 1500 BC AND 1000 BC (continued)

Site name	Submitter/ bibref	National Grid Ref.	Calibrated date (Intcal93)	Context, taphonomy and comments	Material dated	Labcode	Age BP	Sort Age	Error	Error (pref)	d13C
Achnacree, Lorn	Barrett et al. 1976	NM972352	1430 (1259, 1232, 1227) 993	Basal peat overlying cultivated soils with field walls. Dyke C complex, site 1. See also GU–1009A (2520 ± 55 BP).	peat	GU–1009B	3010	3010	85	110	–29.1
Claggan, Morvern	Ritchie et al. 1982	NM697493	1388 (1259, 1233, 1226) 1117	Charcoal from a pit dug into old ground surface and covered with two stone slabs, in kerb cairn 3.	charcoal	SRR–285	3008	3008	40	110	–26.5
Traigh Bhan, Islay	Ritchie and Stevenson 1982	NR215700	1501 (1258, 1235, 1224) 918	Bone from the later of two inhumations in cist 1 (of 3), with a food vessel; the earlier body is dated by GU–1378 (3330 ± 90 BP).	human bone	GU–1379	3005	3005	105	145	–23.3
Upper Largie, Kilmartin	Mercer and Rideout 1987	NR833993	1406 (1256, 1238, 1220) 1009	Charcoal from the fill of a cist on the gravel terrace.	charcoal	GU–1976	3000	3000	65	65	–26.6
Temple Wood, Kilmartin	Scott, J. G. 1989	NR826978	1444 (1251, 1248, 1205) 901	Charcoal from just above natural surface, beneath the outer edge of slab capping, or placed slabs of kerb surrounding cist of burial D, in centre of circle.	charcoal	GU–1045	2980	2980	110	155	–25.4
Upper Largie, Kilmartin	Mercer and Rideout 1987	NR832993	1383 (1196, 1181, 1165, 1141, 1139) 1003	Charcoal from a cist fill on gravel terrace.	charcoal	GU–1977	2970	2970	55	55	–26.4

DATES BETWEEN ABOUT 1500 BC AND 1000 BC (continued)

Site name	Submitter/ bibref	National Grid Ref.	Calibrated date (Intcal93)	Context, taphonomy and comments	Material dated	Labcode	Age BP	Sort Age	Error	Error (pref)	d13C (pref)
Temple Wood, Kilmartin	Scott, J. G. 1989	NR826978	1737 (1196, 1181, 1165, 1141, 1139) 601	Alder and hazel with cremation in pit of burial E Charcoal associated with undisturbed cremation in pit 75 cm below top of cairn material sealing burial within stone circle. In subsoil sealed and undisturbed 1 m below top of cairn.	charcoal	GU-1299	2970	2970	230	320	-25
Temple Wood, Kilmartin	Scott, J. G. 1989	NR826978	1379 (1127) 929	Oak charcoal from upper old ground surface of southern circle.	charcoal	GU-1528	2945	2945	65	65	-23.8
Temple Wood, Kilmartin	Scott, J. G. 1989	NR826978	1676 (1127) 606	Alder from possible stake in stone hole of lower kerb of burial E.	charcoal	GU-1298	2945	2945	215	300	-25
Achnacree Moss, Lorn	Whitting-ton, G.	NM921363	1388 (1120) 905	Base of peat near cairn.	peat	N-1468	2930	2930	80	110	
Claggan, Morvern	Ritchie et al. 1981	NM697493	1264 (1118) 936	Charcoal from stone setting in centre of kerb cairn 1. Old ground surface of Cairn 2 has dates of 2410 ± 60 (SRR-593) and 2540 ± 60 BP (SRR-599).	charcoal	SRR-284	2925	2925	50	110	-26.3
An Sithean, Islay	Barber and Brown 1984	NR252665	1304 (1118) 923	Organic soil immediately below bank of secondary annexe of hut circle E.	soil	GU-1474	2925	2925	60	60	
Cul a'Bhaile, Jura	Stevenson, J. B. 1984	NR549726	1309 (1116) 915	Alder from gully outside period 1 house, with abraded pottery. See GU-1385 (2890 ± 55 BP).	charcoal	GU-1383	2920	2920	65	110	27.0

Site name	Submitter/ bibref	National Grid Ref.	Calibrated date (Intcal93)	Context, taphonomy and comments	Material dated	Labcode	Age BP	Sort Age	Error	Error (pref)	d13C
DATES BETWEEN ABOUT 1500 BC AND 1000 BC (continued)											
Cul a'Bhaile, Jura	Stevenson, J. B. 1984	NR549726	1257 (1034) 909	Alder from gully outside period 1 house, with abraded pottery. See GU–1383 (2920 ± 65 BP).	charcoal	GU–1385	2890	2890	55	110	26.8
Temple Wood, Kilmartin	Scott, J. G 1989	NR826978	1252 (1022) 909	Charcoal on old ground surface beneath stony clay at stone circle. See also SRR–530 (2880 ± 50 BP).	charcoal	SRR–531	2880	2880	50	110	–27.3
DATES BETWEEN ABOUT 1000 BC AND 500 BC											
Achnasavil, Kintyre	Carter and Tipping 1992; Siggins and Carter 1993	NR791386	1154 (999) 861	Charcoal from the fill of a scoop in a scatter of pits and postholes dug into mid-Flandrian river terrace.	charcoal	GU–3075	2850	2850	50	50	–27.0
Achnasavil, Kintyre	Carter and Tipping 1992; Siggins and Carter 1993	NR791386	1154 (987, 956, 944) 830	Charcoal from the fill of a post-pipe in a scatter of pits and postholes dug into mid-Flandrian river terrace.	charcoal	GU–3074	2830	2830	60	60	–26.9
Achnasavil, Kintyre	Carter and Tipping 1992; Siggins and Carter 1993	NR791386	1113 (927) 830	Charcoal from the fill of scoop or hearth in a scatter of pits and post-holes dug into mid-Flandrian river terrace.	charcoal	GU–3073	2810	2810	50	50	–26.5
Temple Wood, Kilmartin	Scott, J. G. 1989	NR826978	1113 (927) 830	Charcoal from the old ground surface beneath stony clay at stone circle. See also SRR–531 (2880 ±50 BP).	charcoal	SRR–530	2810	2810	50	110	–27.1

DATES BETWEEN ABOUT 1000 BC AND 500 BC (continued)

Site name	Submitter/ bibref	National Grid Ref.	Calibrated date (Intcal93)	Context, taphonomy and comments	Material dated	Labcode	Age BP	Sort Age	Error	Error (pref)	d13C
Cul a'Bhaile, Jura	Stevenson, J. B. 1984	NR549726	1031 (895, 876, 856) 797	Charcoal from the capping of the wall of the period 2 house, probably derived from midden or floors	charcoal	GU–1386	2745	2745	70	110	26.7
Cultoon, Islay	MacKie 1977	NR195569	924 (837) 805	Date from overlying peat; which, thus, does not provide a date for the circle except in the loose sense, that it was built before 500 BC. Excavator suggests this is the latest possible date for destruction of the circle.	charcoal	SRR–500	2720	2720	40	110	–27.5
Balloch Hill, Kintyre	Petenburg 1982	NR677760	989 (822) 776	J21, stone-lined bin, date unlikely to be contemporary with J21 or Structure 1.	charcoal	GU–1032	2690	2690	70	110	–26.9
Cultoon, Islay	MacKie 1977	NR195569	Cal. BC 915 (806) 567	Date from charcoal in overlying peat; which, thus, does not provide a date for the circle except in the loose sense, that it was built before 500 BC.	charcoal	GU–1002	2645	2645	70	110	–27.5
Auchategan Glendaruel	Marshall, D. N. 1978	NS002843	928 (799) 409	Later occupation.	charcoal	GaK–2768	2610	2610	100	300	
Kilellan, Islay	Ritchie, A. forthcoming	NR286721	Cal. BC 828 (785) 412	Charcoal from an occupation deposit, which is possibly floor within structure. This layer was covered by sandy soil used for spade-dug cultivation. It sealed earlier pits and other features. The charcoal could derive from a burnt structure represented by post holes, but it seems more likely to derive from domestic activities.	charcoal	GU–3519	2560	2560	70	70	–26.2

DATES BETWEEN ABOUT 1000 BC AND 500 BC (continued)

Site name	Submitter/ bibref	National Grid Ref.	Calibrated date (Intcal93)	Context, taphonomy and comments	Material dated	Labcode	Age BP	Sort Age	Error	Error (pref)	d13C
Kilellan, Islay	Ritchie, A. forthcoming	NR286721	808 (778) 517	The charcoal came from lower fill (black sand 11702 11703) of a substantial pit 117 sealed by upper fill of similar character. The pit deliberately dug and soon filled with sand again, deliberately derived from industrial process, and then the entire pit and fill was sealed by an occupation deposit.	charcoal	GU-3518	2550	2550	50	50	-26.0
Claggan, Morvern	Ritchie et al. 1975	NM697493	826 (769) 402	Charcoal from old ground surface of cairn 2. Same sample as for SRR-593 (2412 ± 55 BP).	charcoal	SRR-599	2536	2536	80	110	-27.2
Achnacree, Lorn	Barrett et al. 1976	NM972352	804 (765) 408	Basal peat overlying cultivated soils with field walls. Dyke C complex, site 1. See also GU-1009B (3010 ±85 BP).	peat	GU-1009A	2520	2520	55	110	-29.1
Balloch Hill, Kintyre	Peltenburg	NR677760	807 (762, 626, 597, 570) 400	Charcoal from K362, a hearth of Structure 4, phase 2.	charcoal	GU-1105	2505	2505	70	110	-26.4
Ballachulish, Lochaber	Sheridan, A. National Museums of Scotland	NN056601	804 (758, 679, 650, 547) 397	Wooden figure found in peat bog in 1880.	wood	HAR-6329	2490	2490	70	70	
MacArthur Cave, Oban	Saville and Hallen 1994	NM859304	791 (750, 746, 526) 397	Left talus from ossuary from the lower shell bed in the cave. See also OxA-4485 (2170 ± 55 BP) from black earth above, OxA-4486 (2365 ± 55 BP from upper shell layer above, and OxA-4488 (2295 ± 60) from the lower shell layer.	human bone	OxA-4487	2460	2460	55	55	-21.9

DATES BETWEEN ABOUT 1000 BC AND 500 BC (continued)

Site name	Submitter/ bibref	National Grid Ref.	Calibrated date (Intcal93)	Context, taphonomy and comments	Material dated	Labcode	Age BP	Sort Age	Error	Error (pref)	d13C
Balloch Hill, Kintyre	Peltenburg 1982	NR677760	793 (519) 391	Area E level 3. Charcoal from an otherwise carbon-free deposit, which may represent a clearance at the beginning of phase 3.	charcoal	GU–1031	2450	2450	65	110	–26.9

DATES BETWEEN ABOUT 500 BC AND 1 BC

Site name	Submitter/ bibref	National Grid Ref.	Calibrated date (Intcal93)	Context, taphonomy and comments	Material dated	Labcode	Age BP	Sort Age	Error	Error (pref)	d13C
Claggan, Morvern	Ritchie et al. 1975	NM697493	765 (409) 388	Charcoal from old ground surface of cairn 2. Same sample as for SRR–599 (2536 ±80 BP).	charcoal	SRR–593	2412	2412	50	110	–28.7
Dun Mor Vaul, Tiree	MacKie 1974	NM042492	792 (406) 206	Charred grain from pre-broch phase 1A.	charred grain	GaK–1098	2395	2395	90	270	
MacArthur Cave, Oban	Saville and Hallen 1994	NM859304	755 (400) 266	Left distal femur from ossuary from the upper shell bed in the cave. See also OxA–4485 (2170 ±55 BP) from black earth above, OxA–4487 (2460 ±55 BP from lower shell layer below, and OxA–4488 (2295 ±60) from the lower shell layer.	human bone	OxA–4486	2365	2365	55	55	–21.3
Dun Mor Vaul, Tiree	MacKie 1974	NM042492	791 (397) 164	Roots from OGS, phase 4. See also GaK–1521 (2240 ±80 BP).	roots	GaK–1092	2350	2350	110	330	
Balloch Hill, Kintyre	Peltenburg 1982	NR677760	513 (391) 201	Charcoal from K6, from a hearth possibly of Structure 5 of phase 3.	charcoal	GU–1104	2320	2320	60	110	27.1
Balloch Hill, Kintyre	Peltenburg 1982	NR677760	BC 767 (387) 62	Charcoal from A21, an entrance barrier in phase 3.	charcoal	GU–1033	2305	2305	110	155	–25.5

DATES BETWEEN ABOUT 500 BC AND 1 BC (continued)

Site name	Submitter/ bibref	National Grid Ref.	Calibrated date (Intcal93)	Context, taphonomy and comments	Material dated	Labcode	Age BP	Sort Age	Error	Error (pref)	d13C
MacArthur Cave, Oban	Saville and Hallen 1994	NM859304	411 (383) 194	Right patella from ossuary from the lower shell bed in the cave. See also OxA–4485 (2170 ± 55 BP) from black earth above, OxA–4486 (2365 ± 55 BP) from upper shell layer above, and OxA–4488 (2460 ± 60) from the lower shell layer.	human bone	OxA–4488	2295	2295	60	60	22.3
Eilean An Dùin, Mid Argyll	Nieke and Boyd 1990	NM792079	414 (381) 188	Below main mass of rampart material. charcoal	charcoal	GU–1814	2290	2290	65	65	–25.9
Dunadd, Mid Argyll	Campbell and Lane 1993	NR836936	404 (377) 195	Base of deposits on summit of Fort A. Metamorphic bedrock, deposit in cleft in bedrock.	charcoal	GU–2464	2280	2280	50	50	–25.9
Balloch Hill, Kintyre	Peltenburg 1982	NR677760	481 (372) 112	Hazel and willow charcoal from 74B3, possible rampart 1 and superstructure of phase 3.	charcoal	HAR–1903	2270	2270	80	80	
Balloch Hill, Kintyre	Peltenburg 1982	NR677760	403 (361, 282, 257) 100	Charcoal, 76J3.	charcoal	HAR–1905	2240	2240	70	70	
Dun Mor Vaul, Tiree	MacKie 1974	NM042492	407 (361, 282, 257) 57	Charcoal from phase 4b. See also GaK–1092 (2350 ±110 BP).	charcoal	GaK–1521	2240	2240	80	240	
Balloch Hill, Kintyre	Peltenburg 1982	NR677760	Cal. BC 756 (361, 282, 257) Cal. AD 13	Hazel charcoal from 74L2AF1, rampart 1 superstructure of phase 3. See also HAR–2043 (2230 ± 90 BP) from the same structure.	charcoal	HAR–1904	2240	2240	120	120	

DATES BETWEEN ABOUT 500 BC AND 1 BC (continued)

Site name	Submitter/ bibref	National Grid Ref.	Calibrated date (Intcal93)	Context, taphonomy and comments	Material dated	Labcode	Age BP	Sort Age	Error	Error (pref)	d13C
Dun Mor Vaul, Tiree	MacKie 1974	NM042492	481 (357, 288, 250) 8	Bone from Phase 1B midden under outer wall.	bone	GaK–1225	2230	2230	100	300	
Cultoon, Islay	MacKie 1981	NR195569	Cal. BC 519 (357, 288, 250) Cal. AD 6	Date from turf; which, thus, does not provide a date for the circle. This date should be about the same as that for overlying peat (GU–1002 2645 ± 70 and SRR–500 2720 ± 40), instead of being 400–500 years younger.	turf	SRR–499	2230	2230	110	155	–29.3
Balloch Hill, Kintyre	Peltenburg 1982	NR677176	392 (196) 35	Charcoal of Area R3 of phase 3. The value quoted here is a primary value.	charcoal	GU–1028	2180	2180	70	110	–26.9
MacArthur Cave, Oban	Saville and Hallen 1994	NM859303	377 (193) 44	From ossuary from the black earth in the cave. See also OxA–4487 (2170 ± 55 BP) from lower shell bed, OxA–4486 (2365 ± 55 BP from upper shell layer above, and OxA–4488 (2295 ± 60) from the lower shell layer.	human bone	OxA–4485	2170	2170	55	55	–21.4
Eilean An Duin, Mid Argyll	Nieke and Boyd 1990	NM792079	373 (189) 40	Below main mass of rampart material in section 1.	charcoal	GU–1815	2160	2160	55	55	–26.6
Balloch Hill, Kintyre	Peltenburg 1982	NR677760	Cal. BC 389 (165) Cal. AD 72	Charcoal, 74B2, from the same structure as HAR–1904 (2240 ± 120 BP), rampart superstructure of phase 3.	charcoal	HAR–2043	2130	2130	90	90	

DATES BETWEEN ABOUT 500 BC AND 1 BC (continued)

Site name	Submitter/ bibref	National Grid Ref.	Calibrated date (Intcal93)	Context, taphonomy and comments	Material dated	Labcode	Age BP	Sort Age	Error	Error (pref)	d13C
Balloch Hill, Kintyre	Peltenburg 1982	NR677760	Cal. BC 369 (157, 137, 125) Cal. AD 54	Charcoal, 75C5F1. Hazel and willow charcoal from gully C51, 75C5F1, of phase 3.	charcoal	HAR–1907	2120	2120	70	70	
Balloch Hill, Kintyre	Peltenburg 1982	NR677760	Cal. BC 361 (50) Cal. AD 120	Charcoal from gully K45 of phase 3.	charcoal	GU–1106	2070	2070	85	120	–26.8
Tormore, Arran	Barber, J. PREPUB		Cal. BC 367 (47) Cal. AD 133	From upper charcoal layer secondary to main occupation of house.	charcoal	GU–1074	2065	2065	95	135	–25.6
Dunadd, Mid Argyll	Campbell and Lane 1993	NR836936	Cal. BC 190 (45) Cal. AD 68	Occupation within the summit Fort A, Phase II B. Thick occupation deposits overlain by rubble, metamorphic bedrock.	charcoal	GU–2461	2060	2060	50	50	–25.9
Balloch Hill, Kintyre	Peltenburg 1982	NR677176	Cal. BC 196 (36) Cal. AD 121	Charcoal from area K level 2 in a layer transitional between phases 3 and 4.	charcoal twigs	GU–1029	2040	2040	70	110	–26.7
Kilellan, Islay	Ritchie, A. forthcoming	NR286721	Cal. BC 183 (31, 18, 9) Cal. AD 116	Undisturbed midden deposit sealed by layer of windblown sand above which a later midden layer. Human deposition domestic refuse contamination unlikely.	animal bone	GU–3516	2030	2030	60	60	–23.8

DATES BETWEEN ABOUT AD 1 AND AD 500

Site name	Submitter/ bibref	National Grid Ref.	Calibrated date (Intcal93)	Context, taphonomy and comments	Material dated	Labcode	Age BP	Sort Age	Error	Error (pref)	d13C
Dunadd, Mid Argyll	Campbell and Lane 1993	NR836936	Cal. BC 104 (Cal. AD 12) Cal. AD 121	Soil underlying Phase I rampart of upper fort (Fort A). Stony loam overlain by drystone wall.	charcoal	GU–2306	2000	2000	50	50	−25.6
Dunadd, Mid Argyll	Campbell and Lane 1993	NR836936	Cal. BC 60 (Cal. AD 26, 42, 53) Cal. AD 131	Hearth in foundation of phase I rampart of upper fort (Fort A). Dry stone walling.	charcoal	GU–2307	1980	1980	50	50	−26.6
Kilellan, Islay	Ritchie, A. forthcoming	NR286721	Cal. BC 115 (Cal. AD 59) Cal. AD 224	Undisturbed midden deposit, sealing abandoned souterrain and itself sealed by extensive cobbled surface. Sample from single discrete deposit within its midden layer. Human deposition, domestic refuse contamination unlikely.	bone	GU–3515	1970	1970	70	70	−26.2
Balloch Hill, Kintyre	Peltenburg 1982	NR677760	Cal. BC 199 (Cal. AD 59) Cal. AD 325	Area CC level 3 (with additional bags of CC 2 which can be amalgamated with CC 3 if there is not enough of the latter.) Boulder clay and stones.	charcoal	GU–1030	1970	1970	110	155	−26.3
Iona	McCormick 1989	NM285240	Cal. BC 92 (Cal. AD 72) Cal. AD 236	Top 5 mm of peat underlying a mineral soil bank.	peat	GU–2593	1950	1950	70	70	−28.5
Dun Mor Vaul, Tiree	MacKie 1974	NM042492	Cal. BC 50 (Cal. AD 125) Cal. AD 375	Primary floor in gallery.		GaK–1097	1890	1890	90	270	

DATES BETWEEN ABOUT AD 1 AND AD 500 (continued)

Site name	Submitter/ bibref	National Grid Ref.	Calibrated date (Intcal93)	Context, taphonomy and comments	Material dated	Labcode	Age BP	Sort Age	Error	Error (pref)	d13C
Iona	McCormick 1989	NM285240	Cal. BC 59 (Cal. AD 141) Cal. AD 420	Top 5 mm of peat underlying mineral soil bank.	peat	GU–2595	1860	1860	110	110	–28.4
Dun Mor Vaul, Tiree	MacKie	NM042492	Cal. AD 59 (244) 433	Rubble in gallery of phase 5.		GaK–1099	1790	1790	90	270	
Dunadd, Mid Argyll	Campbell and Lane 1993	NR836936	Cal. AD 238 (382) 441	Site 3 high in midden deposits. Metalworking middens in acid soil.	charcoal	GU–2462	1700	1700	50	50	–26.2
Achnacree, Lorn	Barrett et al. 1976	NM972352	Cal. AD 250 (409) 540	Basal peat overlying cultivated soils with field walls. Dyke C complex, site 7. See also GU–1010HA (1465 ± 65 BP).	peat	GU–1010	1665	1665	55	110	–28.8
Iona	McCormick 1989	NM285240	Cal. AD 259 (415) 542	Hollow in subsoil.	charcoal	GU–2598	1650	1650	50	50	–25.4
Ardentraive, Cowal	Kendrick, J. RCAHMS 1992, 480, no.228	NS103788	Cal. AD 250 (417) 561	Beneath hillwash and rear bank build-up of a platform cut into steep slope. Cut into natural subsoil of clayey sand.	charcoal	GU–1590	1645	1645	65	65	–25
Dunadd, Mid Argyll	Campbell and Lane 1993	NR836936	Cal. AD 259 (423) 592	Occupation outside Phase I fort rampart, before building of Phase II rampart of upper fort (Fort A). Stony soil.	charcoal	GU–2308	1630	1630	60	60	–26.2

DATES BETWEEN ABOUT AD 500 AND AD 1000

Site name	Submitter/ bibref	National Grid Ref.	Calibrated date (Intcal93)	Context, taphonomy and comments	Material dated	Labcode	Age BP	Sort Age	Error	Error (pref)	d13C
Dunadd, Mid Argyll	Campbell and Lane 1993	NR836936	Cal. AD 426 (596) 660	Bowl hearth in metalworking area of middle fort (Fort D). Overlying sample DA 81/2184. Stony soil, acid environment.	charcoal	GU-2312	1500	1500	60	60	-25.9
Dunadd, Mid Argyll	Campbell and Lane 1993	NR836936	Cal. AD 436 (596) 655	Occupation under rampart of lower fort (Fort F). Waterlogged acid environment.	charcoal	GU-2310	1500	1500	50	50	-26.0
Iona	Barber 1981	NM285240	Cal. AD 437 (605) 666	Highest natural infill layer ditch 2.	charcoal	GU-1281	1480	1480	60	110	-26.0
Dunadd, Mid Argyll	Campbell and Lane 1993	NR836936	Cal. AD 534 (610) 663	Thin occupation layer overlying dismantled Phase I rampart of the highest fort (Fort A). Overlain by stony soil, acid environment.	charcoal	GU-2314	1470	1470	50	50	-26.2
Achnacree, Lorn	Barrett and Hill 1976	NM972352	Cal. AD 440 (614) 675	Basal peat overlying cultivated soils with field walls. Dyke C complex, site 7. See also GU-1010 (1665 ±55 BP).	peat	GU-1010HA	1465	1465	65	110	-27.4
Traigh nam Barc, Colonsay	Ritchie, J. N. G.	NR360914	Cal. AD 447 (614) 671	In hearth material.	charcoal	GU-1641	1465	1465	60	60	-26.1
Dunadd, Mid Argyll	Campbell and Lane 1993	NR836936	Cal. AD 540 (628) 669	Lowest phase of metalworking middens of metalworking debris and rubble.	charcoal	GU-2466	1450	1450	50	50	-26.2

Site name	Submitter/ bibref	National Grid Ref.	Calibrated date (Intcal93)	Context, taphonomy and comments	Material dated	Labcode	Age BP	Sort Age	Error	Error (pref)	d13C
DATES BETWEEN ABOUT AD 500 AND AD 1000 (continued)											
Iona	McCormick 1989	NM285240	Cal. AD 540 (628) 669	Fill of linear feature F 347 in subsoil of site.	charcoal	GU–2597	1450	1450	50	50	–26.5
Dun Mor Vaul, Tiree	MacKie 1974	NM042492	Cal. AD 214 (635) 1011	Bone from rubble in gallery with Norse comb.	bone	GaK–1520	1440	1440	200	600	
Dunadd, Mid Argyll	Campbell and Lane 1993	NR836936	Cal. AD 543 (635) 673	Lowest level of Phase III Site 3 Middens with rubble and metalwork debris.	charcoal	GU–2465	1440	1440	50	50	–25.2
Dunadd, Mid Argyll	Campbell and Lane 1993	NR836936	Cal. AD 547 (641) 678	Small bowl-hearth at base of metal-working deposits in middle fort (Fort D). Lies beneath DA 81/2135. Stony soil acid environment.	charcoal	GU–2313	1430	1430	50	50	–26.0
Dunadd, Mid Argyll	Campbell and Lane 1993	NR836936	Cal. AD 550 (646) 682	Site 3 upper phase of metalworking deposits. Thick middens with rubble.	charcoal	GU–2460	1420	1420	50	50	–26.1
Iona	Barber 1981	NM285245	Cal. AD 599 (660) 773	Lowest natural infill layer ditch 2.	charcoal	GU–1282	1380	1380	55	110	–26.2
Dunadd, Mid Argyll	Campbell and Lane 1993	NR836936	Cal. AD 615 (665) 776	Hearth at highest level of metal-working area of middle fort (Fort D). Stony soil, acid environment.	charcoal	GU–2311	1360	1360	50	50	–26.3

DATES BETWEEN ABOUT AD 500 AND AD 1000 (continued)

Site name	Submitter/ bibref	National Grid Ref.	Calibrated date (Intcal93)	Context, taphonomy and comments	Material dated	Labcode	Age BP	Sort Age	Error	Error (pref)	d13C (pref)
Iona	Barber 1981	NM285245	Cal. AD 615 (668) 783	Layer within the peat deposit lying in the lower 2 m of a *vallum* ditch. Sample lay within peat. There is some indication of prehistoric contamination by fungi. No sign of modern contamination.	wood	GU–1243	1350	1350	55	110	–24.1
Iona	Barber 1981	NM 28582458	Cal. AD 620 (669) 785	Bottom of vallum ditch in a peat deposit. Lies in a peat deposit. Some evidence of ancient fungal infection; otherwise no obvious contamination.	wood	GU–1247	1345	1345	55	110	–23.7
Dunadd, Mid Argyll	Campbell and Lane 1993	NR836936	Cal. AD 633 (671) 783	Site 3, early phase of metalworking. Metalwork middens, acid soil and rubble.	charcoal	GU–2467	1340	1340	50	50	–26.2
Iona	Barber 1981	NM285245	Cal. AD 630 (674) 788	Layer within the peat deposit lying in the lower 2 m of a *vallum* ditch. Sample lay within peat. There is some indication of prehistoric contamination by fungi. No sign of modern contamination.	wood	GU–1246	1335	1335	55	110	–24.4
Iona	Barber 1981	NM285245	Cal. AD 642 (683) 868		wood	GU–1248	1315	1315	55	110	–24.1
Iona	Haggarty 1988	NM287245	Cal. AD 663 (774) 887	F 20. Midden adjacent to ecclesiastical buildings.	charcoal	GU–1984	1265	1265	50	50	–27.1

DATES BETWEEN ABOUT AD 500 AND AD 1000 (continued)

Site name	Submitter/ bibref	National Grid Ref.	Calibrated date (Intcal93)	Context, taphonomy and comments	Material dated	Labcode	Age BP	Sort Age	Error	Error (pref)	d13C
Iona	Barber 1981	NM285245	Cal. AD 662 (776) 891	Layer within the peat deposit lying in the lower 2 m of a *vallum* ditch. Sample lay within the peat. There is some indication of prehistoric contamination by fungi. No sign of modern contamination.	wood	GU–1245	1260	1260	55	110	–23.8
Dunadd, Mid Argyll	Campbell and Lane 1993	NR836936	Cal. AD 653 (782) 984	Summit Fort A, Phase II B occupation layer. Metamorphic bedrock, black occupation layer between rubble spreads.	charcoal	GU–2463	1240	1240	80	80	–26.2
Dunadd, Mid Argyll	Campbell and Lane 1993	NR836936	Cal. AD 679 (883) 1011	Beneath Phase I and II of rampart of lower fort (Fort F). Overlain by drystone walling.	charcoal	GU–2309	1180	1180	70	70	–26.2
Machrins, Colonsay	Ritchie 1981	NR358933	Cal. AD 684 (886) 1014	In a grave sealed by cover slabs. The bones were covered in sand.	human bone	GU–1114	1170	1170	70	110	–19.3
Machrins, Colonsay	Ritchie 1981	NR358933	Cal. AD 709 (891) 1020	In the midden debris within a stone-lined house, eroding from the sand dunes.	animal bone	GU–1115	1150	1150	70	110	–21.1
An Sithean, Islay	Barber and Brown 1984	NR252665	Cal. AD 775 (893) 1017	Basal peat.	peat	GU–1475	1140	1140	60	110	–28.9
Kintra, Islay	RCAHMS 1984, 58 (no. 54)	NR321850	Cal. AD 778 (898, 906, 961) 1026	Extended inhumation in a grave-pit covered by large slabs, in sand dunes.	bone	GU–1624	1120	1120	65	65	–20

Site name	Submitter/ bibref	National Grid Ref.	Calibrated date (Intcal93)	Context, taphonomy and comments	Material dated	Labcode	Age BP	Sort Age	Error	Error (pref)	d13C
DATES BETWEEN ABOUT AD 1000 AND AD 1500											
Ardentraive, Cowal	Kendrick, J. RCAHMS 1992, 480 (no.228)	NS103788	Cal. AD 894 (1018) 1167	From old land surface beneath hill-wash and front bank build-up of the Colintraive platform. Sealed by hillwash/build-up of clean yellow clayey coarse sand.	charcoal	GU-1589	1015	1015	60	60	-25
Brainport Bay, Mid Argyll	MacKie 1981	NR975951	Cal. AD 898 (1028) 1222	The charcoal was on rock and covered by a thin layer of earth and turf.	charcoal	GU-1000	980	980	70	110	-28
Dunadd, Mid Argyll	Campbell and Lane 1993	NR836936	Cal. AD 1031 (1225) 1296	Final midden on summit Fort A, Phase V. Acid soil overlying metamorphic bedrock.	animal bone	GU-2459	830	830	70	70	-26.7
DATES INDISTINGUISHABLE FROM MODERN DATES											
Temple Wood, Kilmartin	Scott, J.G. 1989	NR826780	Cal. AD 1484 (1668, 1788, 1791, 1950, 1952) modern	Juniper twig and pine charcoal from stone bank surrounding circle, beneath black soil and just above yellow clay layer believed to mark and seal top of cairn B.	charcoal	GU-1530	215	215	80	80	-24.4
Port a' Chotain, Islay	DES1974 11	NR397783	modern	Last occupation layer in Cave 1.	shell	GX-3547	240	0	110	330	

Bibliography

Airlie, S. (1994) The view from Maastricht, *in* Crawford, B. E. 1994, 33–46.

Aitken, W. G. (1955) Excavation of a chapel at St Ninian's Point, Isle of Bute, *Trans. Bute Nat. Hist. Soc.*, *14*, 62–76.

Alcock, E. (1992) Burials and cemeteries in Scotland, *in* Edwards, N. and Lane, A. (eds), *The Early Church in Wales and the West* (= Oxbow Monograph 16), Oxford, 125–9.

Alcock, L. (1984) A survey of Pictish settlement archaeology, *in* Friell, J. G. P. and Watson, W. G. (eds) *Pictish Studies* (= British Archaeological Reports 125), Oxford, 7–41.

Alcock, L. and Alcock, E. (1978) Scandinavian settlement in the Inner Hebrides, *Scot. Archaeol. Forum*, *10*, 61–72.

—— (1987) Reconnaissance excavations on Early Historic fortifications and other royal sites in Scotland, 1974–84: 2, Excavations at Dunollie Castle, Oban, Argyll, 1978, *Proc. Soc. Antiq. Scot.*, *117*, 119–47.

Alcock, L., Alcock, E. and Driscoll, S. (1989) Reconnaissance excavations on Early Historic fortifications and other royal sites in Scotland, 3: Dundurn, *Proc. Soc. Antiq. Scot.*, *119*, 189–226.

Allen, J. R. (1882) Notes on some Undescribed Stones with Cup-markings in Scotland, *Proc. Soc. Antiq. Scot.*, *16*, 79–143.

Andersen, P. S. (1991) Norse settlement in the Hebrides: what happened to the natives and what happened to the Norse immigrants? *in* Wood, I. and Lund, N. (eds) *People and Places in Northern Europe: essays in honour of P. H. Sawyer*, Woodbridge, 131–48.

—— (1995) The Norwegian background, *in* Crawford, B. E. 1995, 16–25.

Anderson, A. O. (1922) *Early Sources of Scottish History*, Edinburgh.

Anderson, A. O. and Anderson, M. O. (1961) *Adomnan's Life of Columba*, Edinburgh.

—— (1991) New edition of Anderson and Anderson 1961, revised by M. O. Anderson, Oxford.

Anderson, J. (1874) Notes on the relics of the Viking period of the Northmen in Scotland, *Proc. Soc. Antiq. Scot.*, *10*, 536–94.

—— (1880) Notes on the contents of two Viking graves in Islay ..., *Proc. Soc. Antiq. Scot.*, *14*, 51–89.

284

—— (1883) *Scotland in Pagan Times: the Iron Age*, Edinburgh.

—— (1895) Notice of a cave recently discovered at Oban, containing human remains and a refuse heap of shells and bones of animals, and stone and bone implements, *Proc. Soc. Antiq. Scot.*, *29*, 211–30.

—— (1898) Notes on the contents of a small cave or rock shelter at Druimvargie, Oban; and of three shell mounds on Oronsay, *Proc. Soc. Antiq. Scot.*, *32*, 298–313.

—— (1900) Description of a collection of objects found in excavations at St Blane's Church, Bute ..., *Proc. Soc. Antiq. Scot.*, *35*, 307–25.

—— (1907a) Ship Burial of the Viking time at Kiloran Bay, Colonsay, *Proc. Soc. Antiq. Scot.*, *41*, 443–9.

—— (1907b) Notice of Bronze Brooches ..., *Proc. Soc. Antiq. Scot.*, *41*, 437–43.

Anderson, M. O. (1982) Dalriada and the creation of the kingdom of the Scots, *in* Whitelock, D., Kitterick, R. M., and Dumville, D. (eds), *Ireland in early medieval Europe: studies in memory of Kathleen Hughes*, Cambridge, 106–32.

Anderson, R. S. G. (1939) *The Antiquities of Gigha, a Survey and Guide*, Newton Stewart.

Andrews, J. T. (1970) A geomorphological study of post glacial uplift with particular reference to Arctic Canada, *Inst. Brit. Geogr. Spec. Publ.*, *2*, 156ff.

Andrews, M. V., Gilbertson, D. D. and Kent, M. (1987) Storm frequences along the Mesolithic Coastline, *in* Mellars 1987, 108–14.

Arbman, H. (1961) *The Vikings*, London.

Armit, I. (1988) Broch Landscapes in the Western Isles, *Scot. Archaeol. Rev.*, *5*, 78–86.

—— (1990a) *Beyond the Brochs, Changing Perspectives on the Atlantic Scottish Iron Age*, Armit I. (ed.), Edinburgh, 1990.

—— (1990b) Brochs and Beyond in the Western Isles, *in* Armit 1990a, 41–70.

—— (1990c) Epilogue: the Scottish Atlantic Iron Age, *in* Armit 1990a, 194–210.

—— (1991) The Atlantic Iron Age: five levels of chronology, *Proc. Soc. Antiq. Scot.*, *121*, 181–214.

Atkinson, T. C., Briffa, K. R. and Coope, G. R. (1987) Seasonal temperatures in Britain during the last 22,000 years, reconstructed using beetle remains, *Nature*, *325*, 587–93.

Baillie, M. G. L. (1990) Checking back on an assemblage of published radiocarbon dates, *Radiocarbon 32 (3)*, 361–6.

Balfour, J. A. (ed.) (1910) *The Book of Arran: Archaeology*, Glasgow.

Ballantyne, C. K. (1984) Characteristics and evolution of two relict talus slopes in Scotland, *Scot. Geogr. Mag.*, *100*, 20–33.

Ballantyne, C. K. and Eckford, J. D. (1986) Landslides and slope failures in Scotland: a review, *Scot. Geogr. Mag.*, *102*, 134–50.

Bannerman, J. (1974) *Studies in the History of Dalriada*, Edinburgh.

Barber, J. W. (1978) The excavation of the Holed-stone at Ballymeanoch, Kilmartin, Argyll, *Proc. Soc. Antiq. Scot.*, *109*, 104–11.

—— (1981) Excavations on Iona, 1979, *Proc. Scot. Antiq. Scot.*, *111*, 282–380.

—— (1982) Arran, *Current Archaeol.*, *83*, 358–63.

Barber, J. W. and Brown, M. M. (1984) An Sithean, *Proc. Soc. Antiq. Scot.*, *114*, 161–88.

Barber, J. W. and Crone, B. A. (1993) Crannogs: a diminished resource? A survey of the crannogs of south-west Scotland and excavations at Buiston crannog, *Antiquity*, *67*, 520–33.

Barrett, J. C. (1981) Aspects of the Iron Age in Atlantic Scotland: a case study in the problems of archaeological interpretation, *Proc. Soc. Antiq. Scot.*, *111*, 204–19.

Barrett, J. C., Hill, P. and Stevenson, J. B. (1976) Second millennium B.C. banks in the Black Moss of Achnacree: some problems of prehistoric landuse, *in* Burgess and Miket 1976, 283–7.

Batey, C. (1987) *Freswick Links, Caithness* (=British Archaeological Reports British Series 179), Oxford.

—— (1993) The Viking and late Norse graves of Caithness and Sutherland, *in* Batey *et al.* 1993, 148–72.

Batey, C., Jesch, J. and Morris, C. (eds) (1993) *The Viking Age in Caithness, Orkney and the North Atlantic*, Edinburgh.

Bennett, K. D. (1984) The post-glacial history of Pinus sylvestris in the British Isles, *J. Quat. Sci.*, *3*, 133–55.

—— (1989) A provisional map of forest types for the British Isles 5000 years ago, *J. Quat. Sci.*, *4*, 141–4.

Bersu, G. and Wilson, D. M. (1966) *Three Viking Graves in the Isle of Man* (= Society of Medieval Archaeology Monograph Series 1).

Bibby, J. S., Hudson, G. and Henderson, D. J. (1982) *Soil and land capability for agriculture: western Scotland*, Aberdeen.

Binford, L. R. (1979) Organisation and formation processes: looking at curated technologies, *J. Anthropological Research*, *35(3)*, 255–73.

Birks, H. J. B. (1977) The Flandrian forest history of Scotland: a preliminary synthesis, *in* Shotton, F. W. (ed.), *British Quaternary Studies: Recent Advances*, Oxford, 119–35.

—— (1986) Late Quaternary biotic changes in terrestrial and lacustrine environments, with particular reference to north-west Europe, *in* Berglund, B. E. (ed.), *Handbook of Holocene Palaeoecology and Palaeohydrology*, Chichester, 1–65.

—— (1987) The vegetational context of Mesolithic occupation on Oronsay and adjacent areas, *in* Mellars 1987, 71–7.

—— (1989) Holocene isochrone maps and patterns of tree-spreading in the British Isles, *J. Biogeogr.*, *16*, 503–40.

Bishop, A. H. (1914) An Oronsay shell-mound – a Scottish pre-Neolithic site, *Proc. Soc. Antiq. Scot.*, *48*, 52–108.

Black, G. F. (1890) Notice of a fragment of a rune-incised cross-slab, found on Inchmarnock, Buteshire, *Proc. Soc. Antiq. Scot.*, *24*, 438–43.

Blair, J. and Sharpe, R. (eds) (1992), *Pastoral Care before the Parish*, Leicester.

Bonsall, C. and Robinson, M. R. (1992) Archaeological Survey of the Glenshellach Development Area, Oban: Report to Historic Scotland, University of Edinburgh Department of Archaeology.

Bonsall, C., Robinson, M. R., Payton, R. and Macklin, M. G. (1993) Lón Mór, Oban, *Discovery and Excavation in Scotland 1993*, 76.

Bonsall, C. and Smith, C. (1989) Late Palaeolithic and Mesolithic bone and antler artifacts from Britain: First reactions to accelerator dates, *Mesolithic Miscellany*, *10(1)*, 33–8.

—— (1990) Bone and antler technology in the British Late Upper Palaeolithic and Mesolithic: the impact of accelerator dating, *in* P. M. Vermeersch and P. van Peer (eds), *Contributions to the Mesolithic in Europe*, Leuven, 359–68.

—— (1992) New AMS 14C dates for antler and bone artefacts from Great Britain, *Mesolithic Miscellany*, *13(2)*, 28–34.

Bonsall, C., Sutherland, D. G. and Lawson, T. J. (1991) Excavations at Ulva Cave, western Scotland 1989: a preliminary report, *Mesolithic Miscellany*, *12(2)*, 18–23.

Bonsall, C., Sutherland, D. G., Lawson, T. J. and Russell, N. (1992) Excavations at Ulva Cave, western Scotland 1989: a preliminary report, *Mesolithic Miscellany*, *13(1)*, 7–13.

Bonsall, C. and Sutherland, D. G. (1992) The Oban caves, *in* Walker *et al.* 1992, 115–21.

Bonsall, C., Sutherland, D. G., Russell, N. J., Coles, G., Paul, C. R. C., Huntley, J. P. and Lawson, T. J. (1994) Excavations in Ulva Cave, western Scotland 1990–91: a preliminary report, *Mesolithic Miscellany, 15(1)*, 8–21.

Bonsall, C., Tolan-Smith, C. and Saville, A. (1995) Direct Dating of Mesolithic antler and bone artefacts from Great Britain: new results for bevelled tools and red deer antler mattocks, *Mesolithic Miscellany, 16(1)*, 2–10.

Bradley, J. (ed.) (1988) *Settlement and Society in Medieval Ireland*, Kilkenny.

—— (1988) The interpretation of Scandinavian settlement in Ireland, *in* Bradley 1988, 49–78.

Bradley, R. (1993) *Altering the Earth* (= Society of Antiquaries of Scotland Monograph Series 8), Edinburgh.

Brazier, V. B. (1992) Holocene debris cones in Glen Coe and Glen Etive, *in* Walker *et al.* 1992, 67–73.

Brazier, V. B., Whittington, G. and Ballantyne, C. K. (1988) Holocene débris cone formation in Glen Etive, Western Grampian Highlands, Scotland, *Earth Surf. Process. Landf. 13*, 525–31.

Breuil, H. (1922) Observations on the Pre-Neolithic industries of Scotland, *Proc. Soc. Antiq. Scot., 56*, 261–81.

Bridge, M. C., Haggart, B. A. and Low, J. J. (1990) The history and palaeoclimatic significance of subfossil remains of *Pinus sylvestris* in blanket peats in Scotland, *J. Ecol., 78*, 77–99.

Brøgger, A. W. (1929) *Ancient Emigrants*, Oxford.

Broun, D. (1994) The origin of Scottish identity in its European context, *in* Crawford 1994, 21–32.

Buckley, V. (ed.) (1990) *Burnt Offerings*, Dublin.

Burgess, C. (1990a) The Chronology of Cup-and-ring Marks in Britain and Ireland, *Northern Archaeol., 10*, 21–6.

—— (1990b) The Chronology of Cup- and Cup-and-ring Marks in Atlantic Europe, *Rev. Archaeol. Oest*, Supplement 2, 157–71.

Burgess, C. and Miket, R. (eds) (1976) *Settlement and Economy in the third and second millennia BC* (= British Archaeological Reports 33), Oxford.

Callander, G. J. and Grant, W. G. (1934) The broch of Midhowe, Rousay, Orkney, *Proc. Soc. Antiq. Scot., 68*, 444–516.

Campbell, E. (1987) A cross-marked quern from Dunadd and other evidence for relations between Dunadd and Iona, *Proc. Soc. Antiq. Scot., 117*, 105–17.

—— (1996) Trade in the Dark Age West: A Peripheral Activity? *in* Crawford, B. E. 1966, 79–91.

Campbell, E. and Lane, A. (1993) Celtic and Germanic Interaction: the 7th-century Metalworking Site at Dunadd, *in* Spearman and Higgitt 1993, 52-63.

Campbell, J. F. (1862) *Popular Tales of the West Highlands*, Edinburgh.

Campbell of Kilberry, M. and Ritchie, J. N. G. (1984) Cists from Kilbride, Mid Argyll, *Proc. Soc. Antiq. Scot., 114*, 571–4.

Campbell of Kilberry, M. and Sandeman, M. (1962) Mid Argyll: an archaeological survey, *Proc. Soc. Antiq. Scot., 95*, 1–125.

Campbell of Kilberry, M., Scott, J. G. and Piggott, S. (1961) The Badden Cist Slab, *Proc. Soc. Antiq. Scot., 94*, 46–61.

Carter, S. and Tipping, R. (1992) The Prehistoric Occupation of Carradale, Kintyre, *Glasgow Archaeol. J., 17*, 39–52.

Chapman, J. C. and Mytum, H. C. (eds) (1983) *Settlement in North Britain 1000 BC – AD 1000* (= British Archaeological Reports, British Series 116), Oxford.

Childe, V. G. (1935) *The Prehistory of Scotland, London.*

Childe, V. G. and Thorneycroft, W. (1938a) The vitrified fort at Rahoy, Morvern, Argyll, *Proc. Soc. Antiq. Scot., 72*, 23–43.

Childe, V. G. and Thorneycroft, W. (1938b) The Experimental Production of the Phenomena Distinctive of Vitrified Forts, *Proc. Soc. Antiq. Scot.*, *72*, 44–55.

Christison, D. (1889) The duns and forts of Lorne, Nether Lochaber, and the neighbourhood, *Proc. Soc. Antiq. Scot.*, *23*, 368–432.

—— (1904) The forts of Kilmartin, Kilmichael Glassary, and North Knapdale, Argyle, *Proc. Soc. Antiq. Scot.*, *38*, 205–51.

Christison, D., Anderson, J. and Ross, T. (1905) Report on the Society's excavations of forts on the Poltalloch Estate, Argyll, in 1904–5, *Proc. Soc. Antiq. Scot.*, *39*, 259–322.

Christison, R. (1881) On an ancient wooden image, found in November last at Ballachulish peat-moss, *Proc. Soc. Antiq. Scot.*, *15*, 158–78.

Clancy, T. O. and Márkus, G. (1995) *Iona, the earliest poetry of a Celtic Monastery*, Edinburgh

Clark, J. G. D. (1956) Notes on the Obanian with special reference to antler- and bone-work, *Proc. Soc. Antiq. Scot.*, *89*, 91–106.

Clarke, D. V. (1970) Bone dice and the Scottish Iron Age, *Proc. Prehist. Soc.*, *36*, 214–32.

—— (1971) Small finds in the Atlantic Province: problems of approach, *Scot. Archaeol. Forum*, *3*, 22–54.

Clarke, D. V., Cowie, T. G. and Foxon, A. (1985) *Symbols of Power at the time of Stonehenge*, Edinburgh.

Coles, B. (1990) Anthropomorphic Wooden Figures from Britain and Ireland, *Proc. Prehist. Soc.*, *56*, 315–33.

Coles, J. M. (1960) Scottish Late Bronze metalwork: typology, distributions and chronology, *Proc. Soc. Antiq. Scot.*, *93*, 16–134.

—— (1964) Scottish Middle Bronze Age metalwork, *Proc. Soc. Antiq. Scot.*, *97*, 82–156.

—— (1970) Scottish Early Bronze Age metalwork, *Proc. Soc. Antiq. Scot.*, *101*, 1–110.

—— (1971) The early settlement of Scotland: excavations at Morton, Fife, *Proc. Prehist. Soc.*, *37*, 284–366.

—— (1983) Excavations at Kilmelfort Cave, Argyll, *Proc. Soc. Antiq. Scot.*, *113*, 11–21.

Connock, K. D., Finlayson, B. and Mills, C. M. (1993) Excavation of a shell midden site at Carding Mill Bay near Oban, Scotland, *Glasgow Archaeol. J.*, *17*, 25–38.

Corcoran, J. X. W. P. (1969) Excavation of two chambered cairns at Mid Gleniron Farm, Wigtownshire, *Trans. Dumfries. Galloway Nat. Hist. Antiq. Soc.*, 3rd series, *46*, 29–90.

Cowie, T. G. (1980) Excavations at Kintraw, Argyll, 1979, *Glasgow Archaeol. J.*, *7*, 27–31.

—— (1986) A stone head from Port Appin, Argyll, *Proc. Soc. Antiq. Scot.*, *116*, 89–91.

Craw, J. H. (1930) Excavations at Dunadd and at Other Sites on the Poltalloch Estates, Argyll, *Proc. Soc. Antiq. Scot.*, *64*, 111–46.

Crawford, B. E. (1987) *Scandinavian Scotland*, Leicester.

—— (ed.) (1994) *Scotland in Dark Age Europe*, St Andrews.

—— (ed.) (1995) *Scandinavian settlement in Northern Britain*, Leicester.

—— (ed.) (1966) *Scotland in Dark Age Britain*, St Andrews.

Crawford, I. A. (1981) War or Peace – Viking colonisation in the Northern and Western Isles of Scotland reviewed, *in* Becker-Neilson, H., Foote, P. and Olsen, O. (eds) *The Proceedings of the Eighth Viking Congress 1977*, (1981), Odense, 259–69.

Crawford, I. A. and Switsur, R. (1977) Sandscaping and c14: the Udal, N. Uist, *Antiquity*, *51*, 124–36.

Cubbon, M. (1983) The Archaeology of the Vikings in the Isle of Man, *in* Fell *et al.* 1983, 13–26.

Cuppage, J. (1986) *Archaeological Survey of the Dingle Peninsula*, Ballyferriter.

Curle, A. O. (1921) The broch of Dun Troddan, Gleann Beag, Glenelg, Invernessshire, *Proc. Soc. Antiq. Scot.*, *55*, 83–94.

Currie, A. (1830) *Description of the Antiquities, Etc., of North Knapdale*, Glasgow.

Daniel, D. and Kjaerum, P. (1973) *Megalithic Graves and Ritual* (= Papers presented at the 3 Atlantic Colloquium, Mosegard, 1969), Copenhagen.

Davies, W. (1982) *Wales in the Early Middle Ages*, Leicester.

Dawson, A. G. (1980) Shore erosion by frost: an example from the Scottish Lateglacial, *in* Lowe, J. J., Gray, J. M. and Robinson, J. E. (eds) *Studies in the Lateglacial of north-west Europe*, Oxford, 45–53.

Deith, M. R. (1983) Molluscan calendars: the use of growth-line analysis to establish seasonality of shellfish collection at the Mesolithic site of Morton, Fife, *J. Archaeol. Sci.*, *10*, 423–40.

—— (1985) Seasonality from shells: an evaluation of two techniques for seasonal dating of marine molluscs, *in* Fieller, N. R. J., Gilbertson, D. D. and Ralph, N. G. A. (eds) *Palaeobiological Investigations: Research Design, Methods and Data Analysis* (= British Archaeological Report S266), Oxford, 119–30.

—— (1986) Subsistence strategies at a Mesolithic campsite: evidence from stable isotope analysis of shells, *J. Archaeol. Sci.*, *13*, 61–78.

DMV = MacKie 1994.

Dommasnes, L. (1991) Women, kinship and the basis of power in the Norwegian Viking Age, *in* Samson 1991, 65–73.

Dubois, A. D. and Ferguson, D. K. (1985) The climatic history of pine in the Cairngorms, based on radiocarbon dates and stable isotope analysis, with an account of the events leading up to its colonisation, *Rev. Palaeobot. Palynol.*, *46*, 55–80.

Du Chatellier, P. and Le Pontois, L. (1909) A Ship Burial in Brittany, *Saga Book of the Viking Club*, *6*, 123–61.

Dunbar, J. G. and Fisher, I. (1973) Sgòr nam Ban-Naomha ('Cliff of the Holy Women') Isle of Canna, *Scot. Archaeol. Forum*, *5*, 71–5.

Duns, J. (1881) Notice of an ancient Celtic reliquary ornamented with interlace work, *Proc. Soc. Antiq. Scot.*, *15*, 286–91.

Duplessy, J. C., Delibrias, G., Turon, J. L., Pujol, C. and Duprat, J. (1981) Deglacial warming of the north-eastern Atlantic Ocean; correlation with the palaeoclimatic evolution of the European continent, *Paleogeogr. Palaeoclimatol. Palaeoecol.*, *35*, 121–44.

Edmonds, M. (1992) Their use is Wholly Unknown, *in* Sharples and Sheridan 1992, 179–93.

Edwards, A. J. H. (1934) A Viking cist-grave at Ballinaby, Islay, *Proc. Soc. Antiq. Scot.*, *68*, 74–8.

Eldjarn, K. (1984) Graves and Grave Goods: survey and evaluation, *in* Fenton and Palsson 1984, 2–11.

Fairhurst, H. (1984) *Excavations at Crosskirk broch, Caithness* (= Society of Antiquaries of Scotland Monograph Series 3), Edinburgh.

Fanning, T. (1981) Excavation of an Early Christian cemetery and settlement at Reask, County Kerry, *Proc. Royal Irish Acad.*, *81C*, 67–172.

—— (1988) Three ringed pins from Viking Dublin and their significance, *in* Bradley. J. 1988, 161–75.

Feachem, R. W. (1966) The hill-forts of northern Britain *in* Rivet, A. L. F. (ed.) *The Iron Age in Northern Britain*, Edinburgh, 59–87.

Fell, C. (1984) *Women in Anglo-Saxon England*, London.

Fell, C., Foote, P., Graham-Campbell, J. and Thomson, R. (eds) (1983) *The Viking Age in the Isle of Man: Ninth Viking Congress*, London.

Fellows-Jensen, G. (1984) Viking Settlement in the Northern and Western Isles, *in* Fenton and Palsson 1984, 148–68.

Fenton, A. and Palsson, H. (eds) (1984) *The Northern and Western Isles in the Viking World*, Edinburgh.

Finlayson, B. (1995) Complexity in the Mesolithic of the western Scottish seaboard, *in* Fischer, A. (ed.) *Man and Sea in the Mesolithic: Coastal Settlement above and below Present Sea Level*, Oxford, 261–4.

Fisher, I. (1994) The monastery of Iona in the eighth century, in O'Mahony, F. (ed.) *The Book of Kells: Proceedings of a conference held at Trinity College, Dublin, 1992* (1994), Dublin, 33–47.

Fisher, I. (forthcoming) *Early Medieval Sculpture in the West Highlands*, RCAHMS.

Fojut, N. (1982) Towards a geography of Shetland brochs, *Glasgow Archaeol. J.*, 9, 38–59.

Foote, P. and Wilson, D. M. (1970) *The Viking Achievement*, London.

Fowler, E. and Fowler, P. J. (1988) Excavations on Torr an Aba, Iona, Argyll, *Proc. Soc. Antiq. Scot.*, 118, 181–201.

Fraser, I. (1995) Norse settlement on the north-west seaboard, *in* Crawford 1995, 92–105.

Friell, J. G. P. and Watson, W. G. (eds) (1984) *Pictish Studies: settlement, burial and art in Dark Age Northern Britain* (= British Archaeological Reports, British Series 125), Oxford.

Gaimster, M. (1991) Money and media in Viking Age Scandinavia, *in* Samson 1991, 113–22.

Gair, I. (1995) *Investigating historic sherds with a view to matching with sherds of known provenance*, University of Staffordshire, Stoke on Trent, BSC (Hons)/BSC Applied Science Programme: final year project.

Gordon, K. (1990) A Norse Viking-age grave from Cruach Mhor, Islay, *Proc. Soc. Antiq. Scot.*, 120, 151–60.

Graham, A. (1919) A Survey of the Ancient Monuments of Skipness, *Proc. Soc. Antiq. Scot.*, 53, 76–118.

—— (1948) Some observations on the brochs, *Proc. Soc. Antiq. Scot.*, 81, 49–98.

—— (1949) Notes on some brochs and forts visited in 1949, *Proc. Soc. Antiq. Scot.*, 83, 12–24.

Graham-Campbell, J. (1976) The Viking-age silver and gold hoards of Scandinavian character from Scotland, *Proc. Soc. Antiq. Scot.*, 107, 114–35.

—— (1980) *Viking Artefacts: a select catalogue*, London.

—— (1982) Viking Silver hoards: an introduction, *in* Farrell, R. T. (ed.) *The Vikings*, London, 32–41.

—— (1983) A Viking age gold arm-ring from the sound of Jura, *Proc. Soc. Antiq. Scot.*, 113, 148–68.

—— (1995) *The Viking-age gold and silver of Scotland*, Edinburgh.

Gray, J. M. (1974a) The Main Rock Platform of the Firth of Lorn, western Scotland, *Trans. Inst. Brit. Geogr.*, 61, 81–99.

—— (1974b) Lateglacial and postglacial shorelines in western Scotland, *Boreas*, 3, 129–38.

—— (1975a) The Loch Lomond Readvance and contemporaneous sea-levels in Loch Etive and neighbouring areas of western Scotland, *Proc. Geol. Assoc.*, 86, 227–38.

—— (1975b) Lateglacial in situ barnacles from Glen Cruitten Quarry, Oban, *Quat. Newslett.*, 15, 1–2.

—— (1978) Low-level shore platforms in the south-west Scottish Highlands:

altitude, age and correlation, *Trans. Inst. Brit. Geogr.*, new series *3*, 151–64.

—— (1992) Glacial geology and geomorphology, *in* Walker *et al.* 1992, 4–11.

Gray, J. M. and Brooks, C. L. (1972) The Loch Lomond Readvance moraines of Mull and Menteith, *Scot. J. Geol.*, *8*, 95–103.

Gray, J. M. and Ivanovich, M. (1988) Age of the Main Rock Platform, western Scotland, *Palaeogeogr. Palaeoclimatol. Palaeoecol.*, 68, 337–45.

Greenwell, W. (1866) An account of excavations in cairns near Crinan, *Proc. Soc. Antiq. Scot.*, *6*, 336–51.

Grieg, S. (1940) *Viking Antiquities in Scotland* (= Shetelig, H. (ed.), *Viking Antiquities in Great Britain and Ireland* 2) Oslo.

Grieve, S. (1885) *The Great Auk or Garefowl (Alca impennis, Linn.): Its History, Archaeology and Remains*, London.

—— (1914) Note upon Carn a'Bharraich …, *Proc. Soc. Antiq. Scot.*, *48*, 272–91.

Grigson, C. and Mellars, P. A. (1987) The mammalian remains from the middens, *in* Mellars 1987, 243–89.

Groome, F. H. (1882) *Ordnance Gazetteer of Scotland*, Edinburgh and London.

Guido, M. (1974) A Scottish crannog re-dated, *Antiquity*, *48*, 54–5.

Haggart, B. A. and Bridge, M. C. (1992) Flandrian forest history of Rannoch Moor, with particular reference to the role of pine, *in* Walker *et al.* 1992, 38–50.

Haggart, B. A. and Sutherland, D. G. (1992) Moine Mhor, *in* Walker *et al.* 1992, 143–52.

Haggarty, A. M. (1988) Iona: some results from recent work, *Proc. Soc. Antiq. Scot.*, *118*, 203–13.

—— (1991) Machrie Moor, Arran: recent excavations at two stone circles, *Proc. Soc. Antiq. Scot.*, *121*, 51–94.

Halliday, S. P., Hill, P. J. and Stevenson, J. B. (1981) Early Agriculture in Scotland, *in* Mercer, R. (ed.) *Farming Practice in British Prehistory*, Edinburgh, 55–65.

Hamilton, J. R. C. (1956) *Excavations at Jarlshof, Shetland*, Edinburgh.

—— (1968) *Excavations at Clickhimin, Shetland*, Edinburgh.

Hamlin, A. and Foley, C. (1983) A women's graveyard at Carrickmore, County Tyrone, and the separate burial of women, *Ulster J. Archaeol.*, *46*, 41–6.

Harbison, P. (1992) *The High Crosses of Ireland*, Bonn.

Harding, D. W. (1974) *The Iron Age in Lowland Britain*, London.

—— (ed.) (1976) *Hillforts: Later Prehistoric Earthworks in Britain and Ireland*, London.

—— (1984) The function and classification of brochs and duns, *in* Miket and Burgess 1984, 206–20.

—— (1990) Changing perspectives in the Atlantic Iron Age, *in* Armit 1990a, 5–16.

Harding, D. and Armit, I. (1990) Survey and Excavation in west Lewis, *in* Armit 1990a, 71–107.

Harkness, D. D. (1983) The extent of natural C14 deficiency in the coastal environment of the United Kingdom, in Mook, W. G. and Waterbolk, H. T. (eds) *Proceedings of the First International Symposium 14C and Archaeology* (= PACT 8), Council of Europe, Strasbourg, 351–64.

Harris, E. C. (1979) *Principles of archaeological statigraphy*, London.

—— (1989) *Principles of archaeological stratigraphy* (2nd ed.), London.

Harrington, P. and Pierrepoint, S. (1980) Port Charlotte Chambered Cairn, Islay: An Interim Note, *Glasgow Archaeol. J.*, *7*, 113–15.

Hedges, J. W. (1987) *Bu, Gurness and the brochs of Orkney* (= British Archaeological Reports, British Series 163–5), Oxford.

—— (1990) Surveying the foundations: life after 'brochs', *in* Armit 1990a, 17–31.

Hedges, J. W. and Bell, B. (1980) That tower of Scottish prehistory: the broch, *Antiquity*, *54*, 87–94.

Hedges, R. E. M., Housley, R. A., Law, I. A. and Bronk, C. R. (1989) Radiocarbon dates from the Oxford AMS system: Archaeometry datelist 9, *Archaeometry, 31(2)*, 207–34.

Heggie, D. G. (1981) *Megalithic Science*, London.

Herbert, M. (1988) *Iona, Kells and Derry; the History and Hagiography of the Monastic Familia of Columba*, Oxford.

Henry, F. (1957) Early monasteries, beehive huts, and dry-stone houses in the neighbourhood of Caherciveen and Waterville (Co. Kerry), *Proc. Royal Irish Acad., 58C*, 45–166.

Henshall, A. S. (1963 and 1972) *The Chambered Cairns of Scotland*, Edinburgh.

Hewison, J. K. (1893) *The Island of Bute in the Olden Times*, Edinburgh and London.

Hingley, R. (1992) Society in Scotland from 700 BC to AD 200, *Proc. Soc. Antiq. Scot., 122*, 7–53.

Holmes, G. (1984) *Rock slope failure in parts of the Scottish Highlands*, Unpublished PhD thesis, University of Edinburgh.

Hope-Taylor, B. (1977) *Yeavering: an Anglo-British Centre of early Northumbria*, London.

Hunt, J. (1956) On two 'D'-shaped bronze objects in the St Germain museum, *Proc. Royal Irish Acad., 57C*, 153–7.

Hunter, J. R., Bond, J. M. and Smith, A. (1993) Some aspects of early Viking settlement in Orkney, *in* Batey *et al.* 1993, 272–84.

Innes, J. L. (1983) Lichenometric dating of débris flow deposits in the Scottish Highlands, *Earth surf. Process. Landf., 8*, 579–88.

International Study Group (1982) An inter-laboratory comparison of radiocarbon measurements in tree rings, *Nature, 298 (5875)*, 619–23.

Iversen, J. (1944) Viscum, Hedera and Ilex as climatic indicators. *Geol. Foren. Stock. Forhand., 66*, 463–83.

Jack, R. L. (1875) Notes on a hill or boulder clay with broken shells, in the lower valley of the River Endrick, near Loch Lomond, and its relation to certain other deposits, *Trans. Geol. Soc. Glasgow, 5*, 5–25.

Jacobi, R. M. (1982) Lost hunters in Kent: Tasmania and the earliest Neolithic, *in* Leach, P. E. (ed.) *Archaeology in Kent to AD 1500* (= Council for British Archaeology Research Report 48), London, 12–24.

Jansson, I. (1981) Ecomonic aspects of fine metalworking in Viking Age Scandinavia, *in* Wilson, D. M. and Caygill, M. L. (eds) *Economic Aspects of the Viking Age*, London, 1–19.

Jardine, W. G. (1987) The Mesolithic coastal setting, *in* Mellars 1987, 25–51.

Jardine, W. G. and Jardine, D. C. (1983) Minor excavations and small finds at three Mesolithic sites, Isle of Oronsay, Argyll, *Proc. Soc. Antiq. Scot., 113*, 22–34.

Jesch, J. (1991) *Women in the Viking Age*, Woodbridge.

Johnston, A. (1995) Norse settlement patterns in Coll and Tiree, *in* Crawford, B. E. 1995, 108–26.

Kaland, S. (1993) The settlement of Westness, Rousay, *in* Batey *et al.* 1993, 308–17.

Kaplan, S. A. and Barsness, K. J. (1986) *Raven's Journey; The World of Alaska's Native People*, Pennsylvania.

Kavanagh, R. (1988) The horse in Viking Ireland, *in* Bradley 1988, 89–122.

Kelly, F. (1988) *A Guide to Early Irish Law*, Dublin.

Kermode, P. M. C. (1930) Ship Burial in the Isle of Man, *Antiq. J., 10*, 126–33.

Kruse, S. (1993) Silver storage and circulation in Viking-age Scotland, *in* Batey *et al.* 1993, 187–203.

Lacaille, A. D. (1954) *The Stone Age in Scotland*, Oxford.

Lacy, B. (1983) *Archaeological Survey of County Donegal*, Lifford.

Lamont, W. B. (1966) *The Early History of Islay (500–1726)*, Dundee.

Lane, A. (1984) Some Pictish problems at Dunadd, *in* Friell and Watson 1984, 43–62.

—— (1987) English migrants in the Hebrides: 'Atlantic Second B' revisted, *Proc. Soc. Antiq. Scot., 117*, 47–66.

—— (1990) Hebridean pottery: problems of definition, chronology, presence and absence, *in* Armit 1990a, 108–30.

—— (1994) Trade, gifts and cultural exchange in Dark-age western Scotland, *in* Crawford, B. E. 1994, 103–15.

Lehane, D. (1990) Arran: Machrie North and Glaister, *in* Buckley 1990, 77–9.

Leitch, R. (1989) Travellers' Tents, *Scottish Vernacular Buildings Working Group, 13*, 15–22.

Lethbridge, T. C. (1925) Battle Site in Gorten Bay, Ardnamurchan, *Proc. Soc. Antiq. Scot., 59*, 105–8.

Liestol, A. (1983) An Iona rune stone and the world of Man and the Isles, *in* Fell *et al.* 1983, 85–93.

Loder, J. de V. (1935) *Colonsay and Oronsay in the Isles of Argyll*, Edinburgh and London.

Lowe, J. J. and Walker, M. J. C. (1986) Lateglacial and early Flandrian environmental history of the Isle of Mull, Inner Hebrides, Scotland. *Trans. Roy. Soc. Edinburgh Earth Sci., 77*, 1–20.

Lucas, A. T. (1966) Irish-Norse relations: time for a reappraisal? *J. Cork Archaeol. Hist. Soc., 71*, 62–75.

—— (1967) The Plundering and Burning of Churches in Ireland, 7th to 16th century, *in* Rynne, E. (ed.) *North Munster Studies*, Essays presented to Monsignor Michael Moloney, Limerick, 172–229.

McCann, S. B. (1961) Some supposed 'raised beach' deposits at Corran, Loch Linnhe and Loch Etive, *Geol. Mag., 98*, 131–42.

McCormick, F. (1989) Report on excavations on Iona, *in* Historic Scotland, Archaeological Operations & Conservation, *Annual Report 1989*, 28–30.

McCullagh, R. J. (1989) Excavations at Newton, Islay, *Glasgow Archaeol. J., 15*, 23–52.

Macdonald, A. (1973a) 'Annat' in Scotland: a provisional review, *Scottish Studies, 17*, 135–46.

—— (1973b) Two major early monasteries of Scottish Dalriata: Lismore and Eigg, *Scot. Archaeol. Forum, 5*, 47–70.

—— (1984) Aspects of the monastery and monastic life in Adomnán's Life of Columba, *Peritia, 3*, 271–302.

MacKie, E. W. (1964) New excavations on the Monamore neolithic chambered cairn, Lamlash, Isle of Arran in 1961, *Proc. Soc. Antiq. Scot., 97*, 1–34.

—— (1965a) The origin and development of the broch and wheelhouse building cultures of the Scottish Iron Age, *Proc. Prehist. Soc., 31*, 93–143.

—— (1965b) Brochs and the Hebridean Iron Age, *Antiquity, 39*, 266–78.

—— (1969a) Radiocarbon dates and the Scottish Iron Age, *Antiquity, 43*, 15–26.

—— (1971) English migrants and Scottish brochs, *Glasgow Archaeol. J., 2*, 39–71.

—— (1974) *Dun Mor Vaul: an Iron Age broch on Tiree*, Glasgow.

—— (1975) The brochs of Scotland, *in* Fowler, P. J. (ed.) *Recent Work in Rural Archaeology*, Bradford-on-Avon, 72–92.

—— (1976) The Vitrified Forts of Scotland, *in* Harding 1976, 205–35.

—— (1978) The origin of iron-working in Scotland, *in* Ryan, M. (ed.) *Origins of Metallurgy in Atlantic Europe: Proc. 5th Atlantic Colloquium*, Dublin, 295–302.

—— (1980) Dun an Ruigh Ruaidh, Loch Broom, Ross, and Cromarty: excavations in 1968 and 1978, *Glasgow Archaeol. J., 7*, 32–79.

—— (1981) Wise Men in Antiquity, *in* Ruggles and Whittle 1981, 111–52.

—— (1982) The Leckie broch, Stirlingshire: an interim report, *Glasgow Archaeol. J.*, 9, 60–72.

—— (1983) Testing hypotheses about brochs, *Scot. Archaeol. Rev.*, 2.2, 117–28.

—— (1986) Impact on the Scottish Iron Age of the discoveries at Leckie broch, *Glasgow Archaeol. J.*, 14, 1–18.

—— (1988) Dun Cuier again, *Scot. Archaeol. Rev.*, 6, 116–18.

—— (1992) The Iron Age semibrochs of Atlantic Scotland: a case study in the problems of deductive reasoning, *Archaeol. J.*, 148, 149–81.

—— (1995a) The early Celts in Scotland, *in* Green, M. (ed.) *The Celtic World*, London, 654–70.

—— (1995b) Midhowe and Gurness brochs in Orkney; some problems of misinterpretation, *Archaeol. J.*, 151, 98–157.

MacKie, E. W. and Davis, A. (1989) New Light on Neolithic Rock Carvings: The Petroglyphs at Greenland (Auchentorlie), Dunbartonshire, *Glasgow Archaeol. J.*, 15, 125–56.

MacKie, E. W. and MacAoidh, I. E. (1969) Tuineachas Iarunnaoiseach air Thiriodh, *Gairm*, 67, 276–82.

MacLaren, A. (1969) A Cist Cemetery at Glenreasdell Mains, Kintyre, Argyll, *Proc. Soc. Antiq. Scot.*, 101, 111–18.

—— (1974) A Norse house on Drimore Machair, South Uist, *Glasgow Archaeol J.*, 3, 9–18.

Maclean, D. (1983) Knapdale dedications to a Leinster saint, *Scottish Studies*, 27, 49–65.

McNeill, M. (1891) Notice of excavations in a burial mound of the Viking Periods in Oronsay, *Proc. Soc. Antiq. Scot.*, 25, 432–5.

—— (1892) Notice of the discovery of a Viking interment in the island of Colonsay, *Proc. Soc. Antiq. Scot.*, 26, 61–2.

—— (1910) *Colonsay, One of the Hebrides*, Edinburgh.

Macquarrie, A. (1994) The historical context of the Govan stones, *in* Ritchie, A. 1994, 27–32.

Mann, L. M. (1915) Report on the relics discovered during excavations in 1913 at the cave at Dunagoil, Bute and in 1914 at the fort of Dunagoil, Bute, *Trans. Bute Nat. Hist. Soc.*, 8, 61–86.

—— (1925) Note on the Results of the Exploration of the Fort at Dunagoil, *Trans. Bute Nat. Hist. Soc.*, 9, 56–60.

Mapleton, R. J. (1866) Notice of a cairn at Kilchoan, Argyleshire, and its contents, *Proc. Soc. Antiq. Scot.*, 6, 351–5.

—— (1871) Notice of Remarkable Cists in a Gravel Bank near Kilmartin; and of Incised Sculpturings of Axe Heads, and Other Markings on the Stones of the Cists, *Proc. Soc. Antiq. Scot.*, 8, 378–80.

Marshall, D. N. (1964) Report on the excavations at Little Dunagoil, *Trans. Bute Nat. Hist. Soc.*, 16, 1–69.

—— (1977) Carved stone balls, *Proc. Soc. Antiq. Scot.*, 108, 40–72.

—— (1978) Excavations at Auchategan, Glendaruel, Argyll, *Proc. Soc. Antiq. Scot.*, 109, 36–74.

—— (1983) Further Notes on Carved Stone Balls, *Proc. Soc. Antiq. Scot.*, 113, 628–30.

Marshall, D. N. and Taylor, I. (1977) The excavation of the chambered cairn at Glenvoidean, Isle of Bute, *Proc. Soc. Antiq. Scot.*, 108, 1–39.

Marshall, J. N. (1915) Preliminary note on some excavations at Dunagoil fort and cave, *Trans. Bute Nat. Hist. Soc.*, 8, 42–9.

Martin, M. (1934) *A Description of the Western Islands of Scotland*, Stirling.

Maxwell, G. (1969) Duns and forts: a note on some Iron Age monuments of the Atlantic province, *Scot. Archaeol. Forum*, 1, 41–52.

Meehan, B. (1982) *Shell Bed to Shell Midden*, Australian Institute for Aboriginal Studies, Canberra.

Mellars, P. A. (1972) The Palaeolithic and Mesolithic, *in* Renfrew, C. (ed.) *British Prehistory: a New Outline*, London, 41–99.

—— (1987) *Excavations on Oronsay: Prehistoric Human Ecology on a Small Island*, Edinburgh.

Mellars, P. A. and Wilkinson, M. R. (1980) Fish otoliths as indicators of seasonality in prehistoric shell middens: the evidence from Oronsay (Inner Hebrides), *Proc. Prehist. Soc.*, *46*, 19–44.

Mercer, J. (1971) A regression-time Stone-workers' Camp. 33ft OD, Lussa River, Isle of Jura, *Proc. Soc. Antiq. Scot.*, *103*, 1–32.

—— (1972) Microlithic and Bronze Age camps, 75–26ft OD, N Carn, Isle of Jura, *Proc. Soc. Antiq. Scot.*, *104*, 1–22.

—— (1974) Glenbatrick Waterhole, a microlithic site on the Isle of Jura, *Proc. Soc. Antiq. Scot.*, *105*, 1–32.

—— (1978) The King's Cave, Jura, *Glasgow Archaeol J.*, *5*, 44–70.

—— (1980) Lussa Wood 1: the Late-Glacial and Early Post-Glacial Occupation of Jura, *Proc. Soc. Antiq. Scot.*, *110*, 1–32.

Mercer, R. J. and Rideout, J. (1987) The excavation of a cist-group at Upper Largie quarry, Kilmartin, central Argyll 1982–1983, *Glasgow Archaeol. J.*, *14*, 25–38.

Meyer, K. (1913) *Uber die älteste Irische dichtung*, Berlin.

Miket, R. and Burgess, C., (eds) (1984) *Between and beyond the Walls: essays on the prehistory and history of Northern Britain in honour of George Jobey*, Edinburgh.

Mitchell, A. (1884) On white pebbles in connection with pagan and Christian burials …, *Proc. Soc. Antiq. Scot.*, *18*, 286–91.

Mithen, S. J. (1989) New evidence for Mesolithic settlement on Colonsay, *Proc. Soc. Antiq. Scot.*, *119*, 33–41.

—— (1996) *The Southern Hebrides Mesolithic Project 1996 Progress Report*, Reading.

Mithen, S. J. and Finlayson, B. (1991) Red deer hunters on Colonsay? The implications of Staosnaig for the interpretation of the Oronsay middens, *Proc. Prehist. Soc.*, *57(2)*, 1–8.

Morris, C. D. (1977) Northumbria and the Viking Settlement: the evidence for landholding, *Archaeol. Aeliana*, *54*, 81–103.

—— (1979) The Vikings and Irish Monasteries, *Durham University J.*, *71*, 175–85.

—— (1985) Viking Orkney, *in* Renfrew, C. (ed.) *The Prehistory of Orkney*, Edinburgh, 210–42.

—— (1993) The Birsay Bay Project, *in* Batey *et al.* 1993, 285–307.

Morris, R. W. B. (1969) The Cup-and-ring Marks and Similar Sculptures of Scotland: a Survey of the Southern Counties, Part II, *Proc. Soc. Antiq. Scot.*, *100*, 47–78.

—— (1974) The Petroglyphs at Achnabreck, Argyll, *Proc. Soc. Antiq. Scot.*, *103*, 33–56.

—— (1977) *The Rock Art of Argyll*, Poole.

—— (1993) Cup-and-ring Mark Dating, *Glasgow Archaeol. J.*, *16*, 85–6.

Morrison, A. and Bonsall, C. (1989) The early post-glacial settlement of Scotland: a review, *in* Bonsall, C. (ed.) *The Mesolithic in Europe*. Papers Presented at the Third International Symposium, Edinburgh 1985, Edinburgh, 134–42.

Morrison, I. (1985) *Landscape with Lake Dwellings*, Edinburgh.

Movius, H. L. (1940) An early post-glacial archaeological site at Cushendun, County Antrim, *Proc. Royal Irish Acad.*, *46*, 1–84.

—— (1942) *The Irish Stone Age. Its Chronology, Development and Relations*, Cambridge.

Murphy, G. (ed.) (1956) *Early Irish Lyrics*, Oxford.

NSA (1845) *The New Statistical Account of Scotland*, Edinburgh.

Nicolaisen, W. H. F. (1969) Norse Settlement in the Northern and Western Isles, *Scottish Historical Review*, 48, 6–17.

—— (1982) The Viking Settlement of Scotland, *in* Farrell, P. T. (ed.) *The Vikings*, London, 95–115.

Nieke, M. (1983) Settlement patterns in the first millennium AD: a case study of the island of Islay, *in* Chapman and Mytum 1983, 299–326.

—— (1984) *Settlement Patterns in the Alantic Province of Scotland in the 1st millennium AD: A study of Argyll*, Unpublished PhD thesis, University of Glasgow.

—— (1990) Fortifications in Argyll: Retrospect and Future Prospect *in* Armit 1990a, 131–42.

Nieke, M. R. and Boyd, W. E. (1987) Eilean an Duin, Craignish, Mid-Argyll, *Glasgow. Archaeol. J.*, 14, 48–53.

Nieke, M. and Duncan, H. (1988) Dalriada: the establishment and maintenance of an Early Historic Kingdom in northern Britain, *in* Driscoll, S. and Nieke, M. (eds), *Power and Politics in Early Medieval Britain and Ireland*, Edinburgh, 6–21.

Nisbet, H. C. and Gailey, R. A. (1960) A survey of the antiquities of North Rona, *Archaeol. J.*, 117, 88–115.

O'Cuiv, B. (1988) Personal names as an indicator of relations between native Irish and settlers in the Viking period, *in* Bradley 1988, 79–88.

O'Floinn, R. (1983) The bronze strainer ladle in the Derrynaflan hoard, *in* Ryan, M. (ed.) *The Derrynaflan Hoard, I, A Preliminary Account*, Dublin, 31–4.

O'Kelly, M. J. (1982) *Newgrange: archaeology, art and legend*, London.

O'Sullivan, J. (1994) Excavation of an early church and a women's cemetery at St Ronan's medieval parish church, Iona, *Proc. Soc. Antiq. Scot.*, 124, 327–65.

Peacock, J. D. (1971a) Terminal features of the Creran glacier of Loch Lomond Readvance age in western Benderloch, Argyll, and their significance in the late glacial history of the Loch Linnhe area, *Scot. J. Geol.*, 7, 349–56.

—— (1971b) Marine shell radiocarbon dates and the chronology of deglaciation in western Scotland, *Natur. Phys. Sci.*, 230, 43–5.

—— (1983) A model for Scottish interstadial marine palaeotemperature 13,000 to 11,000 BP, *Boreas*, 12, 73–82.

—— (1989) Marine molluscs and Late Quaternary environmental studies with particular reference to the Late-glacial period in north-west Europe: a review, *Quat. Sci. Rev.*, 8, 179–92.

Peacock, J. D., Graham, D. K. and Wilkinson, I. P. (1978) Late-glacial and post-glacial marine environments at Ardyne, Scotland, and their significance in the interpretation of the history of the Clyde sea area, *Rep. Inst. Geol. Sci.*, 78/17, 25ff.

Peacock, J. D., Harkness, D. D., Housley, R. A., Little, J. A. and Paul, M. A. (1989) Radiocarbon ages for a glaciomarine bed associated with the maximum of the Loch Lomond Readvance in west Benderloch, Argyll, *Scot. J. Geol.*, 25, 69–79.

Peacock, J. D. and Harkness, D. D. (1990) Radiocarbon ages and the full-glacial to Holocene transition in seas adjacent to Scotland and southern Scandinavia: a review, *Trans. Roy. Soc. Edinburgh Earth Sci.*, 81, 385–96.

Peltenburg, E. J. (1972) Excavation of Culcharron cairn, Benderloch, Argyll, *Proc. Soc. Antiq. Scot.*, 104, 63–70.

—— (1979) Two cist burials at Kintyre Nurseries, Campbeltown, Argyll, *Glasgow Archaeol. J.*, 6, 11–19.

—— (1982) Excavations at Balloch Hill, *Proc. Soc. Antiq. Scot.*, 112, 142–214.

Pennant, T. (1790) *A Tour in Scotland; and a voyage to the Hebrides*.

Petersen, J. (1919) De norske vikingesverd. En typologisk-kronlogisk studie over vikingetidens vaaben (= Videnskaps-Selskapets Skrifter, 2, Hist-Filos. Klusse 1919 No.1), Kristiania.
—— (1928) *Vikingetidens smykker*, Stavanger.
Piggott, C. M. (1949) A Note on an Excavation at Dunan na Nighean, Colonsay, *Proc. Soc. Antiq. Scot.*, *83*, 232–3.
Piggott, S. (1954) *The Neolithic Cultures of the British Isles*, Cambridge.
—— (1959) The radiocarbon dates from Durrington Walls, *Antiquity*, *33*, 289–90.
—— (1968) *The Druids*, London.
—— (1972) Excavation of the Dalladies long barrow, Fettercairn, Kincardineshire, *Proc. Soc. Antiq. Scot.*, *104*, 23–47.
—— (1973) Problems in the interpretation of chambered tombs, *in* Daniel and Kjaerum 1973, 9–15.
Piggott, S. and Daniel, G. E. (1951) *A Picture Book of Ancient British Art*, Cambridge.
Piggott, S. and Robertson, M. (1977) *Three Centuries of Scottish Archaeology*, Edinburgh.
Plummer, C. (1892) *Two of the Anglo-Saxon Chronicles Parallel*, Oxford.
Pollard, A. (1990) Down through the Ages: a Review of the Oban Cave Deposits, *Scot. Archaeol. Rev.*, *7*, 58–74.
Powell, T. G. E., Corcoran, J. X. W. P., Lynch, F. and Scott, J. G. (1969) *Megalithic Enquiries in the West of Britain*, Liverpool.
RCAHMS: Royal Commission on the Ancient and Historical Monuments of Scotland.
RCAHMS (1946) *Inventory of Orkney and Shetland. Volume 2: Orkney*, Edinburgh.
—— (1971) *Argyll: an Inventory of the Ancient Monuments. Vol. 1: Kintyre*, Edinburgh.
—— (1975) *Argyll: an Inventory of the Ancient Monuments. Vol. 2: Lorn*, Edinburgh.
—— (1980) *Argyll: an Inventory of the Monuments. Vol. 3: Mull, Tiree, Coll and Northern Argyll*, Edinburgh.
—— (1982) *Argyll: an Inventory of the Monuments. Vol. 4: Iona*, Edinburgh.
—— (1984) *Argyll: an Inventory of the Monuments. Vol. 5: Islay, Jura, Colonsay and Oronsay*, Edinburgh.
—— (1988) *Argyll: an Inventory of the Monuments. Vol. 6: Mid Argyll and Cowal: Prehistoric and Early Historic monuments*, Edinburgh.
—— (1992) *Argyll: an Inventory of the Ancient Monuments. Vol. 7: Mid Argyll and Cowal: Medieval and Later Historic monuments*, Edinburgh.
Radford, C. A. R. (1977) The Earliest Irish Churches, *Ulster J. Archaeol.*, *40*, 1–11.
Raftery, B. (1994) *Pagan Celtic Ireland; the Enigma of the Irish Iron Age*, London.
Ralston, I. (1981) The use of timber in hill-fort defences in France, *in* Guilbert, G., (ed.) *Hill-fort Studies: essays for A. H. A. Hogg*, Leicester, 78–104.
—— (1986) The Yorkshire Television vitrified wall experiment at East Tullos, City of Aberdeen, *Proc. Soc. Antiq. Scot.*, *116*, 17–40.
Randsborg, K. (1980) *The Viking Age in Denmark*, London.
Reece, R. (1981) *Excavations in Iona 1964 to 1974*, London.
Rees, T., Kozikowski, G. and Miket, R. (1994) Investigation of a shell midden at An Corran, Staffin, Isle of Skye. Unpublished report.
Rennie, E. B. (1984) Excavations at Ardnadam, Cowal, 1964–82, *Glasgow Archaeol. J.*, *11*.
Richards, J. D., Jecock, M., Richmond, L. and Tuck, W. (1995) The Viking Cemetery at Heath Wood, Ingleby, Derbyshire, *Medieval Archaeol.*, *39*, 51–70.
Rideout, J., Owen, O., and Halpin, E. (1992) *Hillforts of southern Scotland* (= AOC Monograph 1), Edinburgh.

Ritchie, A. (1977) Excavation of Pictish and Viking-age farmsteads at Buckquoy, Orkney, *Proc. Soc. Antiq. Scot.*, *108*, 174–227.
—— (1993) *Viking Scotland*, London.
—— (ed.) (1994) *Govan and its Medieval Sculpture*, Stroud.
—— (1995) *Prehistoric Orkney*, London.
Ritchie, A., Ritchie, G., Whittington, G. and Soulsby, J. (1974) A prehistoric field-boundary from the Black Crofts, North Connel, Argyll, *Glasgow Archaeol. J.*, *3*, 66–70.
Ritchie, J. N. G. (1967a) Balnabraid Cairn, Kintyre, Argyll, *Trans. Dumfries Galloway Natur. Hist. Antiq. Soc.*, *44*, 81–8.
—— (1967b) Keil Cave, Southend, Argyll: a late Iron Age cave occupation in Kintyre, *Proc. Soc. Antiq. Scot.*, *99*, 104–10.
—— (1968) A Bronze Age cairn at Moleigh, Lorn, Argyll, *Proc. Soc. Antiq. Scot.*, *100*, 190–2.
—— (1970) Excavation of the chambered cairn at Achnacreebeag, *Proc. Soc. Antiq. Scot.*, *102*, 31–55.
—— (1971a) Iron Age finds from Dun an Fheurain, Gallanach, Argyll, *Proc. Soc. Antiq. Scot.*, *103*, 100–12.
—— (1971b) Excavation of a cairn at Strontoiller, Lorn, Argyll, *Glasgow Archaeol. J.*, *2*, 1–7.
—— (1972) Excavation of a chambered cairn at Dalineun, Lorn, Argyll, *Proc. Soc. Antiq. Scot.*, *104*, 48–62.
—— (1974) Excavation of the stone circle and cairn at Balbirnie, Fife, *Archaeol. J.*, *131*, 1–32.
—— (1981) Excavations at Machrins, Colonsay, *Proc. Soc. Antiq. Scot.*, *111*, 263–81.
—— (1987) A cist from Kentraw, Islay, *Proc. Soc. Antiq. Scot.*, *117*, 41–5.
Ritchie, J. N. G. and Crawford, J. (1978) Excavations at Sorisdale and Killunaig, Coll, *Proc. Soc. Antiq. Scot.*, *109*, 75–84.
Ritchie, J. N. G. and Lane, A. M. (1980) Dun Cul Bhuirg, Iona, Argyll, *Proc. Soc. Antiq. Scot.*, *110*, 209–29.
Ritchie, J. N. G. and Shepherd, I. A. G. (1973) Beaker pottery and associated artefacts in south-west Scotland, *Trans. Dumfries Galloway Natur. Hist. Antiq. Soc.*, *50*, 18–36.
Ritchie, J. N. G. and Stevenson, J. B. (1982) Cists at Traigh Bhan, Islay, Argyll, *Proc. Soc. Antiq. Scot.*, *112*, 550–9.
Ritchie, J. N. G., Thornber, I., Lynch, F. and Marshall, D. N. (1975) Small cairns in Argyll: some recent work, *Proc. Soc. Antiq. Scot.*, *106*, 15–38.
Ritchie, J. N. G. and Welfare, H. G. (1983) Excavations at Ardnave, Islay, *Proc. Soc. Antiq. Scot.*, *113*, 302–66.
Robertson, A. S. (1971) Roman Coins found in Scotland, 1961–70, *Proc. Soc. Antiq. Scot.*, *103*, 113–68.
—— (1983) Roman Coins found in Scotland,1971–82, *Proc. Soc. Antiq. Scot.*, *113*, 405–48.
Robertson, D. (1877) Notes on a raised beach at Cumbrae, *Trans. Geol. Soc. Glasgow*, *5*, 192–200.
Romans, J. C. C. and Robertson, L. (1975) Soils and archaeology in Scotland, *in* Evans, J. G., Limbrey, S. and Cleere, H., *The effect of man on the landscape: the Highland Zone* (= Council for British Archaeology Research Report 11), London, 37–9.
Roesdahl, E. (1991) *The Vikings*, London.
Ruddiman, W. F. and McIntyre, A. (1973) Time-transgressive deglacial retreat of polar waters from the North Atlantic, *Quat. Res.*, *3*, 117–30.
Ruggles, C. L. N. *et al.* (1984) *Megalithic Astronomy: a new archaeological and*

statistical study of 300 western Scottish sites (= British Archaeological Reports, British Series 123), Oxford.

Ruggles, C. L. N. and Whittle, A.W. R. (1981) *Astronomy and Society in Britain during the period 4000–1500 BC* (= British Archaeological Reports, British Series 88), Oxford.

Russell, N. J., Bonsall, C. and Sutherland, D. G. (1995) The exploration of marine molluscs in the Mesolithic of western Scotland: evidence from Ulva Cave, Inner Hebrides, *in* Fischer, A. (ed.) *Man and Sea in the Mesolithic. Coastal Settlement above and below Present Sea Level*, Oxford, 273–88.

Russell-White, C. J. and Barber, J. W. (1990) Bute and Islay, *in* Buckley 1990, 82–3.

Sahlins, M.(1974) *Stone Age Economics*, London.

Samson, R. (ed.) (1991) *Social Approaches to Viking Studies*, Glasgow.

—— (1991) Fighting with silver: rethinking trading, raiding and hoarding, *in* Samson, 1991, 123–33.

Saville, A. and Hallen, Y. (1994) The 'Obanian Iron Age': human remains from the Oban cave sites, Argyll, Scotland, *Antiquity*, 68, 715–23.

Saville, A. and Miket, R. (1994) An Corran rock-shelter, Skye: a major new Mesolithic site, *PAST*, 18, 9–10.

Sawyer, P. H. (1962) *The Age of the Vikings*, London.

—— (1971) *The Age of the Vikings* (second edition), London.

—— (1982) *Kings and Vikings*, London.

Scott, J. G. (1956) The Excavation of the Chambered Cairn at Brackley, Kintyre, Argyll, *Proc. Soc. Antiq. Scot.*, 89, 22–54.

—— (1961) The Excavation of the Chambered Cairn at Crarae, Lochfyneside, Mid Argyll, *Proc. Soc. Antiq. Scot.*, 94, 1–27.

—— (1964) The Chambered Cairn at Beacharra, Kintyre, Argyll, *Proc. Prehist. Soc.*, 30, 134–58.

—— (1969) The Clyde Cairns of Scotland, *in* Powell *et al.* 1969, 175–222.

—— (1973) The Clyde Cairns of Scotland, *in* Daniel and Kjaerum 1973, 117–28.

—— (1989) The Stone Circles at Temple Wood, Kilmartin, Argyll, *Glasgow Archaeol. J.*, 15, 53–124.

Scott, Sir L. (1947) The problem of the brochs, *Proc. Prehist. Soc.*, 13, 1–36.

—— (1948) Gallo-British Colonies. The Aisled Round-House Culture in the North, *Proc. Prehist. Soc.*, 14, 46–125.

—— (1954) The Norse in the Hebrides, *in* Simpson, W. D. (ed.), *The Viking Congress, 1950*, Aberdeen, 189–215.

Scott, W. H. (1854) Report on a large hoard of Anglo-Saxon pennies in silver found in the island of Islay, *Proc. Soc. Antiq. Scot.*, 1, 74–81.

Searight, S. (1993) Lussa Bay, Isle of Jura, Argyll: a note on additional tools, *Proc. Soc. Antiq. Scot.*, 123, 1–8.

Sellar, W. D. H. (1966) The origins and ancestry of Somerled, *Scot. Hist. Review*, 45, 123–42.

Sharpe, R. (trans.) (1995) *Adomnán of Iona, Life of St Columba*, Harmondsworth.

Sharples, N. and Sheridan, A. (eds) *Vessels for the Ancestors*, Edinburgh.

Shee-Twohig, E. (1981) *The Megalithic Art of Western Europe*, Oxford.

Shepherd, I. A. G. and Tuckwell, A. N. (1977) Traces of beaker-period cultivation at Rosinish, Benbecula, *Proc. Soc. Antiq. Scot.*, 108, 108–13.

Sheridan, A. (1995) Irish Neolithic pottery: the story in 1995, in Kinnes, I. and Varndell, G. (eds), *'Unbaked Urns of Rudely Shape'* (= Oxbow Monograph 55), Oxford.

Sheridan, A. and Davis, M. (1995) The Poltalloch 'Jet' Spacer Plate Necklace, *The Kist*, 49, 1–9.

Shetelig, H. (1945) The Viking graves in Great Britain and Ireland, *Acta Archaeologica*, *16*, (1945), 1–54 (reprinted *in* Shetelig 1954, 65–111).

Shetelig, H. (ed.) (1954) *The Civilisation of the Viking Settlers in relation to their old and new countries (= Viking Antiquities in Great Britain and Ireland*, 6), Oslo.

Siggins, G. and Carter, S. (1993) The monitoring of an eroding prehistoric site at Achnasavil, Carradale, Kintyre, *Glasgow Archaeol. J.*, *18*, 41–8.

Simpson, D. D. A. (1976) The later neolithic and Beaker Settlement site at Northton, Isle of Harris, *in* Burgess and Miket 1976, 221–32.

Simpson, Sir J. Y. (1868) On Ancient Sculpturings of Cups and Concentric Rings, etc., *Proc. Scot. Antiq. Scot.*, 6, Appendix.

Sissons, J. B. (1982) The so-called high 'interglacial' rock shoreline of western Scotland, *Trans. Inst. Brit. Geogr.*, new series 7, 205–16.

—— (1983a) The Quaternary geomorphology of the Inner Hebrides: a review and reassessment, *Proc. Geol. Assoc.*, *94*, 165–75.

—— (1983b) Shorelines and isostasy in Scotland, *in* Smith, D. E. and Dawson, A. G. (eds) *Shorelines and Isostasy*, London, 209–25.

Smith, B. (ed.) (1994) *Howe: four millennia of Orkney prehistory* (= Society of Antiquaries of Scotland Monograph Series 9), Edinburgh.

Smith, C. (1988) Mid Argyll Cave and Rock Shelter Survey. Report 4, Department of Archaeology, University of Newcastle-upon-Tyne.

—— (1992) *Late Stone Age Hunters of the British Isles*, London.

Smith, S. M. (1971) Palaeoecology of post-glacial beaches in East Lothian, *Scot. J. Geol.*, *8*, 31–49.

Smyth, A. P. (1977) *Scandinavian Kings in the British Isles, 850–880*, Oxford.

—— (1984) *Warlords and Holy Men*, London.

Solberg, B. (1985) Social Status in the Merovingian and Viking periods in Norway from archaeological and historical sources, *Norwegian Archaeol. Review*, *18*, 61–76.

Somerville, J. E. (1899) Notice of an ancient structure called 'The Altar', in the island of Canna, *Proc. Soc. Antiq. Scot.*, *33*, 133–40.

Spearman, R. M. and Higgitt, J. (eds) (1993) *The Age of Migrating Ideas: Early Medieval Art in Northern Britain and Ireland*, Edinburgh.

Spriggs, M. and Anderson, A. (1993) Late colonisation of East Polynesia, *Antiquity*, *67*, 200–17.

Stalsberg, A. (1991) Women as actors in North European Viking Age trade, *in* Samson 1991, 75–83.

Statistical Account of Scotland, 1791–9, Edinburgh.

Stevenson, J. B. (1984) The excavation of a hut circle at Cul a'Bhaile, Jura, *Proc. Soc. Antiq. Scot.*, *114*, 127–60.

Stevenson, R. B. K. (1949) The nuclear fort at Dalmahoy, Midlothian, and other Dark Age Capitals, *Proc. Soc. Antiq. Scot.*, *83*, 186–98.

—— (1951) A hoard of Anglo-Saxon coins found at Iona Abbey, *Proc. Soc. Antiq. Scot.*, *85*, 170–5.

Stokes, W. (1905) *The Martyrology of Oengus the Culdee*, Henry Bradshaw Society, London.

Stuiver, M. and Pearson, G. W. (1986) High precision calibration of the radiocarbon timescale, AD 1950 – 500 BC, *Radiocarbon*, *28*, 805–38.

Stuiver, M. and Reimer, P. J. (1993) University of Washington Quaternary Isotope Lab Radiocarbon Calibration Program Rev 3.0.3, *Radiocarbon 35*, 215–30.

Sutherland, D. G. (1981) The Raised Shorelines and Deglaciation of the Loch Long/Loch Fyne area, western Scotland. Unpublished PhD thesis, University of Edinburgh.

—— (1984) The Quaternary deposits of Scotland and the neighbouring shelves: a review, *Quat. Sci. Rev.*, *3*, 157–254.

Telfer Dunbar, J. (1980) *Herself: the life and photographs of M. E. M. Donaldson*, Edinburgh.

Thom, A. (1967) *Megalithic Sites in Britain*, Oxford.

—— (1971) *Megalithic Lunar Observatories*, Oxford.

Thom, A. and Thom, A. S. (1978) *Megalithic Remains in Britain and Brittany*, Oxford.

Thomas, C. (1971) *The Early Christian archaeology of North Britain*, London.

Thomas, F. W. L. (1882) On Islay Placenames, *Proc. Soc. Antiq. Scot.*, *16*, 241–76.

Thorp, P. W. (1986) A mountain icefield of Loch Lomond Stadial age, western Grampians, Scotland, *Boreas*, *15*, 83–97.

—— (1991) The glaciation and glacial deposits of the western Grampians, *in* Ehlers, J., Gibbard, P. L. and Rose, J., *Glacial Deposits in Great Britain and Ireland*, Rotterdam, 137–49.

Tipping, R. M. (1985) Loch Lomond Stadial Artemisia pollen assemblages and Loch Lomond Readvance regional fernline altitudes, *Quat. Newslett.*, *46*, 1–11.

—— (1987) The prospects for establishing synchroneity in the early post-glacial pollen peak of Juniperus in the British Isles, *Boreas*, *16*, 155–63.

—— (1989) Devensian Lateglacial vegetation history of Loch Barnluasgan, Argyllshire, western Scotland, *J. Biogeogr.*, *16*, 435–47.

—— (1991a) Climatic change in Scotland during the Devensian Late Glacial: the palynological record, *in* Barton, N., Roberts, A. J. and Rose, D. A. *The Late Glacial in North-west Europe: Human Adaption and Environmental change at the End of the Pleistocene* (= Council for British Archaeology Research Report 77), 7–21.

—— (1991b) The climatostratigraphic subdivision of the Devensian Lateglacial: evidence from a pollen site near Oban, western Scotland, *J. Biogeogr.*, *18*, 89–101.

Topping, P. G. (1985) Later prehistoric pottery from Dun Cul Bhuirg, Iona, Argyll, *Proc. Soc. Antiq. Scot.*, *115*, 199–209.

—— (1986) Neutron activation analysis of later prehistoric pottery from the Western Isles of Scotland, *Proc. Prehist. Soc.*, *52*, 105–29.

—— (1987) Typology and chronology in the later prehistoric pottery assemblages of the Western Isles, *Proc. Soc. Antiq. Scot.*, *117*, 67–84.

Vestergaard, E. (1991) Gift-giving, hoarding and outdoings, *in* Samson 1991, 97–104.

Wain-Hobson, T. (1981) Aspects of the glacial and post-glacial history of north-west Argyll. Unpublished PhD thesis, University of Edinburgh.

Walker, M. J. C., Gray, J. M. and Lowe, J. J. (eds) (1992) *The south-west Scottish Highlands: Field Guide*, Quaternary Research Association, Cambridge.

Walker, M. J. C., Lowe, J. J. and Tipping, R. M. (1992) Vegetational history, *in* Walker *et al.* 1992, 21–8.

Wamers, E. (1985) Insularer Metallschmuck in wikingerzeitlichen Gräbern Nordeuropas, *Offa-Bücher*, *56*, Keil.

Waselkov, G. A. (1987) Shellfish gathering and shell midden archaeology, *in* Schiffer, M. B. (ed.) *Advances in Archaeological Method and Theory*, *10*, 93–210, New York.

Watson, W. J. (1926) *The history of the Celtic place-names of Scotland*, Edinburgh.

Welander, R. D. E., Batey, C., Cowie, T. G. *et al.* (1987) A Viking burial from Kneep, Uig, Isle of Lewis, *Proc. Soc. Antiq. Scot.*, *117*, 149–74.

Whittow, J. B. (1977) *Geology and Scenery in Scotland*, Harmondsworth.

Wickham-Jones, C. R. (1990) *Rhum: Mesolithic and Later Sites at Kinloch: Excavations 1984–86* (= Society of Antiquaries of Scotland Monograph Series 7), Edinburgh.

Wickham-Jones, C. R., Brown, M. M., Cowie, T. G., Gallagher, D. B. and Ritchie, J. N. G., (1982) Excavations at Druim Arstail, Oronsay, 1911–12, *Glasgow Archaeol. J.*, 9, 18–30.

Wilson, D. M. (1976b) The Scandinavians in England, *in* Wilson, D. M. (ed.), *The Archaeology of Anglo-Saxon England*, London, 393–403.

—— (1976b) Scandinavian Settlement of the North and West of the British Isles – an archaeological viewpoint, *Trans. Royal Hist. Soc.*, 5th series, 26, 95–113.

Woodman, P. C. (1989) Ireland and Scotland: the Mesolithic of Europe's western periphery. Paper presented at the Conference on Scottish-Irish Links, Edinburgh 1989.

—— (1990) A review of the Scottish Mesolithic: a plea for normality! *Proc. Soc. Antiq. Scot.*, 119, 1–32.

Young, A. (1956) Excavations at Dun Cuier, Isle of Barra, Outer Hebrides, *Proc. Soc. Antiq. Scot.*, 89, 290–328.

Young, A. and Richardson, K. M. (1960) A Cheardach Mhor, Drimore, South Uist, *Proc. Soc. Antiq. Scot.*, 93, 135–73.

Youngs, S. M., Clark, J. and Barry, T. (1985) Medieval Britain and Ireland in 1984, *Medieval Archaeol.*, 29, 188–250.

—— (1986) Medieval Britain and Ireland in 1985, *Medieval Archaeol.*, 30, 114–98.

—— (1987) Medieval Britain and Ireland in 1986, *Medieval Archaeol.*, 31, 111–91.

—— (1988) Medieval Britain and Ireland in 1987, *Medieval Archaeol.*, 32, 225–314.

Zvelebil, M. (ed.) (1986) *Hunters in Transition: mesolithic societies of temperate Eurasia and their transition to farming*, Cambridge.

—— (1986) Mesolithic prelude and the neolithic revolution, *in* Zvelebil 1986, 5–15.

Zvelebil, M. and Rowley-Conwy, P. (1984) Transition to Farming in Northern Europe: a Hunter-Gatherer Perspective, *Norwegian Archaeol. Rev.*, 17, 104–28.

Index